Postmodern Perspectives on Contemporary Counseling Issues

POSTMODERN PERSPECTIVES ON CONTEMPORARY COUNSELING ISSUES

Approaches Across Diverse Settings

Edited by Mark B. Scholl

and

James T. Hansen

OXFORD
UNIVERSITY PRESS

OXFORD
UNIVERSITY PRESS

Oxford University Press is a department of the University of Oxford. It furthers
the University's objective of excellence in research, scholarship, and education
by publishing worldwide. Oxford is a registered trade mark of Oxford University
Press in the UK and certain other countries.

Published in the United States of America by Oxford University Press
198 Madison Avenue, New York, NY 10016, United States of America.

Library of Congress Cataloging-in-Publication Data
Names: Scholl, Mark B., editor. | Hansen, James T., editor.
Title: Postmodern perspectives on contemporary counseling issues : approaches
across diverse settings / editors, Mark B. Scholl, James T. Hansen.
Description: New York, NY : Oxford University Press, [2018] |
Includes bibliographical references and index.
Identifiers: LCCN 2017050205 (print) | LCCN 2017054896 (ebook) | ISBN 9780190621636 (updf) |
ISBN 9780190621643 (epub) | ISBN 9780190621629 (preprinted case cover : alk. paper)
Subjects: LCSH: Counseling psychology. | Counseling. | Psychotherapy.
Classification: LCC BF636.6 (ebook) | LCC BF636.6 .P68 2018 (print) | DDC 158.3—dc23
LC record available at https://lccn.loc.gov/2017050205

9 8 7 6 5 4 3 2 1

Printed by Sheridan Books, Inc., United States of America

To my wife, Kimberly, and my son, Wyatt.
You have both been indispensable sources of optimism,
support, love, and encouragement.
Mark B. Scholl

To my parents, Bill and Gail; my wonderful wife, Mary;
and my two extraordinary sons, Hayden and Hunter.
Thank you for all of your love and support.
James T. Hansen

CONTENTS

CONTRIBUTORS

Allisha M. Berendts, MS, LPCC, is a PhD candidate at The Ohio State University in counselor education with a specialization in disability studies. She has been a clinical counselor in the Columbus, Ohio, area for 6 years in both community and private practice settings. She currently works at The Ohio State University Nisonger Center as a child behavior support specialist conducting functional behavior assessments and developing behavior plans for children with developmental disabilities. As a doctoral student, she has co-taught several counselor education master's-level courses, practicing postmodern techniques in pedagogy.

Juleen K. Buser, PhD, is an associate professor in the Department of Graduate Education, Leadership, and Counseling at Rider University. She has taught courses that focus on clinical skills, addictions counseling, and an orientation to the profession. Her research interests include issues related to eating disorder symptomatology, body dissatisfaction, and nonsuicidal self-injury; much of her research examines the links between spirituality/ religion and these constructs. She has professional experience as a college counselor and has served as a president of the International Association of Addictions and Offender Counselors (IAAOC).

Brian Calhoun, MA, NCC, LPCA, is an assistant professor of the practice in the Department of Counseling at Wake Forest University. He holds an MA in counseling, and an MBA, both from Wake Forest University, as well as an undergraduate degree in business from the Wayne Calloway School of Business and Accountancy. Professor Calhoun teaches the College-to-Career series for undergraduate students at Wake Forest University. He is an active member and presenter in the American Counseling Association and the North Carolina Counseling Association.

Adam M. Clevenger, MA, is a licensed clinical professional counselor in the state of Illinois and currently provides clinical supervision and therapy to individuals, couples, and groups in Chicago. He is a doctoral candidate in counselor education at The Ohio State University and received his Sexual Health Certificate from the University of Michigan in 2017. Adam's area of study includes gender and sexuality issues in counseling, particularly related to men's wellness, sexual health and functioning, and gender socialization. Adam co-developed the Student Civility Program at Ohio State (Columbus), and he is the past president of the Association for Lesbian, Gay, Bisexual, and Transgender Issues in Counseling of Ohio.

Colette T. Dollarhide, PhD, is an associate professor in counselor education at The Ohio State University and de facto school counseling coordinator, and she has been a counselor educator for 20 years. Her main teaching and research focus has been leadership, supervision, school counseling, pedagogy, professional identity, and social justice. It is in the area of social justice that postmodern approaches resonate most. In terms of publications, she has coauthored two textbooks on school counseling (the current book is going into its third edition), two book chapters, and 33 national peer-reviewed journal articles. She has served as the president of the national Association for Humanistic Counseling and the editor of the *Journal of Humanistic Counseling* (JHC). In addition, Colette is a nationally certified counselor, currently holds her LPC with supervisor endorsement in Ohio, and is an approved clinical supervisor.

Todd A. Gibbs, MA, LPC, is a doctoral candidate in counselor education and coordinates the Wellness Coaching program for the Office of Student Life's Student Wellness Center at The Ohio State University. As a licensed professional counselor in the state of Ohio, he has experience working with adolescent and college student populations. Todd has facilitated coursework in multicultural counseling, foundations, practicum and internship, group counseling, and assessment, and regularly provides supervision to counselors-in-training and peer educators. His research interests include motivational theory, college student development, adult learning, and positive psychology.

Sean R. Gorby, MA, is a licensed professional counselor and certified wellness counselor in the state of Ohio, where he is completing his PhD at The Ohio State University. Sean's current research involves understanding meaning and purpose in the lives of clients, counselors, students, and professors and how meaning and purpose impact an individual's ability to live well, to thrive, and to grow. One of Sean's current research projects involves understanding resilience and wellness in aging adults. Sean's clinical and supervisory experience involves working with college students at a college counseling center and with aging adults in care facilities.

James T. Hansen, PhD, is a professor at Oakland University in the Department of Counseling. His primary scholarly interests are philosophical and theoretical issues in counseling and critical examination of contemporary mental health culture. Dr. Hansen has published about 50 refereed articles in leading counseling journals and several books. Two of his books have won awards for their contributions to humanistic philosophy in counseling. Dr. Hansen has over 25 years of experience as a practitioner, supervisor, and consultant.

Michelle S. Hinkle, PhD, LPC, ACS, is an assistant professor and co-coordinator for the mental health counseling track in the Professional Counseling Program at The William Paterson University of New Jersey. She has published and presented on topics related to postmodern approaches to counseling and supervision, including narrative letter writing with children and families and using reflecting teams in group supervision. Dr. Hinkle has applied solution-focused and narrative therapies to her work with children, adolescents, and families in mental health counseling settings.

Matthew E. Lemberger, PhD, is an associate professor of counselor education at the University of New Mexico. He is the current editor of the *Journal of Humanistic Counseling*, the associate editor for the *Journal of Individual Psychology*, and the senior associate editor of the *Journal of Child and Adolescent Counseling*. He has also served as president for the Association of Humanistic Counseling. As a scholar, Matthew has published over 30 peer-reviewed articles, including work pertaining to humanistic and postmodern ideologies. His professional work generally pertains to how counselors can help cultivate executive functioning and feelings of connectedness, particularly targeted to children and families in poverty and in school environments.

Todd F. Lewis, PhD, is an associate professor of counseling and counselor education at North Dakota State University. He is a licensed professional counselor and a national certified counselor. Dr. Lewis is past treasurer and president of the International Association of Addictions and Offender Counselors (IAAOC), a subdivision of the American Counseling Association, and previously served as the IAAOC representative on the Governing Council of the American Counseling Association. Throughout his career, he has taught graduate-level students in motivational interviewing, counseling theory, behavior change, assessment, diagnosis, and treatment planning. Dr. Lewis has presented on these topics at numerous local, state, national, and international venues. He has published numerous research articles related to behavior change, substance abuse, collegiate drinking, and theoretical approaches to addictions treatment and motivational interviewing. He has twice received the Exemplary Research Award from IAAOC for his research.

J. Barry Mascari, EdD, LPC, LCADC, is an associate professor and chair of the Counselor Education Department at Kean University (New Jersey). He came to academia after splitting a 30-year career in schools and outpatient drug treatment. He has held leadership positions in New Jersey and nationally, including president of the American Association of State Counseling Boards and a current CACREP Board member. Publication experience includes coediting a disaster mental health book now in its fourth edition. Trauma treatment experience and research are reflected in his integration of existentialism, Buddhism, and a growing disaffection with traditional theories in a recent ACA presentation, "Entering the Post Theoretical Era."

Gerald Monk, PhD, is a professor in the Department of Counseling and School Psychology at San Diego State University and the director of training for marriage and family therapists. Gerald is a practicing marriage and family therapist in California specializing in couple work and is a mediator and trainer in collaborative divorce practices. He is well known for his contributions to developing and expanding the applications of narrative therapy and mediation with families. Gerald has taught numerous workshops on these subjects over nearly two decades in multiple countries. He has coauthored six books on narrative therapy and narrative mediation with the most recent text, *When stories clash: Addressing conflict in narrative mediation* (Taos Institute, Trans. Japanese, Danish, and Russian).

J. P. Oehrtman, MA, is currently a doctoral student in counselor education at The Ohio State University. He recently earned his school counseling licensure and applies a postmodern perspective to his work with students in grades K–12. He has presented at several national conferences and is continuing to add to his experience as a future counselor educator.

Caroline Perjessy, PhD, LPC (OH and GA), CPCS, is an associate professor at Argosy University and a certified clinical supervisor in Georgia. She has published and presented in the areas of postmodern interventions in counselor education and supervision, including the practice of using reflecting teams in group supervision and postmodern career counseling interventions with college students. Dr. Perjessy has over 10 years of clinical experience working with adolescents and adults who experience a variety of therapeutic issues, and she utilizes a postmodern, humanistic perspective in her clinical work.

Jason Perry, MS, has worked as a probation and parole officer with the North Carolina Department of Public Safety. He holds an MS in counselor education from East Carolina University and is a PhD student in the Counselor Education Program at North Carolina State University. He has worked with Mark B. Scholl to develop career counseling interventions and programs for the ex-offender population, has been involved with the American Counseling Association, and was honored as an Emerging Leader by the Association for Humanistic Counseling in 2013.

Manivong J. Ratts, PhD, is an associate professor of counseling in the College of Education at Seattle University and past president of Counselors for Social Justice, a division of the American Counseling Association. His line of research includes three areas: (1) multicultural and social justice competent care, (2) LGBTI and minority health disparities, and (3) courtesy stigma. His research in these areas has been published in peer-reviewed outlets such as the *Journal of Counseling and Development, Journal of Multicultural Counseling and Development, Counselor Education and Supervision, Journal of LGBT Issues in Counseling, Journal for Specialists in Group Work, Journal for Social Action in Counseling and Psychology,* and *Journal of Humanistic Counseling, Education, and Development.* In 2014, he was selected to chair the Special Committee on the Multicultural Counseling Competencies commissioned by the Association for Multicultural Counseling and Development.

Heidi Robinson, MA, NCC, LPCA, is an assistant professor of the practice in the Department of Counseling at Wake Forest University. She began teaching career development courses at Wake Forest University in 2011. She holds a master's degree in counseling from Wake Forest University and a bachelor's degree in communications from Washington State University. She has presented at programs at the national, regional, and state levels on topics related to career development practices. Her most recent article appeared in a publication of the North Carolina Association of Colleges and Employers on teaching fiscal literacy.

Mark B. Scholl, PhD, LMHC (NY), is an associate professor in the Department of Counseling at Wake Forest University. Dr. Scholl is a past president of AHC, past editor of the *Journal of Humanistic Counseling,* a current associate editor of the *Journal of College Counseling,* and a former chair of the ACA Council of Journal Editors. He is a member of the ACA Governing Council representing the AHC division. He, and his coeditors, received the Hollis Publication Award for their book entitled *Humanistic Perspectives on Contemporary Counseling Issues.* His counseling experience includes the use of postmodern career counseling approaches with high school students, college students, and most recently, members of the ex-offender population. Dr. Scholl has published articles on the use of postmodern career counseling approaches in *Career Development Quarterly* and *Career Planning and Adult Development Journal.*

Megan Speciale, PhD, is an assistant professor of counseling at Palo Alto University. Megan has worked as a professional counselor in a variety of community settings, focusing primarily on lesbian, gay, bisexual, transgender, queer, questioning, intersex, and asexual (LGBTQQIA) individuals, couples, and their families. Her research foci include postmodern perspectives of gender and sexuality in counseling practice and pedagogy, the role of ideology in antioppressive education, and community-informed research methodologies. She currently serves as an editorial board member for the *Journal of Humanistic Counseling* and is a recipient of the AHC Emerging Leaders Award (2015).

Corina Maria Teofilo Mattson, MS, is a licensed marriage and family therapist in the state of Illinois. She is a bilingual couples and family therapist and the director of Programs and Administration at Live Oak, Inc. in Chicago. Corina is an AAMFT approved supervisor. She supervises students in the Marriage and Family Therapy program at The Family Institute at Northwestern University. Corina's areas of clinical expertise include cross-cultural relationships, LGBTQ affirmative practice, trauma-informed practice, intersectional identity work, and intergenerational family therapy.

Jane M. Webber, PhD, LPC, is on the Counselor Education faculty at Kean University (New Jersey) and a licensed disaster response crisis counselor. She coauthored the chapter *Healing Trauma Through Humanistic Connection* in an award-winning book and received the ASCA Writers' Award for *The New Jersey School Counseling Initiative.* She is associate editor of the *Journal of Counseling Preparation and Supervision* and is coediting the fourth edition of a disaster mental health counseling book. Her counseling philosophy is grounded in the stories people share. Her scholarly interests are narrative trauma therapy, postmodern approaches to career and mental health counseling, and sand tray therapy. She has 42 years of experience as an educator and counselor in schools, colleges, and private practice.

Laura S. Wheat, PhD, LPC (GA), NCC, is an assistant professor of counseling at the University of Tennessee, Knoxville. She has served as a school-based counselor and a clinician in a university clinic, applying narrative and constructivist models in her work with children, adolescents, and adults experiencing life crises and transitions, including loss. She has presented and published on grief impacting children and adolescents for

9 years. She currently directs the UT Grief Outreach Initiative for K–12 students and serves on the Board of Directors for the Association for Death Education & Counseling (ADEC).

Peggy P. Whiting, EdD, LPCS (NC), certified thanatologist, licensed school counselor (NC), is professor and coordinator of counselor education at North Carolina Central University within the University of North Carolina system. Dr. Whiting has previously served on the faculty of Vanderbilt and Winthrop Universities. Her primary expertise is in the areas of constructivist models of grief, crisis, and trauma counseling with additional interests in lifespan development and counselor supervision. She is currently serving on the Board of Directors of the Association for Death Education and Counseling, an international organization that credentials grief counselors and educators. For 30 years, she has published, presented, counseled, taught, and supervised in the area of trauma and grief counseling.

Navid J. Zamani, MS, is a licensed marriage and family therapist in San Diego, as well as a faculty member at San Diego State University. He works primarily with populations who have experienced domestic violence and couples in crisis. Navid works closely with immigrant and refugee populations to provide supervision and direct services to support a preferred set of relationships and understandings in their lives. Navid is intimately involved with the narrative therapy communities in San Diego, and he is in conversations that support thickening narrative understandings and integrating contemporary ideas within the narrative/constructionist paradigm.

CHAPTER 1

Introduction to Postmodern Perspectives on Contemporary Counseling Issues

JAMES T. HANSEN AND MARK B. SCHOLL

Helping people who are in a state of emotional suffering can be an incredibly rewarding way to make a living. Changing the course of a life, transforming pain into meaningful insights, and bringing about relational healing are often all in a day's work for counselors and psychotherapists. Decades of research confirm that counseling is, indeed, effective in helping to alleviate psychological pain (Wampold, 2001). The precise reasons that the psychotherapy paradigm consistently works continue to be investigated by researchers, theoreticians, and others in the field who examine the mysteries of the therapeutic process.

In one sense, it is remarkable that counseling is so consistently effective. Imagine the varieties of people who walk into the offices of counselors every day. Each client has unique internal meaning structures, types of problems, and worldviews. An event that is painful to one client may be healing to another; a therapeutic intervention that works well with one client may fail miserably with another. Clients with identical diagnoses and presenting problems are often radically different in terms of their day-to-day concerns, developmental histories, inner psychological lives, values, relationships, self-ideals, and worldviews. Anyone who has experience in the helping professions will surely confirm that no two people are ever truly alike, even if the superficialities of their surface problems appear similar. For professionals who intervene on a psychological level, this extreme variation in clientele makes talk therapy an extraordinarily difficult and complex endeavor. The consistency with which counselors and psychotherapists help, then, is truly remarkable, given the diverse range of their clientele.

Given the staggering complexity of the helping encounter, it is no wonder that numerous theories have been developed to make sense of the bewildering barrage of information that counselors regularly confront. Theories serve to funnel and sort information into various ideological categories, thereby providing counselors with a basis for understanding and helping their clients. For instance, consider a deceptively simple phrase, uttered by a client, such as "I don't like my roommate." This phrase, of course, can have virtually infinite personal meanings and origins depending on the unique psychological constitution of the client. Fortunately, there is a lengthy historical menu of theoretical options to help counselors sort, categorize, and give meaning to this utterance, thereby simplifying its psychological implications. A cognitively oriented helping professional, for example, would hone in on the thought structures inherent in the phrase, a focus that might lead to an intervention that challenges or reframes the idea that the client does not like the roommate. Alternatively, a psychodynamically informed counselor, going on the theoretical assumption that the dislike for the roommate is actually a derivative expression of an unconscious dislike for a developmentally earlier figure, may explore past relationships rather than the contemporary issue with the roommate.

Although the plethora of theories in the helping professions certainly serves to tame the wild ambiguities of the counseling process, theories can also cause their own sets of problems. Practitioners, for instance, may develop a strong allegiance to a particular school of thought, thereby blinding them to useful ways of conceptualizing clients that are outside the scope of their pet theory (Fancher, 1995; Hansen, 2014). To make matters worse, the core assumptions of many of the popular theories of counseling and psychotherapy are entirely incompatible, which makes theoretical integration a difficult, if not impossible, task (Hansen, 2002). For all of their problems, however, theories are arguably a necessary component of professional helping. Without theories, counselors would have no way of making useful, therapeutic meanings out of the dizzyingly complex array of psychological, relational, and cultural information that clients present.

Given the importance of theories to the work of professional helpers, it is a worthwhile scholarly endeavor to systematically examine theories and their relationship to counseling practice. In this regard, extant theories in the helping professions commonly appear to be grossly incompatible when the surface of the theoretical landscape is appraised (Hansen, 2002).

For instance, psychoanalytic theories presume that unconscious conflict is at the root of human behavior (Gabbard, 2010), while humanistic conceptualizations begin with the assumption that people have an inborn drive to self-actualization (Scholl, McGowan, & Hansen, 2012). Cognitive formulations, alternatively, give primacy to thinking and altogether dismiss conceptualizations about actualization or unconscious mental life (Ellis & Grieger, 1977). At first glance, then, various theories appear to be conceptually incompatible, like entirely different forms of plant life, flowers, trees, and weeds, growing wildly in a meadow. However, to continue this botanical metaphor, one can be so struck by the perceived differences in the theoretical plants that it can cause one to miss the commonality that all of the plants in the meadow thrived under the same climatic conditions.

Certain climatic conditions, or philosophical foundations, then, cause particular sets of theories to grow. Traditionally, theories of helping have been sown and grown in an ideological climate of *modernism* (Hansen, 2004), a set of philosophical principles that has given rise to a particular type of theoretical life and, by extension, certain ways of viewing clients and methods to help them. Several decades ago, however, this modernist climate began to be disrupted by postmodernist storms. Gradually, the ideological weather conditions have changed and postmodernist ideologies have begun to encourage the growth of an entirely new set of theories in the conceptual helping garden.

This book is about the postmodernist turn in counseling and psychotherapy. Far from being merely an academic subject, postmodernist theories have generated novel ways of helping that arguably could not have been conceived within a modernist paradigm. The practical implications for helping clients, rather than arid, philosophical topics, are emphasized in the subsequent chapters. Our goal is that, after reading this book, helping professionals will have a variety of new ideas and interventions that they can use to help their clients. Concrete ways that postmodernist conceptualizations can be used in a variety of counseling settings, not cerebral formulations that are disconnected from practice, are the emphasis of this book.

That being said, it is arguably useful for practitioners to have an understanding of the philosophical foundations that gave rise to particular types of theories (Hansen, 2014). The risks are that, without this deeper, ideological understanding, postmodernist treatment recommendations will appear random and conceptually disconnected, thereby limiting the ability of counselors to extend, modify, and apply the treatments to new realms of practice. It is beneficial for helping professionals, then, to not only know the theoretical plants but also the climatic conditions that gave rise to them, so that practitioners can actually work in the conceptual garden to sow new possibilities for helping their clients. To this end, this chapter is about the philosophical foundations of postmodernism. Understanding post-modernism requires a familiarity with modernism. Therefore, modernism serves as the starting point for this discussion.

MODERNISM

The central assumptions of modernism, at least for purposes of this discussion, are that (a) reality is ordered by objective truths that can be accessed in their pristine form by human observers; and (b) people have an internal self-structure that guides and directs their actions (Rosenau, 1992). These assumptions are so baked into the Western mindset that they are usually taken for granted. Indeed, like gravity and oxygen, modernist assumptions operate invisibly, in the background, as forces that structure ideological movements. Consider the scientific enterprise, for example, as a manifestation of the first tenet of modernism. The traditional assumption of scientific investigation is that, by using the scientific method, researchers can discover, or at least approximate, universal laws about the phenomena they investigate (Hansen, 2014). With science as our guide, the objective truth about reality can be known, the forces of nature will gradually be brought under human control, and people will progressively advance to a higher, more desirable state of living.

These modernist assumptions about science may seem self-evident and virtually indisputable, particularly because the scientific enterprise has brought about cures for diseases, technological advances, and other tremendous benefits to humankind. Note, however, that the postulate that the scientific method provides us with an ever clearer view of the pristine laws of the universe is merely an assumption, and that there are, indeed, alternative ways to consider the activities of scientists. Some of these alternatives are reviewed in the section on postmodernism. For now, however, consider that traditional theories of counseling are also structured by modernist assumptions.

Psychoanalytic theory, for instance, presumes that unconscious conflict is at the root of mental health problems (Gabbard, 2010). The objective truth of a client's unconscious conflicts can be ascertained by a trained psychoanalyst. Note that the modernist assumptions about objective truth and the idea that clients have self structures are both inherent in this psychoanalytic model. Likewise, behavioral, cognitive-behavioral, and humanistic theories, at least in their traditional forms, all presume that the counselor can ascertain objective knowledge about clients (Hansen, 2004). These theories, with the arguable exception of orthodox behaviorism, also rely, to varying degrees, on the assumption that clients have an internal self, which guides and directs thoughts, feelings, and actions.

Traditional theories of counseling and psychotherapy, then, developed within a particular assumptive ecosystem. Specifically, the primary assumption is that clients have certain psychological factors, which emanate from their internal self-system, that cause mental health problems. Depending on the theory, these factors may be unconscious conflict or cognitive distortions, to name two examples. Counselors, by virtue of their expertise, heal by objectively ascertaining psychological truths about their clients. After the expert counselor ferrets out the real, objective cause that is lurking behind the symptoms, the counselor encourages client awareness of the true nature of the problem through various technical interventions, such as cognitive reframing or interpretation of unconscious conflict. The types of inferences that are made, and the techniques that are used to share those inferences with the client, are dependent upon the theory that the counselor utilizes. Note, however, that traditional theories of counseling all rely on a modernist paradigm: Objective truths about clients are ascertained by an expert helping professional (Hansen, 2004). The truth sets clients free.

How, though, did these modernist ideals become the foundation of Western intellectual culture? The assumption that humankind advances by acquiring the laws of nature may seem so completely self-evident and commonsensical that it would seem absurd to subject it to critical examination. Ironically, though, the very fact that modernist ideals seem so natural to Westerners is a sign that modernism is a historical and cultural phenomenon, just as analogously, at one time, it seemed completely natural to presume that spirits caused mental health problems, homosexuality was an aberration, or slavery was morally justifiable. Therefore, precisely because modernist assumptions are usually taken for granted, the origins of modernist ideals are worth investigating. By reviewing these origins, it is easier to see that modernism is simply a strong and pervasive historical force, not a self-evident natural paradigm (Rorty, 1979).

Interestingly, our historical journey to discover the origins of modernism begins thousands of years ago in a fictitious cave. The ancient Greek philosopher Plato (2008), in his famous allegory of the cave, invited readers to imagine a cave that was inhabited by people who had been imprisoned there since childhood. Because they were chained in place and unable to turn their heads, the gaze of these cave dwellers had always been fixed on one of the cave walls. A fire burned behind these inhabitants, and people and objects passed in front of the fire, thereby casting shadows on the cave wall. Because they were unable to turn their heads, the imprisoned cave dwellers could only see the shadows on the wall, not the actual entities that were casting them. A primary point of this allegory is that these chained inhabitants would naturally mistake the shadows for the true reality. Unless they were unshackled, and could turn their heads to see the entities that were casting the shadows, they would never know that their idea of truth (i.e., the shadows) was just an illusion. Philosophical investigation, according to Plato, is the way to help people throw off their chains and see the truth.

The allegory of the cave established vital intellectual dualisms, which served as the foundation for the core intellectual ideals of Western civilization (Rorty, 1999). Most notably, there is a distinction between the world that is available to our sense impressions and the true reality that constitutes that world. The key to human progress is to apprehend the objective truths of nature and not be fooled by immediate sense impressions; an essential reality always lurks behind the shadows. This paradigm was so influential that the 20th-century philosopher Whitehead (1979) noted that the history of philosophy "consists of a series of footnotes to Plato" (p. 39). Indeed, the search for truth has informed all traditional Western disciplines, including medicine, physics, literary studies, and philosophy (Anderson, 1990). In this regard, recall that traditional counseling theories are designed to illuminate the truth behind client symptoms. A client's depression, for instance, is only a shadow cast by the true cause, which, if the counselor has a cognitive orientation, for example, is deemed to be cognitive distortions. Just like the cave dwellers, traditional counselors, using theories, unshackle clients and set them free to see the true cause of their troubles (Hansen, 2014).

This search-for-truth paradigm was fortified and elaborated during the Enlightenment, a period of intense intellectual activity that began in the late 17th century (Hicks, 2004). Enlightenment philosophers, such as Descartes, Locke, and Bacon, emphasized reason as the primary way to learn about the world. Rather than blindly accepting royal or religious mandates, these philosophers relied on reason to come to independent conclusions about truth.

Descartes (1988), for example, engaged in a series of meditations that employed radical doubt as a reasoning strategy. Fearing that everything he had learned in his life might not be true, Descartes decided to begin his process of philosophical inquiry by doubting everything, even the fact that he existed. By wiping away everything he had ever learned or taken for granted, Descartes thought that he could gradually build up, through reasoned steps, an edifice of truth that would not be contaminated by any illusions. Through this process, he concluded that the very fact that he was thinking must mean that he existed. Descartes used this central truth as a launching pad to formulate a variety of philosophical tenets, such as mind–body dualism, which have had a tremendous, lasting influence on Western intellectual culture (Custance & Travis, 1980; Stolorow, Atwood, & Orange, 2002).

In at least two important ways, the Enlightenment, with its emphasis on reason, formed the basis of the modernist worldview (Hicks, 2004). First, reason is a property of individuals. Therefore, the Enlightenment was key to establishing the Western emphasis on individualism. Democracy, human rights, and the idealization of self as a willful agent all had their roots in Enlightenment thought. As noted earlier, it is easy to detect this modernist emphasis on individualism in traditional theories of counseling and psychotherapy. Second, the idealization of reason as the path to truth also paved the way for the scientific method to emerge as the preeminent Western way to acquire knowledge. Science, which provides a highly reasoned method of investigation, became idealized as the way to cut through the fog of human illusions, thereby allowing investigators to clearly view the objective laws of nature. This idealization of science was fortified by the incredible discoveries and lifestyle advances made possible by the scientific method in the 19th and 20th centuries. Willful, heroic individuals advancing humankind by making objective discoveries about the hidden laws of nature is an iconic image that symbolizes the essence of the modernist project.

Freud, for instance, whose ideas were formulated at the height of modernism, has been described as a courageous discoverer of the unconscious (Gay, 1988). Despite the tremendous odds against his ideas being accepted, Freud continued to courageously promote the truths he had discovered. Gradually, as the truth of unconscious motivation began to be accepted, advances in mental health treatment were made. Human progression, then, is due to the heroic efforts and supreme dedication of certain individuals who are hell-bent on discovering the truth. Or, at least, so the modernist narrative goes.

What if modernism is only a narrative, though, simply an interesting story that had somehow captivated Western civilization? Certainly, the modernist paradigm has delivered wonderful gifts to the door of humankind, such as cures for horrid diseases. However, without an idealization of science, the atomic bomb and biological weaponry would have never been created. Indeed, the modernist project brought about the first generation of people who had the ability to destroy the planet. Scientific investigation has provided us with longer, more comfortable lives, then, but at what cost? Likewise, an emphasis on individualism has arguably created a culture of alienated, lonely people, who try to compensate for their angst with rampant consumerism and quick, technological fixes that never quite ease their deep sense of isolation. In this regard, perhaps counseling and psychotherapy are an intrinsic part of the modernist project, forged by the ideals of modernism but also designed as an antidote to the darker side of inflated individualism and the relentless pursuit of truth.

Modernism, then, may have run its course. Perhaps it is time for a new paradigm, one that will rescue us from the darker side of the modernist project. But what would this new paradigm entail? The tenets of modernism are so entrenched in Western consciousness that it is hard to imagine an ideology that might replace it. However, the seeds of this new ideology have already been planted. Indeed, this new ideological force has begun to radically change numerous disciplines, including counseling and psychotherapy. Because it followed, and is a response to, modernism, postmodernism is an apt name for this new paradigm.

POSTMODERNISM

The postmodern perspective views human knowing as a process of meaning making in which knowledge is constructed by individuals and communities. By contrast with the traditional modernist perspective, postmodern approaches do not posit the existence of a single truth regarding the client's experience (Hansen, 2014; Ward & Reuter, 2011). From the postmodern perspective it is not sensible to posit singular truths about reality because "reality" is always defined by human perceptions. Perceptions are a function of human meaning-making processes and perceptions continually change to accommodate the way in which people make sense of their experiences (Hansen, 2007).

Because perceptions reflect the unique meaning-making processes of each individual, counselors operating from a postmodern framework do not usually subscribe to the modernist view of human behavior as either normal or abnormal (Ward & Reuter, 2011). Instead, postmodern thinkers are obligated to adopt a more complex view of individuals behaving in accordance with ever-changing perceptions reflecting an active and continual process by which they actively make sense of their experiences (Combs, 1954).

Counselors who view their clients as possessing unique views of reality also incorporate client capacity for meaning making into the counseling process. This capacity is a significant strength that can be utilized to empower clients and enhance their sense of personal agency. Well-known examples of postmodern approaches include, but are not limited to, solution-focused therapies, narrative therapies, and sociodynamic counseling (Peavy, 1998).

A particularly salient historical precedent for postmodernism may be found in Darwin's theory of evolution. Gurmin (2006) observed that

Darwin's theory marked an "anthropological turning point" because it introduced the notion that humans are but one example of a species evolving rather than being created by a single transcendent being (p. 81). Darwin's theory was a precursor to neo-Darwinian notions of socially constructed cultural norms and practices. Darwin's theory has influenced sociobiologists and anthropologists to apply the "survival of the fittest" principle to explain the process by which social values and mores become constructed by members of a society. For example, in *The Whispering's Within* David Barash (1979) makes an analogy between the instinctual reproductive strategy of hoarding wax in honeybees and constructed human status symbols (e.g., owning a Ferrari), which arguably also make reproduction more likely. Also consistent with the postmodern perspective, the theory of evolution has been described as a worldview or metanarrative that can be used as a means for thinking about the universe (Dawkins, 1995).

Freud's psychoanalytic theory constituted another important historical precedent for postmodernism. Freud posited not only that human personality is comprised of three primary components (i.e., the id, ego, and superego) but also that the id is ruled by instinctual desires rather than autonomous reason. Among these instinctual desires, Freud included both erotic and death instincts. Because psychoanalytic theory includes both an ego that operates according to reason and an id that functions to fulfill instinctual desires, postmodernists can cite this theory as support for claims that human perceptions are the product of opposing intrapsychic dynamics rather than representing a copy of some objective truth beyond their perceptions (Tauber, 2012).

Tauber (2012) described the lines of thought by which postmodernists have progressively emphasized the significance of our need to satisfy our biologically determined instinctual desires while also de-emphasizing the significance and autonomy of the rational ego. For example, in Jean-Francois Lyotard's (1974/1993) postmodern take on psychoanalytic theory, he calls for freer expression of libidinal forces as a means for "liberating creativity and vitality" (Tauber, 2012, p. 59).

Critiques of Modernism

The modernist perspective is founded on the belief that absolute truth exists and that the truth can be observed and measured (Ramey & Grubb, 2009). Critiques of modernism generally fall into one of two categories: critiques related to the concept of each individual possessing a singular self, and critiques related to the concept of truth.

With regard to a critique related to the notion of a singular self, this Enlightenment ideal became less plausible as a result of emerging ideological critiques (Hansen, 2014). Immanuel Kant (2007) asserted that the human mind actively shapes what one considers to be reality rather than discovering objective truth. Perhaps the mightiest blow, as previously mentioned, came from Freud's psychoanalytic theory. Rather than being entirely under conscious rational control, Freud asserted, aspects of the human mind operate on a hidden or unconscious level. These theoretical developments rendered modernist notions of a unified, consolidated self at the center of human thought and action untenable (Hansen, 2014).

One noteworthy critique related to the concept of truth pertains to the legitimacy of multiple perspectives. More specifically, modernism fails to account for the fact that there are multiple perspectives of reality, including subjective points of view and cultural differences. Even a concrete concept as simple as a ball cannot be reduced to a single accurate essence. Hansen (2014) observed that a child, an artist, and a scientist would disagree as to whether a ball's essence is recreational, aesthetic, or molecular, respectively, and none of the three individuals has a basis for claiming his or her perspective represents a single objective truth.

Polanyi's Epistemology of Personal Knowledge

A second critique related to modernism's concept of an absolute truth is rooted in philosopher Michael Polanyi's epistemology of personal knowledge (Polanyi, 1962; Polanyi & Prosch, 1975). Polanyi stated that what we choose to believe is inseparable from our biases, values, and feelings. We cannot view the world without some perspective, and because this perspective has been subjectively chosen and adopted, we cannot examine it critically while we are using it. When an individual views the world from a given theoretical perspective, that individual implicitly perceives the theoretical perspective. It is not possible to use a theory and to be focally aware of it. In the words of Polanyi: "You cannot use your spectacles to scrutinize your spectacles. A theory is like a pair of spectacles; you cannot examine things by it, and your knowledge of it lives in this very use of it. You dwell in it as you dwell in your body and in the tools by which you amplify the powers of your body" (Polanyi & Prosch, 1975, p. 37). Modernism fails to account for Polanyi's argument that we are unable to step outside of our perspectives and evaluate them; these "truths" are not truly objective. Perspectives, including theories and worldviews, are examples of ways individuals actively construct meaning (Dean, 1989).

Polanyi stated that all explicit knowledge and skills are grounded in nonexplicit or tacit understanding (e.g., a theory we use as a lens to view phenomena). According to Polanyi (1969), all tacit particulars are marginal or subliminal. Marginal particulars exist just beyond the periphery of conscious experience. They are seen from the corner of our eyes or sensed at the back of our mind and produced by past experience.

Skillful performance is attained by following a set of tacit rules unknown to the person following them (Collins, 2010; Polanyi, 1962). For example, William Miller (Miller & Rollnick, 2013, p. vii) related how the concept of motivational interviewing (MI) grew out of conversations with psychologists in Norway in 1982. Miller was taking a sabbatical from the University of New Mexico and working at a hospital for alcoholism treatment. Part of Miller's experience included meeting regularly with a group of beginning psychologists who would share audiotapes of their counseling sessions with clients coping with substance abuse and related concerns. Miller would demonstrate, through the use of role play, how he would work with the clients. The psychologists would ask questions regarding the content and timing of his counselor responses—for example, why he chose to reflect some client statements rather than others. Their questions caused Miller to verbalize a set of decision rules that he had been using unknowingly with clients (e.g., Rule 1: the client rather than the clinician should be making the arguments for change). As Polanyi would predict, Miller had learned to follow these rules without consciously thinking of them; they were only tacitly understood. These question-and-answer sessions with Norwegian psychologists led Miller to write the 1983 article in which MI was originally described.

Similar to the performance of other complex skills, such as playing the violin, Miller's rules were too numerous and complicated for him to keep in conscious awareness. In Polanyi's words, during skillful understanding or performance, "we know more than we can tell" (Polanyi, 1966, p. 4). Miller's experience also illustrates another important principle—through self-examination or self-reflection we can gain greater awareness of tacitly held knowledge.

According to Polanyi, there are two classes of human awareness: (a) focal awareness and (b) tacit awareness. Polanyi used the example of hammering a nail to illustrate these concepts. While hammering we are focally aware of the nail. That is, we are focusing on the nail to make sure we are hitting it on the head and that it is going in straight. Concomitantly, we are tacitly aware of the feeling of the hammer in our hand. We are tacitly aware of whether we are gripping the hammer tightly or swinging it with enough force. In Polanyi's (1962) words: "I have a subsidiary awareness of the feeling in the palm of my hand which is merged into my focal awareness of my driving the nail" (p. 55).

In all forms of knowing, an individual integrates tacit particulars into a meaningful whole (Manno, 1977). All knowledge is personal because to some extent it is constructed by the individual. This act of construction is essential for knowing to occur and enhances the meaningfulness of knowledge. Polanyi asserted that "into every act of knowing there enters a tacit and passionate contribution of the person knowing what is being known, and that this coefficient is no mere imperfection, but a vital component of this knowledge" (1962, p. vii). The meaningful whole is either a skill (e.g., conducting a counseling session) or a skillful comprehension (e.g., recognizing a face, empathizing). The constructive act of integrating tacit particulars into a whole adds value that is necessary for skillful performance (Polanyi, 1962).

A practicum student's understanding of tacit performance criteria when conducting a counseling session may be used to illustrate the special relationship between tacit knowledge and skills. Performance criteria may include nonverbal attending, reflecting feeling, reflecting meaning, and paraphrasing the client's concerns. The practicum student is focally aware of the criteria when she is reviewing her notes prior to the counseling session. Later, when she is conducting the counseling session, the student is tacitly aware of these criteria. These tacitly held elements are merged into a focal awareness of attending to the client. If the student suddenly shifted her attention to a focal awareness of a given criterion, such as reflecting meaning, then the skillful performance might be momentarily disrupted. Many of us have had the experience of focally attending to our own counseling performance and, as a result, not hearing something the client said.

Polanyi and Prosch (1975) described the functional relationship between tacit knowledge and a focal target as a "from-to relationship" (p. 36). The type of knowledge made possible by this from-to structure is called "from-to knowing" or "indwelling." A tacitly held perceptual whole is made up of smaller tacit particulars. The tacit whole in from-to knowing can be a theory, a tool, or a familiar interpersonal role such as that of counselor. One complex understanding that every student holds implicitly is his or her sense of identity. This sense of identity is made of tacit particulars such as beliefs, values, sense of competence, and sense of purpose.

Knowing a concept by relying on our awareness of it for attending to something else is the same kind of knowledge we have of our bodies by dwelling in them (Polanyi & Prosch, 1975). Thus, just as we dwell in our bodies, we also dwell in our sense of identity. Tacit awareness of a concept can be looked upon as a condition in which the concept forms part of the body. Polanyi explained from-to understanding of concepts in the following statement: "we pour ourselves into them, and assimilate them as part of ourselves" (Polanyi & Prosch, 1975, p. 36). Thus, counselors-in-training assimilate the role of counselor to the act of counseling in much the same way as they assimilate the shoes they wear to the act of walking. This phenomenon of pouring ourselves into assimilated wholes is known as "indwelling." Attempting to learn while dwelling in a role inconsistent with one's sense of identity (e.g., neutral reflecting when one has strong opinions) can be as uncomfortable as attempting to walk while wearing shoes that do not fit properly.

Dwelling in the perspective of another is a special type of indwelling known as empathy. In Polanyi's view, empathy is achieved by the imaginative integration of the particulars of another person's experience into a tacitly held understanding. In empathizing, a person dwells in the imagined attitudes, beliefs, feelings, and conditions of another.

The Role of Language in Knowing

The preceding discussion of Polanyi's personal knowledge provides a powerful critique of modernism because language is fundamental to human knowledge. Moreover, language is both a tool and a noteworthy example of how an individual creates meaning by tacitly integrating particulars into a meaningful whole.

Language was created by humans and is used to convert covert thoughts into the overt written and spoken words that we use to communicate our thoughts with one another (Hansen, 2014; Rorty, 1989). Similar to Polanyi, Rorty (1989) asserted that because all truths must be communicated through language, constructed by humans, it logically follows that all truths are constructed. The fact that truth must be communicated through language is an important of criticism of the assumption that humans can progressively ascertain absolute truth, a central tenet of modernism (Hansen, 2014).

As with other tools, such as eyeglasses, language is a tool that we cannot use and scrutinize at the same time. The fact that language is a tool, invented by humans, which we use for perceiving reality undermines the modernist assumption that a supposed objective reality, beyond our linguistic categories, can be accessed. The perceptions that counselors have of their clients are inextricably bound to language. Because their perceptions are bound to language, counselors cannot claim that their perceptions are objective truths.

Varieties of Postmodernism

Two primary varieties of postmodernism include nihilistic and neopragmatic postmodernism. Nihilism has been defined as the rejection of values and meaning (Woodward, 2002). Woodward explains the relationship between nihilism and postmodernism. She notes that because the postmodern perspective entails a critique of reason and objective truth, values are necessarily relativistic. There is no factual basis for claiming that some values are higher than others. This devaluation of humanity's highest ideals results in reductionistic deconstruction of all values in order to reevaluate them. This reductionistic view of values, in turn, renders values and human life meaninglessness.

However, Woodward (2002) asserted that, similar to existentialists, postmodernists offer a useful response to nihilistic postmodernism. Existentialists, more specifically, embrace the notion that humans have the freedom and capacity to choose what to believe, how to behave, and what values to cherish. By making these choices, sometimes referred to by developmental theorists as *commitments in relativism* (Perry, 1981), humans add meaning to their lives.

In a similar fashion, Rorty (1979) integrated pragmatism with postmodernist thought. This integration is commonly referred to as *neopragmatism* (Hansen, 2014; Polkinghorne, 1992; Rorty, 1999). Unlike nihilistic postmodernism, neopragmatic postmodernism upholds the criterion of *usefulness* as legitimate grounds for endorsing a belief (Hansen, 2014). Usefulness does not require closer and closer approximations of objective truth for a belief to be endorsed. In neopragmatic postmodernism, human progress, Hansen (2014) explains, "is dependent upon learning the lessons of history, avoiding mistakes that were made in the past, and coming together to dialogue about what would be the best course of action in a given situation" (p. 116). Perhaps most important, beliefs that enhance life's meaning meet the criteria of usefulness, and neopragmatism provides a humanistic solution to the nihilistic postmodernism's lack of meaning.

Postmodernism in the Helping Professions

With regard to applications of the postmodern perspective in the helping professions, an important distinction can be made between constructivism and social constructionism. Constructivism is a theoretical counseling perspective positing that individuals create meaning. Constructivism emphasizes the individual's capacity for self-creating. The constructivist perspective is founded on the belief that individuals function within closed meaning-making systems (Hansen, 2004), and it has been criticized for failing to acknowledge the importance of social context in the process of human meaning making (Hansen, 2014; Rudes & Guterman, 2007). Social constructionism, by contrast, posits that our perception of reality is based on the use of language and that reality is constructed by groups of people (Hansen, 2004). Further, Gergen (1999) asserted that words only possess meaning when placed in a social context. Social constructionism has exerted a powerful influence on counseling and psychotherapy practices (Corey, 2013; Hansen, 2014; Murdoch, 2013).

Burr (2003) identified four foundational assumptions underlying the social constructionist perspective. First, individuals should challenge conventions and common beliefs that are assumed to be true without evidence. Second, knowledge is necessarily shaped by its historical and cultural context, and should not be assumed to be objective truth. Third, because knowledge is constructed, we should never fall prey to the mistaken assumption that a single correct way to live one's life can exist. Fourth, social constructions frequently include concrete practices (e.g., who can be legally married; how a family is defined), and these practices should be subjected to scrutiny.

Another foundational assumption underlying social constructionism is that self is always multiple and that a single stable self is a modernist myth. From this perspective, individuals are viewed as having multiple selves (e.g., parent, worker, citizen), and these selves, rather than constant, are continually being modified through the changing perceptions, roles, and choices of individuals (Gergen, 1999; Hansen, 2014; Peavy, 1998).

There are a number of important implications for counseling practice that are a natural outgrowth of the postmodern perspective. One important implication, consistent with social constructionism, is that the counselor's role in postmodern counseling approaches is more collaborative and egalitarian than with the modernist approach. In addition, postmodern therapies sometimes emphasize that the problem lies outside of the client—a principle that is commonly referred to as *externalizing* the problem. Further, the client's life story is sometimes referred to as a narrative and the client is viewed as having the ability to modify, reinterpret, or extend the narrative into the future. In effect, the client is viewed as having the capacity for *reauthoring* his or her life experiences. Sometimes the client is encouraged to *envision* a preferred future reality, counseling outcomes, or self-identity. Processes of reauthoring and envisioning emphasize the client's imagination or creative ability, and they can be facilitated deliberately through processes of *deconstructing* and *reconstructing* the client's current perceptions of reality. The emergence of the postmodern perspective has inspired the recent development of numerous therapies including, but not limited to, narrative therapy, solution-focused therapy, sociodynamic counseling, and motivational interviewing.

Practical Implications of Postmodernism for Counseling Practice

Polanyi's epistemology underscores the importance of personal knowledge in counseling practice and the need to more formally acknowledge and legitimize its role in a counselor's decision-making process and responses in a therapy session. There is a conspicuous divide between the relative status given to personal knowledge and formal counseling theories, with the latter form of knowledge often viewed as more legitimate and more worthy of study by professional counselors. Jensen (2007) argued that counselors and counselor educators should legitimize personal knowledge so that it can be examined directly rather than unconsciously informing counseling practice. More research is needed on the relationships among counselors' personal knowledge (e.g., personal relationships, private experiences, values) and their counseling practice. The field of counseling could potentially be advanced through increased understanding of the ways in which personal knowledge may enhance the counseling process and counselor competence.

The following implications for counseling practice logically follow from the preceding discussion of the tenets of the postmodern perspective:

1. Empathy has been asserted to be the most robust predictor of positive outcomes in counseling (Bohart, 2003). If Polanyi's descriptions of empathy as entailing *imaginative integration* and *dwelling in the perspective of another* are accurate, then the abilities to imagine, to dwell in the other person's perspective, and to integrate elements into meaningful wholes are ones that deserve more emphasis in counselor training programs.
2. Forms of counselor knowing that have an ineffable quality (e.g., intuition, hunches) should be given more consideration by counselors, educators, and researchers (Jensen, 2007). With self-reflection, more tangible bases for these types of personal knowing may be discovered, confirming their usefulness.
3. Counselors should recognize that theoretical perspectives and diagnostic labels potentially impede the process of understanding a client. Dean (1989) advises clinicians to remain humble and recognize the fallibility of assessments and diagnostic labels rather than viewing them as factual (i.e., objectively true).
4. The client's story should be understood as a constructed narrative rather than a strictly factual account (Jensen, 2007). In addition, the counselor

should remain aware of how she or he influences (e.g., through nonverbal encouragement) the nature of the story told by the client. Consistent with Gergen's social constructionism, treatment may be viewed as co-construction of a more adaptive narrative for the client.

5. Polanyi's epistemology of personal knowing indicates that the concept of therapeutic neutrality is impossible to achieve. The therapist listens to the client's story through a subjectively held perspective, which necessarily influences what the therapist hears and how the story is perceived.

6. Polanyi's personal knowledge also emphasizes the important roles played by both focal awareness of subsidiaries (deconstruction) and from-to integration (reconstruction or co-construction). Counselors can utilize understanding of both of these forms of knowing to intentionally assist clients in constructing more useful solutions, counseling outcomes, and social identities.

7. If our personal beliefs and values influence the process of counseling, then counselors arguably have an ethical obligation to be more transparent with regard to sharing personal beliefs and values. This practice, in turn, will potentially result in a counseling relationship that is more mutually respectful (Rhodes, 1986).

8. The postmodern perspective indicates that individuals have the capacity to reinterpret, reframe, or reauthor experiences so as to reduce client dysphoria, which may include feelings of shame, guilt, or culpability. Similarly, the postmodern perspective empowers clients to view their problems as external. By assisting clients in externalizing their problems, counselors can render problems more amenable to change.

Common Criticisms and Limitations of Postmodernism

An important consideration when employing counseling approaches and techniques rooted in the postmodern perspective is that counselors must remember that these techniques are not likely to be effective unless they are integrated with sound foundational counseling skills (Corey, 2013). To implement solution-focused therapy effectively, for example, a counselor must be skilled at establishing a sound working alliance. Without proper training and supervision, a counselor may easily become enamored with isolated postmodern techniques that will be ineffective when used without understanding the importance of an appropriate therapeutic context.

Another common criticism of postmodern counseling approaches is that these approaches commonly neglect the concrete action steps necessary for attaining the client's envisioned goals (Scholl & Cascone, 2010). It is important for counselors to assist clients in developing detailed action steps and plans. Clients commonly benefit from a logical sequence of steps and an appreciation of the level of energy, resources, and resolve necessary for turning an envisioned future into a reality (McMahon & Patton, 2006).

A third criticism that is commonly applied to solution-focused therapy (an approach that is informed by postmodernism) is that this approach is superficial rather than an in-depth approach (Murdoch, 2013). Similarly, postmodern approaches have been criticized for failing to focus on long-term goals (Messer & Gurman, 2011). In response to these criticisms, Piercy, Lipchik, and Kiser (2000) have suggested that solution-focused practitioners pay more attention to in-depth emotions of clients and tailor their use of this approach to meet the needs of the individual client, including the development of appropriate long-term goals.

Another criticism of postmodern approaches is related to limitations when used with some individuals from diverse populations. More specifically, there may be a lack of receptiveness to a counselor's reluctance to assume the role of expert in the counseling process because of the assumption that the client is the expert on his or her subjective impressions and sense of meaning (Corey, 2013; Murdoch, 2013). Corey recommended that counselors bridge this cultural divide by explaining that clients are the experts on what they find meaningful, and the counselor is the expert on counseling process and techniques.

Finally, there is a relatively modest amount of quantitative evidence for the efficacy of postmodern approaches (Gingerich & Eisengart, 2000), though this body of evidence is growing. At the same time, it is important to remember that in most counseling approaches the definition of a successful outcome is provided by the counselor-expert. Outcomes defined by counselors are typically more quantifiable than outcomes in postmodern approaches to counseling characterized by more egalitarian relationships (Messer & Gurman, 2011). In postmodern approaches to counseling, the successful outcome is arguably more dependent upon the perceptions of the client than the counselor. One possible solution to this challenge would be to employ qualitative research investigations of counseling effectiveness or single-case design studies that are supported by quantitative research methods (Scholl, Ray, & Brady-Amoon, 2014). Researchers might also use the outcomes of qualitative research to formulate quantitative research questions.

PURPOSES AND ORGANIZATION OF THE CURRENT TEXT

As previously mentioned, a primary goal of this book is to provide readers with concrete examples of postmodern interventions that can be used in a variety of counseling settings and with a variety of counseling clients. Another important goal of this book is to present strategies for addressing the potential limitations of postmodern counseling approaches. Contributing authors have been mindful of these limitations and addressed them in two primary ways. First, they discuss how their approach addresses or corrects for one or more common limitations. In some instances, they point to future directions for modifying a presented approach in response to criticism. Second, contributors acknowledge limitations of their counseling approaches or identify contraindications signaling that their approach may not be effective or advisable.

The current text's organization reflects the fact that there are well-established postmodern therapies (i.e., solution-focused therapy, narrative therapy) and dozens of additional postmodern therapies that are emerging. Chapters covering the former, well-established therapies are presented in *Section I: Solution-Focused Therapy* and in *Section II: Narrative Therapy*. Three chapters covering emerging postmodern therapies are covered in *Section III: Other Postmodern Therapeutic Models*. In addition, there are still other therapies that might be described as integrative models grounded in postmodern ideology. These integrative models are presented in *Section IV*. Finally, in *Section V: Counselor Education From a Postmodern Perspective*, Dr. Colette T. Dollarhide and her coauthors champion a philosophy of counselor education, rooted in postmodernism, that views the student learner as actively and intentionally constructing his or her identity. In their view, an egalitarian postmodern form of andragogy is essential for ensuring that students develop the attitudes and skill sets needed to make a positive and meaningful difference in the lives of their clients. Due to the dynamic, ever-evolving state of the postmodern therapy landscape, counselor educators are clearly indispensable guides for contemporary counselors-in-training.

REFERENCES

Anderson, W. (1990). *Reality isn't what it used to be: Theatrical politics, read-to-wear religion, global myths, primitive chic, and other wonders of the postmodern world.* San Francisco, CA: Harper & Row.

Barash, D. P. (1979). *The whisperings within.* New York, NY: Harper & Row.

Bohart, A. C. (2003). Person-centered psychotherapy and related experiential approaches. In S. Gurman & S. B. Messer (Eds.), *Essential psychotherapies: Theory and practice* (2nd ed., pp. 107–148). New York, NY: Guilford Press.

Collins, H. (2010). *Tacit and explicit knowledge.* Chicago, IL: University of Chicago Press.

Combs, A. W. (1954). Counseling as a learning process. *Journal of Clinical Psychology, 1,* 31–36.

Custance, A., & Travis, L. (1980). *The mysterious matter of mind.* Grand Rapids, MI: Zondervan.

Dawkins, R. (1995). *River out of Eden.* London, UK: Weidenfeld & Nicolson.

Dean, R. G. (1989). Ways of knowing in clinical practice. *Clinical Social Work Journal, 17*(2), 116–127.

Descartes, R. (1988). *Descartes: Selected philosophical writings.* New York, NY: Cambridge University Press.

Ellis, A., & Grieger, R. (1977). *Handbook of rational-emotive therapy.* New York, NY: Springer.

Fancher, R. (1995). *Cultures of healing: Correcting the image of American mental health care.* New York, NY: Freeman.

Gabbard, G. (2010). *Long-term psychodynamic psychotherapy: A basic text* (2nd ed.). Washington, DC: American Psychiatric Publishing.

Gay, P. (1988). *Freud: A life for our time.* New York, NY: Norton.

Gergen, K. (1999). *An invitation to social construction.* Thousand Oaks, CA: Sage.

Gingerich, W. J., & Eisengart, S. (2000). Solution-focused brief therapy: A review of the outcome research. *Family Process, 39,* 477–498.

Gurmin, J. H. (2006). The theory of evolution from Darwin to postmodernism. *Maynooth Philosophical Paper, 3,* 81–100.

Hansen, J. T. (2002). Postmodern implications for theoretical integration of counseling orientations. *Journal of Counseling & Development, 80,* 315–321.

Hansen, J. T. (2004). Thoughts on knowing: Epistemic implications of counseling practice. *Journal of Counseling & Development, 82,* 131–138. doi: 10.1002/j.1556-6678.2004.tb00294.x

Hansen, J. T. (2007). Counseling without truth: Toward a neopragmatic foundation for counseling practice. *Journal of Counseling & Development, 85,* 423–430.

Hansen, J. T. (2014). *Philosophical issues in counseling and psychotherapy: Encounters with four questions about knowing, effectiveness, and truth.* Lanham, MD: Rowman & Littlefield.

Hicks, S. (2004). *Explaining postmodernism: Skepticism and socialism from Rousseau to Foucault.* Milwaukee, WI: Scholarly Publishing.

Jensen, P. (2007). On learning from experience: Personal and private experiences as the context for psychotherapeutic practice. *Clinical Child Psychology and Psychiatry, 12*(3), 375–384.

Lyotard, J.-F. (1993). *Libidinal economy* (I. H. Grant, Trans.). Indianapolis, IN: Indiana University Press. (Original work published in 1974)

Manno, B. (1977). Michael Polanyi 1891–1976: A remembrance. *Journal of Humanistic Psychology, 17*(3), 65–70.

Messer, S. B., & Gurman, S. (2011). *Essential psychotherapies* (3rd ed.). New York, NY: Guilford.

Miller, W. R., & Rollnick, S. (2013). *Motivational interviewing: Helping people change* (3rd ed.). New York, NY: Guilford Press.

Peavy, R. V. (1998). *SocioDynamic counselling: A constructivist perspective.* Victoria, Canada: Trafford.

Perry, W. G., Jr. (1981). Cognitive and ethical growth: The making of meaning. In A. W. Chickering (Ed.), *The modern American college: Responding to the new realities of diverse students and a changing society* (pp. 76–116). San Francisco, CA: Jossey-Bass.

Piercy, F. P., Lipchik, E., & Kiser, D. (2000). Miller and de Shazer's article on "Emotions in Solution-focused therapy." *Family Process, 39,* 25–28. doi:10.1111/j.1545-5300.2000.39104.x

Plato (2008). *The republic* (B. Jowett, Trans.). New York, NY: Cosimo.

Polanyi, M. (1962). *Personal knowledge: Towards a post-critical philosophy.* Chicago, IL: University of Chicago Press.

Polanyi, M. (1966). *The tacit dimension.* Garden City, NJ: Doubleday.

Polanyi, M. (1969). Knowing and being. In M. Greene (Ed.), *Knowing and being* (pp. 123–137). Chicago, IL: University of Chicago Press.

Polanyi, M., & Prosch, H. (1975). *Meaning.* Chicago, IL: University of Chicago Press.

Polkinghorne, D. (1992). Postmodern epistemology of practice. In S. Kvale (Ed.), *Psychology and postmodernism* (pp. 146–165). Thousand Oaks, CA: Sage.

Rhodes, M. L. (1986) *Ethical dilemmas in social work practice.* Boston, MA: Routledge & Kegan Peel.

Rorty, R. (1979). *Philosophy and the mirror of nature.* Princeton, NJ: Princeton University Press.

Rorty, R. (1989). *Contingency, irony, and solidarity.* New York, NY: Cambridge University Press.

Rorty, R. (1999). *Philosophy and social hope.* New York, NY: Penguin Putnam.

Rosenau, P. (1992). *Post-modernism and the social sciences: Insights, inroads, and intrusions.* Princeton, NJ: Princeton University Press.

Rudes, J., & Guterman, J. (2007). The value of social constructionism for the counseling profession: A reply to Hansen. *Journal of Counseling & Development, 85,* 387–392.

Scholl, M. B., & Cascone, J. (2010). The constructivist resume: Promoting the career adaptability of graduate students in counseling programs. *The Career Development Quarterly, 59,* 180–191.

Scholl, M. B., McGowan, A. S., & Hansen, J. T. (Eds.). (2012). *Humanistic perspectives on contemporary counseling issues.* New York, NY: Routledge.

Scholl, M. B., Ray, D. C., & Brady-Amoon, P. (2014). Humanistic counseling process, outcomes, and research. *Journal of Humanistic Counseling, 53*(3), 218–239.

Stolorow, R., Atwood, G., & Orange, D. (2002). *Worlds of experience: Interweaving philosophical and clinical dimensions in psychoanalysis.* New York, NY: Basic Books.

Tauber, A. I. (2012). Freud's social theory: Modernist and postmodern revisions. *History of the Human Sciences, 25,* 41–70. doi:10.1177/9052695112460045

Wampold, B. (2001). *The great psychotherapy debate: Models, methods and findings.* Mahwah, NJ: Erlbaum.

Ward, C. C., & Reuter, T. (2011). *Strength-centered counseling, integrating postmodern approaches and skills with practice.* Thousand Oaks, CA: Sage.

Whitehead, A. N. (1979). *Process and reality: An essay in cosmology.* New York, NY: Free Press.

Woodward, A. (2002). Nihilism and the postmodern in Vattino's Nietzsche. *An Internet Journal of Philosophy, 6,* 51–67.

SECTION I
Solution-Focused Therapy

INTRODUCTION

Whereas Sigmund Freud's (1949) theory of psychoanalytic therapy emphasized the significance of an individual's history in determining his or her level of functioning, person-centered therapy (Rogers, 1951, 1986) emphasized the importance of being fully present in the here and now. By contrast, the originators of solution-focused therapy (De Shazer, 1982, 1985, 1994; De Shazer & Berg, 1988) asserted that positive growth is promoted when individuals adopt a forward-looking or future-oriented stance. This future-oriented focus is essentially postmodern (i.e., it is about constructing future realities rather than discovering realities that already exist).

Murdock (2017) traced the early roots of solution-focused therapy to Milton Erickson's strategic therapy described in detail in the book *Uncommon Therapy* (Haley, 1973). In his work as a family therapist, Erickson would identify something positive in the family's interactions, call the family's attention to this identified strength, and encourage the family to expand upon, or amplify, the strength. Like contemporary solution-focused therapy counselors, Erickson believed in encouraging clients to celebrate small successes. He recognized that these were significant for two important reasons. First of all, a small change can make a large impact on the family system. Second, a small change can provide the necessary impetus for a client to get unstuck and make changes on a larger scale.

Solution-focused therapy was originally developed by Steve de Shazer in the 1970s and 1980s and by Insoo Kim Berg in the 1990s at the Brief Family Therapy Center in Milwaukee, Wisconsin (Hoyt, 2003). de Shazer and Berg acknowledged they were influenced by Milton Erickson.

Solution-focused therapy and strategic therapy both emphasize the central role of the counselor in promoting a paradigm shift in the client, from focusing on problems to tapping into their natural resources and formulating solutions (Hoyt, 2003).

Philosophy Underlying Solution-Focused Therapy

Solution-focused therapy is grounded in a philosophical belief that solution-focused talk is more therapeutic than problem-focused talk. That is, client–counselor conversations that are centered around solutions provide more therapeutic leverage for change than conversations that are centered around problems (de Shazer, 1991). This focus on creating solutions, rather than discovering problems, makes solution-focused therapy a postmodern inspired approach. Solution-focused therapists believe that the use of problem-focused language, such as the clinical term *depression*, reifies a client's problem, making change more difficult. The emphasis on solution-focused language in solution-focused therapy reflects the foundational belief that problems are transient. This transience logically leads to the conclusion that it is relatively easy for counselors and clients to collaboratively facilitate therapeutic changes in clients' thoughts, behaviors, and emotions. As is true of other humanistically derived therapies, such as person-centered therapy, solution-focused therapy places a premium on the power of client intentionality. The counselor emphasizes that clients are competent and capable of independently constructing or collaboratively co-constructing solutions to their own problems. A hallmark example of this belief is the common solution-focused practice of assisting clients in identifying past *exceptions to the problem*. The client is viewed as capable of identifying these past exceptions and using them to construct viable solutions to the current problem.

Finally, solution-focused therapy is grounded in the optimistic philosophical assumption that making a small change is likely to lead to a larger change. This belief is reflected in the technique known as *pattern intervention* (Cade & O'Hanlon, 1993). Because a problem is contextualized within a larger pattern, even a subtle or small change in one's behaviors or thoughts can potentially ameliorate, or even resolve, the problem.

Early in the process of counseling, a primary role of the therapist is that of helping the client (also known as the complainant) transition from a mindset that emphasizes problems and problem solving to one that emphasizes *solution building* (De Jong & Berg, 2008). Importantly, this process is distinct from a process in which the counselor assumes the role of an expert who is responsible for addressing a client's problems (Saleebey,

2007). Solution building is a strengths-based process (Saleeybey, 2007). The counselor explores, elicits, observes, and affirms the client's strengths in the service of developing viable solutions. The counselor questions the client regarding her or his view of the problem and reframes the problem in a manner that renders it more amenable to change (Guterman, 2013). For example, a clinical term, such as depression, may be rephrased, in terms of the client's language (e.g., feeling blue) in an effort on the part of the counselor to make it less intractable (Cade & O'Hanlon, 1993).

In solution-focused therapy, the client–counselor alliance is an egalitarian one in which the quality of the relationship is integral to effective therapy implementation. The counselor joins alongside the client and shows empathy and respect for his or her competence, expertise, and intentional aims. The counselor cultivates a relationship characterized by the client's trust in her or him. As a result of the establishment of this collaborative relationship the counselor is rendered more capable of empowering the client to build solutions (De Jong & Berg, 2008).

De Jong and Berg described the therapeutic process of solution building as entailing five stages, including "describing the problem, developing well-formed goals, exploring for exceptions, end-of-session feedback, and evaluating client progress" (pp. 17–18). Although the client is viewed as the expert and an emphasis is placed on positive feedback (i.e., compliments), the counselor also provides the client with constructive feedback in the form of suggestions for changing her or his behavior in order to disrupt problematic patterns. Solution-focused counselors view therapeutic goals as attainable within a few sessions, and for this reason counselors commonly approach every session as if it may be the final session (Ratner, George, & Iveson, 2012).

Prior to the advent of solution-focused therapy, psychotherapy theorists had primarily emphasized the importance of factors in a person's past and present. Solution-focused theorists, by contrast, asserted that it is more appropriate for counselors and clients to focus their attention and energy on the future. Although the therapy borrows from earlier approaches such as Erickson's strategic therapy, it has popularized groundbreaking practices such as exploring exceptions to the problem and deconstructing clinical labels to render them more amenable to change. Ultimately, solution-focused therapy is grounded in a forward-looking and decidedly optimistic view of human potential. Motivational interviewing (Miller & Rollnick, 2013) is an example of how easily aspects of solution-focused therapy, such as scaling, can be successfully blended with other counseling approaches. Solution-focused therapy's solution-building approach has been adopted by many helping professionals, including clinical professionals, mentors, and life coaches (Ratner, George, & Iveson, 2012). Because of solution-focused therapy's egalitarian, solution-building, and strengths-based approach, it reduces the likelihood of clients feeling stigmatized, and it has exceptional potential for increasing the numbers and diversity of individuals seeking counseling for generations to come.

Section I of *Solution-Focused Therapy* features two chapters that, through the use of case illustrations, describe applications of solution-focused therapy (also referred to as solution-focused counseling) to two significant counseling concerns in contemporary society. In Chapter 3, Todd F. Lewis discusses solution-focused approaches to the treatment of a client with substance use issues. In Chapter 2, Michelle S. Hinkle and Caroline Perjessy describe the application of solution-focused therapy to counseling adolescent survivors of sexual abuse. Descriptions of solution-focused therapy in counseling theory textbooks may inadvertently lead readers to mistakenly conclude that the use of this approach is simple, or even formulaic (Ratner, George, & Iveson, 2012). However, these authors demonstrate that the application of solution-focused counseling techniques to counseling clients can be challenging, complex, and nuanced. The execution of critical functions such as amplifying exceptions to the problem requires skills and artistry on the part of the counselor, who must adapt her or his approach to the personality and unique needs of the client. The authors of both chapters describe the counseling process in considerable detail so that practitioners may learn from them and replicate their approach to implementation. Moreover, both chapters add significantly to the extant literature on solution-focused therapy.

REFERENCES

Cade, B., & O'Hanlon, W. H. (1993). *A brief guide to brief therapy.* New York, NY: Norton.

De Jong, P., & Berg, I. K. (2008). *Interviewing for solutions* (3rd ed.). Belmont, CA: Brooks/ Cole.

de Shazer, S. (1982). *Patterns of brief therapy.* New York, NY: Guilford Press.

de Shazer, S. (1985). *Keys to solutions in brief therapy.* New York, NY: Norton.

de Shazer, S. (1991). *Putting difference to work.* New York, NY: Norton.

de Shazer, S. (1994). *Words were originally magic.* New York, NY: Norton.

de Shazer, S., & Berg, I. K. (1988). Doing therapy: A post-structuralist revision. *Journal of Marital and Family Therapy, 18,* 71–81.

Freud, S. (1949). *An outline of psychoanalysis.* New York, NY: Norton.

Guterman, J. T. (2013). *Mastering the art of solution focused counseling* (2nd ed.). Alexandria, VA: American Counseling Association.

Haley, J. (1973). *Uncommon therapy.* New York, NY: Norton.

Hoyt, M. F. (2003). In A. S. Gurman & S. B. Messer (Eds.). *Essential psychotherapies: Theory and practice* (pp. 350–399). New York, NY: Guilford.

Miller, W. R., & Rollnick, S. (2013). *Motivational interviewing: Helping people change* (3rd ed.). New York, NY: Guilford.

Murdock, N. L. (2017). *Theories of counseling and psychotherapy: A case approach* (4th ed.). New York, NY: Pearson.

Ratner, H., George, E., & Iveson, C. (2012). *Solution focused brief therapy: 100 key points and techniques.* New York, NY: Routledge.

Rogers, C. R. (1951). *Client-centered therapy.* Boston, MA: Houghton Mifflin.

Rogers, C. R. (1986). Carl Rogers on the development of the person-centered approach. *Person-Centered Review, 1*(3), 257–259.

Saleeybey, D. (Ed.). (2007). *The strengths perspective in social work practice* (4th ed.) Boston, MA: Allyn & Bacon.

CHAPTER 2

Solution-Focused Counseling With Adolescent Survivors of Sexual Abuse

MICHELLE S. HINKLE AND CAROLINE PERJESSY

Clinicians who work with adolescent survivors of sexual abuse may feel ill prepared to work with the complex and multilayered symptoms that their clients present. Survivors of sexual abuse often internalize the experience and struggle with shame, guilt, and low self-esteem (Dube et al., 2005). Although well researched with beneficent outcomes, modern approaches to treating sexual abuse may inadvertently further oppress individuals and support the internalization of resulting symptoms. Therapists working from a modern perspective believe survivors need counselors to guide them to predetermined answers that will help them cope better with the abuse. Alternatively, therapists working from a postmodern perspective will work to empower individuals to find their own personal solutions to problems. Postmodern approaches make room for unique conversations that generate new meaning for clients' experiences and provide ways to move forward from abuse. Solution-focused counseling, in particular, can be useful for adolescent survivors of sexual abuse because the emphasis on egalitarian dialogue invites clients to explore their symptomatology from new perspectives amid the trauma. Further, a primary tenet of the theory is that survivors already possess the necessary strengths and resources to help them be resilient.

This chapter has several goals. First, we introduce the reader to information regarding the impact of sexual abuse on the psychological, social, and emotional development of adolescents. Then, we examine modern, or conventional, approaches to treatment. Following that, we present the benefits of using the postmodern perspective of solution-focused counseling when working with adolescent survivors of sexual abuse. Finally, a case study illustrates how this approach can help clients redefine trauma and identify strengths that can create solutions for symptomology.

SIGNIFICANCE OF ADOLESCENT SEXUAL ABUSE

Adolescent sexual abuse is a pervasive and traumatizing experience that has far-reaching implications for individuals' emotional and psychological development. Those who are sexually abused face immediate adverse consequences and future problems related to their functioning (Vural, Hafızoğlu, Türkmen Eren, & Büyükuysal, 2012). Adolescents who are sexually abused are more likely to develop immediate psychiatric symptoms, such as behavioral outbursts, anxiety, depression, and posttraumatic stress disorder (PTSD), than those who are not sexually abused (Carey, Walker, Rossouw, Seedat, & Stein, 2007; Silverman, Reinherz, & Giaconia,1996; Yüce et al., 2015). In response to trauma, individuals may strive to reduce painful emotions through substance abuse, self-injurious behavior, and other self-harm strategies (McLean, Morris, Conklin, Jayawickreme, & Foa, 2014). Adolescents who experience sexual abuse struggle with a number of long-term issues, including poor self-esteem, shame and guilt surrounding the abuse, substance abuse, suicidal ideation, and relationship difficulties in adulthood (Dube et al., 2005; Vural et al., 2012). In sum, adolescents who experience the trauma of sexual abuse consequently face additional adversities that may have immediate and lifelong implications.

There has been no identified syndrome for adolescents who have experienced sexual abuse; however, studies have found that the rate of PTSD among adolescents who were sexually abused as children is estimated at 38.5% in nonclinical samples (Perkonigg, Kessler, Storz, & Wittchen, 2000) and perhaps as high as 88% in clinical samples (Carey et al., 2007). Not surprisingly, a recent meta-analysis reviewing 78 studies exploring dimensions of injury related to childhood sexual abuse found that the probability of victims suffering from depression and anxiety was 70%. Additionally, dysthymia was found to be more prevalent than major depressive disorder (Amado, Arce, & Herraiz, 2015). Consequently, children and adolescents with such diagnoses are more likely to carry these psychiatric ailments with them into adulthood (Gibb, Chelminski, & Zimmerman, 2007).

Adolescents who experience sexual abuse develop their sense of self and identity differently than those who do not endure sexual trauma. Those who are sexually abused experience the trauma in vastly different ways depending on the individual circumstances of the abuse, family and social supports or influences, and other mitigating factors. Because all adolescents are unique, clinicians working with this population must simultaneously know the existing literature on sexual abuse, while also framing it within the context of their specific clients. The effects of sexual abuse vary based upon the severity and duration of the abuse, as well as survivors' personal characteristics and resiliency (Ratican, 1992). For example, an adolescent who is sexually assaulted by a primary caregiver is going to be impacted in vastly different ways than an adolescent who had an experience with indecent exposure. Some may not suffer from any noticeable negative effects, whereas others may show very adverse reactions with severe psychopathology (Kendall-Tackett, Williams, & Finkelhor, 1993). Sexual abuse may overwhelm children and adolescents who had previously been functioning well. Especially in circumstances in which protective factors are removed, such as when a child is displaced from the primary home and put into foster care, symptoms are likely to emerge (Saywitz, Mannarino, Berliner, & Cohen, 2000). Further, sexual abuse may exacerbate already existing problems.

It is estimated that 20% of women and 8% of men experience sexual abuse prior to age 18 (Pereda, Guilera, Forns, & Gomez-Benito, 2009). It is also estimated that only 50% of sexual abuse in children is disclosed; 15% of cases are reported, and 5% are resolved in court. Therefore, clinicians must be mindful of these statistics when conducting intake assessments, as some victims might not willingly disclose the abuse. Approximately 40% of reported perpetrators are family members and an additional 45% are close to their victims, creating significant challenges in terms of trusting clients' caregivers and establishing relationship boundaries. It also increases the likelihood of being victimized or becoming perpetrators themselves (Kendall-Tackett, 2002). In many instances when victims know their perpetrators, victims may distort or deny the sexual abuse when they come to counseling. Counselors having a clear conceptualization of how a client understands his or her own abuse experiences may be important to maintaining counseling engagement. Counseling for adolescents who suffer sexual abuse is paramount because, if left untreated, individuals may develop into adulthood with maladaptive schemas, possibly leading to revictimization and psychopathology (Molnar, Buka, & Kessler, 2001).

One specific model to conceptualize trauma experiences, the traumagenic model (Finklehor & Browne, 1987), encapsulates the various symptomology associated with sexual abuse. The model suggests abused children and adolescents experience the following: (a) traumagenic beliefs about sexuality (the effects of the abuse on sexual development); (b) feelings of betrayal toward the aggressor, which impact feelings toward other adults; (c) feelings of stigma that emerge from self-blame and shame associated with the abuse, which influence self-image and self-esteem; and (d) feelings of powerlessness caused by lack of control and the inability to put a stop to the abuse, which perpetuate an attitude of withdrawal and passivity and increasing vulnerability to experiencing further abusive sexual experiences. Although this is only one model describing how sexual trauma may impact clients' sense of self, the literature (e.g., Coffey, Leitenberg, Henning, Turner, & Bennett, 1996; Finkelhor, 1990) supports this model's depiction of how individuals' self-esteem and self-concept are radically altered as survivors of sexual trauma.

SELECTION AND EVALUATION
OF DIFFERENT TREATMENT APPROACHES

The treatment of adolescents who experience sexual abuse is often difficult to evaluate for a number of reasons. First, it is challenging to identify symptoms because young people are not able to accurately self-report symptoms due to their limited self-awareness, verbal, and reasoning skills. Caregivers and other adult authority figures may assist in this endeavor, but they often have multiple, and sometimes conflicting, viewpoints on how the abuse occurred and its impact on clients (Kolko & Kazdin, 1993). Second, improvement is not only dependent on the treatment approach but also on the health and stability of adult caregivers. Parental support was found to be a significant predictor in treatment outcomes, indicating that healthy emotional bonds between parents and children may mediate responses to abuse (Kazdin & Weisz, 1998; Limke, Showers, & Zeigler, 2010). Because adolescents are dependent on their adult caregivers, some treatment approaches, such as family therapy, may not be feasible, especially if clients are in foster care.

Adolescents who experience sexual abuse will experience it in disparate ways depending on their functioning prior to the abuse (e.g., temperament, attachment status), the nature of the abuse, and any protective factors such as parental support. Therefore, treatment will vary a great deal depending on the specific context, and it will not yield similar results. Researchers have found that an individualized treatment approach is recommended because of the difficulty in determining the effects of the abuse and the mitigating risk factors that complicate the presentation of symptoms (Target & Fonagy, 1996).

Psychotherapeutic interventions for adolescents with sexual abuse histories require simultaneous consideration of multiple factors, including (a) characteristics of the violence, including duration, intensity, and aggressor relationship; (b) risk factors and protective factors; and (c) symptoms and behavioral and cognitive changes of the adolescent (Saywitz et al., 2000). Sexual abuse is considered a traumatic experience. As such, literature on conventional approaches in treating adolescents who are sexually abused is included within trauma literature. Most therapies target symptoms that are a result of any trauma, sexual or otherwise (e.g., physical abuse, neglect). However, there is a need for targeted treatment specific to sexual trauma, as some treatment approaches were found to be more efficacious with this population than others. A review of the literature revealed that variations of cognitive-behavioral therapy (CBT) are the most frequently used in treating trauma in adolescents, particularly trauma related to sexual abuse (Follette & Ruzek, 2006). CBT has been found effective in reducing symptoms related to depression and anxiety (Cohen, Mannarino, & Knudsen, 2005) and PTSD (Cohen, Deblinger, Mannarino, & Steer, 2004). The literature on adolescent sexual abuse consistently identifies cognitive-behavioral approaches with abuse-focused components as the preferred treatment when working with this population (Child Welfare Information Gateway, 2007).

Several therapies similar to CBT are trauma-informed treatments that were specifically developed for adolescents, such as the multimodal trauma treatment (MMTT) and trauma-focused cognitive-behavioral therapy (TF-CBT) (Cohen, Mannarino, & Deblinger, 2010). MMTT adapts CBT strategies used for adults to adolescents who experience anxiety and have behavioral disorders (Amaya-Jackson et al., 2003). MMTT posits that trauma impacts the development of children and adolescents in negative ways and offers age-appropriate interventions that help children and adolescents overcome the trauma. MMTT is a 14-session group therapy experience that uses CBT techniques, such as psychoeducation, narratives (writing about the trauma), exposure to memories of the trauma, relaxation techniques, and cognitive restructuring (Amaya-Jackson et al., 2003).

Trauma-focused cognitive-behavioral therapy (TF-CBT; Cohen, Mannarino, & Deblinger, 2006) is an evidenced-based practice that is more effective in reducing symptoms than other methods when working with children and adolescents who have experienced sexual abuse (Cohen et al., 2004). This treatment was originally developed for those who specifically experienced sexual abuse, but it has become a treatment of choice for general trauma (Feather & Ronan, 2009). TF-CBT is informed by the assumption that traumatized adolescents will experience disturbances in affective, behavioral, and cognitive functioning (Little & Akin-Little, 2009). TF-CBT is a short-term (12–16 outpatient sessions), structured therapy that attempts to decrease adolescents' negative behavioral and emotional responses and change maladaptive abuse-focused beliefs. The treatment is a combination of psychoeducation about the trauma, skills training for relaxation, and validation and support from the nonoffending caregiver (Webb, Hayes, Grasso, Laurenceau, & Deblinger, 2014). The goals of therapy are to help adolescents master their reactions to reminders of the trauma and help remove them from a victim perspective. Techniques specific to this therapy include teaching clients about trauma narration and how to cognitively process the trauma, in vivo exposure to overcome trauma reminders, and conjoint sessions with clients and caregivers (Cohen et al., 2004).

Another conventional approach in treating adolescent trauma is the Stanford cue-centered therapy (SCCT; Carrion & Hull, 2010). This therapy focuses on the cognitive, affective, behavioral, and physical effects of trauma. The goal of SCCT is to "decrease the adolescent's negative cognitions and sensitivity to traumatic memory while increasing the use of positive emotional expressions and adaptive coping methods" (Black, Woodworth, Tremblay, & Carpenter, 2012, p. 196). It is conducted on an individual basis and utilizes a combination of CBT techniques (e.g., cognitive restructuring, skill building, pscyhoeducation, relaxation) and other interventions, including methods of expression, narrative use, and parental coaching (Stanford School of Medicine, 2010). The treatment is typically 15 to 18 sessions long and the goal is to help adolescents understand how the trauma affects them and control their responses to trauma stimuli (Carrion & Hull, 2010).

Seeking safety (SS; Najavits, Gallop, & Weiss, 2006) is a therapy that addresses both trauma-related symptoms and substance abuse disorders and has been specifically adapted for adolescents. For example, the therapy takes into consideration adolescents' reading levels and uses displacement to talk about the traumatic events. Displacement is a technique that allows adolescents to talk about a traumatic event as if it happened to a friend and provide some distance from the trauma (Najavits et al., 2006). Similar to the other trauma-focused therapies, SS focuses on psychoeducation, relaxation techniques, trigger identification, cognitive restructuring, and trauma narratives. It is effective with adolescent males and females, conducted in a group or individual setting, and includes 25 topics that must be covered over the duration of treatment.

Conventional approaches in treating sexual trauma are primarily CBT based and focus on adolescents' cognitions, behaviors, and affect regulation. CBT carries certain assumptions that influence goals and treatment of therapy. For example, CBT purports that clients' faulty perceptions create symptoms and abnormalities. This belief promotes a pathologizing view of clients, suggesting there is something wrong with them for thinking, behaving, and feeling as they do. It indicates that there is a right way to think, feel, and act about traumatic events. If clients are unable to alter their thinking or feeling about the event, feelings of shame and guilt may increase. For individuals who already struggle with self-acceptance and self-blame, this internalization of the problem can be detrimental to recovery.

Although there have been efforts made to adapt CBT interventions to more diverse populations (Miranda et al., 2005), the majority of the research on the effectiveness of CBT with this population has been conducted on Caucasian, middle-class clients (Bernal, Jimenez-Chafey, & Domenech-Rodriguez, 2009). Cultural sensitivity is important for all clinicians to utilize, and given the contextually diverse circumstances surrounding adolescent sexual abuse, it becomes even more important to do so with these clients. Clinicians must be aware of their own values and beliefs surrounding sexual abuse, as well as their clients' values and beliefs, and how these perceptions impact the trajectory of treatment. Because CBT approaches measure effectiveness through observable, specific, and measureable means, they do not always take into account the unique considerations of adolescents from various cultural backgrounds. As discussed previously, the presentation of trauma can vary widely depending on individuals' predisposition, environmental factors, culture, and resiliency. As such, clinicians working with this population who employ a CBT approach must consider the unique background of adolescents without distorting the trauma. It is also important to remember that adolescents' ages may be significantly different from their developmental stage, both cognitively and socially (De Bellis, Hooper, Woolley, & Shenk, 2010). Additionally, CBT espouses short-term treatment of symptoms, which is not always realistic for those who have suffered traumatic events that have the potential for lifelong developmental changes.

Finally, CBT espouses determinism, in which individuals do not have free will to self-manage or control cognitions (Slife & Williams, 1995). This can perpetuate feelings of shame and guilt for victims of sexual abuse if they are not able, despite their best efforts, to manage their cognitions as a result of external stimuli. For example, a clinician employing the CBT anxiety-reduction technique known as systematic desensitization may instruct a client to visualize the traumatic event. In some instances, especially at the beginning of systematic desensitization process, clients who are attempting to relax may struggle to conjure the image and may experience the same level, or even increased, anxiety with each successive attempt. This experience could, in turn, increase their anxiety surrounding this activity, which may decrease their desire to engage in the intervention. If they continue to feel badly, they may discontinue therapy altogether.

CURRENT TRENDS IN TREATMENT

The literature on sexual abuse treatment in adolescents incorporates alternative treatments for trauma, including art therapy (Krantz & Pennebaker, 2007) and eye movement desensitization and reprocessing (EMDR; Greenwald, 2007). EMDR has been found to significantly reduce trauma-related symptoms among children (Rodenburg, Benjamin, de Roos, Meijer, & Stams, 2009); however, the exact mechanism on how change takes place is unknown. A meta-analysis on the psychological treatment of adolescent sexual abuse discovered that the most tested treatments were (a) CBT and trauma-focused therapy, (b) supportive therapy, (c) psychodynamic treatment, (d) humanistic treatments, and (e) play therapy (Sánchez-Meca, Rosa-Alcázar, & López-Soler, 2011). Results revealed that CBT, in conjunction with supportive therapy, play therapy, or psychodynamic therapies, yielded better results than other treatment options. Play therapy is also effective with this population and enhances treatment (Green, 2012). Although these therapies are helpful in reducing trauma-related symptoms, they are not stand-alone trauma treatments and are usually used in combination with other trauma-focused therapies, such as trauma-focused CBT (Black et al., 2012).

Game-based CBT (GB-CBT) group therapy (Misurell & Springer, 2013), an evidence- and strength-based approach, integrates the three treatment approaches of TF-CBT, play therapy, and group therapy. GB-CBT includes the core components of TF-CBT, including parent management training, cognitive coping, anger management, and relaxation skills, among others. It is designed to highlight the strengths and resources of the adolescent, and it uses positive reinforcement as the primary technique for changing behavior. This approach is more culturally sensitive by considering the collectivist nature of African American and Latino adolescent populations and harnessing this strength to enhance the therapeutic improvement of all group members.

SOLUTION-FOCUSED THEORY AS A POSTMODERN COUNSELING APPROACH

Solution-focused counseling (SFC) is a strength-based and relational counseling approach that uses conversation to deemphasize problem-oriented talk and promote solution-oriented dialogue (de Shazer, 1985, 1988, 1991, 1994). Strength-based counseling approaches help clients see themselves as capable individuals with the capacity to construct their own solutions to problems. Solution-focused counselors assume clients create preferred realities, experience times when complaints do not exist, and have strengths and resources that can be used to eradicate problems (de Shazer et al., 1986).

The theoretical assumptions of SFC are informed by a postmodern framework, which emphasizes social construction and subjective truths (Anderson, 2003). Social construction posits that individuals and communities generate knowledge and meaning through language and dialogue (Gergen, 1985). The belief that language creates realities and provides meaning to experiences is a main component of SFC (Anderson, 2003, Berg & De Jong, 1996; Gergen, 1985, 2009, Walter & Peller, 1996, 2000). Rather than understanding words as an accurate reflection of what exists, postmodern counselors view them as a social contract that has been agreed upon in conversation (Chang & Nylund, 2013; Gergen, 1985, 2009; Walter & Peller, 1996). To a solution-focused counselor, problems endure due to words and conversations that entrap people within a particular narrative. Once entrenched in these stories, individuals see limited possibilities for them to move beyond the identified problem. Counseling conversations in SFC can re-create identities and speak new possibilities into existence (Walter & Peller, 1996, 2000).

Another postmodern perspective that informs SFC is the idea that there is no objective truth, rather there are multiple realities (Hansen, 2002). As such, simultaneous realities coexist, with some truths holding more power and dominance than others (Gergen, 2009). Guided by the idea that pluralistic realities exist, solution-focused counselors will presuppose that there are times when problems, or symptoms of problems, are not present. These times, known as exceptions, are often invisible to clients due to the inflexibility of the language used to describe them (de Shazer, 1991). For example, people might believe that times when problems do not exist are simply flukes or anomalies. During SFC, dialogue that extends from examining exceptions will bring marginalized stories into focus. Clients will hopefully gain awareness that they are part of coexisting realities in which problems are less oppressive or even nonexistent.

When conversations highlight exceptions and build new possibilities, clients are depathologized. Chang and Nyland (2013) pointed out that solution-focused counselors "position themselves outside of dominant pathologizing mental health discourse" (p. 74). One result of this depathologizing process is that clients can begin to externalize their problems or believe that these problems, rather than being a reflection of their core internal identity, are in existence outside of their essential personhood. Postmodern perspectives view problems as external from a person and created through language and descriptions in societal dialogue (Gergen, 2009). Taking this perspective of viewing the complaint as existing apart from clients, rather than within them, opens the possibility of seeing people as healthy with the capacity to overtake problems with their distinct resources and strengths.

Because solution-focused counselors believe there are multiple ways to understand presenting concerns, they also believe there is no singular way problems should be addressed. As a result, counselors do not interpret presenting problems via a particular lens in order to lead clients toward a predetermined route that alleviates symptoms. Instead, clients are seen as the experts who are capable of guiding themselves in unique ways to solve complaints. The counselor takes a curious stance to learn more about clients' unique perceptions and the way they make meaning of experiences (Lipchik, 2002). Although solution-focused counselors may steer conversation toward the future and solutions, clients are expected to have equal participation in constructing the direction of counseling and contributing to the outcomes.

SOLUTION-FOCUSED COUNSELING WITH ADOLESCENT SURVIVORS OF SEXUAL ABUSE

The strength-based nature of SFC makes it an approach that is well suited to counseling individuals who have experienced sexual abuse (Bannink, 2008; Dolan, 1991; Kress & Hoffman, 2008). Trauma survivors are resilient individuals with resources, capabilities, and strengths that enabled them to withstand the sexual abuse and persevere. SFC counselors externalize problems and help clients to see their unique strengths to increase personal agency against the effects of the abuse and resulting symptomology. This might be helpful for clients who often blame themselves, feel shame, and experience low self-esteem as a result of the trauma (Dube et al., 2005).

In SFC, counselors will deemphasize the act of the abuse and instead focus on times in which the trauma and related symptoms are less oppressive. Because retelling and reprocessing traumatic events can often lead to additional stress and increased symptomology (Byrd-Craven, Geary, Rose, & Ponzi, 2008), the solution- and future-oriented talk of SFC may be more fitting for someone who has experienced trauma. By generating supportive and strength-based conversations that re-create the impacts of trauma and redefine its influence, clients can be empowered to increase their sense of control (Carbonell & Parteleno-Barehmi, 1999). This empowerment and ability to make new meaning of the experience may prevent revictimization (Finkelhor & Browne, 1986; Mullen, Martin, Anderson, Romans, & Herbison, 1996). Additionally, the focus on exceptions in solution-oriented counseling is a way to make meaning of past success, which can engender positive self-esteem (Ross & Wilson, 2002).

Because SFC takes into account individuals' uniqueness, as well as the particular meaning clients attribute to events, it is helpful in working with sexual trauma. Adolescents' experiences of sexual abuse can vary greatly due to the multiplicity of circumstances that surround a client's assault (Kendall-Tackett et al., 1993; Ratican, 1992), suggesting individualized treatment is optimal (Target & Fonagy, 1996). Solution-focused counseling is grounded in the belief that individuals' experiences are unique and counselors don't need to understand the etiology of a problem to determine courses of treatment and solutions (de Shazer, 1994). Further, the theory posits that individuals are capable of determining their own course of treatment. As such, solution-focused counselors take a nonexpert stance to allow clients to shape the unique meaning of their experiences and solutions. The collaborative nature of the counseling process will enable clients and counselors to co-create solutions that are specific and distinctive to each person.

Solution-focused family therapy (SFFT) is a natural therapeutic fit when working with adolescents and their families. This collaborative approach assists families in identifying their strengths and resources to bring about positive change (Berg, 2000). SFFT works with family members' personal beliefs and unique family dynamics, while also recognizing that families exist within a broader context and are doing the best they can with the resources that are available to them (Berg, 1994). Further, Wheeler (2001) suggested the usefulness of using SFC with children and adolescents. The author identified the aspects of externalizing the problem, promoting a more balanced view of realities, and reducing blame within the theory as relevant to counseling adolescents. With adolescents, who frequently come to counseling at the request of others, SFC can give them a sense of control over the direction of counseling (Paylo, 2005; Tohn & Oshlag, 1996).

SOLUTION-FOCUSED COUNSELING MODEL

"Solution-focused counseling" is an encompassing term that includes solution-focused brief therapy (SFBT) and its ancillary models. Steve de

Shazer and Insoo Kim Berg, along with their colleagues at the Brief Family Therapy Center in Milwaukee, Wisconsin, developed SFBT. The theory is a strength-based counseling approach that generates solution-oriented discussion. By focusing on solutions and clients' strengths, SFBT counselors believe they can use conversation to help clients create new realities where solutions are more available and they are in control of problems. During SBFT, clients redefine their problems and change their perspectives on themselves.

Fundamental Tenets

SFBT counselors believe that the focus of counseling should be on solutions and the future. de Shazer (1994) believed that no previous knowledge of problems is necessary in order to determine solutions. Solution talk is the main focus of sessions because SFBT counselors believe that talking about life without problems will make life without problems possible. When solutions are discussed, new things can occur for clients. First, they will increase their awareness of times when they are already using solutions so that they can use them more often. Second, by taking into account the times when they are already living without the complaint, they will change their perspective that problems are all encompassing. Finally, by talking about solutions, clients will see them as possible and use them more readily.

SFBT counselors believe that people already possess the resources and strengths required to overcome challenges. These inner strengths have previously helped ameliorate the impact of other problems on clients' lives. Times in which individuals have used strengths to overcome a problem and times in which it doesn't exist are called *exceptions*, and they are a main focus of counseling. During SBFT, counselors will highlight clients' exceptions to their presenting problems by keeping conversations focused on these occurrences. Ensuing conversations will focus on exploring how the exceptions occurred, what happened during the exceptions, the results of the exceptions, and the meaning clients give to these occurrences. These thick, or detailed, descriptions of exceptions make it possible for clients to generate various solutions to problems, and these descriptions empower them to believe they are capable of facilitating more exception times. As a result, clients will be able to externalize their problems and understand them as something that exists outside of themselves, which they have the power to combat. This ability to see a problem as external can be empowering and make the prospect of eradicating problems more feasible. Identifying unique strengths and abilities to overcome complaints can result in clients increasing their personal agency against them.

Language is an important aspect of the process in externalizing problems and discovering solutions. SFBT counselors believe that language is the way knowledge is constructed and meaning can be made. Words used to describe people, problems, and solutions are powerful and can either limit or expand possibility. This is evident in the different meanings that are implied when people who have experienced a sexual trauma are identified as either a victim or a survivor (Bannink, 2008). Bannink suggested that counselors and clients consider the power behind the words *victim* and *survivor* when used to describe someone who has endured trauma (p. 219). For example, he noted that the word *victim* could indicate being preyed upon, vulnerability, weakness, and lacking control. This description can make people feel damaged or fragile, which can limit their range of action and possibilities. Alternatively, Bannink asserted being called a survivor of sexual abuse provides a much different story. The word *survivor* connotes perseverance, strength, life, and control. Being described as a survivor promotes power and the ability to overcome. By making changes to the words used to describe someone or something, new obtainable realities are created.

As clients are empowered to view themselves differently in relation to a problem, they are able to see more readily new possibilities regarding how they might overcome their challenges. This will make it easier to imagine a world in which they are capable of having exceptions happen more often. In SFBT, clients are encouraged to describe their life without the problem and discuss how things would be different if the problem never existed. Clients are encouraged to share their unique perspectives of how problems will be less influential in their life, as well as express their personal desires. Conversations of this nature will lead clients to identify their unique goals (Walter & Peller, 1996). Throughout this process, counselors need to remain curious in order to grasp a strong understanding of what clients want for themselves (Lipchik, 2002).

Through conversations about the future and goals, clients and counselors will find that unique solutions to presenting problems will begin to emerge. When this happens, the focus of conversation will include thick descriptions of the emerging solutions so that clients can become more aware of them. SFBT counselors will instill their belief that clients have expertise in accomplishing their goals through these solutions. Different talk topics will include times when clients will use solutions, how they will use them, how others can promote their use of solutions, and imagined results of the solution. By engaging in talk about ways to overcome problems, clients will use solutions more readily.

Ancillary Theories

Other solution-based theories have derived from SFBT. These theories include solution-oriented therapy (O'Hanlon & Weiner-Davis, 2003) and possibility therapy (O'Hanlon & Beadle, 1997). Many similarities exist between these two approaches to counseling and SFBT. These include an emphasis on solution talk and focus on the future, social construction, and counseling techniques. Minute differences subsist among the theories, such as the acknowledgment and exploration of problems in solution-oriented therapy and the validation of felt experience and sense of self in possibility therapy (Hoyt, 1996).

Techniques

Conversation and language are the main change agents in SFC, and, as a result, there are many techniques that counselors will use to create dialogue. Techniques range from prompts within session to enhance solution-oriented conversations to creative tactics in establishing an audience for clients' new realities. Although counselors use techniques, it is essential they use basic skills like empathy and warmth to maintain and enhance the therapeutic alliance (Lipchik, 2002). Techniques, combined with basic counseling skills, will provide the structure for clients to explore their strengths and solutions to create positive change in their lives.

Future-Oriented Questions and the Miracle Question

Future-oriented questions initiate conversations that focus on a future time, in which problems are no longer a concern. These future conversations are the opposite of problem-talk, which makes the presenting issue and related complaints the focus of counseling. By using future-oriented questions, counselors are able to keep clients envisioning a future without problems in order to speak it into existence, or make it happen. Examples of future-oriented questions are "What will you be doing when you are less depressed?" "What will it feel like when you are able to feel better about your body?" and "What are some signs that you will notice when you decrease your anxiety after a flashback?"

The miracle question is one type of future-oriented question that specifically invites clients to visualize a world in which their problems do not exist. Counselors prompt clients to imagine that a miracle happened while they were sleeping and when they awoke the problem that brought them to counseling was solved. Although there are a variety of ways to deliver the miracle questions, de Shazer (1988) provided a guide: "Suppose that one night, while you were asleep, there was a miracle and this problem was solved. How would you know? What would be different?" (p. 5). The miracle question invites clients to consider various possibilities of how life might be when they are not entrenched in the current problem (De Jong & Berg, 2002). Further, answers to the miracle question can assist with goal setting as it provides counselors with an idea of what clients are looking for in a satisfying life (O'Hanlon & Weiner-Davis, 2003).

Identifying Goals

Co-constructing goals with clients is a way for counselors to understand what clients want out of the counseling process (De Jong & Berg, 1996). Working together on "goaling" (Walter & Peller, 1996, p. 17) is a process in which clients imagine new possibilities and consider new meaning in how they understand their experiences. Although goals are important in all counseling, to a solution-focused counselor goals are not a means to an end. Rather, "goaling" initiates an "evolution of meaning," or a process that changes the way clients understand their experiences and themselves (Walter & Peller, 1996, p. 17). For example, a counselor could ask, "When you experience less anxiety after a flashback, how will it make a difference to you?" This might be followed up with, "What does your ability to alleviate anxiety say about you?"

Exception Questions

Exceptions are instances when problems could have been present but were not (de Shazer, 1985; de Shazer et al., 2007). Fully exploring these times is helpful to begin the process of identifying solutions (de Jong & Berg, 2002). Counselors relay the message that clients should continue to do the things that are already working to keep away complaints. An example of a question that elicits exceptions is, "Over the last week, when was a time that you did not have flashbacks of the sexual abuse?" By asking "when was a time" rather than "was there a time," clients are invited to look for times in which exceptions occurred instead of having an opportunity to say there were none. These presuppositional questions (O'Hanlon & Weiner-Davis, 2003) inherently presuppose that an exception has occurred, thus affirming that clients have inner strengths and the ability to live without the problem.

When exceptions have been identified, solution-focused counselors will amplify them through ongoing dialogue. It will be as though the exceptions to problems are examined through a microscope with the intent to learn as much as possible about these times. O'Hanlon and Weiner-Davis (2003) offered various questions to further explore exceptions, which can be summarized as inquiries into (a) differences between the exception and problematic times, (b) exploring clients' sense of agency in accomplishing the exception, (c) the effects of the exception, (d) creating an audience by asking who else noticed the exception, (e) the behaviors associated with the exception, (f) change that has happened to get the exception to occur, (g) asking about interests to find more exceptions, and (h) asking if clients have eradicated the problem in the past (pp. 85–90).

As clients are sometimes unaware of exceptions, they may struggle to identify times when problems did not exist or were less severe. In these instances, counselors can ask exception questions from another person's perspective. For example, "What would your mom say if I asked her to tell me times over the past couple weeks where anxiety hasn't been a problem for you?" A benefit of asking an exception question from the perspective of someone in the client's life is that new possibilities will be considered and it will begin to create an audience to a new reality for clients (Walter & Peller, 2000). When clients become aware that others notice exceptions, or things they do to combat the problem, they realize that others are supporting a new narrative for their life.

Identifying Strengths and Complimenting

Through conversations about exceptions, client strengths and successes will be revealed (De Jong & Berg, 2002; De Jong & Miller, 1995). Being attuned to hear positive qualities that clients express is an important task for counselors. Amplifying these strengths will lead to co-constructing client competency in accomplishing goals and leading a more satisfying life (Berg & De Jong, 1996). The following are statements that serve as compliments: "I'm impressed with all of the things you've done to keep yourself from becoming anxious after you experience a flashback" and "Spending the afternoon on the anniversary of the trauma with your family and friends was good thinking. It sounds like having their support helped you through the hard day."

Scaling Questions

Scaling questions can be used throughout counseling for clients to reflect on their past and current experiences and approximate their future (Berg &

de Shazer, 1993). They can be used for clients to assess current experiences and measure progress by way of indicating the concrete things they do, or can do, to advance their goals (de Shazer, 1991; De Jong & Berg, 2002). Scaling questions ask clients to rate themselves on a scale of 1 to 10. For example, a counselor might ask, "On a scale of 1 to 10, where 1 indicates no anxiety and 10 indicates unbearable anxiety, how do you rate anxiety after experiencing a flashback?" If the client states that she is usually at a level of 6, the counselor can ask how she would know if her anxiety lowered from a 6 to a 5. Any answers to this question could indicate goals that the client would work toward. Then, if the counselor asked what the client would be doing at a 5 to demonstrate less anxiety, the client would be identifying solutions for achieving her goal.

CASE ILLUSTRATION

Ashley is a 14-year-old adolescent female who struggles with anxiety and depression. She has a history of sexual abuse that took place from the ages of 10–12 by an older boy in the neighborhood. During the sexual abuse, the perpetrator warned her that if she told anyone, he would kill her cat and tell everyone that Ashley was making up the stories about the abuse. Ashley was terrified of him and his threats and felt the need to comply with his demands so that she wouldn't face the consequences. About a year ago, she began to exhibit behavioral symptoms in school, such as crying, lashing out, and social withdrawal. One of her teachers noticed that she had healing cuts on her thigh area. At this point, the teacher referred Ashley to the school counselor. The school counselor met with her several times before Ashley slowly revealed what she had been experiencing. This led to an intervention, where Ashley's parents were encouraged to bring her to a clinical mental health counselor. Ashley has been in weekly counseling since the referral. Her parents are supportive of her treatment, which includes attending individual and group counseling sessions with other young females who were also sexually abused.

Ashley experiences anxiety on an ongoing basis, which affects her ability to sleep and eat. She struggles with poor self-esteem and self-image, and believes she is unattractive and fat, although she is of average weight. She blames herself for the abuse happening. As the abuse occurred, Ashley struggled with anger and alternating feelings of emptiness. In response, she used self-injurious behaviors to help herself feel alive and, simultaneously, to punish herself by acting on the guilt and shame she felt regarding her belief that she contributed to the abuse. These self-injurious behaviors ranged from using scissors to make scratches on her arms and legs to using razor blades. Ashley tended to isolate from her friends and family, but she started enjoying the group process and finding refuge in sharing her experiences in the group setting.

Case Conceptualization

A solution-focused counselor would recognize that Ashley has the strengths and resources to overcome the symptomology she has experienced in the last year. Further, a solution-focused counselor would believe Ashley experiences times without the feelings of depression, anxiety, and low self-esteem, as well as times when she hasn't engaged in self-injurious behaviors or isolation. In fact, she has already revealed an exception to isolation by describing how she enjoys the group she attends with other adolescent girls who have experienced sexual trauma. During counseling this exception will be highlighted, and she will be encouraged to identify more times when problems aren't present. In doing this, the counselor will amplify Ashley's strengths and resources to help her find unique and personalized solutions. Then, she will be able to do more of the same in order to increase times of exceptions until they are a more dominant part of her life.

To a solution-focused counselor, it would be important to create conversation around her ability to overcome the negative impacts of the sexual abuse and restory the trauma so that she no longer blames herself. The counselor will facilitate a process in which an alternative reality for Ashley can be illuminated and strengthened. Through making new meaning of the experience and becoming more aware of how she can live amid the past trauma, she and her counselor will co-create alternative ways to live her life.

Description of the Course of Solution-Focused Counseling with Ashley

Using Questions to Elicit Solution Talk

When working with Ashley, using the miracle question and other future-oriented questions will help to elicit solution talk. The following segment of conversation illustrates how her counselor assessed what she is looking for in counseling and helped her to establish goals.

COUNSELOR: Imagine tonight after you go home and go to bed a miracle occurred while you were sleeping. Since you were sleeping you don't know that it happens, but it causes the problems that you've experienced since the sexual abuse to go away. When you wake up in the morning, what is the first thing you'll notice that tells you the miracle occurred?

ASHLEY: (after some thought) I guess I'd notice while I was getting ready for school. I probably wouldn't change my outfit a bunch of different times.

COUNSELOR: What would you do instead of change your outfit a bunch of times?

ASHLEY: I would feel like I looked good in the first set of clothes I pick.

COUNSELOR: How would you know you felt good in the first outfit?

ASHLEY: Well, I'd look in the mirror and smile at myself. I'd keep the outfit on, and I'd go downstairs to eat breakfast with my sister before school without feeling rushed.

COUNSELOR: So you'd get to spend time eating breakfast with your sister, too?

ASHLEY: Yeah, usually I change so much that I have to eat my breakfast on the bus.

COUNSELOR: So after the miracle your morning would be very different. What do you think your sister would notice about you if you came down to eat with her?

ASHLEY: Well, she'd probably be surprised. She'd be happy, too, because she and my mom are always telling me we should eat together.

COUNSELOR: So you'd surprise your mom and your sister. Anyone else?

ASHLEY: I'd surprise my friends because we'd have time to talk before getting on the bus.

COUNSELOR: When you feel good about yourself in the morning, you spend more time with people you care about. How would life be different if you spent more time with others?

ASHLEY: I'd feel less lonely and sad. When I'm alone, I think about bad things that happened to me. It makes me not like myself.

COUNSELOR: That's an honest answer. It sounds like when you spend time with others, you feel better about yourself and are happier.

In this excerpt, Ashley revealed information about what her life would be like if problems that have emerged since the sexual abuse were eliminated. She began to envision a morning where she felt better about herself and spent more time with others. Future-oriented questions were used to create an attainable reality in which she felt happier and better about herself. Throughout the questioning, the counselor focused on the changes Ashley would see and challenged her to consider what she'd be doing if the miracle occurred and how she'd know it was different. Additionally, Ashley was asked to identify who else in her life might notice changes in order to consider how other people in her life can be witnesses to new realities.

Using Questions to Elicit Exceptions to the Problem

This information can lead the counselor to help Ashley look for exceptions that correspond with answers to her miracle questions, as well as other times when complaints are not as oppressive.

COUNSELOR: So if the miracle occurred, one thing you'd feel is "less lonely and sad." When are times during the day when you already feel less lonely and sad?

ASHLEY: I guess I feel happier when I'm at school during choir practice.

COUNSELOR: What is it about choir practice that makes you happier?

ASHLEY: I like singing, and I have some friends in choir. There's no time to think. In my other classes I zone out while the teacher is talking or when I have to work. When my mind is empty, I get flashbacks.

COUNSELOR: What are some specific things you do during choir that help you feel happier?

ASHLEY: I just really get into the moment, and I like being in the class so it is easier to push thoughts out of my mind.

COUNSELOR: Something that is different about choir is that you're able to push thoughts out of your mind. What other times are you able to do that?

ASHLEY: My dad always makes me go with him on the weekends to run errands. We usually have fun in the car and listen to music together. I don't cut myself when I'm with him.

COUNSELOR: How do you get yourself to avoid injuring yourself when you're with him?

ASHLEY: I can't because he's with me, and there's no way he'd let me. But I don't even really think about it. If the idea does come, I guess I just ignore it.

COUNSELOR: I'm impressed you're able to think of at least two times that you push thoughts out of your mind: in choir and when you're with your dad. You also mentioned music twice. Music helps during choir and you listen to music when you're with your dad, too.

ASHLEY: Yeah, I guess. But the rest of the time is hard, and all I ever want to do is cut.

COUNSELOR: The rest of the day sounds really hard. What do you think it means that you're able to have those other times, though? In choir, with your dad, and when listening to music?

ASHLEY: Well . . . it tells me that I'm not always sad and wanting to hurting myself.

COUNSELOR: Anything else?

ASHLEY: Maybe that I'm stronger than I thought. After what happened to me with that kid I feel really bad all the time. He took something from me. But maybe he didn't take it all.

In this transcript, the counselor uses a series of questions about exceptions to help Ashley identify times when she isn't feeling sad or lonely. The exceptions were drawn from the previous conversation when Ashley revealed that she would feel less lonely and sad when the miracle occurred, and instead feel happier. The counselor sought an exception using a presuppositional question, by asking Ashley to identify a time of the day when she doesn't feel lonely or sad. After Ashley identified choir practice as an exception, the counselor asked follow-up questions to help her examine this time further and amplify the occurrence. The counselor asked Ashley to consider what makes her happier during choir and the things she does to help her in those moments. The answers to these questions thickened her story and offered evidence that she is capable of being happier and less lonely. This then led her to identify another exception in spending time with her dad. The counselor also picked up on a theme of music in the two exceptions. This could uncover an additional resource or solution that could be mined further. As the conversation continued, Ashley identified her ability to "push thoughts (of the trauma and self-harm) out of her mind." The counselor drew attention to this coping skill and sought more exceptions and, using Ashley's own metaphor, invited her to talk about other times when she's able to "push thoughts out of her mind."

The counselor also made use of complimenting in the excerpted transcript by stating how impressive it is that Ashley is able to think of two times when she's able to avoid thoughts of self-injurious behaviors. Through the use of complimenting, the counselor amplified her strengths and abilities. Notice in the transcript that when Ashley began to talk about the difficulty of the rest of the day and how it made her want to engage in self-injurious behaviors, the counselor empathized but then shifted the conversation back to exceptions.

Using Scaling Questions

Scaling questions help clients keep on track with goals and identify ways they have worked toward them. For Ashley, the desire to self-harm has been problematic and difficult for her to overcome. In the previous segment, she alluded to self-injury by sharing that she was able to push the idea out of her mind when she was with her dad. A major goal of counseling was to cease her engagement in self-injurious behavior, and the counselor chose to follow up on the topic.

COUNSELOR: On a scale of 1 to 10, with 10 the worst, how were thoughts to self-harm today?

ASHLEY: Today? I would say I am a 4 today.

COUNSELOR: What does being a 4 mean for you?

ASHLEY: A 4 is pretty good for me. I like being on the lower end of the scale. I think the thoughts are less noticeable on the days I go to counseling.

COUNSELOR: OK, so 4 is pretty good for you. Besides coming to counseling and running errands with your dad, like you mentioned previously, what are some other things that might let you know you're a 4 on that scale?

ASHLEY: This morning I knew that I couldn't cut because I didn't bring my razor to school.

COUNSELOR: A razor is what you usually use, and it's helpful to not have access to one.

ASHLEY: Oh yeah, definitely.

COUNSELOR: Was there a time today that you wanted to cut today but couldn't?

ASHLEY: I had thought of it when I was in the bathroom during lunch.

COUNSELOR: How did you push the thought out of your mind?

ASHLEY: I just started to think about how long it's been since I've cut, and I was glad I didn't have a razor. I'm on a good streak for the past week without doing it.

COUNSELOR: What do you see in yourself now that you didn't see before your good streak?

ASHLEY: I'm proud of myself when I don't cut, and I like that feeling. Today I just told myself that I could keep feeling proud.

COUNSELOR: So, it feels good to have such a nice streak of not cutting.

ASHLEY: It does. In the bathroom I just kept telling myself that. I listened to my music, too, which helped. Afterward, I went to find my friends and the thoughts were gone.

COUNSELOR: You have a plan to get rid of the thoughts! Let me ask you this . . . how would you know if you were at a 3 instead of a 4 on that 10-point scale I described earlier?

ASHLEY: I think the difference would be that the thoughts wouldn't stay as long.

COUNSELOR: How would you make them not stay as long?

ASHLEY: I'd probably listen to my favorite song immediately when the image of cutting came into my head. Maybe I'd replace the image with the word "proud." Today, I gave cutting a split-second thought until I remembered I didn't have the razor. That's when I started to think about my good streak. If I were a 3, I wouldn't give it any thought.

In this excerpt, the counselor used a scaling question to learn more about Ashley's experience with self-harm thoughts specific to that day. The ensuing conversation about the self-harm scale was executed collaboratively between the counselor and Ashley. The counselor facilitated the conversation by bringing up the scale, and Ashley gave personal meaning to the scale by placing herself on it and describing the significance she gave to different numerical ranks (i.e., the difference between a 4 and a 3). The counselor took a curious stance and inquired about the solutions and exceptions that led Ashley to rank herself in the way she did. After she identified herself as being a 4 on the scale, the counselor encouraged Ashley to assign personal meaning to scaling herself as such. The counselor also sought to understand her subjective experience with regard to what being a 4 on the scale meant and looked like, uniquely to her. As a result, Ashley shared the pride she felt about having a lower number to report and provided some concrete solutions that prevented her from cutting and being able to place herself on the low end of the scale. When challenged to consider what would be different if she was a 3 rather than a 4 on the scale, she identified additional solutions of imagining the word "proud" in her mind's eye or listening to music. She also shared that seeing her friends at lunch helped her to avoid thoughts of self-injuring anymore that day. This idea of spending time with others had been a prevalent theme shared by Ashley since the counselor first presented the miracle question (e.g., being with her mom and sister for breakfast, being with her dad, and being with friends at choir or lunchtime).

Exploring Multiple Possible Realities

The idea of being with others is in direct contrast to the fact that she originally characterized herself as being isolated from others in her first counseling session.

COUNSELOR: When we first met, you told me that you kept yourself isolated from others.
ASHLEY: Oh, it's true. I don't really like being with other people.

COUNSELOR: You don't like it but I do notice that when you're feeling good about yourself, and when you avoid thoughts of self-injuring, you happen to be with others.

ASHLEY: Well, I guess so. I hadn't realized that.

COUNSELOR: I wonder if there are times when you like to be with others and times when you like to be with yourself.

ASHLEY: I guess that's probably true. I mean, when I do my homework, I like to be alone because it helps me concentrate, but when I'm with others, I don't think of hurting myself.

COUNSELOR: I see that you are continuing with group counseling, which is another time when you're with other people. How is that going for you?

ASHLEY: It's ok. I really didn't want to talk about this stuff, but it's been helpful to do it.

COUNSELOR: You don't really want to talk about the sexual abuse, but you do anyway, huh? That's neat; you show a lot of courage by talking about it and you've learned that it's helpful for you.

ASHLEY: Yeah, I hate to think about what that kid did to me . . . but I guess it's good to do.

COUNSELOR: So you know that it's good for you, even though it's really hard to talk about. Wow, I am impressed at your determination to do hard things!

ASHLEY: Yeah, well, it is hard, but if I don't talk about it and deal with it, I'll keep it bottled up inside and do bad things to myself.

COUNSELOR: Yes, so you know that even though it is really hard to talk about that stuff, it is still better than the alternative of harming yourself.

ASHLEY: I guess so. It's nice to hear that other people have also gone through what I did.

COUNSELOR: What do you make of that?

ASHLEY: It's just that when I hear other people who are going through similar things to me, it makes me realize that we need to stick together. It makes us stronger than the people who did this to us. I want to be stronger than him.

COUNSELOR: What things show you that you're stronger than him?

ASHLEY: The fact that I am talking about it now. He told me that I couldn't talk about it or he'd lie and he'd hurt my cat. He was in control, but now I'm in control because I do talk.

COUNSELOR: You're really honoring yourself and taking control over the situation. What does this say about your ability to be a survivor?

ASHLEY: It means that I'm in the driver seat now. I have things to share with other girls in my group that are helpful, and I can help myself, too. Things have been hard for me, but I know I have the ability to work through it. I know I can control my happiness and thoughts of self-harm. I can survive that, too.

In the previous transcript, the counselor introduced the idea of multiple realities: liking to be alone and enjoying being with others. Ashley also talked about how she maintains control over the perpetrator by talking about what happened to her rather than staying silent, as he demanded. She described herself as having power, and by doing this she redefined her perception of the trauma. Additionally, the conversation led Ashley to redefine parts of herself by stating that she is in control and a survivor. At the end of the excerpt, Ashley stated that she knows she can feel happier and take control of self-injurious behaviors. This was in response to the counselor's question: "What does this [control] say about your ability to be a survivor?" This question is related to aspects of Walter and Peller's (1996) "goaling," in which clients consider the possibility of assigning new meaning to themselves and experiences (p. 17).

Using Letter Writing to Provide Feedback

In SFC, it is common to provide feedback messages to clients (De Jong & Berg, 2002; de Shazer et al., 1986; O'Hanlon & Weiner-Davis, 2003). In these messages, counselors share observations of counseling and progress to clients. Sometimes this feedback can be in the form of letters (Alexander, Shilts, Liscio, & Rambo, 2008; Reiter, 2010). The following is a letter that was given to Ashley after this session. Within the letter, the counselor has summarized the session and focused on exceptions and alternative realities that were uncovered. There is even an invitation for her to continue to look for exceptions throughout the week and report them to the counselor in the next session. Additionally, the letter includes solutions and strengths that were revealed, and it contains phrases and words that Ashley used in session as a way to honor her unique experiences and ideas.

Dear Ashley,
Something I noticed in our session today was how determined you are to live a life in which you are in control of the trauma you experienced. You frequently mentioned that spending time with people helps you to feel better about yourself and helps you avoid cutting. You also listed various things that helped you to "push ideas of self-injury out of your mind," such as listening to music, remembering your "good streak," flashing the

word "proud" in your mind, and spending time with others. I see strength and determination in you when you talk about these ideas.

Perhaps, the part of your session that stood out to me most was when you said, "Now I'm in control because I talk about what happened." I wonder if this helps you feel strong and empowered? You seem to be showing strength and determination throughout counseling and in your life. I urge you to find more times of strength and determination in your life and report them back to me in our next session. Have a great week.

Warmly,
Counselor

Counseling Outcomes for Ashley

As counseling progressed, Ashley was able to identify more exceptions to the problem. For example, she spoke about times she felt less depressed and anxious, used self-injurious behaviors less frequently, and spent more time with friends and family. Ashley also naturally integrated coping skills and solutions into her life. As such, she used the resources that she has noticed help her to avoid self-injurious behaviors and isolation. While working with her counselor, Ashley also re-created her perspective of the sexual trauma and moved from blaming herself to feeling empowered and in control. As counseling moved closer to termination, Ashley's counselor helped her to avoid slipping into problems again by talking about how she will know when she needs to use her solutions or return to counseling. Examples of this included asking Ashley, "When are you more vulnerable to self-injury and how will you ensure you use your solutions?" and "What will be an indication that you'll need to come back to see me or another counselor?"

RESEARCH FINDINGS SUPPORTING SOLUTION-FOCUSED COUNSELING

There is clear evidence that SFBT is an effective means to treat clients for a range of disorders. In the first systemic review of SFBT, five well-controlled studies reported significant benefits of using the theory in counseling, and researchers noted that more outcome research is needed (Gingerich & Eisengart, 2000). In the last decade, the viability of SFBT has been substantiated by the findings of various meta-analytic studies, all of which reported small to moderate effect sizes. In a study exploring effect sizes of 10 experimental and quasi-experimental studies of SFBT outcomes, five studies showed strong effect sizes supporting the benefits of using SFBT (Corcoran & Pillai, 2009). Stams and colleagues' (2006) meta-analysis included 21 studies that indicated a small to medium effect and found that positive outcomes of SFBT treatment occurred sooner than those from other approaches. Following their randomized trial comparing the relative effectiveness of long-term psychodynamic psychotherapy and SFBT ($n = 326$), Knekt and colleagues (2008) reported that clients treated with SFBT experienced decreased depression symptomology at a relatively faster rate. Over time, however, the participants receiving long-term psychodynamic psychotherapy yielded more benefits as the participants' symptomology improved continuously over the 3-year time period studied, whereas the SFBT group plateaued. In their 5-year follow-up study, Knekt et al. (2015) espoused that long-term psychodynamic psychotherapy does not provide more benefits in quality of life and functioning than SFBT, and those researchers did find that participants who had SFBT had relatively higher levels of optimism and confidence.

Though reporting a small effect size, a 22-study meta-analysis conducted by Kim (2008) determined SFBT was most effective with internalized presenting problems (e.g., anxiety, depression). Similarly, Gingerich and Peterson's (2012) systematic qualitative review of 43 studies yielded 32 studies reporting significant benefits of SFBT and 10 reporting positive trends; SFBT was found most effective in treating depression when compared to other treatment options. Overall, these meta-analytic studies indicate that SFBT is a viable approach for counseling and should be considered when working with clients who experience internalized presenting issues such as anxiety or depression.

In a recent meta-analytic investigation of the effectiveness of SFBT with children and families, only eight out of thirty-eight studies were both methodologically sound and demonstrated that SFBT achieved better outcomes than a control group (Bond, Woods, Humphrey, Symes, & Green, 2013). In their research, Bond and colleagues (2013) determined that the studies with successful outcomes involved children with either internalizing symptoms (e.g., anxiety, depression) or externalizing behaviors with a mild to moderate range of difficulties in functioning. The efficacy of SFBT, specifically in working with the child and adolescent populations in school environments, has also been studied. Although the outcome results were mixed, a meta-analysis of seven studies on the use of SFBT in schools found evidence indicating the approach improved some academic outcomes, managed various externalized behaviors, and reduced internalized negative feelings (Kim & Franklin, 2009). Additionally, exploratory research completed in schools has found that solution-focused interventions combined with motivational interviewing reduced school truancy (Enea &

Dafinoiu, 2009) and increased adolescent self-efficacy, while reducing the urgency of presenting problems (Rakauskiene & Dumciene, 2013).

Investigations of the techniques and aspects of SFBT have yielded mixed results. Lloyd and Dallos (2008), in a client sample consisting of mothers of children with intellectual disabilities, found that the strength-based and collaborative nature of SFBT was useful in strengthening both therapeutic rapport and clients' confidence. Further, Lloyd and Dallos reported that the mothers in their study found future-oriented and scaling questions useful; however, they deemed the miracle question unhelpful and confusing. In their study of deaf clients, Estrada and Beyebach (2007) found clients' levels of depression decreased following solution-focused therapy (Estrada & Beyebach, 2007). This finding is consistent with other studies indicating SFBT is useful for treating internalized symptoms (e.g., Gingerich & Peterson, 2012; Kim, 2008; Knekt, Lindfors, Härkänen, Välikoski, et al., 2008). In a meta-analysis of 33 studies that focused on SFBT techniques, the authors (Franklin, Zhang, Froerer, & Johnson, 2016) reported the majority of studies supported the efficacy of a strength-based approach. Further, the researchers identified SFBT's use of collaborative language, positive language, and solution talk to be elements essential to positive counseling outcomes.

Overall, evidence for the effectiveness of SFBT and its inherent techniques is mixed and modest. However, numerous meta-analyses have indicated small to moderate effect sizes of solution-focused approaches. Empirical evidence of specific interventions is also growing and revealing the usefulness of particular techniques (e.g., positive talk, collaboration, scaling questions).

LIMITATIONS OF SOLUTION-FOCUSED COUNSELING

Due to the structure of SFC, counselors might have a tendency to use isolated techniques without grounding them in the postmodern framework and solution-focused theory. When this happens, clients are less likely to experience positive outcomes. Counselors should be mindful of the therapeutic intent of the foundational theory in order to optimize the potential benefits of specific techniques (Lipchik, 2002). Additionally, a fundamental tenet of SFC is the belief that one does not need to know the underlying cause of a problem in order to solve it. This may cause some to conclude that SFC is a superficial approach to counseling.

Further, even though SFC endorses a highly collaborative relationship between counselor and client, there may be limitations in using this approach with diverse populations. In particular, individuals who are looking to be directed by counselors or view them as the expert may be turned off by the democratic approach. To address this potential limitation, counselors may opt to emphasize their expertise as facilitators of the change process (Corey, 2013). Finally, in general, there is limited empirical evidence for the effectiveness of postmodern approaches. However, as previously mentioned, numerous meta-analytic studies, including dozens of individual outcome studies, have yielded small to moderate effect sizes.

IMPLICATIONS AND RECOMMENDATIONS FOR USE WITH CLIENTS

To use SFC effectively, counselors must use it with basic counseling skills, such as empathy and relationship building (Lipchik, 2002; Miller & de Shazer, 2000). Counselors should also use techniques intentionally and within the context of the solution-focused philosophy. The use of solution-focused techniques in isolation inhibits client change (Lipchik, 2002). Further, counselors should believe in the approach and be able to identify strengths within clients, as well as convey optimism regarding counseling outcomes. For clients who embrace flexible thinking and are capable of exploring different perspectives, as well as mandated clients, SFC may be a good fit. Clients who are reluctant to participate in counseling may find SFC's collaborative, egalitarian approach appealing.

SFC is a versatile and useful form of therapy. Although frequently used with individuals, it has also been applied to couples, family, and group formats. Counselors may choose to use it independently, or with the incorporation of creative arts and play (Kress & Hoffman, 2008; Matto, Corcoran, & Fassler, 2003; Nims, 2007; Riley, 1999). A thorough familiarity with the foundational postmodern ideology is essential for implementing specific techniques effectively.

REFERENCES

Alexander, S., Shilts, L., Liscio, M., & Rambo, A. (2008). Return to sender: Letter writing to bring hope to both client and team, *Journal of Systemic Therapies, 27*, 59–66.

Amado, B. G., Arce, R., & Herraiz, A. (2015). Psychological injury in victims of child sexual abuse: A meta-analytic review. *Psychosocial Intervention, 24*(1), 49–62. doi:10.1016/j.psi.2015.03.002

Amaya-Jackson, L., Reynolds, V., Murray, M. C., McCarthy, G., Nelson, A., Cherney, M. S.,...March, J. S. (2003). Cognitive behavioral treatment for pediatric posttraumatic stress disorder: Protocol and application in school and community settings. *Cognitive and Behavioral Practice, 10*, 204–213. doi:10.1016/S1077-7229(03)80032-9

Anderson, H. (2003). Postmodern social construction therapies. In T. L. Sexton, G. R. Weeks, M. S. Robbins (Eds.), *Handbook of family therapy: The science and practice of working with families and couples* (pp. 125–146). New York, NY: Brunner-Routledge.

Bannink, F. P. (2008). Posttraumatic success: Solution-focused brief therapy. *Brief Treatment and Crisis Intervention, 8*, 215–225.

Berg, I. K., & De Jong, P. (1996). Solution-building conversations: Co-constructing a sense of competence with clients. *Families in society: The Journal of Contemporary Human Services, 77*(6), 376–391.

Berg, I. K., & de Shazer, S. (1993). Making numbers talk: Language in therapy. In S. Friedman (Ed.), *The new language of change: Constructive collaboration in psychotherapy* (pp. 5–24). New York, NY: Guilford.

Bernal, G., Jimenez-Chafey, M. I., & Domenech-Rodriguez, M. M. (2009). Cultural adaptation of treatments: A resource for considering culture in evidence-based practice. *Professional Psychology: Research and Practice, 40*, 361–368.

Black, P., Woodworth, M., Tremblay, M., & Carpenter, T. (2012). A review of trauma-informed treatment for adolescents. *Canadian Psychology, 53*(3), 192–203.

Bond, C., Woods, K., Humphrey, N., Symes, W. Y., & Green, L. (2013). Practitioner review: The effectiveness of solution focused brief therapy with children and families: A systematic and critical evaluation of the literature from 1990–2010. *Journal of Child Psychology and Psychiatry, 54*(7), 707–723.

Byrd-Craven, J., Geary, D. C., Rose, A. J., & Ponzi, D. (2008). Co-ruminating increases stress hormone levels in women. *Hormones and Behavior, 53*, 489–492.

Carbonell, D. M., & Parteleno-Barehmi, C. (1999). Psychodrama groups for girls coping with trauma. *International Journal of Group Psychotherapy, 49*(3), 285–306.

Carey, P., Walker, J., Rossouw, W., Seedat, S., & Stein, D. (2007). Risk indicators and psychopathology in traumatized children and adolescents with a history of sexual abuse. *European Child & Adolescent Psychiatry, 17*(2), 93–98.

Carrion, V., & Hull, K. (2010). Treatment manual for trauma-exposed youth: Case studies. *Clinical Child Psychology and Psychiatry, 15*(1), 27–38.

Chang, J., & Nylund, D. (2013). Narrative and solution-focused therapies: A twenty-year retrospective. *Journal of Systemic Therapies, 32*(2), 72–88.

Child Welfare Information Gateway. (2007). *Trauma-focused cognitive behavioral therapy: Addressing the mental health of sexually abused children.* Washington, DC: US Department of Health and Human Services.

Coffey, P., Leitenberg, H., Henning, K., Turner, T., & Bennett, R. T. (1996). Mediators of the long-term impact of child sexual abuse: Perceived stigma, betrayal, powerlessness, and self-blame. *Child Abuse and Neglect, 20*, 447–455.

Cohen, J. A., Deblinger, E., Mannarino, A. P., & Steer, R. A. (2004). A multisite, randomized controlled trial for children with sexual abuse-related PTSD symptoms. *Journal of the American Academy of Child & Adolescent Psychiatry, 43*, 393–402. doi:10.1097/00004583-200404000-00005

Cohen, J. A., Mannarino, A. P., & Deblinger, E. (2006). *Treating trauma and traumatic grief in children and adolescents.* New York, NY: Guilford Press.

Cohen, J. A., Mannarino, A. P., & Deblinger, E. (2010). Trauma-focused cognitive-behavioral therapy for traumatized children. In J. R. Weisz & A. E. Kazdin (Eds.), *Evidence-based psychotherapies for children and adolescents* (2nd ed., pp. 295–311). New York, NY: Guilford Press.

Cohen, J. A., Mannarino, A. P., & Knudsen, K. (2005). Treating sexually abused children: One year follow-up of a randomized controlled trial. *Child Abuse & Neglect, 29*, 135–145.

Corcoran, J., & Pillai, V. (2009). A review of the research on solution-focused therapy. *British Journal of Social Work, 39*, 234–242. doi:10.1093/bjsw/bcm098

Corey, G. (2013). *Theory and practice of counseling and psychotherapy* (9th ed.). Belmont, CA: Thomson Brooks/Cole.

De Bellis, M. D., Hooper, S. R., Woolley, D. P., & Shenk, C. E. (2010). Demographic, maltreatment, and neurobiological correlates of PTSD symptoms in children and adolescents. *Journal of Pediatric Psychology, 35,* 570–577. doi:10.1093/jpepsy/jsp116

De Jong, P., & Berg, I. K. (2002). *Interviewing for solutions* (2nd ed.). Pacific Grove, CA: Brooks/Cole.

De Jong, P., & Miller, S. D. (1995). How to interview for client strengths. *Social Work, 40,* 729–736.

de Shazer, S. (1985). *Keys to solutions in brief therapy.* New York, NY: Norton.

de Shazer, S. (1988). *Clues: Investigating solutions in brief therapy.* New York, NY: Norton.

de Shazer, S. (1991). *Putting differences to work.* New York, NY: Norton.

de Shazer, S. (1994). *Words were originally magic.* New York, NY: Norton.

de Shazer, S., Berg, I. K., Lipchik, E., Nunnally, E., Molnar, A., Gingerich, W., & Weiner-Davis, M. (1986). Brief therapy: Focused solution development. *Family Process, 25,* 207–222.

Dolan, Y. M. (1991). *Resolving sexual abuse: Solution-focused therapy and Ericksonian hypnosis for adult survivors.* New York, NY: Norton.

Dube, S. R., Anda, R., Whitfield, C., Brown, D., Felitti, V., Dong, M., & Giles, W. (2005). Long-term consequences of childhood sexual abuse by gender of victim. *American Journal of Preventive Medicine, 28,* 430–438.

Enea, V., & Dafinoiu, I. (2009). Motivational/solution-focused intervention for reducing school truancy among adolescents. *Journal of Cognitive and Behavioral Psychotherapies, 9*(2), 185–198.

Estrada, B., & Beyebach, M. (2007). Solution-focused therapy with depressed deaf persons. *Journal of Family Psychotherapy, 18,* 45–63. doi: 10.1300/J085v18n03_04

Feather, J. S., & Ronan, K. R. (2009). Trauma-focused CBT with maltreated children: A clinic based evaluation of a new treatment manual. *Australian Psychologist, 44,* 174–194. doi:10.108000050060903147083

Finkelhor, D. (1990). Early and long-term effects of child sexual abuse: An update. *Professional Psychology: Research and Practice, 21,* 325–330.

Finkelhor, D., & Browne, A. (1987). The traumatic impact of child sexual abuse: A conceptualization. In S. Chess & A. Thomas (Eds.), *Annual progress in child psychiatry and child development, 1986* (pp. 632–648). New York, NY: Brunner/Mazel.

Follette, V. M., & Ruzek, J. I. (2006). *Cognitive-behavioral therapies for trauma* (2nd ed.). New York, NY: Guilford Press.

Franklin, C., Zhang, A., Froerer, A., & Johnson, S. (2016). Solution focused brief therapy: A systematic review and meta-summary of process research. *Journal of Martial and Family Therapy.* doi:10.1111/jmft.12193

Gergen, K. J. (1985). The social constructionist movement in modern psychology. *American Psychologist, 40,* 266–275.

Gergen, K. J. (2009). *An invitation to social construction* (2nd ed.). Thousand Oaks, CA: Sage.

Gibb, B. E., Chelminski, I., & Zimmerman, M. (2007). Childhood emotional, physical, and sexual abuse, and diagnoses of depressive and anxiety disorders in adult psychiatric outpatients. *Depression & Anxiety (1091-4269), 24*(4), 256. doi:10.1002/da.20238

Gingerich, W. J., & Eisengart S. (2000). Solution-focused brief therapy: A review of the outcome research. *Family Process, 39,* 477–498. doi:10.1111/j.1545-5300.2000.39408.x

Gingerich, W. J., & Peterson, L. (2012). Effectiveness of solution-focused brief therapy: A systematic qualitative review of controlled outcome studies. *Research on Social Work Practice 23*(3), 266–283. doi:10.1177/1049731512470859

Green, E. J. (2012). Facilitating resiliency in traumatized adolescents: Integrating play therapy with evidence-based interventions. *Play Therapy, 6,* 10–15.

Greenwald, R. (2007). *EMDR: Within a phase model of trauma-informed treatment.* Binghamton, NY: Haworth Press.

Hansen, J. T. (2002). Postmodern implications for theoretical integration of counseling orientations. *Journal of Counseling & Development, 80,* 315–321.

Hoyt, M. F. (1996). Welcome to possibilityland: A conversation with Bill O'Hanlon. In M. F. Hoyt (Ed.), *Constructivist therapies 2* (pp. 87–123). New York, NY: Guildford Press.

Kazdin, A. E., & Weisz, J. R. (1998). Identifying and developing empirically supported child and adolescent treatments. *Journal of Consulting and Clinical Psychology, 66,* 19–36.

Kendall-Tackett, K. (2002). The health effects of childhood abuse: Four pathways by which abuse can influence health. *Child Abuse and Neglect, 26,* 715–729.

Kendall-Tackett, K. A., Williams, L. M., & Finkelhor, D. (1993). Impact of sexual abuse on children: A review and synthesis of recent empirical studies. *Psychological Bulletin, 113,* 164–180.

Kim, J. (2008). Examining the effectiveness of solution-focused brief therapy: A meta-analysis. *Research on Social Work Practice, 32,* 49–64.

Kim, J. S., & Franklin, C. (2009). Solution focused brief therapy in schools: A review of the outcome literature. *Children and Youth Services Review, 31,* 464–470.

Knekt, P., Heinonen, E., Härkäpää, K. Järvikoski, A., Virtala, E. Rissanen, J., . . . the Helsinki Psychotherapy Study Group. (2015). Randomized trial on the effectiveness of long- and short-term psychotherapy on psychocial functioning and quality of life during a 5-year follow-up. *Psychiatry Research, 229,* 381–388. doi:10.1016/j.psychres.2015.05.113

Knekt, P., Lindfors, O., Härkänen, T., Välikoski, M., Virtala, E., Laaksonen, M. A., . . . the Helsinki Psychotherapy Study Group. (2008). Randomized trial on the effectiveness of long- and short-term psychodynamic psychotherapy and solution-focused therapy on psychiatric symptoms during a 3-year follow-up. *Psychological Medicine, 38,* 689–703. doi:10.1017/S003329170700164X

Kolko, D. J., & Kazdin, A. E. (1993). Emotional/behavioral problems in clinic and nonclinic children: Correspondence among child, parent, and teacher reports. *Journal of Child Psychology and Psychiatry, 34,* 99l–1006.

Krantz, A. M., & Pennebaker, J. W. (2007). Expressive dance, writing, trauma, and health: When words have a body. In J. Graham-Pole (Ed.), *Whole person healthcare: Volume 3, the arts and health* (pp. 201–229). Westport, CT: Praeger.

Kress, V. E., & Hoffman, R. M. (2008). Empowering adolescent survivors of sexual abuse: Application of a solution-focused Ericksonian counseling group. *Journal of Humanistic Counseling, Education, and Development, 47*(2), 172–186.

Limke A., Showers, C. J., & Zeigler, H. V. (2010). Emotional and sexual maltreatment: Anxious attachment mediates psychological adjustment. *Journal of Social Clinical Psychology, 29,* 347–67.

Little, S. G., & Akin-Little, A. (2009). Trauma-focused cognitive behavior therapy. In T. J. Kehle (Ed.), *Behavioral interventions in schools: Evidence-based positive strategies* (pp. 325–333). Washington, DC: American Psychological Association. doi:10.1037/11886-021

Lipchik, E. (2002). *Beyond technique in solution-focused therapy: Working with emotions and the therapeutic relationship.* New York, NY: Guilford Press.

Lloyd, H., & Dallos, R. (2008). First session solution-focused brief therapy with families who have a child with severe intellectual abilities: Mothers experiences and views. *Journal of Family Therapy, 30,* 5–28. doi: 10.1111/j.1467-6427.2008.00413.x

Matto, H., Corcoran, J., & Fassler, A. (2003). Integrating solution-focused and art therapies for substance abuse treatment: Guidelines for practice. *The Arts in Psychotherapy, 30*(5), 265–272.

McLean, C., Morris, S., Conklin, P., Jayawickreme, N., & Foa, E. (2014). Trauma characteristics and posttraumatic stress disorder among adolescent survivors of childhood sexual abuse. *Journal of Family Violence, 29*(5), 559–566. doi:10.1007/s10896-014-9613-6

Miller, G., & de Shazer, S. (2000). Emotions in solution-focused therapy: A re-examination. *Family Process, 39*(1), 5–23.

Miranda, J., Bernal, G., Lau, A., Kohm, L., Hwang, W. C., & LaFromboise, T. (2005). State of the science on psychosocial interventions for ethnic minorities. *Annual Review of Clinical Psychology, 1*, 113–142.

Misurell, J., & Springer, C. (2013). Developing culturally responsive evidence-based practice: A game-based group therapy program for child sexual abuse (CSA). *Journal of Child & Family Studies, 22*(1), 137–149.

Molnar, B. E., Buka, S. L., & Kessler, R. C. (2001). Child sexual abuse and subsequent psychopathology: Results from the National Comorbidity Survey. *American Journal of Public Health, 91*, 753–760

Mullen, P. E., Martin, J. L., Anderson, J. C., Romans, S. E., & Herbison, G. P. (1996). The long-term impact of the physical, emotional, and sexual abuse of children: A community study. *Child Abuse and Neglect, 20*, 7–21.

Najavits, L. M., Gallop, R. J., & Weiss, R. D. (2006). Seeking safety therapy for adolescent girls with PTSD and substance use disorder: A randomized controlled trial. *The Journal of Behavioral Health Services & Research, 33*, 453–463. doi:10.1007/s11414-006-9034-2

Nims, D. R. (2007). Integrating play therapy with the solution focused model. *International Journal of Play Therapy, 16*(1), 54–68.

O'Hanlon, B., & Weiner-Davis, M. (2003). *In search of solutions: A new direction in psychotherapy* (Rev. ed.). New York, NY: Norton.

O'Hanlon, W. H., & Beadle, S. (1997). *A guide to possibility land.* New York, NY: Norton.

Paylo, M. J. (2005). Helping families search for solutions: Working with adolescents. *The Family Journal, 13*(4), 456–258.

Pereda, N., Guilera, G., Forns, M., & Gomez-Benito, J. (2009). The prevalence of child sexual abuse in community and student samples: A meta-analysis. *Clinical Psychology Review, 29*, 328–338.

Perkonigg, A., Kessler, R. C., Storz, S., & Wittchen, H. -U. (2000). Traumatic events and post-traumatic stress disorder in the community: Prevalence, risk factors, and comorbidity. *Acta Psychiatrica Scandinavica, 101*(1), 46–59.

Rakauskiene, V., & Dumciene, A. (2013). Alteration of adolescent self-efficacy when applying brief counseling at school. *Social Behavior and Personality, 41*(6), 893–900. doi:10.2224/sbp.2013.41.6.893

Ratican, K. L. (1992). Sexual abuse survivors: Identifying symptoms and special treatment considerations. *Journal of Counseling & Development, 71*, 33–38.

Reiter, M. D. (2010). Solution-focused marathon sessions. *Journal of Systemic Therapies, 29*(1), 33–49.

Riley, S. (1999). Brief therapy: An adolescent invention. *Art Therapy, 16*(2), 83–86.

Rodenburg, R., Benjamin, A., de Roos, C., Meijer, A. M., & Stams, G. J. (2009). Efficacy of EMDR in children: A meta-analysis. *Clinical Psychology Review, 29*, 599–606.

Ross, M., & Wilson, A. R., (2002). It feels like yesterday: Self-esteem, valence of personal past experiences and judgments of subjective distance. *Journal of Personality and Social Psychology, 82*, 792–803.

Sánchez-Meca, J., Rosa-Alcázar, A. I., & López-Soler, C. (2011). The psychological treatment of sexual abuse in children and adolescents: A meta-analysis. *International Journal of Clinical and Health Psychology, 11*, 67–93.

Saywitz, K. J., Mannarino, A. P., Berliner, L., & Cohen, J. A. (2000). Treatment of sexually abused children and adolescents. *American Psychologist, 55*, 1040–1049.

Silverman, A. B., Reinherz, H. Z., & Giaconia, R. M. (1996). The long-term sequelae of child and adolescent abuse: A longitudinal community study. *Child Abuse and Neglect, 20*(8), 709–723. doi:10.1016/0145-2134(96)00059-2.

Slife, B. D., & Williams, R. N. (1995). *What's behind the research? Discovering hidden assumptions in the behavioral sciences.* Thousand Oaks, CA: Sage.

Stams, G. J. J., Dekovic, M., Buist, K., & de Vries, L. (2006). Effectiviteit van oplossingsgerichte korte therapie: een meta-analyse (Efficacy of solution focused brief therapy: A meta-analysis). *Gedragstherapie, 39,* 81–95.

Target, M., & Fonagy, P. (1996). The psychological treatment of child and adolescent psychiatric disorders. In A. Roth & P. Fonagy (Eds.), *What works for whom? A critical review of psychotherapy research* (pp. 263–320). New York, NY: Guilford Press.

Tohn, S. L., & Oshlag, J. A. (1996). Solution-focused therapy with mandated clients: Cooperating with the uncooperative. In S. D. Miller, M. A. Hubble, & B. L. Duncan (Eds.), *Handbook of solution-focused brief therapy* (pp. 152–183). San Franciso, CA: Jossey-Bass.

Vural, P., Hafızoğlu, Ş., Türkmen, N., Eren, B., & Büyükuysal, Ç. (2012). Perceived parental acceptance/rejection and psychopathology in a group of sexually abused children/adolescents. *Medicinski Glasnik, 9*(2), 363–369.

Walter, J. L., & Peller, J. E. (1996). Rethinking our assumptions: Assuming anew in a postmodern world. In S. D. Miller, M. A. Hubble, & B. L. Duncan (Eds.), *Handbook of solution-focused brief therapy* (pp. 9–26). San Francisco, CA: Jossey-Bass.

Walter, J. L., & Peller, J. E. (2000). *Recreating brief therapy: Preferences and possibilities.* New York, NY: Norton.

Webb, C., Hayes, A., Grasso, D., & Laurenceau, J., & Deblinger, E. (2014). Trauma-focused cognitive behavioral therapy for youth: Effectiveness in a community setting. *Psychological Trauma: Theory, Research, Practice, and Policy, 6*(5), 555–562.

Wheeler, J. (2001). A helping hand: Solution-focused brief therapy and child and adolescent mental health. *Clinical Child Psychology and Psychiatry, 6*(2), 293–306.

CHAPTER 3

Solution-Focused Approaches to the Treatment of Substance Addiction

TODD F. LEWIS

A s many readers are aware, alcohol and other drug (AOD) addiction in the United States is a serious problem that exacts an enormous toll on our society's well-being.[1] The statistics on the frequency of problems and related consequences are indeed mind-boggling. Although it is not the purpose of this chapter to bombard the reader with an avalanche of figures, graphs, and tables, which can be readily accessed online, some basic insights are noteworthy and shed light on the scope and consequences of substance abuse and addiction. According to the National Institute of Drug Abuse (NIDA), abuse of tobacco, alcohol, and illicit drugs costs society approximately $700 *billion* a year in lost wages, productivity, crime, and health care (NIDA, 2015). And this number does not even account for the violent relationships, broken marriages, emotional suffering, mental health issues, and spiritual bankruptcy that arguably no dollar amount could capture. It is probably no surprise that substance abuse and addiction are alive and well in the United States. Excessive substance use is an equal opportunity problem, cutting across ethnicity, gender, social class, and age. It is the fallout from excessive substance use that concerns treatment specialists, researchers, and policy makers the most.

The good news is that there is a collection of treatments for substance abuse problems, ranging from more traditional approaches to emerging trends. Often, 12-step mutual support groups are a necessary adjunct to counseling. In addition, addictions counseling is effective (Miller, Forcehimes, & Zweben, 2011), although all approaches have their strengths and limitations.

In this chapter, I will briefly review conventional methods of substance abuse treatment and introduce an alternative: solution-focused therapy (SFT). The assumptions behind SFT, criteria for effective interventions, rationale for its use with clients abusing substances, and numerous techniques as applied to substance use are explored. The key techniques of SFT are demonstrated through the case of Brian, who struggles with cocaine addiction. Finally, I conclude the chapter with a survey of empirical research, strengths, and limitations of the SFT approach.

CONVENTIONAL SUBSTANCE USE ADDICTION THERAPIES AND THEIR LIMITATIONS

Treatment of substance addiction has an interesting history, as society has grappled with how best to understand this phenomenon. As addiction became more prominent in the 19th and 20th centuries, many felt that it was caused by moral ineptitude and poor choice (i.e., the moral model of addiction; Thombs & Osborn, 2013). However, the medical community eventually saw things differently, describing the addiction as a literal disease (and hence the disease model of addiction; Thombs & Osborn, 2013). Although the disease model is prominent today and adopted by most medical professionals, the moral model still underlies many contemporary treatment approaches. Unfortunately, moral approaches resort to rather harsh confrontation and shame-based tactics to "force" clients to change. For example, Mott and Gysin (2003) described early substance abuse treatment based on Synanon (1958–1991; now defunct), where clients were seen as dangerous and labeled as "addicts," and communities needed to be protected. The client was labeled as a drug abuser and that was it; no other credit was given for his or her life (Mott & Gysin, 2003). The main clinical interventions were designed to increase pressure in the form of harsh confrontation, scorn, and shaming in order to break down client resistance (e.g., rationalization, denial).

Fortunately, the methods of substance abuse treatment are more empathic today, although shades of Synanon can still be seen in an attenuated form (Mott & Gysin, 2003). The disease model of addiction is credited with moving substance addiction out of the moral realm, which has opened the doors to compassion and, importantly, treatment for those who struggle with alcohol and drug problems.

Another characteristic of contemporary substance use treatment is the belief that something is wrong with the client, and that clinicians need to intervene from the outside to "correct" what is malfunctioning, like how one might install software to fix a computer (Miller, 2009). The premise of cognitive-behavioral therapy, for example, is that one's thinking is flawed, and that the clinician must "correct" the client's thinking for healing to take place (Miller, 2009). Much of contemporary chemical dependency treatment follows these protocols, in which clients are viewed as inherently weak and lacking in coping resources to address their disease (Mott & Gysin, 2003).

According to Mott and Gysin (2003), contemporary substance abuse treatment environments too often focus on what is wrong with clients, view them as lacking the internal resources to recover, and fail to acknowledge clients' strengths and what is working. And, as Mott and Gysin pointed out, this deficit perspective can take over the culture of an entire agency, not just the specific consulting room. SFT offers an alternative to contemporary models of substance abuse treatment where client strengths are honored and specific, client-centered goals are identified, all within the framework of a compassionate, empathic therapeutic stance.

SOLUTION-FOCUSED THERAPY: A POSTMODERN PERSPECTIVE AND ALTERNATIVE TREATMENT IN SUBSTANCE ADDICTION

Solution-focused therapy (SFT) is gaining greater recognition as a feasible alternative to more conventional treatment approaches among those who struggle with substance use problems (Linton, 2005). Many clinicians and programs are drawn to its strength-based, positive orientation, which is gaining international appeal in addressing substance use issues (McCullum, Trepper, & Smock, 2003; Smock et al., 2008).

What Makes Solution-Focused Therapy "Postmodern"?

When I was in graduate school in the late 1990s, our counseling department appeared to be going through a philosophical shift in its theoretical emphasis. I kept hearing the word *postmodern* in class discussions and conversations with fellow students but was unclear what the word meant. Through my coursework, I learned that postmodern refers to a philosophical system and unique way of looking at the world, one that utilizes multiple ways of knowing. This underlying philosophy serves as the backdrop of the two popular postmodern counseling approaches: narrative therapy and SFT.

Proponents of these therapies hold that individuals experience their own social "realities," primarily created through forms of communication with others, such as social media and face-to- face conversations. As such, most of our meaning-making processes form through perception and interpretation of language, and thus are shaped and adjusted in conversation with others. According to Gergen (2000), even one's identity is "continually emergent, re-formed, and redirected as one moves through the sea of ever-changing *relationships*" (p. 139; emphasis added). From the postmodern perspective, one's construction of the world is based primarily on these relationships, in addition to other life experiences (White & Epstein, 1990). Being comes into focus through the "ongoing process of relating" (Gergen, 2000, p. 134). Gergen and White and Epstein's emphasis on the concept of relating as a key characteristic of postmodernism is, in essence, what makes SFT postmodern; clinicians seek to help clients find more preferred ways of living by co-constructing alternative social "realities" that emerge within relationships and conversations.

The word *co-construct* is important here; by skillfully asking questions, SFT clinicians help create an environment where counselors and clients negotiate meanings together, and clients are invited to think of strengths, alternatives to the "dominant" story, and solutions to their problems, by using language different from their typical daily interactions.

Practical Advantages of Using Solution-Focused Therapy

De Shazer (1991) reported that SFT should take an average of about five sessions, making it a relatively brief form of intervention. Smock et al. (2008) argued that brief, effective, and cost-efficient treatments are in vital demand in the substance abuse treatment field. Thus, SFT is an ideal approach for busy clinicians working under the demands of managed care, which may preclude longer term treatment. A common perception is that clients need several years of treatment before they finally break out of their substance-using patterns. Certainly, there are occasions when long-term treatment might be the best option for clients; however, researchers have found that brief interventions can be as effective as long-term therapy for problem drinkers, (Berg & Miller, as cited in West, 2010; Miller & Hester, 1986) and with at-risk adolescents (Becker & Curry, 2008). In addition, there is nothing inherently contradictory between long-term aspects of the client's care (e.g., Alcoholics Anonymous [AA] attendance) and SFT. In fact, one positive treatment goal a client might have is to commit to regular AA attendance.

Rationale for Thinking About Substance Addiction
From a Solution-Focused Therapy Perspective

The need for more strength-based approaches in substance abuse treatment, combined with mandates from managed care for brief, effective forms of intervention, makes SFT an attractive treatment option. Transforming one's practice to reflect the strengths, resources, and goals clients bring to the table can have far-reaching consequences. Mott and Gysin (2003) did just that; they converted their substance abuse treatment community (TC) model to a solution-focused model. For years, their TC was based on deficit, "what is wrong with the client" thinking, where clients had limited (or faulty) inner resources to cope with addictive impulses and could not manage their behavior (Lewis, 2014). Mott and Gysin reported that, as a result of the philosophical change, clients became more positive, focused, and inspired. Unexpectedly, they also found that the more strength-based focus generated greater employee fulfilment and more positive staff/personnel attitudes within the agency (Lewis, 2014).

SOLUTION-FOCUSED THERAPY: BRIEF OVERVIEW

The next section provides a brief overview of the major tenets of SFT, including underlying assumptions, the role of the SFT counselor, and how SFT clinicians conceptualize change and progress. Once the basic concepts related to SFT are presented, I turn to the application of SFT with clients who struggle with substance use.

Underlying Assumptions

As with any theoretical approach, a number of underlying assumptions guide the SFT clinician. Aside from the general postmodern assumptions noted earlier, SFT clinicians hold unique views about the relationships between clients and their problems, how problems (and solutions) are generated, and how using language can shape a more positive experience in the counseling setting. The assumptions of SFT are listed next, with a brief description after each.

Change Is Constant

Behavior, including substance use, is not static. Change, such as small successes, happens continually (Linton, 2005; O'Hanlon & Weiner-Davis, 1989; Walter & Peller, 1992). Shifting client thought to become aware of small successes can be quite helpful, because clients can easily become encumbered with a belief system that they will *always* be [fill in the blank]. For example, I once counseled a client who was stuck in a problem-oriented mindset. Abusing alcohol for years, he couldn't possibly see any positives in his life and believed that he would always be a down-and-out alcoholic.

When asked what small changes he had made to break this pattern, he could not think of any. I pointed out that possibly sitting here, in the counseling room, was a type of change that showed he was serious about stopping his alcohol abuse. The client stated that he could not argue that point, and agreed that attending counseling was a step in the right direction. It is interesting how clients will overlook or negate obvious changes they are currently making in their lives, as if somehow counseling didn't count. From the SFT perspective, *any* change, however small, is worth highlighting and serves as a seedling from which future change can grow.

Language and Behavior Have a Reciprocal Influence on Each Other

The language one uses and the corresponding actions one takes each feed on the other in a reciprocal fashion (Walter & Peller, 1992). That is, language influences action, which, in turn, influences language. For example, if a client uses negative self-talk ("I am nobody," "I'm a no-good addict"), this language may perpetuate depressive behaviors and substance use, which only reinforce the client's original negative beliefs. SFT clinicians try to break this circular pattern by introducing new perspectives and possibilities that clients may not have considered, such as recognizing small successes or identifying when the problem was not dominant (Berg & DeJong, 1996).

Every Problem Has Exceptions

SFT clinicians assume there have been exceptions to the problem (i.e., times when the problem was *not* happening or influencing the client's life; Walter & Peller, 1992). For example, clients usually can recall times when they were able to avoid drugs, engage in prosocial behavior, or go to an AA meeting. These exceptions are grist for the therapeutic mill in SFT and are explored in detail to expand their influence. SFT clinicians may, for example, ask a client the factors that led him to go to an AA meeting, the strengths he drew upon, and who encouraged him. Exploring exceptions allows the clinician and client to co-construct a path forward, which includes resources the client can draw upon to reach his goals.

People Are Not Their Problems

Clients who abuse substances often endorse problem-*dominated stories*. That is, their language about their lives not only conveys their struggle with problems in living, but that *they are the* problem! The fallout from excessive substance use makes this story easy to adopt. For example, clients often experience concomitant relationship, familial, occupational, social, financial, and other problems as part of their substance use. Whereas substance use is the primary reason for their clinical visit, clients can easily get overwhelmed with the plethora of other problems surrounding their lives, to the point where they fail to see any possible way out. In conversations with family, the legal system, and peers, negative talk about having problems gradually becomes talk about how the client is the problem. This language becomes internalized and forges a story where the person's failures are global (i.e., due to defects within the whole person). In SFT, clients are conceptualized as separate from their problems. That is, the client is not the problem, but the problem(s) is the problem, and the client is the client (O'Hanlon & Weiner-Davis, 1989). At first glance, this may seem like a play on words, but this reconceptualization of the client and the problem provides a powerful backdrop for SFT.

In this regard, a key conceptual component of SFT is externalization. That is, problems are external to the client (the process of externalization is similar in narrative therapy approaches). As such, the problem is something to be "defeated," like an enemy that is playing wily tricks on the client. SFT counselors use "externalizing language" to promote externalization. For example, a counselor may ask, "How did alcoholism trick you into driving by the liquor store after work? What did it tell you that made you want to go in to buy alcohol?" Here, the clinician is strategically separating the alcoholism (the problem) from the client through language and skillful questioning. As this externalizing conversation continues, the client begins to adopt the externalizing language, which creates a cognitive shift in how the client conceptualizes the problem.

Language also can be used to construct solutions. In SFT, "solution talk" replaces the problem-dominated narrative that clients have been living. Solution talk is language that focuses on positives, strengths, goals, and what is working. According to Walter and Peller (1992), too much focus on problems and pathology actually poses a roadblock to forming solutions; fully comprehending the problem is not necessary for change (Linton, 2005). This is not to say that problems cannot be discussed briefly to give background information; however, if the client continues with a problem-dominated discourse, the SFT clinician steers the conversation toward positives, solutions, and goals. For example, assume a client comes to counseling and talks about what a terrible week she had, that she relapsed using cocaine, and that her husband has given her an ultimatum, saying he will leave her if she doesn't stop using. Giving too much emphasis to the details of these problems risks only reinforcing their grip on the client's life. The SFT clinician might ask the client for a time when the problem was not occurring, when she showed strength, and when she was able to resist the urge to use cocaine. Even small improvements are acknowledged in SFT; if the client could only resist cocaine for 5 minutes, the clinician remains curious about the strength she was able to show (even if for just a moment).

Clients Are Experts on Themselves

Clients are experts on their own decisions, goals, successes, and barriers to change. As such, SFT clinicians assume clients have a valuable perspective to offer in counseling, one that should be honored and encouraged. SFT is a collaborative approach, where clinician and client co-construct goals and a pathway forward. It is hard to do this when a clinician adopts an expert role. This does not negate the use of expertise to help clients who may be stuck; clients can and do ask for advice. However, expertise is offered in a "for what it is worth" posture, and the client is free to take or leave the advice.

Responsibilities of the Solution-Focused Clinician

Walter and Peller (1992) offered several key responsibilities for the SFT clinician. The most prominent of these includes figuring out what the client wants, being aware of what is working and encouraging more of that, and encouraging the client to do something different than what is keeping him stuck. By looking for what is working and encouraging more of this, the clinician and client avoid getting bogged down in figuring out what to change or, worse, changing what doesn't need to be changed.

An additional responsibility of the SFT clinician includes keeping the conversation focused on the present and the future (Lewis, 2014). Client history may be collected at the beginning of counseling, but this is not the focus of SFT therapy. Understanding the etiology of a client's problems is not necessary for change (O'Hanlon & Weiner-Davis, 1989). Co-constructing solutions is a present-oriented activity, where the focus is on identifying what is currently working in the client's life and encouraging clients to do more of these behaviors.

Finally, SFT clinicians help clients generate and clarify counseling goals (the process of goal setting is discussed in a subsequent section; O'Hanlon & Weiner-Davis, 1989). Unfortunately, clinicians can sometimes overlook the importance of setting clear goals and thus miss their usefulness in clinical settings (Seligman & Reichenberg, 2014). With SFT, goals are given a premium, with clinician feedback critical to the SFT process. SFT clinicians reinforce what seems to be working, client accomplishments, positive changes, and affirmations.

Conceptualizing Change and Progress

How does an SFT clinician monitor and conceptualize progress? The path to progress begins with what the client wants. Change and progress occur when clients increase their awareness of when they are getting what they want (i.e., when the problem is not happening) and building on this awareness to create a new way forward. They gain insights into what they were doing, thinking, and feeling (and who they were around) when they were not absorbed in the problem. This insight naturally creates a psychological and behavioral path from which a solution emerges. For example, several years ago I counseled a client who was struggling to address cravings for heroin use. He had relapsed several times, which is not uncommon for people who struggle with addictions. When I asked him about exceptions to the craving problem and when he felt good about his recovery during the past week, he said that when he kept active, either by exercise, work, or seeing his kids, that he felt better about his life. He also felt some excitement about starting meditation. We then talked about how he could do more of these activities through the week to help with his cravings. Essentially, we had co-constructed a solution-oriented plan in which he was intentional about engaging in positive behaviors and noticing small successes. This plan was reviewed in subsequent sessions to see how his new, preferred ways of living were taking hold.

This idea of a "more preferred way of living" is important to stress. SFT is about encouraging action. Many clients believe that they must feel a certain way before they can make behavioral changes. SFT clinicians focus on the what and how of accomplishing goals and problem exceptions that clients can use to their benefit. SFT clinicians attempt to bring about change by encouraging clients to take responsibility for their lives and to stop placing the onus of change on the clinician or others.

USING SOLUTION-FOCUSED THERAPY WITH SUBSTANCE USE PROBLEMS: A CASE ILLUSTRATION

Clients who struggle with substance use often present to counseling with numerous problems, both directly and indirectly related to substance use.

Using SFT, clinicians first focus on what is working in the client's life instead of what is not working (Berg & Miller, 1992). Client resources are mobilized to help improve his or her quality of life. Collaboration between counselor and client also is emphasized. What makes SFT unique is that minimal time is spent discussing what the client already knows—the history and process of their substance use (frequency, quantity, etc.). In this section, I focus specifically on the application of SFT to substance use problems, focusing on key questions to guide the counseling process and setting quality goals, discussing solutions, and emphasizing change before counseling begins. Following these clinical considerations, specific solution-focused techniques as applied to substance use issues are provided followed by a brief review of the empirical research findings supporting the SFT approach. The section concludes with a case illustration demonstrating many of the strategies and techniques discussed in this section.

Key Questions and Setting Quality Goals

SFT clinicians ask four key questions to guide the counseling process: (1) What does the client want? (2) What has the client done to get what he wants? (3) What does the client have to do to get more of what he wants? and (4) What are the client's goals? (Allyn & Bacon Professional, 2001). This does not mean that "anything goes," a charge that is sometimes levied at SFT and postmodern philosophy. According to Berg (Allyn & Bacon Professional, 2001), wants and goals should be consistent with what Alfred Adler called "social interest"—healthy and reasonable within a societal context.

In their book, *Working With the Problem Drinker: A Solution-Focused Approach*, Berg and Miller (1992) outlined a comprehensive, solution-focused strategy to help clients either cut down or abstain from drinking (although their book focused on drinking, it is reasonable to assume their strategy can be applied to other drug problems). The first step in this approach is foundational to SFT: co-constructing clear treatment goals. Goals must be relevant to the client, manageable, and concrete. For example, goals that come solely from the counselor, such as ones that include large, sweeping changes (e.g., stopping use immediately and repairing all harmed relationships), will usually result in little or no progress (Berg & Miller, 1992).

Sometimes *initial* goals may not actually be about substance use, even if that is the obvious major issue. This is especially the case for clients who are precontemplative (Prochaska, DiClemente, & Norcross, 1992) about change, where focusing on substance use from the start may lead to increased resistance. Clients need to feel invested in and passionate about their goals. They may be more comfortable setting goals related to consequences of substance use, such as improving one's marriage, becoming a better father, or experiencing less anxiety, compared to setting goals about substance abstinence. As the fallout from substance use becomes even more evident, the connection of multiple life problems to the substance use becomes clear, in which case clients are more willing to face their addiction. Berg and Miller (1992) called this strategy "finding for the hidden customer" (p. 29: working with what the client wants and, as rapport strengthens, opening the conversation about current drug use).

Another key characteristic of quality goal setting is to help clients add something to their lives rather than just taking something away. In conventional treatment approaches, the focus is typically on removing behaviors: stopping drug use, cutting down on drinking, or avoiding certain relationships. However, stopping addictive behaviors will lead to gaps in clients' lives, and a fair question to ask is what will they be doing instead of these addictive behaviors? The purpose of positive goal setting is to help clients determine what is working, what is positive in their life, or what they could do more of that serves as a substitute for their substance use. Mott and Gysin (2003) argued that clients seem to respond better when imagining a life with positivity and success rather than just being abstinent from drugs.

I use this principle in my Substance Abuse Counseling course I teach to graduate students. In this class, I assign an "abstinence contract" in which students are asked to give up a bad habit, food, substance, or behavior. However, rather than just giving something up, I require them to substitute something positive in place of their "addiction." The positive substitute has to be something they enjoy and not another burden. This last point is an important lesson for our work with clients, too. If we are going to encourage positive behaviors, they must fit with what the client sees as positive and not what we think would be most beneficial. For example, a clinician may encourage more vigorous exercise as a positive substitute for drug use, but the client may hate vigorous exercise and have little motivation to do it. However, he or she may enjoy reading (joining a reading club), yoga (a less intense form of exercise), or reestablishing a long-lost passion.

One final comment about setting goals through the SFT model: Berg and Miller (1992) argued that goals should be perceived as difficult. Perceiving goals as difficult accomplishes two interrelated objectives: First, clients who accomplish small, but difficult goals will build positive momentum in their lives, which increases confidence related to other goals. Second, if clients do not achieve a goal, SFT clinicians stress the difficulties of change and that greater effort may be needed, while at the same time emphasizing that not accomplishing goals does not mean the client is a failure (Berg & Miller, 1992).

Discussing Solutions

After setting goals, Berg and Miller (1992) suggested helping clients move toward exploring solutions to problematic drinking or drug use. Specifically, the SFT clinician skillfully asks questions that take the focus away from the problem narrative toward one of possibilities, strengths, and what is working. Examples of these questions will be covered in more detail under the section "Solution-Focused Techniques."

A unique contribution of SFT is that clinicians emphasize change *even before the client has attended his or her first session*. For example, clinicians may arrange a telephone call with clients before counseling begins to ask them how they already have improved, what small successes they have noticed, and when the problem has not been happening. In my experience, when clients call to set up a counseling appointment, they (a) are trying hard to cut back or stop drug use, (b) realize that their life is not going in a preferred way, (c) have already tried several strategies to stop or cut back, with varying degrees of success, and (d) have been hard on themselves because of their inability to quit (Lewis, 2014). From the SFT perspective, these clients have shown a strong will (corresponding to "a" above), insight into the problems substance use has caused (b), been persistent in trying to stop, but just can't quite get over the hump (c), held themselves to a higher standard and get angry when falling a bit short of this (d). As one can see, what seem like "negatives" in clients' lives are actually strengths to build upon.

Exploring successes and what is working during the first phone conversation is designed to orient the client (and clinician!), consciously or not, to a more positive way of looking at things. Unless the clinician inquires about the positive changes that have already happened, he or she may miss important information that can be used to build solutions (Lewis, 2014). When the client attends the first session, SFT clinicians continue skillful questioning, building on the previous conversation over the phone (e.g., "Since we last spoke, what have you continued to do to keep focused on recovery?" [Lewis, 2014]).

Many of the SFT techniques focus on strategic questioning (Linton, 2005).[2] One of the most well-known strategies is the *miracle question*. According to Berg and Miller (1992) the miracle question looks like this:

> I want to ask you a slightly different question now. You will have to use your imagination for this one. Suppose you go home and go to bed tonight after today's session. While you are sleeping a miracle happens and the problem that brought you here is solved, just like that (snapping a finger). Since you were sleeping, you didn't know that this miracle happened. What do you suppose will be the first small thing that will indicate to you tomorrow morning that there has been a miracle overnight and the problem that brought you here is solved? (p. 78)

This question directs clients to answer in a way that builds their own solution. In essence, clients are asked to visualize what life would be life if they did not have the substance abuse problem. Their ideas for living without drugs or alcohol could then be tested in the real world. For example, if a client says that part of his miracle would be that he would not drive by the alcohol store on the way home, this should be encouraged as something to carry out the next day. From the SFT perspective, no behavior is too small, especially with clients who are in the throes of an addiction and need to build on any small, positive behavioral acts that they can.

Exception to the problem questions include exploring times when the problem is not happening and using these experiences as the foundation for solution generation (Lewis, 2014; Linton, 2005; McCollum et al., 2003). In my clinical experience, most clients are aware of instances where addiction was not happening or did not have its stranglehold on their life. Indeed, humans are not naturally wired to see small successes (see Hanson, 2011, for his work on the negativity bias). Exception questions help clients break away from the fixed mindset that problems are unchangeable and ever-present (Mott & Gysin, 2003). As with scaling questions, the key to successfully using this technique is in the follow-up. When clients provide exceptions, clinicians need to amplify, illuminate, reflect, and remain curious! In other words, explore the exception in detail: What was the client doing? What was the client thinking at the time? Who was the client with? What was going on around him or her? How was this different than when addiction is at its strongest? (Linton, 2005).

Presupposition or "future-oriented questions" encourage clients to presuppose that they have made successful changes sometime in the future. Keep in mind that a key assumption of SFT is that the use of language can help create a new, preferred reality for the client. A clinician may ask, "One year from now, *when you are sober*, what will you see as the one most important influence in accomplishing this goal?" The clinician is presupposing the client will be sober—a delicate, yet powerful strategy to convey confidence, optimism, and hope. A related line of presupposition questioning is *relationship-oriented questions*, which help clients visualize how others might view them without using substances (Mott & Gysin, 2003). An example might be, "When you are no longer using (presupposing change), how will your family respond (relationship oriented)?"

Another type of questioning includes *scaling questions*, which can be used as a way to track progress, encourage clients to think about what they are already doing that is working, and what they can do to improve. There are variations to this line of questioning; however, it is typical to ask clients where they fall on a scale of 1–10 in relation to their goal(s) (Mott et al., 2003). Following is a brief exchange using scaling questions with a client struggling with moderate amphetamine use. His stated goal is to abstain from any drug use:

CLINICIAN: On a scale of 1 to 10, with 1 being no progress on abstaining from amphetamines and 10 being able to completely abstain, where would you rate yourself on this goal?
CLIENT: I would say about a 4. I had a pretty tough week last week!
CLINICIAN: Ok, so a 4. So, what makes it a 4 and not a 1 or a 2?
CLIENT: Well, I did abstain for 3 days straight, so it wasn't a complete waste. Some of the strategies we talked about worked for a while, but then the cravings hit.
CLINICIAN: You were able to abstain for 3 days! What does that say about you that you were able to do that?
CLIENT: I guess I did show some resolve. I just kept reading from the Narcotics Anonymous book and tried some strategies.

This excerpt shows one option the clinician has when using a scaling question. The client was not at 10; however, even at a 4 some progress was acknowledged! The clinician chose to focus on this as a way to orient the client to what is working, which seems to be his resolve, reading the NA book, and other strategies. At the same time, these activities are not enough, so a natural follow-up question might be, "What would it take for you to bump up this scale from a 4 to a 5 or 6?" Here, the client is given the opportunity to brainstorm how he might strengthen his recovery.

Another technique is called *taking a break*. I was first exposed to taking a break in graduate school during my internship. I was so set in the traditional mindset that I had to sit for 50 minutes with no break of any kind, lest I be doing my clients a disservice. What a breath of fresh air to know that, indeed, a break mid-session can actually be a positive therapeutic strategy. Insoo Kim Berg (Allyn & Bacon Professional, 2001) encouraged clinicians to take short breaks (a few minutes) around the middle of counseling sessions. During this time, the clinician gathers his or her thoughts and writes down any positive feedback, strengths, and exceptions. When counseling resumes, the clinician takes a moment to reflect on the session and state these positive observations back to the client. The client is then invited to reflect on the clinician's summary and other positive developments he or she has noticed. As Lewis (2014) noted, this technique does not need to be done in every session with every client. In some instances, taking a break may derail momentum and progress. Clinicians need to use their clinical judgment about this; I have found taking a break particularly useful when the client and I seem stuck and need a moment to gather our thoughts (Lewis, 2014).

One final strategy is encouraging clients to have a *miracle day*. A miracle day incorporates many elements of the previous strategies and is designed to help clients begin to live without the problem. The clinician begins by asking clients what a day without the problem would look like; in essence, what a *miracle* (i.e., no problem) day would be like, particularly in terms of what they would be doing differently. With addiction, clients might say that they would connect with nonusing friends, attend AA, or engage in some other prosocial, positive behavior(s). Once the miracle day is defined, the clinician instructs the client to have one miracle day during the next week. Subsequent sessions explore the miracle day, with a focus on all the positives that happened. Over time, this assignment can expand to 2, 3, 4, or even 7 days a week. I have found this technique to be particularly effective with couples, where one member struggles with addiction.

Research Findings Supporting
the Solution-Focused Therapy Approach

Outcome Research

Treatment effectiveness in the substance abuse field is measured by a multitude of benchmarks, including reduced crime, reduced health care, employment retention, and, of course, reductions in substance use. Taking all of these measures into account, the cost effectiveness of substance abuse treatment is substantial (van Wormer & Davis, 2003). In addition to cost effectiveness, substance abuse treatment seems to be effective in helping clients heal from their addiction, no matter what evidence-based modality is used (Van Wormer & Davis, 2003).

SFT has a rather limited empirical base, in part because it was clinically formulated rather than tested empirically in controlled trials (Allyn & Bacon Professional, 2001). Gingerich and Eisengart (2000) reviewed 15 outcome studies of solution-focused brief therapy (SFBT) to assess its empirical support. Five of these studies were considered well controlled and four found SFBT to be superior to no treatment or standard services. However, only 1 out of the 15 studies examined substance abuse as the presenting concern, and this study was listed as poorly controlled. The researchers concluded that evidence for the effectiveness of SFBT is promising, but a definitive answer could not be provided. In a similar review, Corcoran and Pillai suggested that SFT continues to grow as an evidence-based option among a range of clinical problems. The researchers reviewed outcome research related to SFT and concluded that although clinical evidence remains strong, its effectiveness from an empirical standpoint is not well established and more empirical research is needed.

Polk (1996) studied the effectiveness of solution-focused brief therapy (SFBT) with a 36-year-old problem drinker with a substantial history of alcoholism and work problems. Using a single case AB design, results showed that the client increased both the number of days per week abstinent and number of days attendance at work from baseline to the end of the study. However, this study has been criticized on methodological grounds because of the many threats to internal validity (Gingerich & Eisengart, 2000), precluding strong cause–effect conclusions.

Solution-focused group therapy (SFGT) has shown promise as an evidence-based intervention for substance abuse issues (McCollum et al., 2003). Comparing traditional substance abuse group therapy with SFGT, Smock et al. (2008) found SFGT to be more effective among those who require intensive outpatient services for their substance use. However, the authors noted that more clinical trial research is needed to further substantiate SFGT as an empirically supported approach for substance use. More recently, SFGT was listed as an evidence-based program on the Substance Abuse and Mental Health Services Administration's (SAMHSA) National Registry of Evidence-based Programs and Practices (SAMHSA, n.d.). Key outcomes in which SFGT demonstrated significant effects were depression and psychosocial functioning. Although depression and psychosocial functioning do not include substance abuse, they are often concomitant with substance abuse problems; in addition, SAMHSA lists SFGT as a possible intervention under the broad topic category of substance abuse treatment (SAMHSA, n.d.).

Finally, one must acknowledge the challenge of conducting outcome-based, clinical trial research to an approach like SFT (van Wormer & Davis, 2003). Outcome-based research is traditionally quantitative and based on deductive reasoning models in search of a definite reality. As noted earlier, SFT is based on postmodern assumptions that multiple social realities exist through the medium of language. However, qualitative methodologies seem to be well suited and more consistent with the assumptions of SFT. Understanding how clients experience SFT and what components are most helpful, for example, could lead to more effective, targeted interventions. Whichever methodology is utilized, SFT is becoming a popular alternative to traditional forms of substance abuse counseling, and research on the approach with addiction cases will only increase as this reality grows.

CASE ILLUSTRATION

The following case illustrates the use of SFT techniques with Brian, a 34-year-old mechanic who was charged with marijuana possession and has admitted to severe cocaine use. His substance use has begun to interfere with his job. He has a strong desire to stop his substance use, particularly his use of cocaine. He is married with a 4-year-old daughter and doesn't want to be a poor role model for her. The general format of the case and presentation of techniques is adapted from Lewis (2014).

CLINICIAN: Hello, Brian. Good to see you again.

BRIAN: You, too.

CLINICIAN: Last time you shared a lot about your cocaine use cocaine use and that Amanda has grown increasingly concerned with your substance use. In addition, you noted how substance use has begun to interfere with your job and being a father. I was wondering if you and I could together clarify a goal for coming to counseling (co-constructing goals).

BRIAN: Yup, that sounds like a plan. Like I said, if I continue, I am going to lose my job and maybe Amanda. I know I have to stop using but don't know what to do.

CLINICIAN: And, that seems like a goal—you want to stop! What does "stopping substance use" look like to you? (formulating the goal in behavioral terms)

BRIAN: That is pretty obvious, don't you think?

CLINICIAN: Well, does it mean that you will stop cocaine use altogether, both cocaine and marijuana? How will I or others know that you have stopped? (continuing to facilitate goal formulation).

BRIAN: Ok, I see what you are getting at. The pot doesn't really concern me; I just need to be more careful. Like I said before, I don't think pot is that big a deal. I think stopping cocaine is what I mean. After I get this stuff out of my system, others would see me showing up to work on time, you know, being responsible. I think I would have more energy, just feeling better about myself. And, of course, Amanda would be happy.

CLINICIAN: "Not using" would seem to be very different from how things are now. You would be off of cocaine, have more energy, be more committed to work, and have a happier relationship with Amanda. If you cut out cocaine and attend to work and your marriage, what will you be doing instead of using cocaine, specifically? (identifying potential gaps in recovery plan)

BRIAN: I need to be consistent attending NA; I finally found one that I can tolerate. I guess I would just try to be nicer to Amanda and ask her to help me through this. Recommit to work and have a schedule that gets me there on time.

CLINICIAN: Ok, so attending NA, enjoying life with Amanda, and recommitting to work, which you mentioned before that you enjoyed. Those are positive steps and will require some hard work on your part. (pointing out the difficulty of accomplishing goals)

BRIAN: That is just it. I know what I need to do, and have even tried some of these things, but can't get any consistency.

CLINICIAN: I'd like to ask you a question that I typically ask clients within the first few sessions. It may seem like an odd question at first, and you will have to use your imagination. Suppose you go home and go to bed tonight after today's session. While you are sleeping, a miracle happens and this problem (using cocaine) is solved. Because you were sleeping, you didn't know that this miracle happened. What do you suppose will be the first small thing you will notice tomorrow morning that there has been a miracle overnight and the problem that brought you here, cocaine use, is solved? (Berg & Miller, 1992; miracle question)

BRIAN: The first thing I would notice is that I would get up pretty early and have more energy. I would be a little more motivated for work, you know, have a good breakfast, do all the stuff that regular people do. I know Amanda would feel better because I am no longer using, so our conversation in the morning would be more than it is now, which is almost nonexistent.

CLINICIAN: What else would be different? (continuing to build the miracle)

BRIAN: I would have figured out a way to avoid the bad crowd. And I would have figured out how to handle cocaine cravings. Yeah, that would definitely be a part of any miracle!

CLINICIAN: Are there times when you are already avoiding the bad crowd, handling cravings, and feeling more energy for the day? In other words, you have articulated a pretty comprehensive miracle—what aspects of that are already happening? (exceptions to the problem questions)

BRIAN: The NA meetings help interrupt the cravings. I also have noticed that I get the urge to use when I am bored. When this happens, I have tried to do something different or fun. My friends are my friends, so that one is a toughie!

CLINICIAN: When you have tried to do something different or fun, what have you been able to do to help with the urges?

BRIAN: Well, I love movies, so the past couple of Fridays when I have been off work I have caught an early movie. It helps me relax and I can just enjoy myself. I know I can't do this all the time, though, because of cost, so finding a different activity would be good.

CLINICIAN: Ok, one thing different or fun is going to the movies, which definitely helps you get your mind off of things. And you would like to think of other relaxing activities as well. What is different in your life when you are able to resist the urges and go to a movie or do some other activity?

BRIAN: I don't know, it's kinda strange, but when I anticipate something fun, such as a movie, then the cravings seem to subside. So the anticipation of doing something I enjoy puts me in a positive mood.

CLINICIAN: You are already making some changes, thinking differently, and having some success—very cool! What else have you noticed about your ability to do these things already? (focusing on successes; tapping into abilities).

BRIAN: Sometimes it is sheer willpower . . . I guess I have made some improvements in some areas. But I am just sick and tired of being sick and tired! My job is on the line and who knows with Amanda. She has put up with a lot, but I don't know how long she will do this.

CLINICIAN: Ok, so taking all that in, let me ask you a question related to your goal of stopping the use of cocaine. On a scale of 1–10, with 1 being making no changes to cocaine use and 10 being stopping use, where would you rate yourself? (scaling question)

BRIAN: Right now, about a 5.

CLINICIAN: You are already making some changes toward your goal. Why do you say a 5 and not a 4, for example? (scaling follow-up question)

BRIAN: Now that I think of it, I have minimized some of the things I have been doing. I have fought the urges, tried to mend things with Amanda, been coming to counseling, and have the NA thing going. When you ask it that way, I am better but could be much, much better.

CLINICIAN: You notice some positive changes, but feel you aren't quite there yet. What would it take to bring that number up to a 6? (second scaling question follow-up)

BRIAN: Consistently going to NA would be a start. I feel more motivated about that now. Deleting the number of my dealer would also be a huge step for me, and figuring out a way to block his number. Maybe marriage counseling could be a possibility. I think that would move the dial on the scale, for sure.

CLINICIAN: Sticking with NA, getting rid of your dealer's contact info, and counseling for you and Amanda would help increase that number. All of these would help move you toward your goal of stopping cocaine use. (simple reflection)

BRIAN: Right. But I haven't stopped cocaine completely. I have had brief moments, but struggle with confidence.

CLINICIAN: Stopping use might take more hard work than some of the behaviors you mentioned. At the same time, you listed several actions that would at least help you begin to move up the scale. Brian, I can tell that you are seriously thinking about your goals and how to improve your life. We are about halfway through our session, and I would like to take a break for a few minutes to gather my thoughts and reflect on our session so far. Sound ok? You can stay here or take a stretch/water break. Feel free to reflect on our conversation as well. (taking a break)

Taking a break may not be a desirable option with every client. However, the clinician felt that a lot of positives and strengths had been discussed, but feared losing sight of them as the session moved on. After the short break, the session resumes.

CLINICIAN: Let me take a moment to summarize my thoughts and observations. You have really opened up about sharing some difficult thoughts and feelings surrounding your substance use, showing persistence, courage, and determination. You recognize that if you continue on the same path, there may be problems with your work and Amanda. You can see that if you accomplish your goal, you will have more energy and better relationships. You will feel greater commitment in your job. Your "miracle" was clearly articulated and you identified some specific behaviors that would be different if you stopped using cocaine. And, you are already doing some of these things! You also have identified ways to do even more to strengthen your recovery. (reflective summary on strengths, successes discussed so far; positive observations)

BRIAN: I actually feel better about my goals and what I have already done. I feel a little more confident. Can you help me brainstorm ways to get to a 10?

CLINICIAN: We can certainly explore your strengths and how to use them to move up the scale! Remember how I mentioned that change is hard work? Well, let's say you worked really hard to abstain from cocaine, and at the end of the year, when you have *quit cocaine completely*, what steps would you have taken to get to that point? (presupposition question)

BRIAN: I think consistency is the key. Just doing the things I mentioned on a consistent basis. Also, putting all of my energy into my wife and daughter, and work, and stop hanging around bad people.

Brian is at a point where he is feeling more confidence and momentum. The SFT clinician might continue to help Brian expand on what he means by consistency and what putting more energy into his family and job would look like. All of these insights will help Brian move up the scale toward his ultimate goal of stopping cocaine use. One further point: note how Brian is clearly doing more than he thought or recognized, but he didn't see things that way until this conversation with the clinician. This is quite common among clients, who greatly underestimate how much progress they are already making, instead choosing to focus on all the negativity in their lives. Whereas problem recognition is important, the negativity bias precludes thoughtful reflection on the aspects of life that are working and how to parlay them into solutions. Let's now pick up this case illustration at the five-session mark. Here, the clinician assigned Brian and Amanda (who attended the previous session) to have a miracle day during the previous week. Recall that a miracle day is a day when the problem does not happen and is not discussed. Instead, the focus is on activities, behaviors, and thoughts that would constitute a "miracle" (e.g., having a conversation about mutual goals instead of arguing or fighting). The clinician opens the session (Amanda is again in attendance) by exploring how the miracle day went for the couple.

CLINICIAN: Hello, Amanda and Brian. If you recall during the last session, I assigned a *miracle day* for you. You both agreed that a miracle day would include spending more time together, not arguing, and doing something fun together. I am curious how it went!

BRIAN: Well, we picked Wednesday to have our miracle day, because we both get off work early and have generally more time to go out. We got a babysitter for that night, which was a big step for us. We went out to dinner—first time in several months—and then went to a movie we both agreed to see. I must say, it was the best time we had in months! We kept to the rules—no fighting or talking about the "problem."

AMANDA: I can't believe we were able to do it! Usually either we don't go out or, if we do, we end up fighting about money, his substance use, or something else. We had our first normal conversation in quite a while. Of course, the "problems" are still there, but we weren't feeding them, if you know what I mean.

COUNSELOR: That is really interesting. I am curious about what you were doing differently during the miracle day? What was it that made it so successful? What did you notice?

AMANDA: I just didn't have the expectation of fighting. I tried hard not to criticize or be negative. I am sure he did, too. It is just awareness, I guess. How about you (looking at Brian)?

BRIAN: It was a big relief knowing that the problem is off limits. Like she said, the "problem" is still there, but we are showing that it does not run our lives. It felt really good not to get blamed again. We even complimented each other, as part of the miracle. This may sound strange, but my resolve to get clean is even stronger now.

CLINICIAN: It does not sound strange at all! You had different expectations, fought off urges to argue, had greater awareness, complimented each other, and did something fun! That to me sounds like a pretty good blueprint for living a more preferred life! How about for the next week you continue having a miracle day? Let's make sure we take some time at the end of the session to visualize what this might continue to look like.

In subsequent sessions, the clinician could explore miracle days and suggest any adjustments as needed. It is important that the clinician and client(s) clarify what would constitute a miracle day. If possible, help clients be as behavioral and specific as possible. If this clinician continued to see Brian (and Amanda, as needed), he or she could encourage having 2 or more miracle days over time. The goal is to build enough "miracles" together that the client or couple ends up creating their own solution.

STRENGTHS AND LIMITATIONS RELATED TO SOLUTION-FOCUSED THERAPY

SFT offers one alternative to traditional methods of substance abuse counseling that tend to operate from a deficit perspective, focusing on confrontation and breaking down client defenses. Solution-focused therapy is brief, strength-based, and shifts client perspectives to a more solution-oriented (or sober-oriented) life (Lewis, 2014). It moves away from "problem talk" and embraces client strengths, resources, and inner talents. Solution-focused therapy can be used in combination with other approaches as necessary (Lewis, 2014). For example, clinicians may use the miracle question to assess how the client envisions a solution to his substance use, and then use CBT to explore cognitive mechanisms that currently block the realization of that solution. Another strength of SFT is that clients are allies in their own care, and this respectful stance allows for them to make significant contributions to their own recovery. This can only empower clients, helping them to regain their self-efficacy in the recovery process. Finally, as noted, SFT is well suited for a brief therapy format (Lewis, 2014).

Solution-focused therapy is not without its limitations as a treatment approach for substance abuse issues. Solution-focused interventions may not be enough to address the multifaceted complexities of substance abuse problems (Lewis, 2014). As SFT is intended to be brief, clinicians may need additional interventions when clients clearly need longer term care and follow-up. The limited empirical research on the effectiveness of SFT with clients who abuse substances could also be a limitation (Lewis, 2014). Traditional substance abuse treatment providers may argue that SFT does not adequately address the biological mechanisms of substance addiction (Lewis, 2014). Whereas this would be the case for any psychotherapy, new discoveries in the neurobiology and neuroscience of addiction suggest that clinicians need to take these discoveries seriously. Finally, Linton (2005) argued that clinicians and staff trained in traditional substance abuse treatment models may not fully grasp the SFT philosophy and thus raise questions regarding its suitability for substance abuse problems.

IMPLICATIONS AND RECOMMENDATIONS FOR USE WITH CLIENTS

Situations and Client Characteristics in Which Solution-Focused Therapy Is Most Effective

SFT may be well suited for any client struggling with substance addiction issues; its philosophy of honoring client wants, goals, and resources is applicable to a wide range of clientele. Clients who have faced systematic bigotry and intolerance may find the SFT focus on context, cooperation, and client-generated goals a positive and affirmative approach (Archer & McCarthy, 2007). Clients who are motivated to change and ready to take action would be good candidates for SFT.

One situation where SFT has shown some success in substance abuse treatment is within the group therapy setting (solution-focused group therapy [SFGT]; McCollum et al., 2003; Metcalf, 1998; Smock et al., 2008; West, 2010). All the techniques discussed in this chapter could be applied to a group setting, particularly looking for exceptions (West, 2010). In an interesting take on this technique, West proposed a slight adjustment in that exceptions should be reframed as "periods of success" or "periods of sobriety," rather than moments when the problem is not occurring. This makes sense, in that one way those struggling with addiction count success is by the number of days (or hours, or minutes) sober. Smock et al. (2008) provided an outline of a typical SFGT group session focusing on the miracle question and exceptions, one that I have adopted in my own work with clients (Lewis, 2014). In subsequent SFGT group sessions, however, this focus may continue or extend to other strategies, such as setting goals or exploring a miracle day.

Situations and Client Characteristics in Which Solution-Focused Therapy May Not Be the Best Approach

Clients who struggle with severe emotional difficulties in addition to their substance addiction may need more than SFT to address chronic comorbidity and physiological problems related to substance abuse (Seligman & Reichenberg, 2014). For example, whereas focusing on what is working and co-creating solutions can be clinically useful, clients also may need interventions outside the realm of SFT, such as medical attention to address cravings or more cognitive-based interventions to address irrational thinking. Seligman and Reichenberg pointed out the difficulty in implementing SFT if clients lack internal coping skills and resources. Many clients who present with substance addiction struggle with the inability to cope with experiences such as negative emotions, cravings, and low frustration tolerance. The empirical literature strongly supports relapse prevention strategies, based on CBT models, as established procedures to address these difficult experiences (Lewis, 2014). Substance addiction can be a long-term, chronic problem that is often associated with many other problems in living. Whereas focusing on successes can be a start, clinicians need to be mindful of systematic racism, injustice, and chronic problems that may need long-term attention.

With that being said, I personally believe that exploring exceptions, honoring successes, and developing positive goals can be clinically useful by helping clients shift from a problem-focused to a solution-focused mindset. As such, even if one is not adopting a pure SFT approach with addiction clients, he or she can infuse some principles into longer term care.

CONCLUSION

Solution-focused therapy reminds clinicians (and clients!) that successes, however small, need to be illuminated and explored using many of the techniques outlined in this chapter. I find this insight extremely helpful when working with clients. It is easy to fall into the trap of reifying the problem by talking endlessly about what is not working. In my experience, the miracle questions are quite effective in setting the stage for new solutions to become the fabric of clinician–client conversations. Even if the client continues to use substances, or experiences a full-blown relapse, small improvements can still be explored.

Critics of strength-based approaches may see benefit in exploring what is working, but they may argue that additional interventions are needed to address the biological, psychological, and spiritual aspects of chemical dependency. Whereas this may indeed may be the case, elements of SFT can serve as a foundation for formulating counseling goals no matter what approach is used and supplement longer term approaches.

NOTES

1. There are many ways that authors speak of alcohol and other drug (AOD) use. For example, common terms include substance use, substance addiction, drug use, drug addiction, chemical dependency, substance use problems, illicit drug use, and others. Although I try to remain consistent in my language, the reader should assume that when he or she comes across any of these terms, I am referring to a person whose substance use is out of control and interfering significantly with his or her life.

2. There is some debate as to whether the miracle question originated with SFT. For example, Alfred Adler often asked his patients "the question" (the structure of which was quite similar to the current miracle question), which was designed to determine if problems had a psychological or physical origin. Regardless, the miracle question is most commonly associated with SFT because of its use as a strategy to help clients build solutions.

REFERENCES

Allyn & Bacon Professional (Producer). (2001). Solution-focused therapy for the addictions with Insoo Kim Berg [video tape]. (Available from Allyn & Bacon, A Pearson Education Company, Needham Heights, MA). Retrieved from http://www.abacon.com/professional

Archer, J., & McCarthy, C. J. (2007). Theories of counseling and psychotherapy: Contemporary applications. Columbus, OH: Pearson.

Becker, S. J., & Curry, J. F. (2008). Outpatient interventions for adolescent substance abuse: A quality of evidence review. Journal of Consulting and Clinical Psychology, 76, 531–543.

Berg, I. K., & DeJong, P. (1996). Solution-building conversations: Co-constructing a sense of competence with clients, Families in Society, 77, 376–391.

Berg, I. K., & Miller, S. D. (1992). Working with the problem drinker: A solution-focused approach. New York, NY: Norton.

de Shazer, S. (1991). Putting differences to work. New York, NY: Norton.

Gergen, K. J. (2000). The saturated self: Dilemmas in identity in contemporary life. New York, NY: Basic Books.

Gingerich, W. J., & Eisengart, S. (2000). Solution-focused brief therapy: A review of the outcome research. Family Process, 39, 477–499.

Hanson, R. (2011). *Buddha's brain: The practical neuroscience of happiness, love, and wisdom.* PESI Seminars: Online webcast.

Lewis, T. F. (2014). *Substance abuse and addiction treatment: Practical application of counseling theory.* Columbus, OH: Pearson.

Linton, J. (2005). Mental health counselors and substance abuse treatment: Advantages, difficulties, and practical issues to solution-focused interventions. *Journal of Mental Health Counseling, 27,* 297–310.

McCollum, E. E., Trepper, T. S., & Smock, S. (2003). Solution-focused group therapy for substance abuse: Extending competency-based models. *Journal of Family Psychotherapy, 14,* 27–42.

Metcalf, L. (1998). *Solution-focused group therapy.* New York, NY: The Free Press.

Miller, W. R., Forcehimes, A. A., & Zweben, A. (2011). *Treating addiction: A guide for professionals.* New York, NY: Guilford.

Miller, W. R., & Hester, R. (1986). Inpatient alcoholism treatment: Who benefits? *American Psychologist, 41,* 794–805.

Mott, S., & Gysin, T. (2003). Post-modern ideas in substance abuse treatment. *Journal of Social Work Practice in the Addictions, 3,* 3–19.

NIDA. (2015). Trends and statistics. http://www.drugabuse.gov/related-topics/trends-statistics

O'Hanlon, W. H., & Weiner-Davis, M. (1989). *In search of solutions: A new direction in psychotherapy.* New York, NY: Norton.

Polk, G. W. (1996). Treatment of problem drinking behavior using solution-focused therapy: A Single-subject design. *Crisis Intervention, 3,* 13–24.

Prochaska, J. O., DiClemente, C. C., & Norcross, J. C. (1992). In search of how people change: Applications to addictive behaviors. *American Psychologist, 47,* 1102–1114.

Seligman, L., & Reichenberg, L. W. (2014). *Theories of counseling and psychotherapy: Systems, strategies, and skills* (4th ed.). Columbus, OH: Pearson.

Smock, S. A., Trepper, T. S., Wetchler, J. L., McCollum, E. E. et al. (2008). Solution-foucsed group therapy for level 1 substance abusers. *Journal of Marital and Family Therapy, 34*(1), 107–120.

Substance Abuse and Mental Health Services Administration. (n.d.). Intervention summary: Solution-focused group therapy. Retrieved from http://legacy.nreppadmin.net/ViewIntervention.aspx?id=281

Thombs, D. L., & Osborn, C. A. (2013). *Introduction to addictive behaviors* (4th ed.). New York, NY: Guildford.

van Wormer, K., & Davis, D. R. (2003). *Addiction treatment: A strengths perspective.* Pacific Grove, CA: Brooks/Cole.

Walter, J. W., & Peller, J. E. (1992). *Becoming solution-focused in brief therapy.* Levittown, PA: Brunner/Mazel.

West, E. C. (2010). Solution focused group treatment with publicly funded alcohol/other drug abuse clients in rural settings. *Alcoholism Treatment Quarterly, 28,* 176–183.

White, M., & Epstein, D. (1990). *Narrative means to therapeutic ends.* New York, NY: Norton.

SECTION II
Narrative Therapy

INTRODUCTION

It is perhaps easy to miss just how revolutionary narrative therapy is in the history of psychotherapeutic ideas. If one did not know about the radical foundational shifts that came with this movement, it might be tempting to characterize narrative therapy as simply another treatment orientation, which merely tossed some new therapeutic techniques on top of a century-old pile. Although it has provided practitioners with useful techniques, the contributions of narrative therapy have been far greater than just technical innovations. Rather, narrative therapy represents an extraordinary shift in how we think about counseling and the potential for human transformation. To recognize the profound theoretical and technical innovations of this novel orientation, the history, philosophical underpinnings, and treatment approaches of narrative therapy must be reviewed.

First formally introduced in the classic *Narrative Means to Therapeutic Ends*, White and Epston (1990) founded narrative therapy on the radical notion that people should be understood according to their stories, not by some supposed objective, scientific reality. In other words, people live according to their life stories, which crystallize into routine ways of being (Polkinghorne, 2004). Drawing from the poststructuralist philosophical movement, which rejected the structuralist assumption that observable phenomena have deep, underlying structures (Combs & Freedman, 2012), pioneering narrative therapists attended to the unique nuances of their clients' narrations. The impact of this conceptual shift has far-reaching consequences. That is, narrative therapists refused to engage in a therapeutic search for the universal structures that were supposedly responsible for their clients' problems, a strategy that was advocated by virtually all previous orientations to counseling (Hansen, 2006). Rather, narrative therapists rejected the assumption of universal, foundational structures and, instead, listened for the unique storied creations that animated the lives of their clients.

This shift from foundational client realities to narrational productions opens some interesting conceptual doors. Notably, it leads to the insight that clients often adopt culturally dominant narratives as their life stories (White & Epston, 1990). For instance, if a woman adopts a cultural message that women should be homemakers, this narrative might conflict with her lived experience of wanting a meaningful career. Drawing from the philosopher Foucault (1984), pioneering narrative therapists viewed these cultural messages as a societal means of empowering certain people and disempowering others. Knowledge and truth claims, from this Foucaultian perspective, are always entangled with power. When people adopt certain culturally prominent narratives as their life stories, these stories may violate their lived experience, keep them oppressed, and cause them suffering (Combs & Freedman, 2012; White & Epston, 1990).

Narrative therapy, then, draws from two, novel assumptions about counseling: (a) client stories should be the focus of therapeutic attention, not supposed objective, underlying realities; (b) people adopt societally dominant stories, which may create problems of living. When these therapeutic assumptions are endorsed, they naturally lead to a particular therapeutic posture, certain techniques, and an interesting vision of therapeutic change.

Unlike many traditional forms of therapy, narrative therapists do not view themselves as experts (Murdock, 2017). Because client stories are the center of treatment concern, the client is the expert, not the therapist (White & Epston, 1990). The role of the narrative therapist is to draw out and define client stories so that the narrational factors that have created client problems can emerge as therapeutically workable material. People may not be entirely aware that they have been enacting a story until that story is brought to light and concretely defined.

Narrative therapists use a method known as externalizing the problem (White & Epston, 1990) to make the influence of stories more obvious, to help clients develop strategies to deal with them, and to promote the identification of unique outcomes (i.e., instances when the problem did not occur). In short, when clients come to therapy, they are often identified with the problem; clients believe that they are the problem. By deliberately locating the problem outside of the client, narrative therapists help clients gain a useful psychological distance from the problem, a process that can reveal effective solutions that the client was unable to see when the problem was conceived as identical to the client's self (White, 2007). For example, White and Epston review the case of a 6-year-old who suffered from encopresis. By externalizing the problem and naming it "sneaky poo" (p. 47), the child and his family were able to view the problem in a new light, which was not identified with the child. This externalization helped the family to expand on unique outcomes, develop strategies to minimize the problem, and redefine the problem as an enemy to resist, not an intrinsic part of the child.

Note that when problems are externalized, they can be seen as oppressive forces that threaten to dominate clients. Moving from identifying with problems to defining them as external, enemy oppressors enables clients to find ways to resist their allure, liberate themselves, and define preferred stories, which are consistent with their lived experience. It is no coincidence that the language in the earlier description sounds political. As noted earlier, narrative therapists believe that people often adopt dominant societal narratives, which are inconsistent with their lived experience. This emphasis on oppressive narratives conceptually links narrative therapy to important movements in counseling, particularly social justice and multiculturalism (Combs & Freedman, 2012; Monk & Gerhart, 2003). People are indeed disempowered by culturally dominant storylines. Narrative therapy is uniquely sensitive to oppressive, societal forces and offers techniques aimed at personal liberation. Therefore, narrative therapy is not just another counseling orientation in a long, historical line of treatment approaches. Rather, narrative therapy represents a profound shift in the way that therapy is conceptualized, a shift that philosophically embeds narrative therapy within contemporary movements which recognize that societal forces may have an oppressive impact on client well-being.

Obviously, it is impossible to provide a detailed overview of the narrative therapy movement, with all of its conceptual nuances and creative techniques, in this brief, introductory section. Some of the important general points to remember, however, are that narrative therapy (a) views stories, not objective realities, as the source of client problems and solutions; (b) presumes that dominant, societal stories are adopted by clients, often to their detriment; and (c) provides a variety of techniques (e.g., externalizing the problem) to liberate clients from the damaging stories that hold them captive.

With its radical conceptual shifts from traditional counseling orientations, it is no wonder that narrative therapy has been an incredibly generative system of thought. The chapters in this section are signs of this generativity. Webber and Mascari outline a narrative therapy approach for the treatment of trauma. The implications of narrative therapy to help children and adolescents with grieving is offered by Wheat and Whiting. These chapters provide evidence that narrative therapy is an extraordinarily fertile treatment approach, which will surely continue to inspire innovative approaches to helping.

REFERENCES

Combs, G., & Freedman, J. (2012). Narrative, poststructuralism, and social justice: Current practices in narrative therapy. *The Counseling Psychologist, 40,* 1033–1060.

Foucault, M. (1984). P. Rabinow (Ed.), *The Foucault reader.* New York, NY: Pantheon.

Hansen, J. T. (2006). Counseling theories within a postmodernist epistemology: New roles for theories in counseling practice. *Journal of Counseling & Development, 84,* 291–297. doi:10.1002/j.1556-6678.2006.tb00408.x

Monk, G., & Gerhart, D. R. (2003). Sociopolitical activist or conversational partner? Distinguishing the position of the therapist in narrative and collaborative therapies. *Family Process, 42,* 19–30.

Murdock, N. L. (2017). *Theories of counseling and psychotherapy: A case approach.* New York, NY: Pearson.

Polkinghorne, D. (2004). Narrative therapy and postmodernism. In L. Angus & J. McLeod (Eds.), *The handbook of narrative and psychotherapy: Practice, theory, and research,* (pp. 53–67) Thousand Oaks, CA: Sage.

White, M. (2007). Maps of narrative practice. New York, NY: Norton.

White, M., & Epston, D. (1990). *Narrative means to therapeutic ends.* New York, NY: Norton.

CHAPTER 4

Sacred Privilege

Using Narrative Reconstruction as a Postmodern

Approach With Grieving Children and Adolescents

LAURA S. WHEAT AND PEGGY P. WHITING

Each year in the United States, thousands of children and adolescents suffer the death of someone they love. The New York Life Foundation, in conjunction with the National Alliance for Grieving Children (NAGC), estimates that approximately one in seven Americans will lose a sibling or parent before they reach adulthood (New York Life Foundation/ National Alliance for Grieving Children, 2012). Additionally, while exact numbers of children and adolescents impacted by the death of a peer are not known, adolescents between the ages of 15 and 19 are dying at the rate of 49.4 per 100,000 and children between the ages of 5 and 14 die at the rate of 12.9 per 100,000, suggesting that significant numbers of friends and classmates may be affected (US Department of Health & Human Services, Health Resources & Services Administration, 2013). Add to these losses the deaths of grandparents or pets as well as other losses related to divorce, blending families, homelessness, addiction in the family, and traumatic events involving abuse, domestic violence, bullying, incarceration of a family member, and the cycle of deployment, and it becomes obvious how much loss affects the lives of young people.

Despite the many losses they typically experience in their lives, however, children and adolescents tend to be "forgotten mourners" (Grollman, 1995, p. xi; Rosen, 1984–1985). Helping professionals rarely receive education or training in the specifics of grief and its multifaceted impact and therefore may have trouble recognizing the face of grief in young mourners. Additionally, much of the research in *thanatology*—the study of death, dying, and bereavement—has until very recently tended to focus mainly on adult grief, leaving the wilderness of childhood and adolescent grief largely unexplored. Caring adults surrounding children grieving a loss may not want to see them in pain and therefore deny their grief, or they may believe that because of children's shorter attention spans, they will "get over it" quickly and do not need further attention. Finally, adolescents in particular may hide their reactions in an effort to blend in (Balk, 2011), causing surrounding adults to assume they are doing well or are not impacted by a loss. Young people can be tremendously impacted by loss, however, and helping professionals who fail to recognize this or seek to understand their experience can inadvertently isolate them at a time when they most need adult support. When this occurs, *disenfranchised grief* results, a concept described as making illegitimate either the grief or the griever (Doka, 2002).

Reconciliation of grief in disenfranchised situations is more difficult and positions the griever in a vulnerable position regarding future emotional well-being and health. Older ways of viewing grief as something to be resolved or "finished" within a certain time frame may also contribute to the disenfranchisement of child and adolescent grief. As development proceeds and young people learn to process their life experiences in more complex ways, they often experience a resurgence of grief from years past. Fortunately, postmodern approaches to counseling offer a uniquely egalitarian, client-focused way of helping that accepts young clients where they are and positions them as the experts rather than counselors. In this chapter, we will introduce and explore one of these approaches, narrative reconstruction, and its specific applicability to working with grieving children and adolescents. In order to reduce the disenfranchisement of young people and their grief, however, it is first necessary to understand how grieving a loss interacts with typical child and adolescent development.

THE LOSS STORY WITHIN THE DEVELOPMENTAL NARRATIVE

As we know, understanding developmental progression across the life span, particularly during childhood and adolescence, can be a complex endeavor and may be viewed through multiple theoretical and empirical lenses. These varied perspectives include attention to such aspects as attachment, developmental domains, maturational tasks, common characteristics of defined development age groupings, structures of cognition, and processes of learning. Contemporary developmentalists generally view development as a flexible process, with continuous learning and information processing, and with the idea that interpretation (making meaning) of events in our lives is as significant as the particular event itself (Balk, 2014; Bowlby, 1982; Corr & Balk, 2010; Goldman, 2014; Meagher & Balk, 2013; Neimeyer, Klass, & Dennis, 2014; Piaget, 1954; Rubin, 2011; Stillion & Attig, 2015; White, 2005).

The direction of development is, therefore, toward expansion of cognitive complexity, healthy interpersonal and social relating, appropriate emotional expression and regulation, complex perspective-taking skill, resilient coping mechanisms, and richer self-concept and esteem—a sophistication of the developmental resources necessary to navigate and mitigate experiences such as grief. Children and adolescents both benefit from and need collaboration with informed adults in order to transform difficult loss events into catalysts for developmental maturity (Adler & McAdams, 2007; Balk, 2014; Goldman, 2014; James, Oltjenbruns, & Whiting, 2008; Machin, 2014; Neimeyer, 2012; White & Morgan, 2006; Whiting, Wheat, & Bradley, 2008; Yuen, 2007).

It is critical to understand that loss is experienced within the child or adolescent's developmental level of functioning at the time of the event. Functioning is multifaceted and includes the emerging worldview framed in part by the sophistication of her or his cognitive ability and the social and cultural associations and meanings encountered thus far. One of the fascinating aspects of working with children and adolescents is that the interpretation of the loss event will change as levels of maturity shift with time (Biank & Werner-Lin, 2011).

The journey of development also includes the limitations of any special individual needs and environmental deficits as well as some vulnerability due to the lack of sophistication and maturity of a given age. Simply stated, a 10-year-old child will not grieve with the same structure of meaning and resource as a 16-year-old adolescent. Counselors must meet the grief story of a particular child or adolescent cognizant of that client's development and must prepare to revisit and rework past grief with the client's newly acquired developmental lens. The child or adolescent's grief story meets the developmental narrative already in operation as she or he is making meaning out of life experience through the resources and limitations of the present worldview.

For the purposes of this chapter, we will examine the differences in the developmental world of a child in early childhood, middle childhood, and adolescence, in order to discuss the paradigm within which the loss event and the interpretive story of that situation occur. Many individual variations can occur, and the power of the cultural, familial, and other diversity factors present within each child or adolescent's situation shifts the general developmental understanding of any individual. Therefore, we will discuss more generalized age-related but not age-specific comments on these three broad categories.

Early and Middle Childhood

Issues of attachment and separation are at the forefront of the emotional landscape in early childhood, making abandonment and survival insecurity a central fear and trust the central task (Bowlby, 1982; Erikson, 1980). The verbal and conceptual skills of this age group are introductory and limited, representing a developmental vulnerability for limited expressions of grief, making meaning of what is happening, and seeking what is needed. The lack of cognitive sophistication impacts concepts such as finality, causality, and irreversibility (Piaget, 1954), so the child finds it nearly impossible to embrace a loss as signifying something is permanently over or that events are caused through a variety of means sometimes defying understandable explanation. The imagination, magical thinking, and fantasy common in early childhood leave children vulnerable to inaccurate and sometimes harmful ideas of what happened and why, notions that could set the stage for a storyline about their loss that is harmful if left uncorrected.

The young child, therefore, needs adult comfort and reassurance and profits from attachment figures who offer the consistency of routines, the reassurance that life will go on, and the soothing that results when grief is given words and emotional outlet. The story of loss at this juncture meets the developmental story of the young child, one that is highly sensory and intuitive, given trust and security are not fully formed (Bowlby, 1982; Erikson, 1980; Piaget, 1954). Events that take place in early childhood set the stage for the child's initial learning about grieving, adapting to change, and feeling safe receiving support from others. Whatever is learned becomes part of the child's story of the self, others, and life.

The developmental world of middle childhood contains the accumulation of resources through task mastery that occurs in interaction with the child's environment. The emerging narrative the child is creating is more mature and increasingly sophisticated. Concrete operational thinking as Piaget (1954) described allows the child to not only experience the sensory aspects of loss events but the aspects made literal, detailed, and specific. The counselor listening for the developmental story of this child will hear questions such as "Was there a lot of blood?" or "Can Mom breathe now that she died?" The child's focus is on the details of the event and how those details literally affect her or him. Egocentrism is expected developmentally, yet it does not serve the child well if the story is, "I caused this to happen." This kind of storyline would be an opportunity for a counselor to use narrative techniques focused on separating the child from the event (White, 2005).

Fear and anxiety often begin to manifest verbally. Questions such as "Will you die, too?" may illustrate how the story is being constructed. However, the child still often appears minimally affected because of short attention span and differences in processing information (Piaget, 1954). It would not be uncommon to hear the grieving child comment, "I'm tired of this and want to go outside," only to pose questions a few hours later about the loss. Again, the loss story is being constructed within the developmental world of middle childhood. A counselor assists a child this age to learn how to put grief into appropriate words and behaviors. The child's natural tendency to imitate allows an opening for the counselor to utilize creative techniques to assist the grieving child in feeling expression and coping (Piaget, 1954).

Adolescence

A cross-generational and cross-cultural portrait of adolescent development highlights a widely accepted view of this life stage as unique in multiple domains of functioning. Most theorists discuss identity formation as a key component of adolescence, the journey for differentiation around self-concept (Erikson, 1980). The narrative is becoming more focused on questions such as "Who am I?" and "Who am I now that I've had a loss?"

Adolescents will seek technological avenues to experiment with who they are, seek comfort, express vulnerable feelings, and receive feedback, and they often do so from unknown sources quite autonomously and without adult supervision (James et al., 2008; Sofka, Cupit, & Gilbert, 2012). The impulsivity and lack of discernment many adolescents may have when seeking immediate relief and solace from the complexity of grief frequently concern adults. At a life stage when identity formation is developmentally new, grieving teens may have the difficult task of reforming their self-perception as a result of the death of significant adult figure or peers.

The social and interpersonal style of adolescence focuses on group acceptance and independence from adult figures. Adolescents desire some anonymity and privacy, such that adult monitoring may be difficult or perceived as intrusive (Oltjenbruns, 2001). This is against the notion that the most notable predictor of positive outcome of an adolescent's grief is the availability of a responsible and responsive adult (Worden, 2009). Cognitively, the adolescent is shifting toward greater sophistication in comprehending the finality, causality, and universality of death through the onset of abstract reasoning (Piaget, 1954).

However, the importance of belonging can exaggerate the self-focused belief of the *imaginary audience*, the idea that peers are watching and evaluating them at all times (Oltjenbruns, 2001). This belief contributes to increased fear of being perceived as different, perhaps denied a coveted social place or acceptance with others. Certainly, the notion of expressing feelings considered out of the norm by the peer group will result in censorship by the grieving adolescent. Technology may provide ways for an adolescent to experiment with feeling expression without the self-consciousness inherent in face-to-face interaction but may set up a camouflage for real intimacy. The intensity of grief expressed in less authentic relationships is a phenomenon of today's technological structures.

Additionally, the concept of the *personal fable* is another example of the impact of cognition upon the adolescent's experience of bereavement (Oltjenbruns, 2001). The belief that "this cannot happen to me" creates a pronounced feeling of disbelief and shock when an adolescent is confronted with making sense of bereavement events, especially untimely deaths of parents, siblings, and peers. While disbelief may be a normative response for all ages, it is particularly potent for the adolescent who has a sense of endless time to live, find a destiny, establish self-image, belong, and feel confident about the direction of her or his future.

The stark reality of bereavement during this period can influence an adolescent's coping with the core issues of predictability, personal control, justice and fairness, self-confidence, and connections symbolic of belonging (Balk, 2014). Researchers have reported such influences as an increase in fear associated with a lack of predictability over life events (Worden, 2009), a dismissal of support and connection from peers who find the bereaved adolescent to be wearisome and tiring (Oltjenbruns, 2001), and a lowered sense of self-efficacy accompanying a higher sense of self-doubt (Balk, 2011). Counselors must consider the possibility that the grieving adolescent's outreach for Internet support and comfort may contribute to increased fears around predictability, increased social dismissal, and elevated self-doubt. Adolescents are better served when encouraged to adopt a "restoration orientation" (Stroebe & Schut, 1999), and this can be the goal of narrative interventions with grieving adolescents.

Mourning, therefore, can be viewed as restoration and adaptation within changing developmental capacities. The mourning process includes four tasks influenced by the developmental issues of the maturing child: (a) accepting the reality of the loss; (b) experiencing, expressing, and managing the emotional intensity of grief; (c) adjusting to the resultant change; and (d) continuing and completing a bond through repositioning and memorializing the loss (Worden, 2009). The counselor, then, should direct appropriate interventions toward these aims.

CONVENTIONAL APPROACHES TO GRIEVING CHILDREN AND ADOLESCENTS

Most evidence-based treatment approaches with grieving children have emphasized a more traditional cognitive-behavioral model that is action and goal oriented and counselor directed, evaluated, assessed, and corrected (Currier, Holland, & Neimeyer, 2010). These conventional approaches match the emerging developmental capacities and needs as described previously in early childhood, middle childhood, and adolescence. Additionally, they translate well into current clinical practice in many settings. "In the era of managed care, evidence-based practice, and short term solution focused interventions, clinicians in agency based settings generally do not have the luxury of long-term contact with bereaved children" (Biank & Werner-Lin, 2011, p. 271). Unquestionably there is value in correcting distortions in thinking, learning specific coping strategies, increasing emotional identification and expression, distinguishing between feeling and acting, and adapting to inevitable changes when children and adolescents grieve (Corr & Balk, 2010; Currier et al., 2010; Currier, Holland, & Neimeyer, 2007; Currier, Neimeyer, & Berman, 2008; Goldman, 2014; Nadar & Salloum, 2011; National Child Traumatic Stress Network, 2015; Salloum, 2015; Steele & Malchiodi, 2012; Winokuer & Harris, 2016).

Edgar-Bailey and Kress (2010) reviewed creative interventions with children and adolescents confronting traumatic grief and link these to evidence-based cognitive-behavioral therapy (CBT) models. Additionally, it is clinically accepted that trauma-focused CBT (TF-CBT) is perhaps the treatment of choice when children and adolescents lose significant others in a traumatic manner and present symptoms of trauma that complicate and take precedence over interventions aimed at assisting a more normative grieving process (Steele & Malchiodi, 2012). *Trauma-informed care* is a new and necessary paradigm and contains widely accepted principles, including trauma awareness, emphasis on safety, opportunities to rebuild control, and strengths-based approach (Guarino & Bassuk, 2010; Hopper, Bassuk, & Olivet, 2010; McKenzie-Mohr, Coates, & McLeod, 2012; Saul, 2013; Steele & Malchiodi, 2012). Trauma-specific services address the estrangement from others and imply that traumatized individuals and families need to connect more effectively with others if healing is to occur.

Psychological first aid (PFA) is a culturally responsive best practice model and essentially a cognitive-behavioral approach for disaster and trauma survivors, including children and adolescents (National Child Traumatic Stress Network, 2015). Used with schools, community agencies, and Medical Reserve Corps, PFA emphasizes the provision of safety and comfort, education about psychological reactions to traumatic experiences, empowerment around resilience-based present and future choices, and the integration of community service linkages. PFA also builds social connections for support and intervention for developmental issues, anger management, sleep difficulty, and co-occurring mental health and substance abuse complexities. In these ways, PFA is one model based on trauma-informed care principles and offering trauma-specific services. These emerging models hold great promise, and future outcome research will judge the efficacy of their use with grieving children and adolescents.

Cautions do exist, however, with the more conventional interventions often used to assist children and adolescents. The aim of these interventions is one of conforming thinking and behavior to adaptive standards within the structured environments of the child or adolescent. This approach is more problem and corrective focused than narrative tenets espouse. Even when play therapy has been utilized, it is often not child-centered play and heavily relies upon the direction and interpretation of the therapist. Interventions with grieving children often occur through a diagnostic lens when grieving is complicated and symptomatology has shown itself in injurious ways in the grieving child or adolescent's life at home and school.

Furthermore, research has asserted serious questions as to "whether bereavement interventions actually promote children's adjustment to loss and help to improve their post-loss functioning" (Currier et al., 2007, p. 254). Additionally, the integration of developmental understanding and immediate and longer term response to childhood and adolescent grief and mourning is scant (Biank & Werner-Lin, 2011; Nader & Salloum, 2011).

THE POSTMODERN RATIONALE FOR A NARRATIVE RECONSTRUCTION ALTERNATIVE

Conventional approaches, then, tend not to represent the most congruent ways of helping grieving children and adolescents because they originate from a counselor-centric, diagnostic lens. An individual child or teen's unique perspective and the nuances of their grief may be ignored in favor of a "cookbook" approach meant to help them return to appropriate functioning as quickly as possible. Postmodern approaches, however, represent a very different attitude altogether on the part of the helper.

Counselors working with grieving children and adolescents can utilize narrative reconstruction in particular to understand their experience and collaborate to coauthor a story of hope and healing in the midst of pain. This postmodern approach acknowledges the subjective nature of the story, the primary goal of meaning making as a catalyst for healing, and the salient importance of the relationship between client and counselor in building a resilient narrative (Neimeyer, 2001). Counselors operating from a postmodern perspective embody a way of being that is honoring of the young person's story and curious about it, allowing the young client to be the expert rather than the counselor (White & Morgan, 2006). Helping is a collaborative process rather than a prescriptive one, and it is the present-oriented, ever-changing relationship between client and counselor that facilitates adaptation and healing rather than merely the specific tools a counselor chooses to use. Within the context of this therapeutic relationship, the goal is not about "resolving" grief; instead, counselor and client together move toward co-creating a resilient narrative, one that expresses an evolving meaning-making process (Gillies & Neimeyer, 2006; Machin, 2014).

Because postmodern approaches, including those based in the narrative therapeutic tradition, emphasize empowerment of clients, counselors who want to help grieving young people cannot operate from an assumption of expertise. This does not mean counselors should ignore whatever knowledge about grief they may have gleaned from personal and professional experience, however. It means an attitudinal shift into continuous curiosity about a client's subjective experience, the story of her or his grief, and an acknowledgment that counselors never have the "whole story," that the narrative is continually changing. Though research and theoretical concepts necessarily inform counselors' thinking, the primary focus is on bearing witness to the current story as well as co-creating the evolving resilient narrative. This attitude shifts the balance of power in the therapeutic relationship from a counselor-centered one to a more egalitarian one—an experience not likely typical of most other relationships between young clients and the adults in their lives. Rather than the implicit message that adults are in control and children and adolescents are powerless to change by themselves, they receive the message that they can change and can see themselves as resilient survivors rather than victims with problem-saturated stories.

From the standpoint of a more egalitarian, collaborative therapeutic relationship between client and counselor, the goal of helping shifts from directing the young client to fit into an objective definition of "doing well" in grief to assisting with a process of meaning making that will result in a more hopeful narrative (Gillies & Neimeyer, 2006). Until the time of the loss, a young person's personal narrative includes elements of predictability to a greater or lesser extent (Janoff-Bulman, 1992). Even for those who live in unstable homes or experience constantly changing environments, there may be a kind of constancy present in the instability itself. A loss disorganizes the story and increases uncertainty. A counselor operating from a postmodern approach is well situated to help young people see the strengths they already possess both within themselves and in their surrounding systems. They can then help them make sense of what happened and transform the narrative into a balanced story of grief and hope. Because current research suggests that positive meaning making increases the likelihood of better adaptation to grief (Holland, Currier, & Neimeyer, 2006), a postmodern approach to counseling with grieving children and adolescents, one that is attentive to the subjective developmental and cultural aspects of a given client's story, is a strong alternative to more conventional approaches to counseling.

NARRATIVE RECONSTRUCTION IN GRIEF

Narrative reconstruction provides an alternative approach to the more conventional CBT interventions, although CBT techniques can be utilized within a narrative reconstruction approach. Narrative reconstruction has dominated contemporary models of grief recovery and yet is often unknown to counselors (Ober, Granello, & Wheaton, 2012). This social constructivist model is built upon meaning-making interpretive activity wherein the child or adolescent's narrative evolves within a social context and contains metaphors and themes that offer autobiographical coherence and identity to the emerging story of her or his life (Figley & Kiser, 2012; Neimeyer et al., 2014; Rubin, Malkinson, & Witzum, 2011; Saul, 2013). Narrative reconstructionists argue that loss and trauma challenge existing constructions of reality about the self, others, and life in ways that demand a constitutional reconstruction of who one is presently, given the experience (Neimeyer, 2009).

Experiences in the child or adolescent's life are organized into a plot, perhaps originating within sensory and intuitive aspects from early childhood; negotiated in social and cultural interactions, meanings, and responses; and communicated with others (Neimeyer, Burke, Mackay, & Stringer, 2010; Neimeyer, Torres, & Smith, 2011; White, 2005; White & Morgan, 2006; Yuen, 2007). The premise is that meaning is made by story making and storytelling, thereby defining narrative construction as the evolving personal activity of constructing and transforming meaning in one's life story within a social context.

The formation of the narrative does not happen for the child or adolescent in isolation but rather in relationship with others. The interpretive activity she or he engages in can result in fractures to the self, such as victimization, marginalization, and disenfranchisement so severe that resilience for the future is compromised (Neimeyer, 2009; Rubin et al., 2011; Saul, 2013). Resilient narratives are constructed more easily when interventions are strength based, mastery oriented, and competency driven. The individual's future is more hopeful when self-efficacy is high. Simultaneously, the therapeutic environments within which children and adolescents construct and reconstruct a sense of self and future most assuredly have to rewrite the contextual narrative for this population as one of survivorship, welcome, and respectful place. Healing of grief is movement toward resilient narrative transformation, an application of narrative reconstruction in grief given the disruption to the story resulting from loss (Neimeyer, 2014).

When working with grieving children and adolescents within the concepts, processes, and techniques of the narrative reconstructive approach, the counselor can best be described as a collaborator with the client. It is a curious exploration process with respectful listening and honoring without judgment (Neimeyer et al., 2014; White, 2005; White & Morgan, 2006; Yuen, 2007). The child or adolescent is changed in the action of story sharing, as is the counselor who witnesses the meanings within the plot. There is a kind of coauthoring happening between client and counselor that implies both that the client is active and that the counselor assists with an alternative storyline if an injurious, nonresilient narrative is told. The experiential world of the grieving child or adolescent has center stage. It may be described as a creative and dynamic process, a sacred privilege for counselors willing to embrace this approach.

Narrative therapists tend to agree with Carl Rogers in the notion that the therapeutic relationship and the personhood of the counselor are more primary than a prescribed set of intervention techniques. However, the literature includes poignant examples of how to structure the process with questions that elicit the experience of the client rather than the information of the event of loss. Counselors utilize myriad techniques to express the narrative; to deconstruct problematic meanings; to externalize the problem as a way of creating distance between what has been lost and either self-blame, self-effacing, and self-shaming; and to suggest preferred stories of identity for the child or adolescent's resilience for the future. Reauthoring alternate stories and assisting the client to find responsive audiences who might witness and support those narratives is also a critical activity. Narrative themes that lead to *benefit finding* (Holland et al., 2006) within a difficult situation such as grief parallel the findings of the Harvard Bereavement Study, a longitudinal study of children who lost parents. Children displayed better coping and adaptation to death when some positive outcome could be generated (Worden, 2009).

RESEARCH AND PRACTICE FROM THE LITERATURE

Expressive arts interventions are being used more widely with grief across the life span (Thompson & Neimeyer, 2014), and they may be uniquely suited to facilitating the exploration of the story and the process of meaning making within a narrative reconstruction framework. They represent creative, collaborative means of helping children and adolescents examine the elements of their story, identify areas of confusion or disorganization, and coauthor a new, resilient narrative. In addition, expressive arts interventions allow counselors to participate with clients in a concrete way by serving as witnesses to the evolving story. Examples from recent literature on expressive arts interventions illustrate current modalities currently used with grieving children and adolescents.

Muselman and Wiggins (2012) discuss the function of ritual creation as a way to engage with others in meaning making around a significant death. They also advocate bibliotherapy, art therapy, memory expressions through art, journaling, and letter writing as techniques that may be modified for developmental appropriateness. Scaletti and Hocking (2010) describe the use of sandtray as "one approach recommended to assist children to externalize their grief" (p. 67) from which a storybook might be created to capture, share, and remember important aspects of the sandtray intervention. Whiting et al. (2008) discuss how counselors can be creative advocates for bereaved children and adolescents and present a variety of examples of expressive interventions for use with this population.

Additionally, Wheat and Whiting (2015) present creative possibilities for school counselors assisting children whose parents are deployed. Slyter (2012) discusses creative interventions with adolescents that might assist in *continuing bonds*, widely recognized as part of repositioning a relationship of presence into a relationship of memory (Klass, Silverman, & Nickman, 1996) through the use of music, visual arts such as photography, and cinematherapy. Finally, Philpott (2013) posits that the use of dance movement therapy (DMT) may create a shared experience where "kinesthetic empathy" can be built with the counselor or others. Philpott writes, "perhaps it could mean the surrender into moving grief: trusting the vitality of the heart's empathic resonance while dancing through the complexity and transformative power of emotion" (p. 165). These examples from the literature illustrate how a variety of expressive arts may be used specifically in conjunction with narrative reconstructive approaches and with grieving children and adolescents.

Narrative approaches in general are best known from the work of White (2005) and subsequent colleagues who represent social constructionists in the concepts of meaning construction, truth as substantiated through interpretive stories, dominant cultural narratives, and the therapeutic techniques used in narrative intervention (White & Morgan, 2006). The social constructivist literature has extensive contributions rooted in ideas such as that of *personal constructs* (Holland, Currier, Neimeyer, & Berman, 2007; Kelly,

1955/1991) and *meaning making* (Bruner, 1990) and continued in recent years in ideas such as narrative reconstruction (Adler & McAdams, 2007; Neimeyer, 2008) and *narrative-dialogical processes* (Neimeyer, 2006b; Ribeiro, Bento, Gonçalves, & Salgado, 2010). The research and practice literature related to grieving in general, and grieving children and adolescents specifically, consistently presents Neimeyer's model of narrative reconstruction as a contemporary, innovative, and highly promising model of grief reconciliation (Corr & Balk, 2010; Goldman, 2014; Meagher & Balk, 2013; Neimeyer, 2014; Neimeyer et al., 2010; Neimeyer, Harris, Winokuer, & Thornton, 2011; Stillion & Attig, 2015; Winokuer & Harris, 2016).

More research will undoubtedly continue to examine the efficacy of these approaches, the outcomes of narrative reconstruction with grieving individuals at unique life phases across the life span and in diverse settings, the use of narrative reconstruction ideas and techniques in various loss events (death and otherwise), and the application of these to both typical and complicated grief and mourning. Meaning making and narrative reconstruction as conceptualized with grieving individuals is an emerging base of both research and practice in recent literature (Bragin, 2010; Coleman & Neimeyer, 2010; Currier et al., 2008; Currier et al., 2010; Gerrish, Steed, & Neimeyer, 2010; Gillies, Neimeyer, & Milman, 2015; Holland & Neimeyer, 2010; Holland et al., 2006, 2007; Johnson, 2014; Laurie & Neimeyer, 2010; Lichtenthal, Burke, & Neimeyer, 2011; Lichtenthal, Currier, Neimeyer, & Keesee, 2010; Neimeyer, 2006a, 2006b, 2006c; Neimeyer, Burke, Young, & McDevitt-Murphy, 2015; Neimeyer & Wogrin, 2008; Neimeyer et al., 2010; Pearce, 2011; Piazza-Bonin, Whiting, 2012; Whiting & Bradley, 2007; Williams, Burke, McDevitt-Murphy, & Neimeyer, 2012; Yuen, 2007).

CASE ILLUSTRATION—WORKING WITH ALEXIS, AGE 16

To clarify the somewhat nebulous concepts of narrative reconstruction, it is useful to see them in action through a representative case. The following case demonstrates work with a grieving adolescent; however, it should be noted that this case is a composite of several clients in order to protect the confidentiality of any one client.

The Client

Alexis J. was a tall, lanky girl with long, dark brown hair and large brown eyes. Her younger brother Mateo had died at 8 years old several months before, in a car accident involving several other members of her family.

Alexis's mother had been driving the younger siblings home from soccer practice; she stopped at a four-way stop, started into the intersection, and was hit by someone speeding through. She was badly injured herself, and the other two siblings showed minor cuts and bruises, but Mateo was directly impacted and died on the scene.

At the time of the accident, Alexis was at home making dinner for the family. Her father, who she assumed was on his way home from work, called her cell phone to be sure she was at home and told her to wait there for him. When her father arrived, he sat down with Alexis at the kitchen table and told her that he had gotten a call from the hospital, that there had been an accident, and that they needed to go to the hospital right away. Alexis was immediately flustered and anxious, peppering her father with questions, but he either didn't know anything or wouldn't say. At the hospital, Alexis saw her mother looking weak in a hospital bed, with multiple injuries. In the midst of her anguished reaction, a hospital social worker appeared and led Alexis and her father to a small room where a doctor was waiting with her younger sisters. This was when Alexis learned that her brother Mateo hadn't made it.

In the weeks and months that followed the accident, Alexis silently withdrew. At first, she still went to school and did all the things she normally did, such as watching her younger siblings and attending football games, but her heart didn't seem to be in it anymore. Her grades slipped and she began to appear listless. She gradually isolated herself from her friends, spending increasing amounts of time alone in her room. Her grandmother, who had moved in with the family to keep it functioning, grew concerned and spoke with the parish priest about what to do. He met with Alexis at her grandmother's request and afterward recommended that Alexis participate in more intensive counseling.

Process Description

Sessions One and Two

The first time I (LSW) met Alexis, she sat across from me finishing a text on her phone and then looked up expectantly as though waiting for me to "therapize" her. She, like most people, assumed I was going to do something magical and "fix" her. I remember smiling and asking her what she had heard about counseling and what she imagined would happen. She seemed surprised and perhaps caught off guard that I hadn't jumped into asking her about herself. She told me what she expected based on what she had heard, and I surprised her again by asking her what she wanted it to be like.

Together we decided on the parameters of our relationship, and I let her know that my philosophy as a counselor leads me to treat my clients like partners and that I believed that she was the expert on her life and her story, but that I could help by listening and working together with her to help her. This exchange seemed to relax Alexis, and she shifted her position on the couch to a more casual one.

For the rest of that session and most of the next one, the main focus was on hearing Alexis's story and on bearing witness to that story. Initially, the story she told was thin and factual, with very few expressive details, as if she were reporting for the newspaper. For example, when once I ventured to ask about her family and her culture, she responded by saying simply, "Well, I have a mom and a dad; my grandmother lives with us; and I have two little sisters. I guess you could say I'm Latina, but I don't really know what that means. We do go to church and my grandmother makes this soup called menudo on New Year's, supposedly an old family recipe, but that's about it. I don't know, I guess that's all." Her face was fairly expressionless, though I noticed she fiddled with something in her pocket while she was speaking. The picture she drew with her words was essentially made up of stick figures—and she hadn't mentioned her brother at all. I felt compelled to mention his absence and asked her about it. Alexis shrugged and said, "Well, that is why I'm here, right?" I thought I noticed a challenge in her eyes and in the tone of her voice, though outwardly she still appeared comfortable. She was not quite ready to include Mateo in her story again; it was too painful, I guessed. I changed my focus back to building rapport and asked instead about some other aspect of her story that she might feel safer telling.

As Alexis continued with her stories, I increasingly asked more specific questions, encouraging her to enrich and enliven the narrative with greater detail. She began to weave a more complex tapestry as she talked and grew accustomed to the nature of storytelling. Close to the end of the second session, Alexis finally spoke her brother's name aloud. In the middle of a story about a humorous incident that happened when she was babysitting her siblings, she hesitated for the barest second before saying with a slight hitch in her voice, "And then Mateo came crawling out of the laundry basket, rubbing his eyes—he fell asleep in the middle of the game." Nearly a minute before, she had been laughing, her eyes dancing as she described a game of hide and seek gone awry, and then in the moment she spoke her brother's name, her aspect changed and she seemed to waver, uncertain whether she felt safe to unlock her deepest door. She looked confused, almost frightened, and after a quiet beat, I reflected that to her. The acknowledgment and acceptance of her present emotion appeared to remove the last barrier and the floodgates opened. Without seeming to change her countenance at all, suddenly tears spilled down her face and her breathing became labored. "Oh my God I miss him so much!" was all she could manage to get out.

Sessions Three Through Five

Alexis and I continued to build on her story, and by this time I started to notice some themes in what she related. She was not always the main character, frequently playing a supportive role to someone else. For instance, she once spoke of how she and her friends liked to go shopping, and she focused on a story about how her best friend, Sarah, had once egged them on to talking to some boys they thought were cute at the mall. She talked all about how Sarah convinced them, Sarah's first move, and how Sarah had giggled and pretended to faint afterward. Another example was the previous story about hide and seek with her siblings. The focus was continually on her siblings' antics and not as much on any plot-advancing action on her part. I wondered about her seeming lack of agency in her story. At one point during a natural break in the third session, I asked her about what I was noticing, framing it as a question about whether I was perhaps misperceiving a family value or cultural characteristic. She seemed surprised, thought about it, and said she didn't think so, that she hadn't noticed. I then wondered aloud how it might change the story if she told it with herself as the main character instead. Alexis liked this idea and switched her focus. I hoped she would feel empowered by this change, and after she finished another story, I asked her what it was like to tell it that way. She responded with a grin and a shy "Good!"

I usually began our sessions with a question: "How should we start today?" This allowed her to take the lead and gave me the role of "professional witness" and coauthor. I noticed in session four that although she had started our time together with a couple of vignettes that were lighter and more superficial, Alexis quickly delved deeper into her memories of her brother and her lost relationship with him. These stories were full of anguish, confusion, and yearning, with a hint of anger. The image coming to my mind as she talked was of a bewildered witness to a natural disaster talking to a news reporter who asked incomprehensible questions. She couldn't seem to make sense of the accident and "why" questions filled her narrative. It was as though she was barely in touch with other aspects of her grief because the desire, the need, to fix the plot hole created by the accident was so dire. I was curious about who Mateo was in her story outside of the accident, and I thought expanding on his character might give her some relief from the questions momentarily as well as help her acknowledge other aspects of her grief. Additionally, in a previous session, I had learned of Alexis's interest in photography. So I carefully broached the subject with a question: "It is so hard to live all the time with this terrible wish to know what really happened in the accident and why Mateo had to die! It's so obvious how much you love him. You were his big sister! I'd love to know more about him and what you remember . . . did you ever take pictures of him?" She responded that she had a lot of pictures of her own, and some from when she was younger and didn't take pictures yet. I told her of my idea, to bring in some of her favorites that she would like to share with me and tell me about what was happening in the pictures—but I also asked her whether she thought that might be helpful and whether she was willing to do that. Alexis thought about it seriously for a few minutes in silence, again fiddling with something in her pocket. She finally replied, "I think I would like to bring a few in. Actually I haven't looked at them much; I just haven't been able to."

In session five, Alexis used two pictures of her brother brought from home to tell me all about him, and Mateo began to take shape between us. The more she talked, the more she seemed to relish helping me get to know him. Mateo's character in her stories was a funny, impish little boy who loved practical jokes and getting dirty. He had a huge heart and he wanted to be a doctor someday "to help all the little kids who are sick." As her story took a wistful turn, Alexis grew sad and began to cry. Her "why" questions were returning. "It's so hard to live with questions that don't have answers. And it's so terribly unfair to have to let go of your little brother before he had a chance to grow up, isn't it?" I asked her. She nodded, once again digging her fingers into her pocket. She told me she didn't know what to do, that it was driving her crazy. She pulled a white shoelace from her pocket, and looking down at it in her hands, she said that besides the pictures, it was all she had left of Mateo. Shortly after his death, Alexis had sneaked into his room and taken the shoelace out of one of his tennis shoes. She carried it with her now wherever she went, as a way to stay connected with him, to feel as though he was still with her. I reflected gently that it felt as though he had disappeared from the story and now she had to hang on to anything that would confirm he was once there. She got up and paced a little before returning to the couch and setting her head in her hands. I stayed quiet, trusting that she needed a moment's space. Finally, without looking up, she said chokingly, "My job was to take care of him. I wasn't even there! If I had been there, I would have done something, I don't know covered him up or something. He wouldn't have died!" She was revealing what she saw as the toughest problem in the story—her role was to be the protector, and she had failed. Alexis seemed to feel hopeless as she left this session and I worried about her a bit.

In session six, I noticed Alexis had put her hair up in a loose ponytail tied with a shoelace. She told me, after I inquired about it, that it was Mateo's and that she had decided to do something different with it. I was honestly relieved to see her, as she had missed the previous week due to illness, but there was something a little different about Alexis besides the shoelace. She told me she had thought a lot about our last session, to the point of even dreaming about it. In her dream, I was the failed protector—I had failed to keep her from her grief and guilt. But when she awoke, feeling weepy, she remembered what I had said in the first session about our being partners in our work, which meant she could make choices. She said she thought about Mateo and how he would run up to her and hug her when she was sad, and that he was probably looking down from heaven and sending her one of those hugs right now, not wanting her to be sad. She reported that in that moment, still lying in bed, she really thought she could feel his arm around her. That was when she decided to put her hair up with the shoelace, rather than keeping it in her pocket. She had been doing it every day since then. She couldn't explain why she wanted to do it. I wondered aloud whether maybe she sensed that it was okay not to feel guilty or to have to hide her brother's death and her grief from people. She looked skeptical and shrugged.

Later that same session, Alexis and I were again talking about her role in her story and how the story would change now that Mateo was no longer an active character. We had reached a point of silence in which Alexis seemed to be unable to move forward. I took the opportunity to ask whether she could think of a way for Mateo to remain in the story even though his character couldn't interact in the same ways. She looked confused and for a moment I thought she was going to tell me I was crazy. I explained that even though he was physically gone, she didn't just erase him from her life. Maybe there was a way to keep him in the story in a different way. We discussed this for a couple of minutes, during which time Alexis grew pensive. Finally she said, "Well, I guess that's kinda like how I'm using his shoelace in my hair, right? I mean, I do feel better in a weird way knowing people can see it now, like you said before. So he's already still in the story because I put him in my hair." She laughed, for the first time in a long time.

By the end of the session, Alexis had decided she wanted to keep Mateo in her story by remembering him and imagining what he might say or do sometimes. She had an idea to make a scrapbook with the pictures she had and to decorate it with mementos from their life together such as a treasure map she had once drawn on a napkin for her siblings to find or stickers from her Mickey Mouse hat, which came from a family trip to Disney World. As we ended the session, I remarked on how different she seemed that day, how she seemed to be slowly taking charge of writing her own story. She smiled shyly as she went out the door.

The majority of session seven was spent in much the same vein. Alexis brought part of her scrapbook with her as well as some materials so she could work on it as we talked. She told me about her process while she worked, occasionally saying things such as "Mateo would hate this page, it's too girly. He would say 'Ewwww!' But I can't help it; it's my scrapbook, I'll put flowers in it if I want!" At one point, Alexis said quietly that she had been to Mateo's grave for the first time since the funeral. I asked what it was like for her, and she replied that she was sad going there, but that it wasn't as terrible as she had thought it might be. She hesitated, and then said in a confessional tone that she had talked to him and told him everything he had missed to that point. It had felt relieving, as though she had taken off a large burden and left it at the cemetery. We discussed what it meant for her to have done these things, how she was changing. The session ended on a thoughtful note with Alexis beginning to think about Mateo's continued presence in her life.

Session Eight

Alexis walked in with her scrapbook, completed over the last week, and showed me page by page what was in it, telling me any stories I hadn't yet heard. Finally, closing the book, she said that she thought she would be okay without coming to counseling anymore. I could see she was serious and asked about her thought process. Alexis responded that even though she was still sad, it wasn't unbearable anymore, and it was sometimes mixed with happy memories. When I asked her what was different, what caused those changes, she paused for a few moments and seemed to think hard. Finally she said, "I don't know about all of it, I just know that Mateo doesn't blame me for what happened. And I know that no matter what, he's always gonna be with me." I told her sincerely that I had great respect for the work she had done, that she had turned into her own protector and heroine. We spent the rest of the session discussing what she could do when she had hard times or when she felt herself slipping back into a supporting character role. At the end, she hugged me and smiled on her way out.

Counseling Outcomes and Discussion

This case demonstrates a nearly ideal use of narrative reconstruction with a grieving adolescent client. I (LSW) approached working with Alexis from an egalitarian standpoint, attempting to empower her by emphasizing her ability to choose the direction our sessions took as frequently as possible. I framed our working relationship as a partnership in which she was the expert on her story and I was a helpful professional witness to the evolving story. Rather than setting a goal to help her feel better, confronting what I might perceive to be cognitive distortions or unhealthy adaptations, all of which might be congruent with more conventional approaches, I trusted that she already had some wisdom within herself to know what she needed in her grief. My work as a counselor was to remain present with her, to help her express her narrative, and to help her to make sense of her story by resituating what was lost. Additionally, though we primarily did this verbally because she was willing and able to do so, Alexis did use expressive arts in the form of the scrapbook to help her with her process. As she created it, my goal as witness and coauthor was to ask questions about her choices and help her look at emerging themes. I did at one point have the idea to incorporate Alexis's photography as a method of expressive storytelling; however, because the scrapbook idea came from Alexis herself rather than me as the counselor, it was much better suited to the theme of agency beginning to surface in her narrative.

By the time she ended counseling, Alexis had achieved a great deal. She was no longer withdrawn; in fact, she was beginning to reengage with some of the clubs and activities she had been a part of before Mateo's death. She also felt a little less vulnerable around her friends and classmates, choosing to open up to Sarah about aspects of her grief, though she still watched carefully for any sign that Sarah was scared or "freaked out." The biggest gains she made, however, were in her understanding and ability to tolerate her grief. Mateo was the first significant person Alexis had ever lost, and she was blindsided by her own reaction, caught in a maelstrom with a desperate need to understand what happened. Through our work, she was able to come to terms with Mateo's death and transform her relationship with him. He would live on in her memory, and this could be comforting to her rather than merely a torment. The scrapbook helped her with that transformation because it gave her a way to allow grief to coexist with happiness and humor. In essence, she had reclaimed Mateo as she knew him before his death and invited him back into her story in new ways (Hedtke & Winslade, 2004).

Alexis did face some challenges to her new narrative, however. Mateo's death impacted everyone in the family, hitting the mother especially hard. Alexis's relationship with her mother deteriorated as she felt she needed to take care of her mother and be strong for her. As she originally did with her friends, she tended to mask her feelings when she could and withdraw when she couldn't. The family's emotional turmoil was fairly constant as they dealt with not only losing Mateo but participating in the legal system, a brief burst of media attention, and some serious financial difficulty. In retrospect, it would have been most helpful if I had convinced Alexis and some of her family members to participate in counseling together. Children and adolescents need the support of adults around them; in addition, when a loss impacts an entire family, the family narrative is disrupted along with each individual's personal narrative. Supporting each of them as they work to rebuild together would be the best way to ensure that Alexis's changes took hold and that the family relationships were strengthened. Fortunately, Alexis was resilient and had a number of people outside her family from whom she could seek support.

LIMITATIONS OF NARRATIVE RECONSTRUCTION AS A POSTMODERN APPROACH FOR WORKING WITH GRIEVING CHILDREN AND ADOLESCENTS

As the previous case example demonstrates, postmodern approaches can certainly be fruitful in working with children and adolescents. The precepts of narrative reconstruction specifically represent a unique method for joining with a child or teenager to rebuild storylines disrupted by loss. As with any approach, however, there are some definite limitations. First, postmodern counseling approaches generally receive very little attention in counselor training programs; when they are included, it is usually in a theories of counseling course in a section for alternative or emerging methodologies. Narrative reconstruction specifically has roots in constructivism and contains some philosophical similarities to narrative therapy, but as a stand-alone approach is not typically considered in counselor training. Consequently, most counselors have no familiarity with this approach. The few who may have been exposed to it perhaps understand the tenets of narrative reconstruction but may experience a disconnect with how to practice it or how to integrate it with other counseling skills such as reflective listening. In addition, at the core of the approach is an assumption that the nature of truth is subjective, and that is why the client is assumed to be the expert on her or his reality rather than the counselor; but this assumption is in direct opposition to many conventional approaches to counseling, which start from an assumption that an objective truth can be known. It may be very difficult, therefore, for counselors with little experience in other postmodern approaches to learn and practice narrative reconstruction.

Another possible limitation of this approach, particularly as it applies to working with children and adolescents, is its primary aim of long-term change. Reconstructing a personal narrative that is situated within a family narrative and influenced by larger cultural and societal narratives tends not to be short-term work. This reality conflicts with the current need to have brief, evidence-based approaches because of insurance compliance issues for clinically based counselors or multiple demands on time for school counselors. Counselors should consider whether this approach is a fit based on the requirements of their role.

Finally, client characteristics should be considered. As with many other approaches to counseling, there is little research regarding applicability of narrative reconstruction to clients of diverse ethnicities, genders, or cultural backgrounds. A collaborative approach such as this one may not work for some individuals or populations. Counselors therefore should take care to consider what might be the best fit for their clients. Additionally, the developmental characteristics of typical children and adolescents mean that some may not be able to comprehend or fully participate in reconstructing a narrative because they may not possess the requisite cognitive capacity to do so. The nature of identity construction itself, as well as meaning making, depend on abstract thinking—a skill that is virtually unknown in childhood and that gradually emerges throughout the course of adolescence. Though this is certainly a limitation, it may be possible for counselors to modify the usage of this approach so that the focus is on reconstructing storylines or individual elements of a narrative rather than attempting to reconstruct an entire personal narrative that may or may not even be comprehensible to a given client. The case illustration of working with Alexis is an example of this process; it would have taken much longer to reconstruct her personal narrative and may not have fit with her developmental stage. Again, however, there is little research in this arena, and counselors are urged to use caution.

IMPLICATIONS AND RECOMMENDATIONS FOR USE WITH CLIENTS

Although there are certainly some limitations to the use of narrative reconstruction with children and adolescents, it is flexible enough for counselors to be able to adapt it to the needs of their clients and the availability of resources. As such, it can be employed in multiple settings in which counselors work. School counselors, for instance, should tailor their interventions to the developmental level of their students and must work within their time limitations as well, so attending to specific elements of a storyline may be especially helpful. Expressive arts techniques can be particularly effective for younger clients who may not be able to tell their story in words, and for older children and teens who may feel more comfortable with indirect methods of expression. Numerous examples of expressive arts interventions exist in the literature (e.g., Slyter, 2012; Thompson & Neimeyer, 2014; Whiting et al., 2008); however, counselors should continually keep in mind the purpose for the intervention and its applicability to narrative reconstruction.

In clinical settings, counselors frequently have more time with their clients, but they are often pressured to provide results relatively quickly, so again concentrating on storyline elements through the use of expressive arts methods may be helpful. Counselors in clinical settings with young clients can involve family members as well, particularly if the loss was shared by multiple members of the same family. Although each member of the family carries a personal narrative which contains her or his own understanding of the context of the loss, this narrative is influenced by the family narrative as well, and this larger systemic narrative will also undergo reconstruction. Counselors in clinical settings are well positioned to help families reconstruct their narrative together in a process that seeks the perspective of all members.

Regardless of setting, however, it is even more imperative for counselors to become knowledgeable about grief. This area of human experience is typically given short shrift in counselor preparation programs (Ober et al., 2012) and is not mentioned at all in the current CACREP standards (2015) or their immediate predecessor (2009). Without proper training in how to recognize grief and work with grieving people, particularly children and adolescents, counselors run the risk of unintentionally harming their clients—or at the very least, failing to help them. Narrative reconstruction was developed specifically for use with those mourning significant losses, so counselors seeking to use this approach should take care to increase their competence in grief as well. It is also important to realize that though grief is a typical response to loss and that most people naturally move toward reconciliation of their grief, in some cases people do not move in that general direction, instead getting stuck in their pain, going through a delayed reaction, or experiencing a mixture of grief and trauma (Worden, 2009). These may be indications of complicated grief, in which case specific treatment through grief therapy would be warranted (Neimeyer et al., 2010). This is an area in need of continued research, especially in the recognition and treatment of children and adolescents who may be experiencing complicated grief.

CONCLUSION

Postmodern approaches to counseling, specifically narrative reconstruction, possess clear advantages over conventional approaches to grieving children and adolescents by empowering young clients; working from a subjective, not necessarily time-limited definition of grief; and facilitating expression of the evolving story in a manner most suited to the individual client. Conventional approaches such as CBT tend to be counselor directed and goals are primarily set by the counselor according to adaptive standards and diagnostic criteria. These approaches may fail to consider an individual child or adolescent's story and therefore may miss the meaning inherent in grief as well as the myriad specific pieces of the shattered assumptive world. By approaching a grieving young client as an equal, with shared responsibility for putting the pieces together again in a new way, the whole of the client's experience is respected, rather than merely focusing on distorted thoughts or problematic behaviors. Perhaps more than in conventional approaches with their selective focus, postmodern approaches such as narrative reconstruction have the power to plant seeds of self-reliance and agency because of their empowering stance toward young clients. Perhaps as these clients grow and other losses impact them over time, they will come to see their healing as arising from within as well as without.

As has been noted in direct and indirect ways throughout this chapter, counselors hold a sacred privilege when they work with children and adolescents who are grieving. We are chosen to provide a precious holding environment, a safe space for young clients to present their most vulnerable and tender selves. By using a postmodern approach such as narrative reconstruction, we are privileged to bear witness to and co-create a resilient narrative, one that balances acknowledgment of mourning with hope in the future.

REFERENCES

Adler, J. M., & McAdams, D. P. (2007). The narrative reconstruction of psychotherapy. *Narrative Inquiry, 17*(2), 179–202. doi:10.1075/ni.17.2.03adl

Balk, D. (2011). Adolescent development and bereavement: An introduction. *The Prevention Researcher, 18*(3), 3–9. Retrieved from https://www.highbeam.com/publications/the-prevention-researcher-p408642

Balk, D. E. (2014). *Dealing with dying, death, and grief during adolescence.* New York, NY: Routledge.

Biank, N. M., & Werner-Lin, A. (2011). Growing up with grief: Revisiting the death of a parent over the life course. *Omega, 63,* 271–290. doi:10.2190/OM.63.3.e

Bowlby, J. (1982). *Attachment.* New York, NY: Basic Books.

Bragin, M. (2010). Can anyone here know who I am? Co-constructing meaningful narratives with combat veterans. *Clinical Social Work Journal, 38,* 316–326. doi:10.1007/s10615-010-0267-4

Bruner, J. (1990). *Acts of meaning.* Cambridge, MA: Harvard University Press.

Coleman, R. A., & Neimeyer, R. A. (2010). Measuring meaning: Searching for and making sense of spousal loss in late life. *Death Studies, 34,* 804–834. doi:10.1080/07481181003761625

Corr, C. A., & Balk, D. E. (Eds.). (2010). *Children's encounters with death, bereavement, and coping.* New York, NY: Springer.

Council for the Accreditation of Counseling and Related Educational Programs (2009). *2009 standards.* Alexandria, VA: Author.

Council for the Accreditation of Counseling and Related Educational Programs (2015). *2016 standards.* Alexandria, VA: Author.

Currier, J. M., Holland, J. M., & Neimeyer, R. A. (2007). The effectiveness of bereavement interventions with children: A meta-analytic review of controlled outcome research. *Journal of Clinical Child & Adolescent Psychology, 36,* 253–259. doi:10.1080/15374410701279669

Currier, J. M., Holland, J. M., & Neimeyer, R. A. (2010). Do CBT-based interventions alleviate distress following bereavement? A review of the current evidence. *International Journal of Cognitive Therapy, 3,* 79–95. doi:10.1521/ijct.2010.3.1.77

Currier, J. M., Neimeyer, R. A., & Berman, J. S. (2008). The effectiveness of psychotherapeutic interventions for bereaved persons: A comprehensive quantitative review. *Psychological Bulletin, 134,* 648–661. doi:0.1037/0033-2909.134.5.648

Doka, K. J. (Ed). (2002). *Disenfranchised grief: New directions, challenges and strategies for practice.* Champaign, IL: Research Press.

Edgar-Bailey, M., & Kress, V. E. (2010). Resolving child and adolescent traumatic grief: Creative techniques and interventions. *Journal of Creativity in Mental Health, 5,* 158–176. doi:10.1080/15401383.2010.485090

Erikson, E. H. (1980). *Identity and the life cycle.* New York, NY: Norton.

Figley, C. R., & Kiser, L. J. (2012). *Helping traumatized families* (2nd ed.). New York, NY: Routledge.

Gerrish, N. J., Steed, L., & Neimeyer, R. A. (2010). Meaning reconstruction in bereaved mothers: A pilot study using the biographical grid. *Journal of Constructivist Psychology, 23,* 118–142. doi:10.1080/10720530903563215

Gillies, J., & Neimeyer, R. A. (2006). Loss, grief, and the search for significance: Toward a model of meaning reconstruction in bereavement. *Journal of Constructivist Psychology, 19,* 31–65. doi:10.1080/10720530500311182

Gillies, J. M., Neimeyer, R. A., & Milman, E. (2015). The grief and meaning reconstruction inventory (GMRI): Initial validation of a new measure. *Death Studies, 39,* 61–74. doi:10.1080/07481187.2014.907089

Goldman, L. (2014). *Life and loss: A guide to help grieving children* (3rd ed.). New York, NY: Routledge/Taylor & Francis Group.

Grollman, E. A. (1995). *Bereaved children and teens: A support guide for parents and professionals.* Boston, MA: Beacon Press.

Guarino, K., & Bassuk, E. (2010). Working with families experiencing homelessness: Understanding trauma and its impact. *Zero to Tree, 30*(3), 11–20. Retrieved from http://www.zerotothree.org/about-us/areas-of-expertise/zero-to-three-journal

Hedtke, L., & Winslade, J. (2004). *Re-membering lives: Conversations with the dying and the bereaved.* Amityville, NY: Baywood.

Holland, J. M., Currier, J. M., & Neimeyer, R. A. (2006). Meaning reconstruction in the first two years of bereavement: The role of sense-making and benefit-finding. *Omega, 53,* 175–191. doi:10.2190/FKM2-YJTY-F9VV-9XWY

Holland, J. M., & Neimeyer, R. A. (2010). An examination of stage theory of grief among individuals bereaved by natural and violent causes: A meaning-oriented contribution. *Omega, 61,* 103–120. doi:10.2190/OM.61.2.b

Holland, J. M., Neimeyer, R. A., Currier, J., & Berman, J. (2007). The efficacy of personal construct therapy: A comprehensive review. *Journal of Clinical Psychology, 63*, 93–107. doi:10.1002/jclp.20332

Hopper, E. K., Bassuk, E., & Olivet, J. (2010). Shelter from the storm: Trauma-informed care in homelessness services settings. *The Open Health Services and Policy Journal, 3*(2), 80–100. Retrieved from http://benthamopen.com/tohspj/home

James, L., Oltjenbruns, K., & Whiting, P. (2008). Grieving adolescents: The paradox of using technology for support. In K. Doka (Ed.), *Living with grief: Children and adolescents* (pp. 299–316). Washington, DC: Hospice Foundation of America.

Janoff-Bulman, R. (1992). *Shattered assumptions: Towards a new psychology of trauma.* New York, NY: The Free Press.

Johnson, C. M. (2014). The loss of friends to homicide and the implications for the identity development of urban African American teen girls. *Clinical Social Work Journal, 42*, 27–40. doi:10.1007/s10615-012-0425-y

Kelly, G. A. (1955). *The psychology of personal constructs.* New York, NY: Norton.

Klass, D., Silverman, P. R., & Nickman, S. (Eds.). (1996). *Continuing bonds: New understandings of grief.* New York, NY: Brunner-Routledge.

Laurie, A., & Neimeyer, R. A. (2010). Of broken bonds and bondage: An analysis of loss in the slave narrative collection. *Death Studies, 34*, 221–256. doi:10.1080/07481180903559246

Lichtenthal, W. G., Burke, L. A., & Neimeyer, R. A. (2011). Religious coping and meaning-making following the loss of a loved one. *Counselling and Spirituality, 30*(2), 113–136. Retrieved from http://www.counsellingandspirituality.com/english/journal.php

Lichtenthal, W. G., Currier, J. M., Neimeyer, R. A., & Keesee, N. J. (2010). Sense and significance: A mixed methods examination of meaning-making following the loss of one's child. *Journal of Clinical Psychology, 66*, 791–812. doi:10.1002/jclp.20700

Machin, L. (2014). *Working with loss and grief: A theoretical and practical approach* (2nd ed.). Washington, DC: Sage.

McKenzie-Mohr, S., Coates, J., & McLeod, H. (2012). Responding to the needs of youth who are homeless: Calling for politicized trauma-informed intervention. *Children and Youth Services Review, 34*(1), 136–143. doi:10.1016/j.childyouth.2011.09.008

Meagher, D. K., & Balk, D. E. (Eds.). (2013). *Handbook of thanatology: The essential body of knowledge for the study of death, dying, and bereavement* (2nd ed.). New York, NY: Routledge.

Muselman, D. M., & Wiggins, M. I. (2012). Spirituality and loss: Approaches for counseling grieving adolescents. *Counseling & Values, 57*, 229–240. doi:10.1002/j.2161-007X.2012.00019.x

Nader, K., & Salloum, A. (2011). Complicated grief reactions in children and adolescents. *Journal of Child & Adolescent Trauma, 4*, 233–257. doi:10.1080/19361521.2011.599358

National Child Traumatic Stress Network. (2015). Psychological First Aid (PFA). Retrieved from http://www.nctsnet.org

Neimeyer, R. A. (Ed.). (2001). *Meaning reconstruction and the experience of loss.* Washington, DC: American Psychological Association.

Neimeyer, R. A. (2006a). Complicated grief and the reconstruction of meaning: Conceptual and empirical contributions to a cognitive-constructivist model. *Clinical Psychology: Science and Practice, 13*, 141–145. doi:10.1111/j.1468-2850.2006.00016.x

Neimeyer, R. A. (2006b). Narrating the dialogical self: Toward an expanded toolbox for the counselling psychologist. *Counselling Psychology Quarterly, 19*, 105–120. doi:10.1080/09515070600655205

Neimeyer, R. A. (2006c). Complicated grief and the quest for meaning: A constructivist contribution. *Omega, 52*, 37–52. doi:10.2190/EQL1-LN3V-KNYR-18TF

Neimeyer, R. A. (2008). Presence, process and procedure: Principles of practice for constructivist psychotherapy. *Constructivism in the Human Sciences, 12*, 172–188. Retrieved from https://sites.google.com/site/constructingworlds/journal

Neimeyer, R. A. (2009). *Constructivist psychotherapy*. London, UK: Routledge.

Neimeyer, R. A. (Ed.). (2012). *Techniques of grief therapy: Creative practices for counseling the bereaved*. New York, NY: Routledge.

Neimeyer, R. A. (2014). The changing face of grief: Contemporary directions in theory, research and practice. *Progress in Palliative Care, 22*(3), 125–130. doi:10.1179/1743291X13Y.0000000075

Neimeyer, R. A., Burke, L., Mackay, M., & Stringer, J. (2010). Grief therapy and the reconstruction of meaning: From principles to practice. *Journal of Contemporary Psychotherapy, 40*, 73–83. doi:0.1007/s10879-009-9135-3

Neimeyer, R. A., Harris, D. L., Winokuer, H. R., & Thornton, G. F. (Eds.). (2011). *Grief and bereavement in contemporary society: Bridging research and practice*. New York, NY: Routledge.

Neimeyer, R. A., Klass, D., & Dennis, M. R. (2014). A social constructionist account of grief: Loss and the narration of meaning. *Death Studies, 38*, 485–498. doi:10.1080/07481187.2014.913454

Neimeyer, R. A., Torres, C., & Smith, D. (2011). The virtual dream: Rewriting stories of loss and grief. *Death Studies, 35*, 646–672. doi:10.1080/07481187.2011.570596

Neimeyer, R. A., & Wogrin, C. (2008). Psychotherapy for complicated bereavement: A meaning-oriented approach. *Illness, Crisis and Loss, 16*, 1–20. doi:10.2190/IL.16.1.a

New York Life Foundation/National Alliance for Grieving Children. (2012). *National poll of bereaved children and teenagers*. Retrieved from https://childrengrieve.org/national-poll-bereaved-children-teenagers/

Ober, A. M., Granello, D. H., & Wheaton, J. E. (2012). Grief counseling: An investigation of counselors' training, experience, and competencies. *Journal of Counseling & Development, 90*, 150–159. doi:10.1111/j.1556-6676.2012.00020.x

Oltjenbruns, K. A. (2001). Developmental context of childhood: Grief and regrief phenomena. In M. S. Stroebe, R. O. Hansson, W. Stroebe, & H. Schut (Eds). *Handbook of bereavement research: Consequences, coping, and care* (pp. 169–197). Washington, DC: American Psychological Association.

Pearce, C. (2011). Girl, interrupted: An exploration into the experience of grief following the death of a mother in young women's narratives. *Mortality, 16*, 35–53. doi:10.1080/13576275.2011.536000

Philpott, E. (2013). Moving grief: Exploring dance/movement therapists' experiences and applications with grieving children. *American Journal of Dance Therapy, 35*, 142–168. doi:10.1007/s10465-013-9158-x

Piaget, J. (1954). *The construction of reality in the child*. New York, NY: Basic Books.

Piazza-Bonin, E., Neimeyer, R. A., Burke, L. A., Young, A., & McDevitt-Murphy, M. (2015). Disenfranchised grief following African American homicide loss: An inductive case study. *Omega, 70*, 369–392. doi:0.1177/0030222815573727

Ribeiro, A. P., Bento, T., Gonçalves, M. M., & Salgado, J. (2010). Commentary: Self-narrative reconstruction in psychotherapy: Looking at different levels of narrative development. *Culture & Psychology, 16*, 195–212. doi:10.1177/1354067X10361400

Rosen, H. (1984–1985). Prohibitions against mourning in childhood sibling loss. *Omega, 15*, 307–316.

Rubin, S. S., Malkinson, R., & Witzum, E. (2011). *Working with the bereaved: Multiple lenses on loss and meaning*. New York, NY: Brunner-Routledge.

Salloum, A. (2015). *Grief and trauma in children: An evidence-based treatment manual*. New York, NY: Taylor & Francis.

Saul, J. (2013). *Collective trauma, collective healing: Promoting community resilience in the aftermath of disaster*. New York, NY: Routledge.

Scaletti, R., & Hocking, C. (2010). Healing through story telling: An integrated approach for children experiencing grief and loss. *New Zealand Journal of Occupational Therapy*, 57(2), 66–71. Retrieved from http://www.otnz.co.nz/public/publications/new-zealand-journal-of-occupational-therapy

Slyter, M. (2012). Creative counseling interventions for grieving adolescents. *Journal of Creativity in Mental Health*, 7, 17–34. doi:10.1080/15401383.2012.657593

Sofka, C., Cupit, I., & Gilbert, K. (2012). *Death, dying, and grief in an online universe: For counselors and educators*. New York, NY: Springer.

Steele, W., & Malchiodi, C. A. (2012). *Trauma-informed practices with children and adolescents*. New York, NY: Routledge.

Stillion, J. M., & Attig, T. (Eds.). (2015). *Death, dying, and bereavement: Contemporary perspectives, institutions, and practices*. New York, NY: Springer.

Stroebe, M., & Schut, H. (1999). The dual process model of coping with bereavement: Rationale and description. *Death Studies*, 23, 197–224. doi:10.1080/074811899201046

Thompson, B. E., & Neimeyer, R. A. (Eds.). (2014). *Grief and the expressive arts: Practices for creating meaning*. New York, NY: Routledge.

US Department of Health & Human Services, Health Resources & Services Administration. (2013). *Child health USA 2012*. Rockville, MD: Author.

Wheat, L. S., & Whiting, P. P. (2015). The forget-me-not book of reminders during deployment. In S. Degges-White & B. Colon (Eds.), *Expressive arts interventions for school counselors* (pp. 239–243). New York, NY: Springer.

White, M. (2005). Children, trauma, and subordinate storyline development. *International Journal of Narrative Therapy & Community Work*, 3(4), 10–22. Retrieved from http://dulwichcentre.com.au/publications/international-journal-narrative-therapy

White, M., & Morgan, A. (2006). *Narrative therapy with children and their families*. Adelaide, South Australia: Dulwich Centre Publications.

Whiting, P. (2012, December). Authoring a story of meaning after the suicide of a son: The case of Renee. *Texas Association for Adult Development and Aging Today*, 2 (2), 2–5. Retrieved from http://www.txca.org/tca/TAADA_Home.asp

Whiting, P., & Bradley, L. J. (2007). Artful witnessing of the story: Loss in aging adults. *Adultspan Journal*, 6, 119–128. doi:10.1002/j.2161-0029.2007.tb00037.x

Whiting, P. P., Wheat, L. S., & Bradley, L. J. (2008). The storyteller's companion: Counselors as creative advocates for bereaved children. In G. Walz, J. Bleuer, & R. Yep (Eds.), *Compelling counseling interventions: Celebrating VISTAS' fifth anniversary* (pp. 21–30). Alexandria, VA: Counseling Outfitters, LLC & American Counseling Association.

Williams, J. L., Burke, L. A., McDevitt-Murphy, M. E., & Neimeyer, R. A. (2012). Responses to loss and health functioning among homicidally bereaved African Americans. *Journal of Loss and Trauma*, 17, 358–375. doi:10.1080/15325024.2011.635583

Winokuer, H., & Harris, D. (2016). *Principles and practice of grief counseling* (2nd ed.). New York, NY: Springer.

Worden, J. W. (2009). *Grief counseling and grief therapy* (4th ed.). New York, NY: Springer.

Yuen, A. (2007). Discovering children's responses to trauma: A response-based narrative practice. *International Journal of Narrative Therapy & Community Work*, 2007(3/4), 3–18. Retrieved from http://dulwichcentre.com.au/publications/international-journal-narrative-therapy

CHAPTER 5

Restorying the Survivor Narrative With Sexually Abused Adolescents

JANE M. WEBBER AND J. BARRY MASCARI

With the growing awareness of the impact of trauma, counselors and mental health professionals are likely to work with individuals or families affected by interpersonal trauma. The most horrific form of interpersonal victimization may well be the sexual abuse of children and adolescents, "the most powerless of victims" (Herman, 2015, p. 345). In the landmark 10-year Adverse Childhood Experiences Study with 17,337 participants, the total prevalence of sexual abuse was 21%, with 25% female and 16% male victims (Anda et al., 2006). Of the 70% of sexually abused individuals who knew their abuser at the time of the abuse, 93% were children (Pereda, Guilera, Forns, & Gómez Benito, 2009).

Interpersonal trauma can lead to such overwhelming physical, emotional, and existential suffering that it profoundly affects our identity as "a disruption so serious that it threatens our existence, shaking the foundation of who we are and who we once were" (Serlin & Cannon, 2004, p. 314). Sexual abuse can trigger debilitating reactions ranging from intrusive thoughts, flashbacks, and nightmares, to numbing and dissociation, leaving a pernicious imprint on the life stories of young victims. Sexually traumatized children and adolescents may go through life ruled by stories of victimization and hopelessness (Adams-Westcott, Dafforn, & Sterne,

1993; Durrant & Kowalski, 1990). This impact is magnified by paralyzing shame and intense fear that the secret of sexual abuse might be exposed and the perpetrator will repeat the abuse.

In response to the increasing demand for counselors skilled in trauma-informed practices, particularly with victims of sexual abuse, students in counseling programs accredited by the Council for Accreditation of Counseling and Related Educational Programs (CACREP, 2009, 2015) are required to meet trauma and crisis standards. In a content analysis of trauma articles, sexual abuse was the most frequent trauma-related topic addressed in the *Journal of Counseling & Development* and the *Journal of Mental Health Counseling* from 1994 to 2014 (Webber, Kitzinger, Runte, Smith, & Mascari, 2017). In a content analysis of more than 15,000 American Counseling Association conference sessions in 1977–2008, Helwig and Schmidt (2011) ranked *abuse* as the seventh most frequent category of all sessions in the period 1985–1992, fourth in 1993–2000, and fourth in training sessions in 2001–2008.

Stories and storytelling have been an essential part of all cultures from the beginning of time, especially in times of crisis and trauma. People make meaning of their life experiences through the stories they tell, but not all stories that direct the daily lives of abused children and adolescents are their authentic narratives. Dominant, problem-saturated stories maintain control over sexually abused minors, destroying their trust in relationships and hope for a positive future without the stigma, pain, and shame of sexual trauma. However, through narrative therapy, a postmodern approach centered on changing the stories that shape people's lives (White & Epston, 1990), victims of sexual abuse can find their voice to redescribe the trauma narrative as *their* preferred story. In this chapter, we examine the differences between using conventional and postmodern therapies with adolescent survivors of sexual trauma. We describe narrative practices to help victims of sexual abuse externalize and separate from the problem, deconstruct perpetrators' stories, and reauthor their preferred stories. Narrative trauma practices are illuminated in the story of a teenager who was sexually abused.

SEXUAL TRAUMA AS A TREATMENT CHALLENGE

Ideally in therapy, survivors of sexual trauma should be able to transform past victimization stories into present and future survivor stories; however, the severe psychological and relational consequences of sexual trauma often make it virtually impossible for victims to conceive of themselves as healed survivors. For example, many children and adolescents experienced extreme forms of sexual abuse by trusted caregivers that destroyed relationships, disrupted attachments, and compromised their develop-ment (Ford, 2009). In a study of sexual abuse survivors in support groups, Anderson and Hiersteiner (2008) found that although they viewed recovery as an obtainable goal, healing was perceived as unachievable "because participants could not imagine a future where their trauma and its effects would no longer impact their lives or identities" (p. 422). Conventional trauma treatment sometimes leads to retraumatization; "techniques that require the person to 'relive' traumatic events can replicate the experience of powerlessness and, hence, have the potential to reinforce disempowering stories about self" (Adams-Westcott et al., 1993, p. 263).

In her landmark book, *Trauma and Recovery: The Aftermath of Violence— From Domestic Abuse to Political Terror*, Herman (2015) described three phases of trauma recovery: developing safety and stabilization, remembering and telling the trauma story, and reconnecting to family and community. In the first phase, a sense of personal safety must be established both within one's body and in the therapeutic relationship. Entering an inti-mate counseling relationship may be an extremely difficult step for victims of sexual trauma whose fundamental trust in relationships was destroyed by perpetrators.

> They breach the attachments of family, friendship, love, and community. They shatter the construction of the self that is formed and sustained in relationship to others. They undermine the belief systems that give meaning to human experiences . . . . The trau-matic event thus destroys the belief that one can be *oneself* in relationship to others. (Herman, 2015, pp. 51, 53)

In the second phase, victims tell their story with the counselor as a witness and supporter. Sharing the trauma of sexual abuse can be so terrifying that victims often perceive danger even when it is not present; therefore, maintaining safety and managing emotional and somatic dis-tress triggered by trauma memories are essential before sharing their story. Sexual abuse survivors are unlikely to want to relive the emotional intensity of sexual assault in therapy. "If remembering makes someone worse, then they are likely to do best by avoiding their memories, at least as long as those memories hurt rather than heal. The goal of trauma healing must be to *relieve*, not intensify, suffering" (Rothschild, 2010, p. xi). Remembering their story without retraumatization requires a new kind of discourse, safe space, and therapeutic partnership.

As they struggle with shame, helplessness, and guilt, trauma victims often isolate themselves from family members and friends, cutting off sup-portive trusting relationships. Therefore, in the third phase of trauma re-covery survivors gradually reconnect to their world with a new sense of meaning and hope. In the transition from the safety and intimacy of the therapeutic relationship to family and community life, individuals begin to reestablish relationships with persons they can trust to honor and validate their preferred trauma story publicly. Otherwise, victims may outwardly appear to have moved on with their lives without healing the trauma wound within. Herman emphasized the critical importance of reconnecting to family members and friends in the resolution of the trauma story: "Trauma isolates; the group re-creates a sense of belonging. Trauma shames and stigmatizes; the group bears witness and affirms. Trauma degrades the victim; the group exalts her. Trauma dehumanizes the victim; the group restores her humanity" (Herman, 2015 p. 214). This social testimony is in stark contrast to the perpetrator's demand for secrecy and control, and we are just beginning to understand the neurological and interpersonal effects of community validation that promote emancipation from the stigma of sexual abuse.

CONVENTIONAL AND POSTMODERN APPROACHES TO TRAUMA THERAPY

Conventional trauma therapies typically view the counselor as an expert who diagnoses traumatized clients according to standardized criteria and provides treatment with manualized procedures (Foa, Keane, Friedman, & Cohen, 2008). With traditional treatments for posttraumatic stress disorder (PTSD), "reliving trauma may offer an opportunity for mastery, but most survivors do not consciously seek or welcome the opportunity. Rather, they dread and fear it" (Herman, 2015, p. 42). Conventional therapies interpret the human experience through the lens of a central defining internal construct, such as personality, cognition, behavior, or the unconscious. These approaches view trauma symptoms as maladaptive behavior and define the problem in intrapsychic language that points to the source of the disorder within the victim. Therapists may fail to recognize how victims of abuse internalized the perpetrator's story as the truth, instead of their own inner story. Although some survivors may need to revisit details of the trauma story, Rothschild (2010) cautioned that "a good portion of trauma victims suffer a worsening of symptoms when encouraged or forced to remember their traumas" (p. x).

In contrast to conventional treatment that posits one all-encompassing truth, the cornerstone of postmodern narrative trauma therapy is grounded in victims' subjective responses to traumatic experiences (Grand, 2013; White, 1997, 2005). Instead of following conventional prescribed techniques, the narrative counselor draws from a wealth of verbal and sensory practices to facilitate externalizing the problem, analyzing the dominant story, and restorying the trauma narrative.

> If therapists are paying too much attention to getting a method's protocols and procedures right, how can they closely follow the client's process? . . . Thus each therapy process—in fact, each session—is different. What remains the same is that the client needs to be listened to very carefully. (Grand, 2013, p. 76)

Moreover, conventional therapy is generally limited to scheduled face-to-face sessions, while narrative sessions (i.e., conversations) continue after the session through letters that document the client's quotes and unique outcomes and deepen the conversation with additional questions. As an equal partner in the conversation (i.e., session), the client can also write back to the therapist between sessions.

Narrative trauma practices focus on discovering alternative meanings to the dominant problem-saturated story and envisioning future possibilities for living (Combs & Freedman, 2012; O'Hanlon, 1993). For example, traditional behavioral treatment approaches for anorexia focus on the control of eating and weight through monitoring meal charts, food diaries, and weigh-ins; these techniques typically parallel the disorder's control of the victim. Postmodern approaches help victims externalize and change their relationship with the problem by distancing themselves from its control, instead of identifying with it (Scott, Hanstock, & Patterson-Kane, 2013; M. White, 2011).

NARRATIVE THERAPY PRACTICE

Narrative therapy originated in Australia and New Zealand and spread rapidly throughout the world. The cofounders of narrative therapy, Michael White (1997) from Australia and David Epston (2011) from New Zealand, were inspired by the anthropological view of humanity as *homo narrans*, meaning "storytellers" (Myerhoff, 1982, p. xv). White and Epston (1990) created their narrative process as "a storied therapy" that respects and honors the meaning of people's experiences shared through their stories (p. 77). In their transition from family systems, narrative practices evolved from their trauma work with families, children, and marginalized groups, particularly Aboriginal and other indigenous communities. White and Epston's narrative therapy "largely by-passes psychological explanations and interventions, and instead seeks to help people by working with the ways in which they talk about issues, and the ways in which they participate in social life" (McLeod, 2006, p. 206).

Postmodern approaches assume that people gain knowledge and meaning about their world through their lived experiences rather than from universal truth or a fixed reality. Narrative practices are grounded in existential, feminist, and Foucauldian ideas that criticize dominant stories used to maintain control over victims (Foucault, 1980). Although narrative therapy provides a special context for therapeutic conversations, each person's recovery path is unique, warranting different practices and interventions (Denborough, 2014; Rothschild, 2010; C. White, 2011).

A foundational assumption of narrative therapy is that "the problem is the problem. The person is not the problem" (Winslade & Monk, 2007, p. 2). Fundamental to the narrative relationship is a respectful, nonpathological view of the client who experiences concerns about a problem; thus, the sexual abuse victim is not labeled as the problem (e.g., *He is damaged goods.*) or blamed for causing the problem (e.g., *She didn't fight back. She deserved it.*). In narrative therapy the client and counselor are both experts with a "reciprocal exchange of gifts" (Epston, 2011):

> Clients are experts on their own experiences, including their pain, suffering, and concerns. They also have expertise about their memories, goals, and responses. The counselor neither interprets the client's experiences nor holds the solution. Counselors are experts in creating a conversational and interactional climate for change and results in therapy. (O'Hanlon, 1993, p. 12)

After narrative, counselors ask questions from a genuinely nonknowing and curious view; they listen for nuances in the problem-saturated story and encourage the client to recall exceptions to the problem. With the conventional hierarchical structure removed from the therapeutic relationship, the counselor's role dramatically shifts to "expert companion" (Calhoun & Tedeschi, 2008, p. 327) In this partner role, the counselor is "double-listening" for both the trauma story and the client's very thin story of response that may be just a trace or hint of resistance and coping. "It is vitally important that we do get onto this trace, and that we assist people to thicken . . . what it is that people continued to give value to despite everything they have been through (White, 2004, p. 30). These "double-storied" conversations of survival are the heart of narrative trauma restorying in which the client is the storyteller, as well as the narrator, director, actor, protagonist, hero, and agent of change. Any attempt to free oneself from the problem's power is an "absent but implicit" sign of survival and is added as a critical "subordinate storyline" in the victim's new chapter (White, 2006, p. 155). Through narrative conversations clients discover exceptions to the dominant story and become aware that they can alter the meaning of the story and shift their life role from victim to survivor.

When the client and counselor discuss the problem's impact, they create a name or metaphor for the problem that reflects the client's experience, such as *The Dictator* or *The Big A* (Abuse). As a result, labeling the problem and its intentions begins to externalize the problem and diminish its power. Using creative and often lighthearted expressions reflects the way White (1997) played with a problem and encouraged clients to find exceptions when they refused to submit to the problem's control, for example, *The Big A was so weak he couldn't break down my bedroom door.* As victims transform their relationship with the problem, they re-create their identity apart from the problem, for example, *I am not damaged goods*, or *I am who I am; I am not my sexual abuse.*

In the restorying process, the survivor and counselor coauthor a self-story using the client's language in the first person using *I* and *we.* Questions play an important role in narrative trauma therapy to help victims find their hidden voice and their self-story. As the alternative story develops, "landscape of action" questions generate new understandings about events of abuse in the victim's life and "landscape of identity" questions promote new meanings as the story is redescribed (Madigan, 2011, p. 82). Through relative influence questions, the therapeutic partners map the extent of the problem's impact on family members and other relationships. For example, *How is your new assertive voice changing your relationship with the problem?* Reflexive questions affirm the client's equitable role in the course of narrative conversations, such as "Have any of my responses in this conversation put limits on what you feel you can talk about here?" (White, 1997, p. 138).

As they deconstruct the problem-saturated dominant story, the counselor listens for moments of courage and resilience. These hints of emancipation encourage remembering forgotten mini-stories when victims confronted the problem or distanced themselves from its control (e.g., *How have you escaped from the Big A's hold over you?*). As clients recall these incidents of courage, they thicken the story with exceptions "that do not leave people trapped in victimhood and that encourage them to have a voice in the kind of relations they would like to see develop in their lives" (Winslade & Monk, 2007, pp. 101–102). This narrative restorying process continues to strengthen the power of the victim in becoming a survivor.

To facilitate Herman's (2015) third phase of reconnection and reintegration, survivors are encouraged to write letters to friends and relatives, inviting them to be an audience to hear the new story, and build a network of supporters who write letters to "re-member back into situations from which the problem has most often dis-membered them" (Madigan, 2011, p. 119). The group spirit and momentum created at community ceremonies mirror Frankl's (1946/2006) survival message: "For what then matters is to bear witness to the uniquely human potential at its best, which is to transform a personal tragedy into triumph, to turn one's predicament into a human achievement" (p. 135). Publicly sharing knowledge and recommendations with sexual abuse survivor groups affirms the survivor's liberation from domination and creates a new sense of purpose by helping others with similar trauma.

NARRATIVE THERAPY WITH SEXUALLY ABUSED ADOLESCENTS

Storytelling is a natural form of communication for adolescents who are in transition between childhood and young adulthood. As they move through the process of separation and individuation from parents, teenagers continue to seek adult approval and support. There are myriad stories created in teenagers' lives every day, but the dominant problem-saturated story sexual abuse victims initially bring to therapy is not likely to be their preferred story. Victims of sexual trauma who struggle to verbalize their traumatic experiences may be judged by traditional therapists as treatment resistant or not ready for therapy. These judgments can be devastating to teenagers who have lived under the tenets of perpetrators' stories that blame victims for the abuse that was forced upon them. Stories of resistance by teenagers are often hidden or twisted into blaming narratives, and victims of sexual abuse may be unable to tell their trauma story within traditional counselor-directed treatment. "Whether or not a person adopts a victim life story depends on the meaning that is ascribed to the traumatizing events" (Adams-Westcott et al., 1993, p. 262).

A Safe and Protected Relationship

Before victimized teenagers can share their story, they need to experience total safety, validation, and acceptance in the therapeutic relationship (Duvall & Beres, 2007). Sexually abused teenagers begin therapy in a room with the door closed and are asked to talk to a strange adult in an intimate relationship about how another adult who most likely cared for them also abused them. In narrative therapy, they can move at their own pace, choose what to say, when to disclose, and whom to invite. Adolescents respond more positively to the narrative therapist who respects and recognizes their knowledge and expertise about themselves (Gil, 1996). They relate more to the therapist who asks their permission to be questioned about their personal experiences and feelings (Winslade & Monk, 2007). With developmental hypersensitivity to judgment and criticism, repeated questioning can quickly lead to the teenager shutting down. Asking young abuse survivors about their hopes and dreams and "what they hold precious" redirects conversations away from the traumatic past and toward subordinate storylines with a possible future (White, 1006, p. 148). Using expressive materials, such as art, clay, sand tray, and music, helps develop the relationship and open channels for communication without the pressure of talk therapy. Sending narrative letters after conversations strengthens the relationship with teenagers, and choosing to write letters back to the therapist validates their egalitarian partnership with the therapist. Instead of trying to fix them or tell them what to do, partnering and negotiating with abused teenagers validates their newly found power as survivors.

In the first phase of trauma recovery (safety and stabilization), victims of sexual trauma experience therapeutic conversations in a new protected space. For several sessions, teenagers may talk on a superficial level without mentioning abuse until they trust the counselor and feel confident that they will not be judged. They may test the counselor's commitment and attempt to undermine the safety of the relationship. Sexual abuse can create feelings of overwhelming self-blame and guilt in both children and teenagers. Although we reaffirm to victims that they are not to blame and were powerless to stop the abuse, many adolescents continue to ruminate about how they should have tried harder to escape from the perpetrator while protecting their families from shame or harm. Sexually abused teens may feel damaged, useless, and worthless to parents, relatives, and friends, as well as the counselor.

Dysregulation and Reliving the Trauma Story

Teenagers may not understand how sexual trauma has affected their brain and body. A traumatic event is stored with its intense sensory memories and recalled differently than other memories (Rothschild, 2000; van der Kolk, 1996, 2014). The verbal narrative becomes separated from sensations and images of the traumatic memory in the brain, and victims can literally become scared speechless, unable to express their emotions and experiences in words. A teenager may not be physically able to talk about sexual trauma; as one client wrote to me, "I tried, but when I opened my mouth, it wouldn't come out." Their verbal story may remain silent or hidden until expressive narrative practices are used to jump-start the storying process (Petersen, Bull, Propst, Dettinger, & Detwiler, 2005; van der Kolk, 2014). Once they perceive that they are truly safe from reliving the trauma, sometimes teenagers cannot stop the flood of stories that pour out that had been silenced by their fear of the perpetrator. The counselor slows down their restorying to prevent victims from becoming emotionally overwhelmed and retraumatized. Narrative practices integrated with emotion regulation can expand the opportunities for trauma recovery so that "trauma healing takes place through the process of telling one's story in order to reconstruct the experience" (Webber, Mascari, & Runte, 2010a, p. 205). Since each trauma story is subjective and unique to the adolescent survivor, it is important that the counselor and client view the problem story from multiple personal dimensions: relational, affective, cognitive, as well as somatic, as teenagers might not connect their physical symptoms (e.g., stomach ache, trembling, choking) to the impact of sexual trauma.

As they begin the process of trauma therapy, victims are frequently, if not constantly, fearful of being overwhelmed by intrusive memories and flashbacks. Persons with symptoms of posttraumatic stress disorder (PTSD) can live each day continuously experiencing high levels of arousal and hyperarousal. The amygdala acts as a "smoke alarm" that signals danger and plays a key role in arousal of the sympathetic nervous system even when there is no threat (van der Kolk, 2014; Webber & Mascari, 2014b, p. 33). When the amygdala triggers a false positive, the brain starts the stress hormone secretion process outside of the client's awareness, reinforcing teenagers' beliefs that they are in danger even when the danger is no longer present.

Rothschild (2000) reminded us of the importance of learning to brake before accelerating the trauma story; staying calm and emotionally regulated is essential in avoiding retraumatization. Teaching teenagers to use the subjective unit of distress (SUD) gives them a concrete tool to know when to pause and calm before becoming overwhelmed. With the SUD scale, individuals rate their distress on a scale of 1 to 10, with 1 being very calm, and a rating of 9 or 10 being very distressed (Rothschild, 2010; Wolpe, 1969). Suppressed intrusive thoughts can continue to surface like a "snooze alarm," reminding survivors that their trauma memory has not been fully resolved (Webber & Mascari, 2014b, p. 30). When overwhelmed, adolescents may overreact with risky behaviors, such as driving fast, using alcohol and drugs, running away, or attempting suicide. Practicing emotion regulation when adolescents are parasympathetic-dominant and their cognitive processes are engaged is critical to breaking the cycle of sympathetic arousal and avoiding continual emotional overdrive. After learning what the distress they experience is about and how the brain processes and stores traumatic memories, teenagers gradually understand that their feelings of fear and avoidance are actually normal coping responses to a horrific abnormal event, and they can better manage intense somatic reactions as they tell their own story.

Asking young sexually traumatized victims about their unique needs, personal hopes, and unspoken dreams shifts their focus from the past to the present and future, and they begin to realize that the dominant story ruling their life is *not* their story (White, 2006). This new awareness is liberating, and a glimpse of hope leads to remembering sparkling moments (unique outcomes) when they outwitted the perpetrator (Adams-Wescott et al., 1993; O'Hanlon, 1993). Adolescents typically like their new detective role in narrative conversations seeking to unearth evidence about how they escaped the problem's control. Instead of horrific details of sexual abuse, their stories become rich in their discovery of exceptions to the abuse. As they move from the role of victim to survivor and thriver in their new story, teenagers can remember the event(s) without automatically triggering the sympathetic nervous system (Rothschild, 2000; van der Kolk, 2014). The traumatic experience eventually becomes just one remembered story among many stories instead of a relentless activated memory with intense posttraumatic intrusive thoughts and flashbacks.

INTEGRATING EXPRESSIVE PRACTICES IN RESTORYING

In our work with adolescent survivors of sexual trauma, we have found that integrating multisensory techniques expands narrative therapy practices by jump-starting the restorying process (Webber, Mascari, & Runte, 2010b). Sensory fragments of trauma memory that were separated from the verbal story need to be integrated into a consistent narrative to promote resolution (Gil, 2006; van der Kolk, 2014). Therapeutic conversations can be expanded beyond verbal discourse using multisensory practices, such as drawing (van der Velden & Koops, 2005), genograms (Chrzastowski, 2011; Gil, 2006; White, 1997), sand tray (Gallerani & Dybicz, 2011; Gil, 2006, 2010; Webber et al., 2010b), scenes and chapters (Webber & Mascari, 2014a; White & Epston, 1990), story maps (Duvall & Beres, 2011; White, 2007), theater and drama (van der Kolk, 2014), timelines (Webber & Mascari, 2014a), and visualization (Webber & Mascari, 2014b). Even in a safe protected space with the therapist, the restorying process may trigger intense memories and reactions; survivors can distance themselves from the problem and its intense feelings by visualizing a container that holds the problem. For example, one teenager sealed her drawing of the perpetrator in a large envelope, covered the surfaces with shipping tape, and stapled all the edges; another teen pictured a garbage truck that loaded the enormous problem and drove it to the dump.

Teenage sexual abuse survivors can record their new stories with a variety of modalities, including dictation, video- or audio-recording, script, illustration, sand tray, and graphic or photo story. We have witnessed self-stories created and presented in several expressive forms. For example, one teenager wrote her trauma story in calligraphy; another painted scenes on a hand-crafted triptych; and an artist and poet wrote a series of haiku, each illustrated in watercolor. Other adolescents created personal diaries, one-act plays, vision boards, and photo stories. One teenager delivered his story in a monologue on stage with only his best friends and counselor in the theater. Another teen, with supporters listening and cheering in the theater, celebrated her alternative narrative as a "success story rather than the 'sad' format of many psychotherapy narratives" (White & Epston, 1990, p. 163).

Creating a timeline with yarn or ribbon on the floor outlines the survivor's life story before, during, and after the sexual abuse. Painful or negative events are marked below the timeline with a symbol, such as a stone, and positive events and supporters are represented above the time-line with a positive metaphor, such as a flower, heart, or photograph. As they *walk* the timeline with the therapist, victims tell their life story, pausing at the end where a ball of yarn or ribbon reflects the future. By presenting their autobiographical timeline and photographing it, survivors can witness that the sexual trauma is one of many events that they experienced on their life's path, and they can move beyond it.

We have used sand tray therapy extensively with teenagers to facilitate the restorying process, especially when they become stuck in telling the story and cannot use words. Survivors frequently select figures and objects that represent the traumatic event (e.g., nurse, police, ambulance, or monster for the perpetrator) and arrange them as a story in the sand tray. Free to move figures around in the tray, they can add storylines to the alternative story, create new outcomes, and develop a sense of mastery and empowerment (Gallerani & Dybicz, 2011; Gil, 1996, 2010).

Teenagers often begin their stories describing their life before the abuse happened: where they lived, who their friends and supporters were, and what they liked to do. This is generally followed by a brief statement of the problem, for example, *Something very bad happened.* In narrative restorying, sparkling moments are usually described next, testifying to how they escaped from the problem or outwitted the perpetrator. Teens can add trauma details in later chapters when they are ready to manage any distress that may be triggered. Others include only their accomplishments in separating from the problem and revising their relationship to it. The ending is dynamic and future-oriented, reflecting how they continue to cope (e.g., *I can talk about it with my counselor when I need a booster shot*) or made changes in their story (e.g., *We moved to another house for a fresh start*).

In the third phase of trauma recovery, the teenage survivor begins to re-connect with family members and friends by inviting them to a session that helps to normalize talking about sexual abuse that had been a taboo subject. The survivor's story is thickened through conversations about family support genograms and circles of support using miniatures. For example, supportive relationships can be illustrated on a large newsprint genogram where the survivor selects miniature figures to represent how family members intervened, protected, and supported the victim (Chrzastowski, 2011; Webber & Mascari, 2014a; White, 1997). Using miniature figures and objects, Gil (2006) invited relatives to find and place a figure on a small circle that represents their reactions to the sexual abuse and a second figure on a larger outer circle that represents how they responded and helped the victim. The teenager and counselor also invite family members and friends to a ceremony to hear the new story, honor the survivor's recovery, and destigmatize the abuse. Herman (2015) emphasized the importance of reentering family and community in the process of healing from trauma: "Repeatedly in the testimony of survivors there comes a moment when a sense of connection is restored by another person's unaffected display of generosity. . . . Mirrored in the actions of others, the survivor recognizes and reclaims a lost part of herself" (p. 214). These group sessions facilitate restarting family traditions and activities that were curtailed after the sexual abuse was revealed. Support groups in high school and college promote reentry into the community and provide strength and support during this transition.

RESEARCH FINDINGS SUPPORTING NARRATIVE THERAPY

Whereas conventional empirical research methods focus on objective outcomes of success, narrative therapy research prioritizes subjective processes, including collaboration with clients (Etchison & Kleinst, 2000; Madigan, 2011). Therefore, research on narrative therapy generally uses qualitative and ethnographic methods, case studies, and co-research (Combs & Freedman, 2012; Denborough, 2004; Etchison & Kleinst, 2000). Adler (2012) studied 600 personal narratives written before and after each therapy session and found that the personal agency of the participants increased and was positively related to improvements in mental health. In a grounded theory study of the trauma recovery stories of sexual abuse survivors by Anderson and Hiersteiner (2008), meaningful processes emerged, including breaking the silence and disclosing the abuse, and participating in supportive relationships. Duvall and Beres (2011) conducted a naturalistic evaluation of a 10-month narrative training experience and identified the storied process, circulation of language, pivotal moments, the reflecting team, and outsider witnesses as purposeful elements.

Narrative conversations are actually a form of collaborative investigation and co-research where "the person consulting the therapist is an equal partner in the process and it is *their* knowledge and skills about their own life and relationships that are the focus of the conversation" (Denborough, 2004, p. 33). Instead of moving toward an intense emotional breakthrough or catharsis, a critical element of co-research is the continuous process of gathering knowledge about the client's relationship with the problem in order to advocate for new solutions (Epston, 2004). A major strength of narrative therapy is the collaborative and egalitarian therapeutic relationship between the counselor and client. Researchers studying common factors found the helping relationship, rather than techniques of an approach, contributes most to treatment outcomes (Benish, Imel, & Wampold, 2008; Wampold, 2001).

> Therefore, the basic paradigm for healing that is effective across cultures, and the progressive enhancement of the quality of a relationship, which is the factor most associated with positive outcomes in counseling, are both highly dependent upon the introduction and gradual co-construction of cohesive, internally consistent narratives. This is the precise opposite of the disconnected implementation of techniques that is advocated by current mental health culture and its emphasis on so-called best practices. (Hansen, 2007, p. 427)

The equitable counselor–client partnership and collaborative therapeutic conversations in co-authoring the story are unique elements of the narrative relationship that differ substantially from conventional therapies, particularly with traumatized adolescents. Herman (2015) emphasized that "the principle of restoring human connection and agency remains central to the recovery process and no technical therapeutic advance is likely to replace it" (p. 241). Similarly, Gil (1996) recognized the power of narrative practices in developing "a strong therapeutic relationship that over time can provide a "safe, rewarding, corrective, and reparative experience to abused adolescents" (p. 88).

AN EXAMPLE OF NARRATIVE TRAUMA THERAPY: ANGEL'S STORY

The following case illustrates the process of narrative therapy, moving through the three phases of narrative trauma recovery: developing a safe and trusting relationship, remembering and restorying the trauma experience with her preferred story, and reconnecting to family, university, and community. In this case, the names and identifying information have been changed, and the story elements have been drawn from several cases.

Angel was a 16-year-old high school female who lived with her mother, a pediatric nurse who worked the night shift, and her mother's boyfriend, a salesperson who worked primarily at home. Angel struggled to adjust to life without her dad, an Army major killed in combat in Iraq 5 years earlier. When her mother brought Jack into their small family 3 years later, Angel was immediately put off by him and frequently talked about how much she missed her father when Jack was present. Since elementary school, Angel and her two best friends wrote in a secret journal, sharing everything with each other. When a journal was full, they placed it in a lockbox that they rotated from house to house. After they began their junior year, Angel wrote in the journal that she felt weird around Jack and suddenly moved the lockbox to Julia's house, saying it was no longer safe in her house.

Just before Christmas, Angel wrote that she lost all hope and wanted to die. When she would not talk with her best friends, they took Angel to the school counselor who had helped her after her father was killed. Angel sat on the counselor's couch wedged in between her two friends. They held her hands as she whispered, "He keeps hurting me. I can't go on anymore." Jack had sexually abused Angela for 7 months and threatened to harm her mother if Angel revealed their secret. Angel could not bear the sexual assaults any longer; she would rather kill herself than put her mother in harm's way. Angel was overwhelmed with shame and guilt, "Mom will hate me for not stopping it, I'll lose her too."

Angela's disclosure started a roller coaster ride of crisis intervention, child protective services, legal depositions, and counseling sessions. She testified in court, hoping the trial would end her nightmares and flashbacks. Even though the perpetrator was incarcerated, Angel could not escape the fear, shame, and self-blame she felt when she was on the stand. As Angel became increasingly silent and withdrawn, her friends were worried and stayed close to her. One day, when she did not arrive at school, they texted Angel's mother, who raced home and found her unconscious on the bathroom floor after an overdose. During her hospitalization, a psychiatrist prescribed medications that relieved immediate symptoms but did not resolve her on-going intrusive thoughts and feelings of dread. In her first therapy session, when the counselor directed her to tell her story, filling in as many details as she could remember, Angel broke down and cried uncontrollably. During the next month of therapy, she repeatedly tried to recount the abuse but could not get past the horrible memories; the therapist suggested that she was not making progress because she was not trying hard enough.

When she returned to school, Angel felt ashamed and could not talk to her friends. She believed she no longer fit in and thought everyone knew her secret. Angel avoided her high school counselor whom she thought could not help her anymore. Angel dyed her hair purple, dressed in punk rock clothing, and separated from her best friends. Her two best friends remained steadfast supporters, and although they tried to convince her to go with them, Angel did not attend prom or graduation. Her responses to her mother's pleas to talk were superficial and strained, resulting in *yes* and *no* answers as she retreated to her bedroom, closing the door. Later, Angel then changed her looks to goth with black hair, lipstick, and clothes so that people would stop offering to help and leave her alone. Angel still could not shake the cloud of doom and distress, and after a year of taking medications that made her continually feel distant and out of her body, she stopped taking them.

Angel started college in the fall where she majored in psychology and continued to live at home. She disclosed her trauma history and suicide attempt to her college advisor, who assured Angel that she was not the problem and was suffering like veterans traumatized by combat experiences. Angel accompanied her advisor to a weekly support group for students who had been sexually abused where she instantly felt safe and protected. Although she did not speak openly in the support group, Angel enjoyed the expressive narrative activities, including drawing, movement, and sand tray, that helped her manage most trauma symptoms from rendering her nonfunctional in classes. After group members suggested she try a different kind of therapy, Angel and I met for the first time. She immediately started to list her disorders and describe the sexual abuse, and I asked her to pause. "Angel, you are describing disorders that others told you that you had. Tell me what you need today from your own perspective, what you are experiencing now, and how it feels inside."

Angel burst into tears, relieved that she did not have to retell everything about the sexual abuse, at least not the way she had in earlier therapy sessions. "I couldn't stand the pain. Each time, I felt I was being ripped apart."

When Angel asked what she should say in counseling, I responded, "You are the expert of Angel, the survivor! Tell me what you want me to know about you. What do you cherish? What are your hopes and dreams?"

Although Angel was certain she had no hope of feeling better, her dream was to "feel normal again. I wish I could erase the memories, but they will never go away." I explained to Angel that narrative conversations are different and hopeful for the future she wished for.

"We can work together to help you free yourself from this problem, but we first need to practice braking before accelerating the process so you don't become overwhelmed again. This means being able to keep calm and not moving too fast with your story."

On a scale of *1* to *10*, Angel was at *9*, and her subjective unit of distress (SUD) was never lower than 8, regardless of where she was. Each time she started to talk about the perpetrator or the sexual abuse, her SUD rapidly elevated, but now Angel was confident that she knew how to push her "pause button" and breathe to lower her anxiety (Snel, 2013, p. 11). At first, Angel was reluctant to talk about her real feelings, believing that I would eventually withdraw my unconditional acceptance and blame her just as the previous therapist had. She continually questioned me as to whether she was really an equal partner in our conversations. Thus, this first phase of narrative trauma therapy was long, as we gradually repaired her distrust of therapists, disbelief in healing, and fear of retraumatization.

Angel liked our *conversations,* a word that appealed to her more than being in *therapy* or *treatment* where the therapist had talked at her and tried to fix her. She looked forward to reading my letters summarizing our conversations and highlighting her unique outcomes, and Angel often wrote back. As we deconstructed the problem-saturated story, Angel called herself the source of the problem less frequently and she no longer blamed herself using diagnostic labels like MDD, GAD, and PTSD. After we named the problem the *Big A* (Abuse), our conversations evolved into the second phase of trauma recovery, remembering and restorying the trauma experience. By externalizing the problem, Angel realized the immense power the perpetrator held over her, even though he was in prison. To distance herself, Angel painted a bright-red, 3-foot, high-heeled shoe on newsprint and imagined stuffing the Big A in the massive shoe, and hurling it into outer space. Each time Angel and I met, she retaped the shoe painting on the back of the door to keep the problem out of the room.

Starting to separate from the problem's control was a liberating experience for Angel, and I asked if she had ever been able to outwit The Big A even for one night. Angel remembered trying to escape from the problem while protecting her mother from physical and emotional abuse, especially when the perpetrator had been drinking. After Angel described a sparkling moment when she pretended to dance in a 24-hour marathon to avoid being home with him, I created a certificate for *Outstanding Marathon Dancer in Red High Heels* that she decorated with red glitter. Angel recalled another unique outcome when she had faked forgetting to charge her cell phone so that the perpetrator could not locate her. One evening when she was cornered at home, Angel forced herself to vomit in front of the perpetrator to feign illness. We documented these unique outcomes in an award for *Expert Escape Artist.* As our conversations deepened, Angel realized her punk and goth identities were creative ways to isolate herself when she felt humiliated and to avoid talking to others about the problem. She also selected gothic-style miniature figures to represent her alternate personas in sand tray scenes and chose a three-headed fire-breathing monster to represent the perpetrator. Angel painted each sand tray scene as an illustration in her story. As she thickened the story with her hopes and dreams for the future, Angel created a series of *dream scenes* in the sand tray for her future: "No more terrifying nightmares, convince my mom I'm getting better, tell my friends I love them, someday have a boyfriend I trust, get my life back, and never forget my dad."

In spring, Angel told her support group that she changed her major from psychology to art and theater and gave away her abnormal psychology textbooks, which she had used to confirm her earlier diagnoses. As we moved to the third phase of trauma recovery, several story-based narrative practices helped Angela reconnect to her mother, relatives, and friends. At her first definitional ceremony, Angel read her new story to her mother and showed her the powerful illustrations. Later she invited her two friends to hear her story and awarded them glittery certificates honoring their steadfast support and loyalty even when Angel had avoided and dissed them. Angel's most significant celebratory ceremony was telling her story to the college support group that had become her circle of support. Later, Angel volunteered as a peer facilitator for the group, where she shared her wisdom and suggestions; this group involvement strengthened her reconnection to family members and friends. Angel revised the title of her story to *My Survivor Story: Artist, Actress, Daughter, Friend* and painted portraits of her four restoried roles.

LIMITATIONS OF NARRATIVE THERAPY

The egalitarian counselor–client relationship and the freedom to choose from a variety of techniques rather than use a manualized procedure are strengths of narrative therapy; however, these could raise treatment challenges for counselors working in a conventional psychotherapy framework or a managed-care environment. When counseling teenagers who endured sexual trauma, counselors could misunderstand that the reluctance or inability to express emotions or to engage in talk therapy was the result of traumatic impact. The equitable partnership in narrative therapy might increase the potential for an enmeshed relationship or overshadow the client's need to learn emotion regulation before telling the trauma story. With narrative therapy's emphasis on verbal discourse, the affective and somatic impact of trauma has been addressed only recently in narrative practices (Angus & Greenberg, 2011; Beaudoin & Zimmerman, 2011; Webber & Mascari, 2014a, 2014b; Webber et al., 2010b; White, 2005; Zimmerman & Beaudoin, 2015).

IMPLICATIONS AND CONCLUSION

Sexual trauma violates all dimensions of adolescents' lives—physical, sexual, cognitive, relational, emotional—stripping them of their integrity, selfhood, and future. Narrative trauma therapy provides a unique relational space and discourse in which teens can safely resolve their trauma story without reliving the pain and terror of the abuse. Its nonpathologizing process provides "'news of difference,' so that clients can see possibilities for new solutions and new self-narratives" (Gil, 1996, p. 86). As adolescents move through the phases of trauma recovery, they restory their experience of sexual abuse and victimization to one of healing and survivorship. In the following, we summarize our insights and recommendations for using narrative practices with teenagers who have been sexually abused.

- A genuinely egalitarian and trusting relationship is essential for therapeutic conversations with adolescents about sexual abuse.
- The therapist's nonshaming, nonblaming presence promotes a safe space in which sexually abused teenagers can tell their story in their own way.
- In narrative conversations, the counselor honors unique outcomes of existential courage when a teen disengaged from the adult perpetrator.
- To prevent retraumatization, adolescent survivors need to learn how to manage distress and emotional dysregulation before moving through the restorying process.
- The teenager's knowledge and expertise as a survivor of sexual trauma are respected and valued.
- When traumatized teenagers are unable to speak, expressive storying modalities, such as art, sand tray, clay, music, and drama, facilitate the narrative process and open pathways to the trauma story.
- Restorying a narrative of victimization to one of survival requires a paradigm shift from using a structured protocol to being open to myriad possibilities of narrative practices that can uniquely support the survivor.
- Sexual abuse survivors are validated as they tell their story to supporters, family members, outside observers, and others who have experienced sexual abuse.
- Narrative conversations are dialogic and bidirectional: The counselor and client are equal partners in the relationship and both will be affected in the healing process.
- Counselors who work with sexually abused adolescents are at risk for vicarious traumatization; they are also open to the potential for posttraumatic growth in co-creating the alternative story (Calhoun & Tedeschi, 2008).

The postmodern partnership between counselor and client decenters the conventional therapist's position of power and affirms the client's expert knowledge, which is essential to restoring the self after sexual abuse. Teenagers may struggle to envision relationships without the pain and memory of being sexually abused; therefore, White situated the healing role of the counselor "to revere the other doubly: for their suffering and for their *unsuffering* of themselves" (as cited in Epston, 2011, p. xxviii). In this compassionate bond, sexually abused adolescents can feel whole again, emerging as survivors who hope for healthy and intimate relationships in the future no longer tainted by the problem story of the past.

Narrative conversations are dynamic and empowering: Both the teenage client and adult counselor experience profound changes while restorying the trauma experience together with a new sense of purpose and relationships. Survivors experience true healing and validation through "an ongoing autobiography . . . an ever-changing expression of narratives, being and becoming through language and storytelling as we continually attempt to make sense of the world and ourselves" (Rober, 2005, p. 480).

REFERENCES

Adams-Westcott, J., Dafforn, T. A., & Sterne, P. (1993). Escaping victim life stories and co-constructing personal agency. In S. Gilligan & R. Price (Eds.), *Therapeutic conversations* (pp. 258–271). New York, NY: Norton.

Adler, J. (2012). Living into the story: Agency and coherence in a longitudinal study of narrative identity development and mental health over the course of psychotherapy. *Journal of Personality and Social Psychology, 102*(2), 367–389. doi:10.1037/a0025289

Anda, R. F., Felitti, V. J., Bremner, J. D., Walker, J. D., Whitfield, C., Perry, B. D., . . . Giles, W. H. (2006). The enduring effects of abuse and related adverse experiences in childhood: A convergence of evidence from neurobiology and epidemiology. *European Archives of Psychiatry Clinical Neuroscience, 256,* 174–186. doi:10.1007/s00406-005-0624-4

Anderson, K., & Hiersteiner, C. (2008). Recovering from childhood sexual abuse: Is a 'storybook ending'" possible? *American Journal of Family Therapy, 36*(5), 413–424. doi:10.1080/01926180701804592

Angus, L. E., & Greenberg, L. S. (2011). *Working with narrative in emotion-focused therapy: Changing stories, healing lives.* Washington, DC: American Psychological Association.

Beaudoin, M.-N., & Zimmerman, J. (2011). Narrative therapy and interpersonal neurobiology: Revisiting classic practices, developing new emphases. *Journal of Systemic Therapies, 30*(1), 1–13. doi:10.1521/jsyt.2011.30.1.1

Benish, S. G., Imel, Z. E., & Wampold, B. E. (2008). The relative efficacy of bona fide psychotherapies for treating post-traumatic stress disorder: A meta-analysis of direct comparisons. *Clinical Psychology Review, 28*(5), 746–758. doi:10.1016/j.cpr.2007.10.005

Calhoun, L. G., & Tedeschi, R. G. (2008). The paradox of struggling with trauma: Guidelines for practice and directions for research. In S. Joseph & P. A. Lindley (Eds.), *Trauma,* recovery, and growth: Positive psychological perspectives on posttraumatic stress (pp. 325–338). New York, NY: Wiley.

Chrzastowski, S. K. (2011). A narrative perspective on genograms: Revisiting classical family therapy methods. *Clinical Child Psychology and Psychiatry, 16*(4), 635–644. doi:10.1177/1359104511400966

Combs, G., & Freedman, J. (2012). Narrative, poststructuralism, and social justice: Current practices in narrative therapy. *The Counseling Psychologist, 40*(7), 1033–1060. doi:10.1177/0011000012460662

Council for Accreditation of Counseling and Related Educational Programs. (2009). *2009 CACREP accreditation manual.* Alexandria, VA: Author.

Council for Accreditation of Counseling and Related Educational Programs. (2015). *CACREP 2016 standards.* Alexandria, VA: Author.

Denborough, D. (2004). Narrative therapy and research. *International Journal of Narrative Therapy and Community Work, 2,* 29–36. Retrieved from http://dulwichcentre.com

Denborough, D. (2014). *Retelling the stories of our lives: Everyday narrative therapy to draw inspiration and transform experience.* New York, NY: Norton.

Durrant, M., & Kowalski, K. (1990). Overcoming the effects of sexual abuse: Developing a self-perception of competence. In M. Durrant & C. White (Eds.), *Ideas for therapy with sexual abuse* (pp. 65–110). Adelaide, Australia: Dulwich Centre Publications.

Duvall, J., & Beres, L. (2007). A map for thematic conversations about trauma. In C. Brown & T. Augusta-Scott (Eds.), *Narrative therapy: Making meaning making lives* (pp. 229–250). Thousand Oakes, CA: Sage.

Duvall, J., & Beres, L. (2011). *Innovations in narrative therapy: Connecting practice, training and research.* New York, NY: Norton.

Epston, D. (2004). From empathy to ethnography: The origin of therapeutic co-research. *The International Journal of Narrative Therapy and Community Work, 2,* 31. Retrieved from http://dulwichcentre.com

Epston, D. (2011). Introduction. In M. White (Ed.), *Narrative practice: Continuing the conversation* (pp. xxi–xxxviii). New York, NY: Norton.

Etchison, M., & Kleinst, D. M. (2000). Review of narrative therapy: Research and utility. *Family Journal, 8*(1), 61–27. doi:10.1177/1066480700081009

Foa, E. B., Keane, T. M., Friedman, M. J., & Cohen, J. (2008). *Effective treatments for PTSD: Practice guidelines from the International Society for Traumatic Stress Studies* (2nd ed.). New York, NY: Guilford.

Ford, J. D. (2009). Defining and understanding complex trauma and complex traumatic stress disorders. In C. A. Courtois & J. D. Ford (Eds.), *Treating complex traumatic stress disorders: An evidence based guide* (pp. 13–30). New York, NY: Guilford.

Foucault, M. (1980). *Power/knowledge: Selected interviews and other writings, 1972–1977.* New York, NY: Vintage.

Frankl, V. (2006). *Man's search for meaning.* New York, NY: Beacon Press. (Original work published in 1946)

Gallerani, T., & Dybicz, P. (2011). Postmodern sandplay: An introduction for play therapists. *International Journal of Play Therapy, 20*(3), 165–177. doi:10.1037/a0023440

Gil, E. (1996). *Treating abused adolescents.* New York, NY: Guilford.

Gil, E. (2006). *Helping abused and traumatized children: Integrating directive and nondirective approaches.* New York, NY: Guilford.

Gil, E. (2010). *Working with children to heal interpersonal trauma: The power of play.* New York, NY: Guilford.

Grand, D. (2013). *Brainspotting.* Boulder, CO: Sounds True.

Hansen, J. T. (2007). Counseling without truth: Toward a neopragmatic foundation for counseling practice. *Journal of Counseling and Development, 85,* 423–430. doi:10.1002/j.1556-6678.2007.tb00610.x

Helwig, A. A., & Schmidt, L. L. P. (2011). Content analysis of 32 years of American Counseling Association convention programs. *Journal of Counseling & Development, 89,* 148–153. doi:10.1002/j.1556-6678.2011.tb00072.x

Herman, J. (2015). *Trauma and recovery: The aftermath of violence: From domestic abuse to political terror* (1R ed.). New York, NY: Basic Books. (Original work published in 1992)

Madigan, S. (2011). *Narrative therapy.* Washington, DC: American Psychological Association.

McLeod, J. (2006). Narrative thinking and the emergence of postpsychological therapies. *Narrative Inquiry, 16*(1), 201–210. doi:10.1075/ni.16.1.25mcl

Myerhoff, B. (1982). Life history among the elderly: Performance, visibility, and remembering. In J. Ruby (Ed.), *A crack in the mirror: Reflexive perspectives in anthropology* (pp. 99–117). Philadelphia, PA: University of Pennsylvania.

O'Hanlon, W. H. (1993). Possibility therapy: From iatrogenic injury to iatrogenic healing. In S. Gilligan & R. Price (Eds.), *Therapeutic conversations* (pp. 4–17). New York, NY: Norton.

Pereda, N., Guilera, G., Forns, M., & Gómez-Benito, J. (2009). The prevalence of child sexual abuse in community and student samples: A meta-analysis. *Clinical Psychology Review. 29*(4), 328–338. doi:10.1016/j.cpr.2009.02.007

Petersen, S., Bull, C., Propst, O., Dettinger, S., & Detwiler, L. (2005). Narrative therapy to prevent illness-related stress disorder. *Journal of Counseling & Development, 83,* 41–47.

Rober, P. (2005). The therapist's self in dialogical family therapy: Some ideas about not-knowing and the counselor's inner conviction. *Family Process, 44,* 477–495. doi:10.1111/j.1545-5300.2005.00073.x

Rothschild, B. (2000). *The body remembers: The psychophysiology of trauma and trauma treatment.* New York, NY: Norton.

Rothschild, B. (2010). *8 keys to safe trauma recovery.* New York, NY: Norton.

Scott, N., Hanstock, T. L., & Patterson-Kane, L. (2013). Using narrative therapy to treat eating disorder not otherwise specified. *Clinical Case Studies, 12*(4), 307–321. doi:10.1177/1534650113486184

Serlin, I., & Cannon, J. T. (2004). A humanistic approach to the psychology of trauma. In D. Kanfo (Ed.), *Living with terror, working with trauma: A clinician's handbook* (pp. 313–330). Landham, MD: Rowman & Littlefield.

Snel, E. (2013). *Sitting still like a frog: Mindful exercises for kids and their parents.* Boston, MA: Shambhala.

van der Kolk, B. A. (1996). Trauma and memory. In B. A. van der Kolk, A. C. McFarlane, & L. Weisaeth (Eds.), *Traumatic stress: The effects of overwhelming experience on mind, body, and society* (pp. 279–302). New York, NY: Guilford.

van der Kolk, B. A. (2014). *The body keeps the score: Brain, body, and mind in the healing of trauma.* New York, NY: Viking.

van der Velden, I., & Koops, M. (2005). Structure in word and image: Combining narrative therapy and art therapy in groups of survivors of war. *Intervention: International Journal of Mental Health, 3*(1), 57–64.

Wampold, B. E. (2001). *The great psychotherapy debate: Models, methods, and findings.* Mahwah, NJ: Erlbaum.

Webber, M., Kitzinger, R., Runte, J. K., Smith, C. M., & Mascari, J. B. (2017). Traumatology trends: A content analysis of three counseling journals from 1994 to 2014. *Journal of Counseling & Development, 95,* 249–259.

Webber, J., & Mascari, J. B. (2014a, March). *Four expressive techniques that jumpstart the trauma story.* Presentation to the American Counseling Association Conference, Honolulu, HI.

Webber, J., & Mascari, J. B. (2014b, September). *Top ten concepts counselor educators should be teaching about trauma and neurobiology*. Presentation to the North Atlantic Region Association for Counselor Education and Supervision Conference, Providence, RI.

Webber, J., Mascari, J. B., & Runte, J. (2010a). Psychological first aid: A new paradigm for disaster mental health. In J. Webber & J. B. Mascari (Eds.), *Terrorism, trauma and tragedies: A counselor's guide to preparing and responding* (3rd ed., pp. 201–205). Alexandria, VA: American Counseling Association Foundation.

Webber, J., Mascari, J. B., & Runte, J. (2010b). Unlocking traumatic memory through sand tray therapy. In J. Webber & J. B. Mascari (Eds.), *Terrorism, trauma, and tragedies: A counselor's guide to preparing and responding* (3rd ed., pp. 13–17). Alexandria, VA: American Counseling Association Foundation.

White, C. (2011). Epilogue: Continuing conversations. In M. White (Ed.), *Narrative practice: Continuing the conversation* (pp. 157–180). New York, NY: Norton.

White, M. (1997). *Narratives of therapists' lives*. Adelaide, Australia: Dulwich Center Publications.

White, M. (2005). Attending to the consequences of trauma. In *Workshop notes* (pp. 19–22). Retrieved from http://dulwichcentre.com.au/michael-white-workshop-notes.pdf

White, M. (2006). Children, trauma and subordinate storyline development. In D. Denborough (Ed.), *Trauma: Narrative responses to traumatic experience* (pp. 143–165). Adelaide, South Australia: Dulwich Centre Publications.

White, M. (2007). *Maps of narrative practice*. New York, NY: Norton.

White, M. (2011). On anorexia: An interview with Michael White. In In M. White (Ed.), *Narrative practice: Continuing the conversation* (pp. 87–97). New York, NY: Norton.

White, M., & Epston, D. (1990). *Narrative means to therapeutic ends*. New York, NY: Norton.

Winslade, J. M., & Monk, G. D. (2007). *Narrative counseling in schools: Brief and powerful* (2nd ed.). Thousand Oaks, CA: Sage.

Wolpe, J. (1969). *The practice of behavior therapy*. New York, NY: Pergamon Press.

Zimmerman, J. L., & Beaudoin, M. N. (2015). Neurobiology for your narrative: How brain science can influence narrative work. *Journal of Systemic Therapies, 34*(2), 59–74. doi:10.1521/jsyt.2015.34.2.59

SECTION III
Other Postmodern Therapeutic Models

INTRODUCTION

There are literally dozens of postmodern, or constructivist, therapies (Neukrug, 2015). The three *primary* postmodern therapies are commonly considered to be solution-focused therapy, narrative therapy, and collaborative therapy (Neukrug, 2015). Some additional postmodern therapies include coherence therapy, Ericksonian therapy, feminist therapy, personal construct therapy, and gender aware therapy (Raskin, 2015). The three chapters in Section III present an overview and case illustrations representing collaborative therapy, dialectical humanism, and the counselor–advocate–scholar model.

Dr. Robert A. Neimeyer, the editor-in-chief of the *Journal of Constructivist Psychology,* is one of the foremost international authorities on postmodern therapies. He has described the defining features of these therapies in a manner that is accessible to practitioners who are less familiar with postmodern ideology. In his book, entitled *Constructivist Psychotherapy: Distinctive Features* (Neimeyer, 2009), he discusses 30 distinctive features of postmodern therapies, including both theoretical (e.g., "redefining reality," "living in language," and "deconstructing the self") and practical features (e.g., "tracking evolving goals," and "re-authoring the self-narrative") (pp. v–vi).

A number of the distinctive features identified by Neimeyer are also illustrated in the three chapters in this section on Other Postmodern Therapies. In Chapter 6 of this section, Dr. Juleen K. Buser discusses the characteristics and conceptual foundation underlying collaborative therapy. She describes the application of collaborative therapy to the treatment of a client with symptoms of an eating disorder. Her chapter clearly illustrates the defining theoretical feature known as *personal knowledge* (Neimeyer, 2009). That is, the therapist is careful to adopt a not-knowing stance and shows deep respect for the client's story as unlike any other story she has ever encountered. In addition, the counselor uses basic attending skills and suggestions to facilitate a shift to a more empowering self-definition on the part of the client. Though the collaborative counselor's approach is subtle and nuanced, her approach clearly represents the distinctive practice feature known as *reauthoring the self-narrative* (Neimeyer, 2009).

In Chapter 7, Drs. Megan Speciale and Matthew E. Lemberger present an application of a less well-known postmodern model to sexuality counseling. More specifically, they discuss the course of treatment with Parker and Renee, a couple experiencing difficulties in their sexual relationship. They describe the process as the "dismantling . . . [of] heteronormative definitions of sexuality" to make it possible to reimagine new sexual possibilities. This description closely resembles the distinctive conceptual feature Neimeyer (2009) referred to as *living on the frontier*. More specifically, Neimeyer describes a process in which clients' "forward movement entails confronting challenges and innovating solutions as [they] move forward, pushing back the boundaries of the known world" (p. 11). In a manner similar to that recommended by Neimeyer, the counselor in the case illustration supports and encourages the couple to accept the ongoing anxiety associated with *living on the frontier* by co-constructing their definition of a mutually satisfying sexual relationship.

Finally, in Chapter 8, Dr. Manivong J. Ratts presents his counselor–advocate–scholar (CAS) model, which he applies to the case of a Vietnamese American client (Van) who is coping with workplace discrimination. His application illustrates the distinctive theoretical feature *systems within systems* (Neimeyer, 2009, p. v) by showing that meaningful and adaptive actions vary as a function of the level of system in which the client is operating (i.e., microlevel, mesolevel, macrolevel). In addition, Dr. Ratts's CAS model exemplifies the theoretical feature, *redefining reality,* by demonstrating the inherent power in deconstructing and challenging social constructions, such as those constraining Van's potential for career advancement.

A client typically can find solutions by looking past conventional social constructions. The three chapters in this section provide a generous breadth of perspective on less well-known postmodern therapies. They reflect the ever-expanding repertoire of therapies contemporary counselors can employ to help clients reveal and reclaim their inner strengths and past solutions. These building blocks are essential for co-constructing innovative, individualized solutions.

REFERENCES

Neimeyer, R. A. (2009). *Constructivist psychotherapy: Defining features.* New York, NY: Routledge.

Neukrug, E. S. (Ed.). (2015). *The SAGE encyclopedia of theory in counseling and psychotherapy.* Thousand Oaks, CA: SAGE.

Raskin, J. D. (2015). Constructivist therapies: Overview. In E. S. Neukrug (ed.), *The SAGE encyclopedia of theory in counseling and psychotherapy* (pp. 221–225). Thousand Oaks, CA: SAGE.

CHAPTER 6

Acceptance, Empowerment, and Meaning

A Collaborative Therapy Approach for College-Age Clients Struggling With Eating Disorder Symptoms

JULEEN K. BUSER

The postmodern approach of collaborative therapy is useful for addressing key concerns of clients struggling with eating disorder symptomatology. In particular, clients struggling with eating disorder symptoms commonly experience emotions of shame and guilt (Gee & Troop, 2003; Oluyori, 2013), feel labeled and stigmatized (Becker et al., 2010), seek control (Humphry & Ricciardelli, 2004; Schuler & Kuster, 2011), experience addiction to their symptoms (Cassin & von Ranson, 2007), and feel a void of meaning (Buser, Parkins, & Buser, 2014; Hardman, Berrett, & Richards, 2003; Kater, 2010; Sandoz, Wilson, & Dufrene, 2010). As will be explicated in this chapter, the philosophical underpinnings of collaborative therapy are well suited to assist clients facing these concerns.

Individuals who struggle with eating disorder symptomatology have reported feelings of shame (Gee & Troop, 2003; Oluyori, 2013) and guilt (Oluyori, 2013) related to their experiences with problematic eating practices. Struggling individuals have also reported feeling a sense of stigma related to their eating disorder symptoms; this stigma was identified as a factor that may inhibit treatment seeking (Becker et al., 2010). Given this potential vulnerability of clients struggling with eating disorder symptoms, a counseling approach grounded in a nonjudgmental posture would likely be beneficial. Collaborative therapy is an approach based in a lack of external judgement and an approach that eschews pathologizing client behaviors; in fact, Anderson (2007c) put it this way: "Each client is simply thought to present with an everyday, ordinary life situation (e.g., a difficulty, a misery, a dilemma, a challenge, a pain, or a decision) that any of us could similarly encounter" (p. 53).

Other elements of collaborative therapy also make it well suited to work with clients struggling with eating disorders. Based in a postmodern philosophical stance, collaborative therapy values a cooperative learning-centered therapy atmosphere and use of dialogue to co-create new meanings and new options with clients (Anderson, 1997, 2007b). For clients whose eating disorder symptoms are related to a desire for control (Humphry & Ricciardelli, 2004; Schuler & Kuster, 2011), such a counseling atmosphere may present a new way to feel empowered (Anderson, 2007c). For clients who feel addicted to their eating disorder (Cassin & von Ranson, 2007) and may deny the seriousness of their eating disorder symptoms (Vandereycken & Humbeeck, 2008), a collaborative therapy counseling approach may neutralize resistance due to its emphasis on the client's point of view. For clients who are struggling with disconnection from values or meaning in their lives (Buser et al., 2014; Hardman et al., 2003; Kater, 2010; Sandoz et al., 2010), this approach may assist them in formulating new meanings and identities.

In this chapter, I will discuss collaborative therapy in terms of its application to clients struggling with eating disorder symptoms, with an emphasis on college-age clients. First, I will define and summarize eating disorder symptomology, that is, symptom presentation and prevalence rates. Then, I will review and illustrate the main features of collaborative therapy, in addition to discussing how these collaborative therapy features apply to clients facing eating disorder symptoms. In particular, I will explain why collaborative therapy is well suited for addressing the issues that may be faced by clients struggling with eating disorder symptomatology: (a) shame, guilt, and stigma; (b) control; (c) addiction; (d) and a separation from a sense of meaning and/or values. Last, I will discuss the research base behind collaborative therapy and potential limitations of this approach.

EATING DISORDER SYMPTOMATOLOGY

A range of problematic eating behaviors and attitudes comprise the construct of *eating disorder symptomatology*. These symptoms may be clinical or subclinical in nature (American Psychiatric Association [APA], 2013; Eisenburg, Nicklett, Roeder, & Kirz, 2011; Stice, Marti, & Rohde, 2013). Researchers have found that subclinical and clinical symptoms do not represent two different taxonomies of symptoms; instead, they represent different levels of severity (Tylka & Subich, 1999).

The *Diagnostic and Statistical Manual of Mental Disorders,* fifth edition (*DSM-5;* APA, 2013), defines the pattern of symptomatology required for a clinical diagnosis of an eating disorder. In particular, a diagnosis of anorexia nervosa (AN) is characterized by (a) an excessively low weight; (b) fear of weight gain or efforts to prevent weight gain; and (c) failure to recognize the severity of low body weight, extreme value placed on body weight or shape, or disordered perception of weight or shape. In a national population-based prevalence study, researchers reported lifetime prevalence rates for AN as ranging from .3% (males) to .9% (females; Hudson, Hiripi, Pope, & Kessler, 2007). Researchers have noted a potential increase in AN prevalence rates, due to changes in diagnostic criteria in the *DSM-5* (Mustelin et al., 2016). These researchers reported that, among female participants in their study, lifetime AN prevalence rates rose by 60%, specifically increasing to 3.6% using the *DSM-5* criteria versus 2.2% using the *DSM-IV* criteria.

Individuals who struggle with bulimia nervosa (BN) exhibit the following cluster of symptoms: (a) binge eating, wherein an individual feels out of control and consumes a large number of calories in a specific period of time; (b) compensatory actions to stave off weight gain, for example, vomiting, laxative use, diuretic use, overexercising; (c) symptoms have occurred, at minimum, once weekly over a 3-month period; and (d) self-assessment highly dependent on weight and shape. Clinical BN is more common than clinical AN, with lifetime prevalence rates of .5% (males) to 1.5% (females; Hudson et al., 2007). Trace et al. (2012) reported little expectation of major prevalence rate changes for BN based on the *DSM-5* criteria.

Clinical levels of binge eating disorder (BED) must meet the following criteria: (a) binge eating symptoms, that is, lack of control over eating and ingesting large amounts of food in a distinct time period; (b) abnormally fast eating, experiencing an unpleasant sensation of fullness, eating without hunger, eating alone due to shame and/or emotions of disgust, depression, or guilt (at least three of the preceding symptoms required); (c) feeling troubled by eating patterns; (d) binge eating once weekly over a 3-month period; and (e) lack of compensatory actions. BED has the highest lifetime prevalence rate, compared to AN and BN, ranging from 2% (males) to 3.5% (females; Hudson et al., 2007). These prevalence rates are unlikely to be drastically altered due to the *DSM-5* criteria (Hudson, Coit, Lalonde, & Pope, 2012; Trace et al., 2012).

The clinical criteria described earlier do not capture all individuals who struggle with eating disorder symptoms. A client's symptom presentation may not conform to all the criteria for AN, BN, or BED as described previously; the "Other Specified Feeding and Eating Disorders" category in the *DSM-5* may be appropriate for such clients (APA, 2013). Subclinical levels of eating disorder symptoms (e.g., reduced frequency of binge eating or bulimic symptoms) represent a mental health struggle for numerous individuals (Eisenburg et al., 2011; Stice et al., 2013). For example, Stice and colleagues (2013) conducted a longitudinal study of female adolescents ($N = 496$). Participants were aged 12 to 15 years at the start of the study and took part in this research for 8 years. Researchers reported that participants' lifetime prevalence rates were as follows: subclinical BN (4.4%), subclinical BED (3.6%), and frequent purging behaviors (3.4%). These prevalence rates indicate how many participants reported eating disorder symptomatology at the start and/or during the 8-year study. Eisenburg et al. (2011) surveyed college students on their eating behaviors ($N = 2,822$) and reported high levels of endorsement of problematic symptoms: concern related to lack of control over eating (26.4% women; 8.4% men), significant and sudden weight loss (4.8% women; 5.2% men), and feelings of fullness resulting in self-induced vomiting (13.7% women; 4.3% men).

COLLABORATIVE THERAPY AND EATING DISORDER SYMPTOMATOLOGY

Anderson (1997, 2007a, 2007b, 2007c) created collaborative therapy, framing it as a postmodern approach that is best understood as a philosophy instead of a theory. In this chapter, I will focus on three distinctly postmodern elements of collaborative therapy (as described by Anderson, 1997, 2007a, 2007b, 2007c), which have specific applicability to the treatment of clients struggling with eating disorders. First, collaborative therapy stresses a lack of judgement for client difficulties, refusing to label or pathologize clients. This is an attitude directly related to its postmodern sensibilities, as counselors are encouraged to view clients as struggling with understandable and routine concerns, prioritize the client's language, and engage in a process of authentic listening to client stories. Second, collaborative therapy stresses client agency; clients are viewed as authorities and experts on their lives and counselors are encouraged to be inquisitive about and interested in clients' constructed narratives, knowledge, and meanings. Third, counselors and clients engage in a mutual process of meaning making in collaborative therapy work; client storytelling is used as a way to facilitate this co-creation. These three postmodern elements of collaborative therapy are well suited to working with clients struggling with eating disorder symptomatology. The lack of judgement and genuine listening is compatible with the needs of clients struggling with shame, stigma, and guilt; the focus on client agency and authority is compatible with the needs of clients who desire control in their lives and/or are struggling with addictive elements of eating disorder symptoms; the mutually created meaning is compatible with the needs of clients who are experiencing a lack of meaning in their lives. In the following section, I will discuss each of these features in detail, contrasting the collaborative therapy approach to forms of cognitive-behavioral therapy that have been applied to eating disorder treatment (e.g., Fursland et al., 2012).

Stigma, Shame, and Guilt

Researchers have documented the feelings of shame, guilt, and stigma that those struggling with eating disorder symptoms may experience. Specifically, individuals struggling with eating disorder symptoms may have a tendency to be self-critical (Oluyori, 2013), sense that others view them as unimportant (Gee & Troop, 2003), feel guilty for struggling with eating disorder symptoms (Oluyori, 2013), and avoid or hide treatment-seeking efforts due to a sense of the stigma of eating disorders (Becker et al., 2010; Oluyori, 2013). Clients struggling with eating disorder symptoms may therefore be in a vulnerable state upon entering treatment. Any hint of judgement or diagnostic labeling may damage efforts to build a therapeutic bond with a client who already feels ashamed, guilty, and stigmatized. Traditional counseling approaches such as cognitive therapy may unintentionally suggest judgement or stigma to a client. A main premise of cognitive therapy is to identify and challenge illogical thought patterns (e.g., Beck, 1995; Ellis, 1999; Fursland et al., 2012). The language used in this approach implies a sense of normal versus abnormal and is also focused on the negative elements of client thoughts (e.g., *irrational* thoughts, *faulty* beliefs; Beck, 1995; Ellis, 1999). Thus, this language may feel labeling and judgmental to a client who is already sensitive to those issues.

Collaborative therapy, on the other hand (as described by Anderson, 1997, 2007b, 2007c), approaches clients from a place of openness, acceptance, and a refusal to label something as pathology. Client concerns are viewed as issues to which no one is immune, thereby destigmatizing the concern. Moreover, the collaborative therapist strives to use the client's language. Diagnostic terms and clinical language may enhance a client's sense of guilt, shame, or stigma; rooting the therapeutic conversation in client words and phrases diminishes the sense of counselor judgement. Additionally, the collaborative therapist genuinely listens to the client, communicating an authentic desire to understand the client's experience. The counselor does this by tracking with the client's story—offering responses that phrase the client's words in a somewhat different manner so as to corroborate understanding. The counselor also engages in active listening by asking questions that help the client "clarify and expand" the story, rather than directing or guiding the conversation (Anderson, 2007b, p. 36). This fully present listening, wherein the counselor ideally becomes fascinated and engrossed in the client's story, can be a powerful antidote to client feelings of shame, guilt, and stigma. In genuine listening, there is no focus on judgement, labeling, or diagnosis.

Control

Authors have discussed that clients who struggle with eating disorder symptoms may engage in these symptoms in an effort to establish a sense of control in their lives (Humphry & Ricciardelli, 2004; Schüler & Kuster, 2011). As these authors discuss, some individuals who feel very out of control in one or more areas of their lives use eating disorder symptomatology to gain a degree of control. Given this desire for control experienced by some clients struggling with eating disorder symptoms, collaborative therapy may be particularly appropriate. In contrast to counseling approaches that emphasize the expertise of the counselor and prescribe certain activities for the client to undertake, collaborative therapy values the client's authority and insight.

Cognitive therapy works from a premise of counselor expertise and unique knowledge. In this approach, counselors help the client identify illogical or maladaptive thought patterns and then work to change these thought patterns (Beck, 1995; Ellis, 1999; Fursland et al., 2012). The counselor is thus the one who defines rational versus irrational thoughts and thereby sets up a degree of power and control in the counseling environment.

As Anderson (1997, 2007a, 2007b, 2007c) explicated, such a dynamic is discarded in collaborative therapy. The client's own perspective and opinions are prioritized; although the constructed knowledge of the counselor is not dismissed, it is not given inordinate priority over the client's constructed knowledge. This counseling atmosphere may be affirming and empowering for clients who desire a sense of control in their lives. Rather than cultivating a counseling setting where clients may feel disempowered, collaborative therapists aim to make clients feel that their voice and experience are deeply important.

Addiction

Eating disorders have been conceptualized as process or behavioral addictions (Hagedorn, 2009). Individuals struggling with eating disorder behaviors (e.g., binge eating) and attitudes (e.g., determining one's personal worth by body size and shape) have reported addiction symptoms such as a continuation of eating disorder behaviors and attitudes despite adverse consequences, an experience of tolerance to the behavior, and a loss of control over the behavior (Cassin & von Ranson, 2007). These addictive symptoms suggest that struggling clients may lack motivation to seek treatment—a commonly discussed issue in the addictions field (Miller & Rollnick, 2002; Prochaska, DiClemente, & Norcross, 1992; Rollnick & Miller, 1995). Moreover, authors have noted the ways in which clients struggling with eating disorder symptoms may be in denial of their symptoms (Vandereycken & Humbeck, 2008) and may be hesitant to engage in treatment (Becker et al., 2010; Oluyori, 2013).

Collaborative therapy is well suited to working with unmotivated clients. As discussed previously, this counseling approach prioritizes the client's experience and authority. Rather than imposing the counselor's perspective on the problem or the solution, collaborative therapy corresponds with the motivational interviewing concept of meeting the client at his or her stage of change (Miller & Rollnick, 2002; Prochaska et al., 1992; Rollnick & Miller, 1995).

As discussed in the prior section, Anderson (1997, 2007a, 2007b, 2007c) specified that collaborative therapy places priority on the client's constructed knowledge. The counselor is not seen as an expert working to teach the client new strategies or skills. Instead, a counselor working from a collaborative therapy stance expresses interest in and curiosity about the client's experience and approaches client concerns from a "not-knowing" perspective (Anderson, 2007c, p. 48). This not-knowing perspective includes valuing the client's constructed knowledge, refusing to assume familiarity with the client's experience, and posing suggestions tentatively and cautiously so as not to communicate expertise and authority over the client's constructed knowledge (Anderson, 2005, 2007c). Such an approach may defuse client resistance to treatment. Rather than fighting against the client's denial, collaborative therapists embrace it and become curious about this denial and hesitation to change. Clients who are resistant to change and hesitant to engage in treatment may experience a sense of relief at not having to fight against a counselor's assertions that they are mentally ill (Anderson, 1997).

Void of Meaning

Clients struggling with eating disorder symptoms may experience a loss of meaning in their lives. The eating disorder symptoms may have consumed their lives to such a degree that space for values, hopes, and dreams is un-available (Hardman et al., 2003; Kater, 2010; Sandoz et al., 2010). Clients may also feel a spiritual void and/or a disconnection from God or a Higher Power (Buser et al., 2014; Hardman et al., 2003). Traditional therapies for eating disorders do not always address this sense of meaninglessness. For example, cognitive therapy focuses on client thought patterns and does not emphasize a client's spiritual vacancy as contributing to symptoms.

Collaborative therapists, on the other hand, spend considerable time working with clients to co-create meaning. Specifically, through allowing and encouraging clients to tell their stories in an ongoing, repetitive manner, collaborative therapists engender a "self-story transformation" (Anderson, 1997, p. 234). Clients may find new, untapped meanings through this sto-rytelling process, finding sources of self-agency and freedom previously ignored. As Anderson (1997) explicated,

> From an interpretive, meaning-generating perspective, change is inherent in dia-logue: change is the telling and re-telling of familiar stories; it is the redescriptions that accrue through conversation; it is the different meanings that are conferred on past, pre-sent, and imagined future events and experiences. (p. 233)

Practical Applications in Counseling

As the prior discussion of collaborative therapy suggests, this counseling approach is not technique heavy. Collaborative therapy emphasizes the creation of a supportive counseling environment and relationship rather than specifying techniques and strategies. Yet there are recommendations for ways in which counselors can create a nonjudgmental, open, client-affirming space, provided by Anderson (1997, 2007b, 2007c). Some ini-tial practical considerations include setting up an informal and comfortable space, having the counselor and the client seated in comparable chairs where they can see each other, and generally avoiding note taking, which can establish a barrier in sessions (Anderson, 1997).

In addition, counselors can be intentional about the way they welcome a client to counseling. A sense of respect is crucial in this initial interaction; Anderson (2007c) framed the counselor as a "host who meets and greets the client as a guest while simultaneously the therapist is a guest in the client's life" (p. 45). Collaborative therapy's emphasis on a nonjudgmental atmosphere accords well with this sense of the client as a guest in coun-seling and the counselor as a guest in the client's experience. Also, a view of the client as struggling with an issue that anyone might face at some point in their life is more likely to foster this welcoming, hospitable atmosphere.

An inherent respect for the client's experience, story, and personally constructed knowledge permeates all aspects of collaborative therapy. When counselors listen in collaborative therapy, they do so without an agenda—eschewing even an agenda of clinical assessment (Anderson, 2007b). Client communications are approached as stories. Counselors are urged to "primarily attend to the whole of the story" and loosen their focus on gathering details for a clinical assessment (Anderson, 2007b, p. 37). Such details and facts, while important, will naturally come from the client's organic storytelling. As Anderson (2007b) explained it: "Picture how you would listen to a story if you truly believed that you had not heard it before and were hearing it for the first time. The unfamiliarity of it invites curiosity and anticipation" (p. 37). The counselor is encouraged to take on a posture of captivation and inquisitiveness as the client speaks, using skills to facilitate continued client openness and communication, such as questions about the client's story (not questions that lead the story into new directions), clarifying statements and paraphrases that communicate counselor understanding of the client's story (not mere parroting responses, which cannot establish mutual understanding), and attention to nonverbal communication and use of silence to encourage (versus discourage) client discussion. Despite this effort to accurately understand the client, a counselor is also cognizant of the client's unique experience; a counselor does not claim to have a perfect understanding of what the client is experiencing (Anderson, 1997).

Collaborative therapists also view the client as an expert. They communicate and behave in ways that foster an egalitarian relationship. The client's own language is used and counselors approach a client's story with a genuine desire to understand the concern from the client's point of view. In particular, the collaborative therapist spends a lot of time listening to a client with deep respect for the story, and with a genuine belief that the client can teach the therapist something. Counselors also may offer their own suggestions in a tentative manner. As Anderson (2007b) emphasized, the not-knowing stance of the collaborative therapist does not mean that the therapist's own expertise is devalued or ignored. Collaborative therapists are not silent bystanders in counseling. But when they do offer their own constructed knowledge, it is done carefully, thoughtfully, and tentatively.

Collaborative therapists also encourage client storytelling. In an effort to help clients create new and/or different self-stories, counselors urge clients to tell their stories multiple times. In this retelling process, clients may notice new possibilities in a story. For example, Anderson (1997) noted how clients who experienced incest may feel tension between clashing identities and may also struggle with disempowering individual and/or societal narratives that cast them as a "survivor" and/or a "victim" (p. 232).

Through the telling of their stories, clients can shift their personal narratives so as to allow for multiple identities to coexist and to also open up space for different, more empowering self-definitions.

CASE STUDY

In the following section, I present a hypothetical case of a college student struggling with habits and attitudes that likely represent subclinical levels of eating disorder symptomatology. Following this case, I provide details on how a counselor (Sylvie) working from a collaborative therapy stance would approach this client and conduct counseling. Sylvie is a 35-year-old Asian American master's-level clinician who has been working at a college counseling center for 5 years. She recently attained her clinical license and is starting to develop a specialty in eating disorder treatment. She has attended postdegree trainings and workshops in this area, in addition to making a consistent effort to be aware of current research and literature in the field. The case discussion that follows is based on the principles and premises of collaborative therapy presented by Anderson (1997, 2007a, 2007b, 2007c).

Chloe is an 18-year-old, Caucasian, first-year college student. She is attending a large public university about 3 hours from her hometown. She has come to the college counseling center reluctantly; she noted that she went home for winter break and her mom expressed serious concern about her weight loss. She insisted that Chloe attend several counseling sessions at college and Chloe agreed (despite some reservations). Chloe is dieting frequently and often skips meals. She is also exercising regularly—sometimes up to 2 hours per day. She noted that she has lost about 15 pounds since beginning college in the fall (it is now February) and reported that she feels "more confident, more secure, and stronger" due to this weight loss. She noted that her "dieting and exercise habits" have added some stress to her life, namely around difficulties going out to eat with friends, emotions of guilt if she feels she overeats, and a sense of panic if she does not strenuously exercise daily. Chloe noted that she didn't "plan" to start dieting or lose weight; she mentioned feeling stressed out due to the demands of classes, feeling lonely at college, and feeling worried that her parents' investment in her education would not pay off, that is, that she would not find a job after graduation.

Sylvie begins her work with Chloe by asking her to tell her story fully and thoroughly. Sylvie validates the notion that Chloe is not here completely of her own accord, but she emphasizes that Sylvie is providing a space (for however long Chloe should choose to use it) for the purpose of honoring her perspective. In carrying out this session, Sylvie keeps in mind the unstructured, instinctive nature of collaborative therapy. Anderson (1997) clearly stated that "The structure of the therapy conversation is spontaneous, determined by moment-to-moment exchanges that zigzag and crisscross. It does not follow a predetermined script such as a structured question guideline or sequenced action" (p. 126).

Sylvie talks about Chloe's concern as her "dieting and exercise habits," avoiding clinical terminology such as "eating disorder symptoms," which may stigmatize Chloe's concern and dissuade her from continuing counseling. Sylvie says to Chloe, "Tell me more about these dieting and exercising habits," aware that terming them "subclinical eating disorder symptoms" would be imposing her own viewpoint on Chloe's experience (Anderson, 1997). This immediate acceptance of Chloe's worldview may feel freeing and relieving, as Chloe does not have to argue to convince Sylvie that she does not have an eating disorder (Anderson, 1997).

Being careful not to direct Chloe's story, Sylvie asks Chloe to expand on her story, endeavors to communicate understanding of her experience, and conveys a fascination with her narrative. Anderson (1997) discussed the importance of being patient so as to allow the client to direct the dialogue and also noted the value of well-phrased questions in the counseling session. These questions should be open, inquisitive, and nonjudgmental. Rather than inquiries that presuppose a counselor's expertise (e.g., questions about a desire for control in life that may correlate with her symptoms), these questions should be focused on "learning more of what distressed and worried" the client (Anderson, 1997, p. 148).

Sylvie also uses skills that reflect back the client's statements in slightly different language (e.g., paraphrases, summaries) in order to communicate understanding. In session, Sylvie is attuned to being sure she accurately understands Chloe's story. Continually checking in with the client to ascertain mutual understanding is important. Moreover, Sylvie also uses the skill of scanning, wherein she brings up issues Chloe mentioned at another point in session (Anderson, 1997). In this way, Sylvie is careful not to inadvertently lead the session in a direction not chosen by the client; scanning gives the client the opportunity to change direction and direct the session to a different domain of focus (Anderson, 1997). At some point in the session, Sylvie seeks to more overtly confirm that she and Chloe are following the same trajectory regarding what to discuss in session. Anderson (1997) termed this getting "a sense of [the client's] agenda" (p. 170).

Through Chloe's storytelling, openings for new meanings may become available. Importantly, this new meaning is not counselor led, but rather emerges through the client's own words about her experience (Anderson, 1997). For example, Chloe shifts the discussion of her "dieting and exercise habits" into a discussion about how stress, loneliness, worry, and self-doubt sometimes fuel her urge to restrict food and exercise strenuously. Sylvie decides to reflect this back to Chloe, saying "it sounds like you are saying that dieting and exercising a lot might be a way to silence feeling overwhelmed at school, feeling distant from others, and feeling pressured to succeed after graduation." Through continued storytelling, Chloe may gradually understand a new identity that reduces the need for coping through these dieting and exercise habits.

For example, as Chloe reflects on the ways in which her stress, loneliness, and self-doubt trigger her dieting and exercise habits, she also comments on her strong sense of family loyalty, her powerful value of friendship, and her commitment to education. After reflecting back these issues and asking Chloe to expand on them, Sylvie decides to offer a tentative insight: "As you've been telling me your story, I have noticed we have been discussing two related, but also contrasting, things. If this sounds correct to you, it seems that you are struggling in this new atmosphere of college, but you're also aware of certain strengths and values that led to this struggle. I'm curious about your thoughts on this." Through continued dialogue, Chloe expands her self-identity so that it includes both her feelings of unhappiness at college and her recognition of important underlying strengths and values.

Collaborative therapy is specifically attuned to the development of client agency through storytelling and how shifting self-identities can move toward increased self-agency (Anderson, 1997). Thus, as Chloe talks about this new identity that combines both unhappiness and strengths/values, she may feel that this self-identity is "liberating" compared to an identity wherein her unhappiness was paramount (Anderson, 1997, p. 233). Optimally, with a new awareness of her complex self, the need to cope via dieting and exercise will diminish.

RESEARCH ON COLLABORATIVE THERAPY

Anderson (2007c) noted that collaborative therapy has primarily been examined through the use of qualitative studies and anecdotal accounts. For example, authors have shared anecdotal and case study examples to support the helpfulness of collaborative therapy approaches with a range of clients and client concerns, such as grief (Penn, 2007), eating disorders (Fernández, Cortés, & Tarragona, 2007), older adults (Andrews, 2007), and family therapy with children (Gehart, 2007; McDonough & Koch, 2007). Authors have also provided anecdotal and case study accounts of the success of collaborative therapy approaches as consultation methods in a prison (Wagner, 2007) and with teachers (London &

Rodriguez-Jazcilevich, 2007) and have discussed the utility of a collaborative approach in education (McNamee, 2007), supervision (London & Tarragona, 2007), research (Gehart, Tarragona, & Bava, 2007), and in case report writing (St. George & Wulff, 1998).

Beyond case studies and anecdotal reports, some researchers have qualitatively or quantitatively examined collaborative therapy approaches. For example, Gehart-Brooks and Lyle (1999) used interpretive ethnography to examine the clinical experiences of client and therapists; these therapists reported using a collaborative therapy approach. Clients identified several elements as being beneficial in the therapy experience, such as (a) the listening efforts of the therapist, which included feeling heard, understood, connected, validated, and accepted; (b) the freedom to express oneself verbally; and (c) gaining a novel perspective, which was facilitated through therapist questions, suggestions, and mediation and which was understood as leading to the client's ability to alter emotional or behavioral responses. Therapists identified forming a therapeutic bond and listening as important for client change; forming a therapeutic bond included accepting the client, providing a space for client expression, and serving as a model of mutual communication. Therapists also noted that clients were able to take on new perspectives, which led to change: "From the therapists' perspective, clients experienced change when they found a new story that redefined the connections between themselves and others" (p. 70).

Feinsilver, Murphy, and Anderson (2007) conducted a project they termed "research-as-part-of-everyday-practice" (p. 270). They explored the impact of a collaborative research and therapeutic process with "women identified as 'homeless'" (p. 269). The authors summarized a variety of benefits clients experienced, such as "a sense of personal worth," an appreciation for community, and a transition from "initial deficient labels" to "expanded and more useful notions of self" (p. 285).

Moreover, collaborative therapy approaches have been empirically examined with individuals struggling with psychosis. Specifically, an approach started in Finland and termed *open dialogue* has been studied with those facing psychosis; this approach contains seven main components: intervening quickly, prioritizing client supports, altering the approach to fit the client's needs, a team of accountable clinicians, stability of care, willingness to accept uncertainty, and creation of a mutual dialogue with the client and family that open up space for novel meanings (Haarakangas, Seikkula, Alakare, & Aaltonen, 2007). Many of the components of open dialogue are rooted in collaborative therapy; qualitative and quantitative researchers have found this approach to be beneficial in the treatment of individuals struggling with psychosis (e.g., Seikkula, 2002; Seikkula, Alakare, & Aaltonen, 2001; Seikkula et al., 2003). For a summary of the evolution of this approach and its use with clients facing psychosis, see Haarakangas et al. (2007).

Research on Collaborative Therapy and Eating Disorders

A small body of literature has specifically explored collaborative therapy concepts and their application to treating clients struggling with eating disorder symptoms. For example, Geller, Brown, Zaitsoff, Goodrich, and Hastings (2003) examined client preference for directive versus collaborative interventions in eating disorder treatment. These authors did not specifically examine collaborative therapy per se, but instead examined principles of working cooperatively with clients that accord with the underlying philosophy of collaborative therapy. For example, these authors established that a collaborative approach to treatment specifies that the client has an important, active place in treatment decisions. In this study, 48 clients in an eating disorder treatment program were asked to rate their responses to eight vignettes about treatment for a variety of client situations, such as being admitted to an inpatient facility or dealing with a client's need for weight gain. Participants rated their reactions to these vignettes across several domains and reported that the collaborative approaches were more acceptable than directive approaches and were more likely to encourage clients to remain in treatment and complete treatment recommendations. As compared with clients who were more certain about change, clients who were uncertain about change rated the directive approaches as less appealing, less acceptable, and less likely to lead to follow-through on treatment recommendations. In another article, Fallon and Wisniewski (2013) described a case study of a client struggling with anorexia nervosa. Undergirding their treatment model (which used a variety of techniques from evidence-based therapies) was an approach of collaboration. In particular, these authors discussed the importance, for the client, of "a feeling that her voice would be heard" (p. 505).

Fernández and colleagues (2007) presented a discussion of their collaborative therapy treatment approach to their work with clients struggling with eating disorder symptoms. These authors carried out a reflecting team approach in their clinical care; they worked with clients who were also seeing individual therapists and thus viewed their sessions as consultation meetings. In these consultations with clients, the authors noted the salience of cultural definitions of *beauty* and *attractiveness*. In fact, clients seemed especially interested in discussing the ways in which the larger culture idealized certain body types. These authors also noted the clinical relevance of biological and medical information about eating disorders (e.g., the link between self-starvation and increased anxiety) and the place of gentle education on these issues in meetings with clients. In general, these authors commented that the collaborative spirit of their interaction with clients was vital; they noted that, particularly for clients who had sought treatment previously for eating disorder symptoms, this approach, entailing cooperation, mutuality, and honoring the client's voice, was surprising and helpful to clients.

Overall, additional empirical studies are needed in order to establish the clinical usefulness of collaborative therapy in successfully treating client concerns. Quantitative studies are particularly important. Although some quantitative investigations have been conducted, these have been primarily focused on work with clients struggling with psychosis (e.g., Seikkula, 2002; Seikkula et al., 2001, 2003). There is a need for quantitative investigations on the use of collaborative therapy with a range of client difficulties. Such studies (with large numbers of participants) can do more to establish a warrant for generalizability of findings. An expansion of the qualitative research base is also merited. Additional qualitative studies can help clinicians develop an enhanced understanding of client reactions to specific elements of collaborative therapy.

LIMITATIONS OF COLLABORATIVE THERAPY

In addition to the aforementioned strengths of collaborative therapy for working with clients struggling with eating disorders, this approach has some limitations that are important to address. As Hansen and Scholl (in Chapter 1 of this volume) noted, postmodern approaches to counseling are often dependent on the strong core counseling skills of the practitioner. This is extremely pertinent to collaborative therapy. As collaborative therapy de-emphasizes techniques and stresses the creation of a certain therapy atmosphere and relationship, the fundamental counseling skills of empathy and relationship building are crucial to successful collaborative therapy. This therapy has few techniques and strategies for counselors to implement; much of its work is natural, spontaneous, and guided by the client's story. Thus, some trainees and practitioners may find the openness of this approach overwhelming and may gravitate to more clear-cut methods of intervening with clients.

Also, although it is well suited to clients with eating disorder symptoms in general, several characteristics of collaborative therapy, such as client–counselor mutuality, the counselor's stance of not-knowing, and cooperation, may come into conflict with more directive approaches required for addressing the physical risks of eating disorder symptoms. Counselors should be aware that best practices in the eating disorder field recommend concomitant medical care for clients and, consequently, counselors should recommend that their clients seek appropriate medical assessment and care (APA, 2010). Recommendations include physical examinations by doctors competent in the varied effects of eating disorder symptomatology, including attention to dental damage, heart irregularities, bone thinning, and reproductive concerns (APA, 2010). Such mandated medical interventions may not wholly accord with the client-as-expert focus of collaborative therapy (Fernández et al., 2007). However, these medical concerns and interventions can still be approached in a collaborative manner, with counselors beginning by mutually discussing the risks and interventions with the client (Fernández et al., 2007). Moreover, as Geller et al. (2003) noted, clients reported a preference for a collaborative approach to issues like weight gain and discussion of physical damage; counselors may be able to consult with medical professionals to convey the value of speaking with the client in a mutual, open, nonjudgmental fashion rather than solely prescribing a weight gain goal or chastising a client for not decreasing his or her exercise.

CONCLUSION

Collaborative therapy, a distinctly postmodern approach, has a potentially powerful application to clients struggling with eating disorder symptoms. Crafted as an approach that prides itself on a cooperative effort between a counselor and a client, values the expertise and knowledge of the client, and eschews a pathological view of clients, collaborative therapy can offer a potent perspective to clients. Specifically, clients who feel stigmatized, ashamed, or guilty about symptoms are likely to benefit from the counselor's nonjudgmental stance. Clients with a low motivation to seek treatment and/or clients searching for control are likely to benefit from the emphasis on the client's voice and point of view. Finally, clients who experience a sense of meaninglessness are likely to benefit from working with a collaborative therapist who encourages them to tell their stories in order to illuminate and co-create new meanings.

REFERENCES

American Psychiatric Association. (2010). *Practice guideline for the treatment of patients with eating disorders* (3rd ed.). Retrieved from http://psychiatryonline.org/pb/assets/raw/sitewide/practice_guidelines/guidelines/eatingdisorders.pdf

American Psychiatric Association. (2013). *Diagnostic and statistical manual of mental disorders* (5th ed.). Washington, DC: Author.

Anderson, H. (1997). *Conversation, language, and possibilities: A postmodern approach to therapy.* New York, NY: Basic Books.

Anderson, H. (2005). Myths about "not-knowing." *Family Process, 44*(4), 497–504. doi:10.1111/j.1545-5300.2005.00074.x

Anderson, H. (2007a). A postmodern umbrella: Language and knowledge as relational and generative, and inherently transforming. In H. Anderson & D. Gehart (Eds.), *Collaborative therapy: Relationships and conversations that make a difference* (pp. 7–19). New York, NY: Routledge/Taylor & Francis Group.

Anderson, H. (2007b). Dialogue: People creating meaning with each other and finding ways to go on. In H. Anderson & D. Gehart (Eds.). *Collaborative therapy: Relationships and conversations that make a difference* (pp. 33–41). New York, NY: Routledge/Taylor & Francis Group.

Anderson, H. (2007c). The heart and spirit of collaborative therapy: The philosophical stance— "A way of being" in relationship and conversation. In H. Anderson & D. Gehart (Eds.), *Collaborative therapy: Relationships and conversations that make a difference* (pp. 43–59). New York, NY: Routledge/Taylor & Francis Group.

Andrews, J. (2007). Honoring elders through conversations about their lives. In H. Anderson & D. Gehart (Eds.), *Collaborative therapy: Relationships and conversations that make a difference* (pp. 149–166). New York, NY: Routledge/Taylor & Francis Group.

Beck, J. S. (1995). *Cognitive therapy: Basics and beyond.* New York, NY: Guilford.

Becker, A. E., Hadley Arrindell, A., Perloe, A., Fay, K., & Striegel-Moore, R. H. (2010). A qualitative study of perceived social barriers to care for eating disorders: Perspectives from ethnically diverse health care consumers. *International Journal of Eating Disorders, 43*(7), 633–647. doi:10.1002/eat.20755

Buser, J. K., Parkins, R. A., & Buser, T. J. (2014). Thematic analysis of the intersection of spirituality and eating disorder symptoms. *Journal of Addictions and Offender Counseling, 35,* 97–113. doi:10.1002/j.2161-1874.2014.00029.x

Cassin, S. E., & von Ranson, K. M. (2007). Short communication: Is binge eating experienced as an addiction? *Appetite, 49,* 687–690. doi:10.1016/j.appet.2007.06.012

Ellis, A. (1999). Why rational-emotive therapy to rational emotive behavior therapy? *Psychotherapy: Theory, Research, Practice, Training, 36*(2), 154–159. doi:10.1037/h0087680

Fallon, P., & Wisniewski, L. (2013). A system of evidenced-based techniques and collaborative clinical interventions with a chronically ill patient. *International Journal of Eating Disorders, 46*(5), 501–506. doi:10.1002/eat.22108

Feinsilver, D., Murphy, E., & Anderson, H. (2007). Women at a turning point: A transformational feast. In H. Anderson & D. Gehart (Eds.), *Collaborative therapy: Relationships and conversations that make a difference* (pp. 269–290). New York, NY: Routledge/Taylor & Francis Group.

Fernández, E., Cortés, A., & Tarragona, M. (2007). You make the path as you walk: Working collaboratively with people with eating disorders. In H. Anderson & D. Gehart (Eds.), *Collaborative therapy: Relationships and conversations that make a difference* (pp. 129–147). New York, NY: Routledge/Taylor & Francis Group.

Fursland, A., Byrne, S., Watson, H., La Puma, M., Allen, K., & Byrne, S. (2012). Enhanced Cognitive behavior therapy: A single treatment for all eating disorders. *Journal of Counseling & Development, 90*(3), 319–329. doi:10.1002/j.1556-6676.2012.00040.x

Gee, A., & Troop, N. A. (2003). Shame, depressive symptoms and eating, weight and shape concerns in a non-clinical sample. *Eating and Weight Disorders, 8*(1), 72–75. doi:10.1007/BF03324992

Gehart, D. (2007). Creating space for children's voices: A collaborative and playful approach to working with children and families. In H. Anderson & D. Gehart (Eds.), *Collaborative therapy: Relationships and conversations that make a difference* (pp. 183–196). New York, NY: Routledge/Taylor & Francis Group.

Gehart-Brooks, D. R., & Lyle, R. R. (1999). Client and therapist perspectives of change in collaborative language systems: An interpretative ethnography. *Journal of Systemic Therapies, 18*(4), 58–77.

Gehart, D., Tarragona, M., & Bava, S. (2007). A collaborative approach to research and inquiry. In H. Anderson & D. Gehart (Eds.), *Collaborative therapy: Relationships and conversations that make a difference* (pp. 367–387). New York, NY: Routledge/Taylor & Francis Group.

Geller, J., Brown, K. E., Zaitsoff, S. L., Goodrich, S., & Hastings, F. (2003). Collaborative versus directive interventions in the treatment of eating disorders: Implications for care providers. *Professional Psychology: Research & Practice, 34*(4), 406. doi:10.1037/0735-7028.34.4.406

Haarakangas, K., Seikkula, J., Alakare, B., & Aaltonen, J. (2007). Open dialogue: An approach to psychotherapeutic treatment of psychosis in northern Finland. In H. Anderson & D. Gehart (Eds.), *Collaborative therapy: Relationships and conversations that make a difference* (pp. 221–233). New York, NY: Routledge/Taylor & Francis Group.

Hagedorn, W. B. (2009). The call for a new Diagnostic and Statistical Manual of Mental Disorders diagnosis: Addictive disorders. *Journal of Addictions & Offender Counseling, 29*(2), 110–127. doi:10.1002/j.2161-1874.2009.tb00049.x

Hansen, J. T., & Scholl, M. B. (2018). Chapter 1: Introduction to postmodern perspectives on contemporary counseling issues. In M. B. Scholl & J. T. Hansen (Eds.), *Postmodern perspective on contemporary counseling issues: Approaches across diverse settings.* New York, NY: Oxford University Press.

Hardman, R. K., Berrett, M. E., & Richards, P. S. (2003). Spirituality and ten false beliefs and pursuits of women with eating disorders: Implications for counselors. *Counseling & Values, 48*(1), 67–78. doi:10.1002/j.2161-007X.2003.tb00276.x

Hudson, J. I., Coit, C. E., Lalonde, J. K., & Pope, H. G. (2012). By how much will the proposed new DSM-5 criteria increase the prevalence of binge eating disorder? *International Journal of Eating Disorders, 45*(1), 139. doi:10.1002/eat.20890

Hudson, J. I., Hiripi, E., Pope, H. G., & Kessler, R. C. (2007). The prevalence and correlates of eating disorders in the national comorbidity survey replication. *Biological Psychiatry, 61*, 348–358. doi:10.1016/j.biopsych.2006.03.040

Humphry, T. A., & Ricciardelli, L. A. (2004). The development of eating pathology in Chinese-Australian women: Acculturation vs. culture clash. *The International Journal of Eating Disorders, 35*, 579–588. doi:10.1002/eat.10269

Kater, K. (2010). New pathways: Applying acceptance and commitment therapy to the treatment of eating disorders. In M. Maine, B. McGilley, & D. W. Bunnell (Eds.), *Treatment of eating disorders: Bridging the research–practice gap* (pp. 163–180). San Diego, CA: Elsevier Academic Press. doi:10.1016/B978-0-12-375668-8.10010-5

London, S., & Rodríguez-Jazcilevich, I. (2007). The development of a collaborative learning and therapy community in an educational setting: From alienation to invitation. In H. Anderson & D. Gehart (Eds.), *Collaborative therapy: Relationships and conversations that make a difference* (pp. 235–249). New York, NY: Routledge/Taylor & Francis Group.

London, S., & Tarragona, M. (2007). Collaborative therapy and supervision in a psychiatric hospital. In H. Anderson & D. Gehart (Eds.), *Collaborative therapy: Relationships and conversations that make a difference* (pp. 251–267). New York, NY: Routledge/Taylor & Francis Group.

McDonough, M., & Koch, P. (2007). Collaborating with parents and children in private practice: Shifting and overlapping conversations. In H. Anderson & D. Gehart (Eds.), *Collaborative therapy: Relationships and conversations that make a difference* (pp. 167–181). New York, NY: Routledge/Taylor & Francis Group.

McNamee, S. (2007). Relational practices in education: Teaching as conversation. In H. Anderson & D. Gehart (Eds.), *Collaborative therapy: Relationships and conversations that make a difference* (pp. 313–335). New York, NY: Routledge/Taylor & Francis Group.

Miller, W. R., & Rollnick, S. (2002). *Motivational interviewing: Preparing people for change* (2nd ed.). New York, NY: Guilford.

Mustelin, L., Silén, Y., Raevuori, A., Hoek, H. W., Kaprio, J., & Keski-Rahkonen, A. (2016). The DSM-5 diagnostic criteria for anorexia nervosa may change its population prevalence and prognostic value. *Journal of Psychiatric Research, 77,* 85–91. doi:10.1016/j.jpsychires.2016.03.003

Oluyori, T. (2013). A systematic review of qualitative studies on shame, guilt and eating disorders. *Counselling Psychology Review, 28*(4), 47–59.

Penn, P. (2007). Listening voices. In H. Anderson & D. Gehart (Eds.), *Collaborative therapy: Relationships and conversations that make a difference* (pp. 99–107). New York, NY: Routledge/Taylor & Francis Group.

Prochaska, J. O., DiClemente, C. C., & Norcross, J. C. (1992). In search of how people change: Applications to addictive behaviors. *American Psychologist, 47*(9), 1102–1114. doi:10.1037/0003-066X.47.9.1102

Rollnick, S., & Miller, W. R. (1995). What is motivational interviewing? *Behavioural and Cognitive Psychotherapy, 23*(4), 325–334. doi:10.1017/S135246580001643X

Sandoz, E. K., Wilson, K. G., & Dufrene, T. (2010). *Acceptance and commitment therapy for eating disorders: A process-focused guide to treating anorexia and bulimia.* Oakland, CA: New Harbinger.

Schüler, J., & Kuster, M. (2011). Binge eating as a consequence of unfulfilled basic needs: The moderating role of implicit achievement motivation. *Motivation & Emotion, 35*(1), 89–97. doi:10.1007/s11031-010-9200-y

Seikkula, J. (2002). Open dialogues with good and poor outcomes for psychotic crises: Examples from families with violence. *Journal of Marital and Family Therapy, 28*(3), 263–274. doi:10.1111/j.1752-0606.2002.tb01183.x

Seikkula, J., Alakare, B., & Aaltonen, J. (2001). Open dialogue in psychosis II: A comparison of good and poor outcome. *Journal of Constructivist Psychology, 14*(4), 267. doi:10.1080/107205301750433405

Seikkula, J., Alakare, B., Aalotonen, J., Holma, J., Rasinkangas, A., & Lehtinen, V. (2003). Open dialogue approach: Treatment principles and preliminary results of a two-year follow-up on first episode schizophrenia. *Ethical Human Sciences & Services, 5*(3), 163–182

St. George, S., & Wulff, D. (1998). Integrating the client's voice within case reports. *Journal of Systemic Therapies, 17*(4), 3–13.

Stice, E., Marti, C. N., & Rohde, P. (2013). Prevalence, incidence, impairment, and course of the proposed DSM-5 eating disorder diagnoses in an 8-year prospective community study of young women. *Journal of Abnormal Psychology, 122*(2), 445–457. doi:10.1037/a0030679

Trace, S. E., Thornton, L. M., Root, T. L., Mazzeo, S. E., Lichtenstein, P., Pedersen, N. L., & Bulik, C. M. (2012). Effects of reducing the frequency and duration criteria for binge eating on lifetime prevalence of bulimia nervosa and binge eating disorder: Implications for DSM-5. *International Journal of Eating Disorders, 45*(4), 531–536. doi:10.1002/eat.20955

Tylka, T. L., & Subich, L. M. (1999). Exploring the construct validity of the eating disorder continuum. *Journal of Counseling Psychology, 46*(2), 268–276. doi:10.1037/0022-0167.46.2.268

Vandereycken, W., & Van Humbeeck, I. (2008). Denial and concealment of eating disorders: a retrospective survey. *European Eating Disorders Review: The Journal of the Eating Disorders Association, 16*(2), 109–114. doi:10.1002/erv.857

Wagner, J. (2007). Trialogues: A means to answerability and dialogue in a prison setting. In H. Anderson & D. Gehart (Eds.), *Collaborative therapy: Relationships and conversations that make a difference* (pp. 203–220). New York, NY: Routledge/Taylor & Francis Group.

CHAPTER 7

The Practice of Possibilities

Using Dialectical Humanism to Help Clients

With Sexual Concerns

MEGAN SPECIALE AND MATTHEW E. LEMBERGER

Sexuality is woven into the tapestry of all human experience, serving as a source of vitality and motivation, a contributor to health and wellness, an identity, and a channel for human connection. Although sexuality is thoroughgoing in people's lives, the treatment of sexuality has generally been relegated to an area of therapeutic specialization (i.e., sex therapy or sexology), and many nonspecializing mental health professionals report receiving little to no sexuality-specific education or supervision during their careers (Russell, 2012; Sansone & Wiederman, 2000). This is problematic given that the majority of mental health professionals, regardless of clinical setting and population, will encounter clients with myriad sexuality- and gender-related concerns numerous times throughout their career (Southern & Cade, 2011). Without appropriate training, many generalist counseling professionals feel unprepared to discuss and treat sexual concerns with clients and often report feeling embarrassed, uncomfortable, and hesitant to discuss sexual issues with clients (Harris & Hays, 2008; Miller & Byers, 2010; Weerakoon, Jones, Pynor, & Kilburn-Watt, 2004).

Unease when talking about sexuality is common throughout the mental health field and, indeed, throughout the majority of society. Social and cultural value systems tend to prohibit or hinder the open discussion of sexuality topics, and it is unsurprising that many clients have internalized considerable shame and guilt that often reflect the dubious moral, political, and personal messages affixed to sexuality. This is especially true for nondominant and traditionally oppressed groups, such as women, sexual minorities, gender-nonconforming individuals, people of color, children and the elderly, and people with disabilities, whose sexuality has been marginalized and silenced in society (Hall & Graham, 2014). Thus, there is great potential in the humanistically oriented therapeutic space, which could offer a liberating and empowering counternarrative to negative cultural messages and may facilitate opportunities for exploration of clients' sexual wants, desires, and emotional reactions without judgment. Central to this endeavor is the counselor's recognition of the social, cultural, historical, and political contexts by which sexuality is shaped, and the simultaneous recognition of the client's agentic capacity to influence her or his life and generate positive therapeutic change.

Despite the unique and ever-evolving personal and social aspects of sexuality, traditional models of sex therapy have been criticized as rigidly defining the activity and experience of sex by adopting a single and exact cause, expression, and meaning of sexual experiences (Kleinplatz, 2011). Such modernistic conceptualizations of sexuality have been critiqued as reductionistic and symptom focused, unresponsive to social and cultural factors of sexual health, and rooted in predominantly Western, male/phallus-centric, and heteronormative conceptualizations of sexual functioning (Kashak & Tiefer, 2001). Heteronormativity may be described as the "overarching system for organizing and regulating sexuality, whereby certain ways of acting, thinking and feeling about sex are privileged over others" (Cameron & Kulick, 2006, p. 9). For example, genital performance (e.g., erection, vaginal lubrication, orgasm) has been used as a hallmark of healthy or "successful" sexual functioning, as described in the pioneering work of Masters and Johnson (1966, 1970). In these early studies, the human sexual response was positioned as the linear metric of healthy and normal sexual functioning, a script utilized to assign highly directive behavioral interventions directed toward the alleviation of immediate physical symptoms. Feminist scholars have since argued that such a posture undermines the holism of a person— the totality of a person's unique positionality in the world—and omits the psychological, relational, and sociopolitical context (e.g., gender/power differences and cultural subjectivity) from etiological and diagnostic criteria (Kashak & Tiefer, 2001; Kleinplatz, 2012; Tiefer, 2010). Conversely, rather than pathologize or medicalize clients' sexual concerns, postmodern conceptualizations of sexuality are cognizant of the plurality of sexual experiencing and the dynamic relationship between sexual satisfaction and individual, relational, and environmental factors (Aanstoos, 2012).

Rarely are conversations pertaining to sexuality completely coherent or sequential; instead, they contain uncertain, emergent, or even seemingly contradictory elements. Given these complexities, linear, conventional, modernist versions of sexuality counseling, which generally prescribe particular goals and outcomes, often fail to take the richness of sexual experience into account. More specifically, in the spirit of modernistic ideology, many of the historical approaches to counseling (e.g., person-centered therapy; Rogers, 1957) endorse concepts such as an authentic relationship shared between counselor and client, a certain insight or actualized way of being as a laudable client outcome, or even new and specific ways of thinking, feeling, or behaving as the measure of therapeutic success (see Hansen, 2010, 2015; Slife & Fisher, 2000). Given the complexity of sexuality, postmodern counseling approaches that affirm multiple client experiences can be a useful alternative to modernist approaches.

Although there is great utility in emergent and nonprescriptive therapeutic approaches, critics of radical postmodern approaches have cautioned that, without an anchor to the tangible and ultimately quantifiable aspects of a client's narrative, one may fall into the trappings of nihilistic subjectivity—a sort of falling down the rabbit hole of the unknowable, constantly changing nature of human experience (Sokal & Bricmont, 1998). In the case of sexuality, there are fundamental biological and phenomenological qualities of sexual experience that are undeniably true (i.e., the role of selective serotonin reuptake inhibitors in diminishing libido or the painful influence of misogynist ideology on an adolescent female client's experience of being "slut shamed" at school). Therefore, just as modernist conceptions of sex and sexuality are insufficient, radical postmodern versions of counseling may be similarly lacking. As an alternative, an approach that serves to bridge modern and postmodern epistemology can oscillate between the certain and uncertain, the settled and impermanent, the profane and the political, and so on to more thoroughly support the client.

THE BASES OF A DIALECTICAL HUMANISM

Dialectical humanism is not a new or conclusive approach to counseling practice; rather, it was conceived as a framework to reconcile shortcomings in extreme modern or postmodern forms of counseling. The shortcomings of radical adherence to either strict modernism or postmodernism are particularly problematic in the context of sexuality counseling. An unwavering affiliation to modernism might lead the practitioner to believe that there is a distinct and quintessential sexuality, or a universally acceptable way to diagnose, treat, and evaluate sexual difficulties. Alternatively, adopting un-regulated postmodern conceptions of sex can be unhelpful, as there might be a lack of core principles to guide treatment. Although both manners of conceiving reality are useful, one without the other might lead to a myopic practice of sex therapy, which would not be useful to clients, counselors, or even the larger society.

The authors suggest an alternative to sex therapy approaches that stand exclusively on modernist or postmodernist suppositions. Dialectical humanism is a conceptual frame that incorporates both modernism and postmodernism (see Lemberger & Lemberger-Truelove, 2016). As it applies to therapeutic practice, dialectical humanism posits certain basic, humanistic assumptions about clients, but, at the same time, the therapeutic content is always understood flexibly and dynamically over time and across circumstances. For example, the dignity of the client is regarded as a patent truth, and yet two very divergent ways of being can be equally dignified, even if they are in conflict with each other or the pre-vailing social mores.

Firmly modernist conceptions of people provide a certain stability and comfort in what is true and nonnegotiable, but this can also result in ideologies or practices where one person or group marginalizes others in the name of so-called truth or righteousness. In fact, radically modernist conceptions of people are preposterous. That is, even if there are objective truths, the perception and communication of these truths would neces-sarily be contaminated by the structure of language, perceptual processes, unique perspectives, and sociocultural mores (Hansen, 2007b). Therefore, there can never be a pristine understanding or communication of a hy-pothetical objective truth. In a similar way, if one were to take postmod-ernism to its logical conclusion, the lack of postmodern criteria to select from among multiple possibilities might ultimately paralyze therapeutic decision making. Dialectical humanism, as a third way, endorses certain humanistic principles (e.g., dignity of all clients) but also has the ideolog-ical flexibility to accept multiple, and even contradictory, perspectives. In short, dialectical humanism therapists oscillate between modernist and postmodernist conceptions, practices, and evaluations at each stage of the therapeutic process.

In practice, dialectical humanism is not as complex as it might seem; in fact, dialectical humanism is consistent with prevailing practices in therapy, whether or not these practices are specific to sex therapy. When a therapist attempts to help a client, it is useful to employ modernist cer-tainty that the client exists and that this existence has in some manner affected what they bring to the therapeutic relationship. The paradig-matic base of the dialectical humanism framework is consistent with traditional humanistic psychology in that the following postulates are maintained:

1. Human beings supersede the sum of their parts. They cannot be reduced to components.
2. Human beings operate in a human relational context.
3. Human beings are aware and aware of being aware—that is, they are conscious. Human consciousness always includes an awareness of one-self in the context of other people.
4. Human beings have some choice and, with that, responsibility.
5. Human beings are intentional, aim at goals, are aware that they cause future events, and seek meaning, value, and creativity. (Greening, 2007, n.p.)

While valuable, each of these postulates implies the existence of a stable and potentially knowable self and therefore risks falling into a number of modernist philosophical traps (see Hansen, 2007a, 2009). Dialectical humanism reshapes the modernistic elements of traditional humanistic psychology by allowing for a flexible, postmodern interpretation of core humanistic assumptions. Stated otherwise, modernistic implications such as a knowable truth, teleology, reflexive understanding between people, and so on are simultaneously maintained but also recolored to include personal and social complexity and variation. From this perspective, counselors deemphasize the search for essential client truths by focusing on the client's total phenomenological experiencing of sexuality, while recognizing that sexuality, race, gender, class, ability status, and other identity constructions exist within hegemonic power structures.

Consistent with traditional postmodern ideology, dialectical humanism endorses multiple truths as permissible; in fact, in dialectical humanistic counseling, multiple truths are almost always pursued. In this way, dialectical humanism encourages and legitimizes multiple possibilities and outcomes.

Just as the modernistic elements of humanism must be examined, post-modern ideology must also be reconsidered or risk falling into irrelevance for counseling. On the surface, postmodern approaches by themselves are useful by providing the grounds to accept a variety of client experiences or narratives. Unfortunately, what this ideology lacks is a rope back to reality. If one considers an extreme postmodern position (i.e., there are multiple truths, influences, or ends pertaining to singular events or circumstances), the sheer vastness of possibilities may preclude a focused direction of treatment. This is to say, either there are limits to the number of possible truths or postmodernism remains open to infinite truths into perpetuity.

In this regard, contemporary philosophers Dreyfus and Taylor (2015) illustrate the shortcomings of postmodernism when they describe this ideology as largely mediational between the self and the world. This is to say, mediational knowledge for any given individual and the external world is indirect, and therefore uncertain and subject to varied interpretation. As an alternative, they suggest that "the phenomenological description of our direct coping with everyday things shows that we are not imprisoned in our skins or minds, but are open to a shared world, there may be phenomena revealed in our scientific practice that show that our true theories correspond to an independently existing universe" (Dreyfus & Taylor, 2015, p. 147). Their alternative contact theory suggests that the self is always embodied with the world, in dialogue with others within that world, and that truth in science predicates multiple experiences of that truth. Dialectical humanism adopts this position of the self's access to the truth of the world and also acknowledges the disorienting effects of a world that is in flux, generally unfair, and subject to time.

The praxis of dialectical humanism is influenced by a version of the philosopher Hegel's dialectical method: the thesis, antithesis, and synthesis. For Hegel, an individual's perception of almost any initiating experience or proposition may constitute the formation of a thesis. The thesis must be recognizable and comprehendible to the self and others and, for each thesis derived from one's experience, an antithesis (i.e., an alternative proposition juxtaposed to the thesis) exists. Put simply, the thesis and antithesis are alternating perceptions of the initiating experience. To complete the dialectical scheme, a synthesis ensues where both the thesis and antithesis sustain their distinctness and province, yet the combined influence of each perpetuates a new, more mature experience or personal phenomenology. For the praxis of dialectical humanism, unlike Hegel, the synthesis is not a newfangled blend of the thesis and antithesis; rather, it more closely reflects a metamodernist position (see Vermeulen & Van Den Akker, 2010), where the self can oscillate between the thesis and antithesis, and therefore any synthesis is always wholly each but never completely one or the other. The practical implication of this very complex dynamic is something similar to critical thinking for the client and counselor. The proclivity to oscillate between what might be true and how that truth is unavoidably affected by the influences of relationships, epoch, and the immeasurable other social factors provides the client the stability to operate in the world yet remain open to its complexity.

There are a number ethical and praxis considerations that follow from dialectical humanism. First, one thesis cannot ascend or dominate the other thesis. For example, what initially appears to be a thesis pertaining to self-interest must be dialectically influenced by an antithesis that emphasizes an obligation to take the interests of others into account. This is especially pertinent for sexuality counseling, as sexual activity involves gratification of one's impulses while, at the same time, consideration of the needs of a partner. For example, hedonistic sexual drives cannot justify predatory sexual behaviors, as such behaviors unequivocally limit the self-interests of others. Social stigmas may similarly infringe upon the experience of a person or group of people, such as beliefs that condemn or demonize certain sexual identities. Dialectical humanism maintains the concept of self enough to protect clients from dehumanization; on the other hand, it does not reify a stable self to the point where it risks becoming stuck in a single identity (e.g., heteronormativity).

Dialectical Humanistic Techniques for Practice

Because dialectical humanism is a metasystem in which other counseling orientations may operate, it can easily overlay and inform most therapeutic techniques. Consider one of the most basic counseling techniques: the open-ended question. The general purpose of an open-ended question is to elicit important information from a client, but the question is also framed in a way that is designed to cause the client to reconsider his or her suppositions. Unfortunately, open-ended questions are often asked in a manner whereby the counselor is leading the client to one or two reasonable responses, as opposed to the question being open enough to elicit a wide array of client responses.

A modernistic manner of asking an open-ended, sexuality-focused question might be the following:

COUNSELOR: What sexual activities do you find to be most satisfying with your partner?

At first blush, this example question appears to focus on the client's perspective, but a deeper consideration illustrates the modernistic value of singularity and stability. For example, the question presumes that sexual behaviors satisfy the client, and she or he possesses a clear hierarchy of preferred sexual activities. Furthermore, this manner of asking the question assumes that preferred sexual behaviors are stable for the client over time, or across varying contexts.

A postmodern alternative to this question might be something like the following example:

COUNSELOR: How do you experience your sexual relationship with your partner?

From this question, the counselor might elicit the same client responses as the modernistic question. However, this postmodern style of questioning may facilitate client responses that are not limited by the assumptions of singularity and stability.

From a dialectical humanistic perspective, neither the modern nor postmodern form of the question is preferred; instead, each may have utility based on the unique counseling relationship. Dialectical humanism affords the counselor the latitude to oscillate between these two types of questions. For example, it is generally desirable that the postmodern form of the question is asked first, as to provide the greatest number of client responses. In this way, the client's values and experiences drive the session, not the assumptions of the counselor. Using the client's response to the initiating postmodern question, the counselor can then include specific (modernistic) aspects of the client's response to ask a question that is more directional or certain. Finally, the counselor can then follow the more specific modernistic question with a third open-ended question that integrates both elements. An example of a synthesis question might be, "Considering your description of your current sexual relationship, how might this insight shape the satisfaction you experience with your partner?"

Another dialectical humanistic technique is demonstrated in the therapeutic reflection of feeling, a communication strategy commonly used to convey accurate empathic understanding and deepen the emotionality of the counseling session. For major humanistic counseling models, therapeutic empathy hinges upon the therapist's ability to correctly discern and reflect the client's emotional state (Rogers, 1957). Conversely, postmodernism dictates that the accuracy of the counselor's reflection is impossible to discern; therefore, the validity of reflective statements is judged by client resonance with the statement, not by their supposed truth value. From the dialectical humanist perspective, the counselor acknowledges that therapeutic reflection must resonate with the client so it may be experienced as personally relevant. In this way, the inexactitude of the counselor's reflection does not indicate therapeutic failure but is regarded as a generative opportunity for the client to form new truths and possibilities of experience.

Dialectical Humanism in Research

Dialectical humanism exists outside of the standard modernist and postmodernist research divide. In this way, philosophically it is difficult to fit dialectical humanism within so-called evidence-based research. Also, dialectical humanism is an emergent metatheoretical framework. Therefore, no field tests have been conducted to measure the efficacy of this approach.

Although the dearth of specific evidence appears to be a limitation of the dialectical humanistic approach, there does appear to be some inferential evidence in support of its effectiveness. Discussing his systematic analyses of psychotherapy outcome research, Wampold (2012) asserted that all effective psychotherapies have key humanistic elements. As such, the inclusion of dialectical humanism as an overlay into extant counseling practices endorses and draws from the vast literature in support of counseling outcomes.

DIALECTICAL HUMANISM IN PRACTICE: THE CASE OF PARKER AND RENEE

To illustrate the principles of dialectical humanism, the authors propose the case of Parker and Renee, a composite illustration of previous clients with identifying details altered for anonymity. At the start of therapy, Parker and Renee had been partnered monogamously for almost 4 years. Parker was a White, bisexual female in her mid-30s and worked as a freelance website designer and part-time barista at a local coffee shop. Renee, a Mexican American transgender man, was in his late 30s and worked as a substance abuse counselor at a nearby homeless shelter. When Parker first called to schedule an appointment, she reported that they were seeking counseling to address increasing feelings of disconnection sparked from work stress, financial strain associated with buying their first home, and asymmetrical intimacy needs. Parker indicated that long-standing conflicts led to frequent bickering and confirmed that there had been no previous physical or emotional abuse in the relationship.

The couple was warm and affectionate to one another in the first session, recalling with fondness memories of the early stages of their relationship. Parker and Renee reported that their relationship had been mostly joyous and invigorating, though they described facing several stressful events together that had weighed heavily on their intimate connection. At the end of their first year, Parker pursued a lifelong dream and began attending a master of fine arts program, which she described as the most rigorous and challenging experience of her life. Producing art was a deeply vulnerable and passionate process for her, which sometimes detracted from her ability to connect with Renee. Around Parker's second semester in school, Renee was unexpectedly let go from his job as a school counselor when the charter school where he had worked for 6 years lost funding for his position. As the major financial provider while Parker was in graduate school, Renee's unemployment was a major blow to the couple's financial well-being. Renee finally found work at the homeless shelter after about 6 months of searching.

In the early stages of these major transitions, the couple expressed that their sexual connection had remained passionate and intense. However, after Renee began working again, the couple indicated that sex had become less frequent, which they both assumed was normal, considering the circumstances. Parker reported feeling satisfied with their sexual relationship, which she described as "a whole other world" compared to her previous relationships, in part because her sexual experiences had mostly been with cisgender men (i.e., men whose biological sex and gender identity aligned as male). She felt that Renee's experiences as a transgender person contributed to his sensitivity and reverence of physical intimacy, evidenced by his attunement with her body and his attentiveness to her sexual pleasure. When asked about his sexuality with Parker, Renee expressed satisfaction with the quality and frequency of sex in the relationship. He also indicated feeling uncomfortable with sexual touch on his chest and genitals, which he attributed to his experiences of being transgender and the general incongruence he felt with the biologically female parts of his body. He described Parker as a responsive, intuitive lover who worked hard to respect and value these boundaries, though she would sometimes feel hurt and embarrassed when he had to remind her that certain sex acts were off limits. Parker agreed and explained that her attraction to Renee included the masculine and feminine parts of him, and she would often "get carried away and forget the rules."

In the year preceding counseling, the couple reported that they were having sex about once per month and more frequently shared other forms of intimacy, such as cuddling, sharing massages, showering, and cooking meals together. Though the couple conceded that sex was at an all-time low, both partners reported feeling generally satisfied with their level of physical intimacy. The issue, they stated, was that not having sex instigated other problems in their relationship. Parker described:

> I know it doesn't make sense. I mean, I'm in my 30s—my sexual prime, right? But if I'm honest, I really am happy with our physical connection. It's not all about having orgasms anymore. It's about feeling Renee next to me in bed, holding his hand at the supermarket. Yet I feel like something might be wrong with us, like we should want to have sex with each other, if we were really as happy as we think we are.

Renee described similar feelings, as well as the impression that the lack of sexual intimacy had triggered feelings of insecurity. Namely, he feared that his unemployment had caused Parker to lose respect for him and that she was no longer sexually attracted to him. Parker ensured that this was not the case and the couple agreed that their decreased sex life was sparking internal feelings of shame and guilt for both of them. Renee described, "All of our friends talk about this headboard-rocking, mind-numbing sex and it makes me feel like Parker and I have gotten off track somehow. That's why we're here. We want to get that passion back."

Therapeutic Process

Establishing the Therapeutic Relationship

From a dialectical humanistic perspective, the therapeutic relationship shared between the counselor and client(s) is essential, the foundation upon all other therapeutic work transpires. Consistent with humanistic and postmodern approaches to counseling, the relationship should be collaborative, supportive, engaged, and empathic. The dialectical nature of a postmodern form of humanism suggests that the counselor elicit the client's personally held perceptions of experience while tasking the client to consider different possible story arcs. With Parker and Renee, the counselor first learns about each partner's experiences that have contributed to them seeking counseling—the decreasing physical intimacy, reoccurring conflicts, troubling insecurities—then each partner is asked to consider the implications of these feelings of distress: "How do you experience shame within the context of your friends versus when you are alone or with Parker? How do the dynamics of these relationships shape your sense of insecurity?" In this way, the development of the therapeutic relationship is more than mere information gathering but, instead, it is a period of allegiance aimed at expanding conceptions of self, others, and the world, including the client's history and extending into the therapeutic relationship.

Clarifying Sexual Meanings

Practitioners who utilize a dialectical humanistic perspective acknowledge that any therapeutic relationship that does not take into account the ever-evolving nature of the client's worldview may run the risk of forcing the client toward potentially inappropriate, limiting, or unnecessary therapeutic processes and outcomes. The idea that a lone, reducible *cause* of disturbance is expunged as the counselor and client introduce the idea that each disturbance can contain multiple histories, influencers, limitations, and interpretations. In this way, as the therapeutic relationship is cultivated, the client can experience acceptance, as each story possibility in the dialectic is permitted. This process of dialectical relationship building thus extends into other therapeutic functions, including acceptance of diverse interventions and outcomes in the counseling process.

In the preceding case illustration of Parker and Renee, a differently orientated counselor might hastily assume that the many stressors reported by the clients were necessarily the factors that had caused their decline in sexual connection. Simply reducing the couple's problems to financial stress neglects the individual, shared, and emergent influences that led to these happenings. Furthermore, reductions of the couple's experiences would imply that a single and stable therapeutic remedy is possible. For instance, the clients reported feeling distressed by their decreasing physical intimacy, though it was unclear whether either partner's distress had resulted from the actual lack of sex or rather from the fears and negative assumptions they associated with "not having enough sex." Despite describing feelings of satisfaction elsewhere in her relationship, Parker reported fearing that there was something inherently broken about a sexless relationship; the dialectical humanistic counselor elicits Parker's further clarification of the implied meanings beneath these experiences. Societal mores about sexual frequency in a relationship are mixed and often confusing. Self-help books and other mainstream media outlets imply that too much sex is a sign of unhealthy coping or some impulse pathology, whereas too infrequent sexual episodes with a partner are a sign of disconnection, sublimated resentment, or evidence of an extrarelational affair. By learning more about how these cultural messages influence Parker's sexual belief system, the therapist comes to see the distress as a dynamic constellation of assumptions about what is considered "ideal" sexuality.

Deconstructing Sexual Scripts

The postmodern aspect of a dialectical humanistic approach further compels the counselor and client(s) to challenge reductionist and normative beliefs pertaining to definitions of healthy/diseased or normal/abnormal sexuality. The postmodern aspect of this approach results in critical reflection of the influences of social mores and habits, particularly oppressive and hegemonic social influences that affect the client's conceptions of self, others, the world, and one's behaviors and beliefs. By questioning and critically examining heteronormative influences, the counselor and client are able to consider and adopt alternative definitions of sexuality. In this regard, the dialectical humanistic perspective also allows the counselor and client to consider the personal and social utility of myriad sexual preferences, values, and expressions. From the case example, challenging the socially constructed meaning of "enough sex" might shed light on the potentially performance-focused and heteronormative values that have contributed to the clients' feelings of relational doubt and failure. Such influences might lead the couple to conflate the health of their relationship with these social mores, thus influencing both partners to judge the validity of the relationship based on standards that may be in misalignment with the couple's unique needs or desires.

Reimagining Sexual Possibilities

The humanistic adjunct to the largely postmodern design of a dialectical humanistic therapeutic encounter is the significance placed on personal phenomenology. The dismantling of heteronormative definitions of sexuality stokes new perceptual possibilities for the couple, but the unique manner in which it is internalized and expressed is filtered through the uniqueness of each partner's being. In this way, the client's experiences in counseling, as a social influence colored by the introduction of postmodern possibilities, is not simply a consequence of her or his exposure, but rather the unique merger of historic, emergent, personal, and social possibilities of meaning structures.

The dialectical reconstruction of meaning also affords a new possibility of acceptance, both personal and social, that is not necessarily passive or complicit with past experiences of disturbance. For example, through counseling, Parker and Renee may come to recognize the many implicit and overt factors influencing their sexual relationship and, readied with this new insight, experience new possibilities of intimate satisfaction. Equipped with a more mindful state of consciousness, the clients are able to generate various personal and social possibilities, which, given that multiple narratives are reasonable in any client circumstance, process, or outcome, contribute toward continued mindful acceptance of the clients' evolving reactions and internal experiences.

Summary of Therapeutic Process

In working with Parker and Renee from a dialectical humanistic perspective, the counselor is able to ameliorate the philosophical tensions between modern and postmodern frames of counseling. Upon establishing the therapeutic relationship, the counselor calls upon the clients to offer their respective conceptualizations of the issue, emphasizing the fallible, ever-changing, and multifaceted decisions and meanings the clients may present. In this sense, the clients are unburdened by the task of finding the exact nature of the problem, which renders an exact cure or solution to the couple's dilemma unnecessary. Contrary to modernistic approaches, the counselor entertains numerous possible reasons for the sexual problem rather than attempting to excavate a singular, inerrant explanation.

IMPLICATIONS AND LIMITATIONS OF DIALECTICAL HUMANISM

An important consideration when implementing this approach is that dialectical humanism is not intended as a stand-alone counseling intervention. Therefore, as a metatheoretical model, dialectical humanism is effectual insofar as it is coupled with the basic factors of the therapeutic alliance, such as empathy, authenticity, respect, and cultural responsivity. The dialectical humanist approach may also serve as a foundational theoretical base for most evidence-based counseling approaches. Consider, for example, a client with sexual distress originating from a strong physiological component, such as in the case of medicine- or hormone-induced erectile difficulties, sexual arousal issues, and some genito-pelvic pain disorders. Though the therapeutic protocol may require more modernistic behavioral interventions, dialectical humanism would serve as a useful guide to the assessment, intervention, treatment planning, and goal-setting stages of the counseling process. As such, the client's visceral or embodied experience of her sexuality may be more wholly understood by exploring how distressing sexual responses and sensations have been affected perceptually by any number of things, including individual perspective, cultural mores, epoch, or otherwise.

A common critique of postmodern therapeutic approaches is that the practice of eliciting several evolving and conflicting client truths may in fact hinder the development of a specific therapeutic action plan during initial stages of treatment. From the dialectical humanistic perspective, the counselor strives to cultivate a therapeutic milieu that evokes a complex understanding of the client's phenomenological worldview and thus recognizes that the treatment plan will likely shift and mature, reflecting the client's evolving meaning-making system. In turn, it is important that the dialectically oriented counselor collaborate with the client to delineate a therapeutic timeline with detailed and future-oriented steps for individual growth.

REFERENCES

Aanstoos, C. (2012). A phenomenology of sexual experiencing. In P. J. Kleinplatz (Ed.), *New directions in sex therapy: Innovations and alternatives* (pp. 51–67). London, UK: Routledge.

Cameron, D., & Kulick, D. (2006). *The language and sexuality reader.* New York, NY: Routledge.

Dreyfus, H., & Taylor, C. (2015). *Retrieving realism.* Cambridge, MA: Harvard University Press.

Greening, T. (2007). Five basic postulates of humanistic psychology. *Journal of Humanistic Psychology, 47*(1), NP.

Hall, K., & Graham, C. (2014). Culturally sensitive sex therapy: The need for shared meanings in the treatment of sexual problems. In M. Binik & K. Hall (Eds.), *Principles and practice of sex therapy* (5th ed., pp. 334–374). New York, NY: Guilford.

Hansen, J. T. (2007a). Epistemic contradictions in counseling theories: Implications for the structure of human experience and counseling practice. *Counseling and Values, 51*(2), 111–124.

Hansen, J. T. (2007b). Counseling without truth: Toward a neopragmatic foundation for counseling practice. *Journal of Counseling & Development, 85*(4), 423–430.

Hansen, J. T. (2009). Self-awareness revisited: Reconsidering a core value of the counseling profession. *Journal of Counseling & Development, 87*(2), 186–193.

Hansen, J. T. (2010). Consequences of the postmodernist vision: Diversity as the guiding value for the counseling profession. *Journal of Counseling & Development, 88,* 101–107.

Hansen, J. T. (2015). The relevance of postmodernism to counselors and counseling practice. *Journal of Mental Health Counseling, 37,* 355–363.

Harris, S. M., & Hays, K. W. (2008). Family therapist comfort with and willingness to discuss client sexuality. *Journal of Marital and Family Therapy, 34,* 239–250.

Kashak, E., & Tiefer, L. (Eds.). (2001). *A new view of women's sexual problems.* Binghamton, NY: Haworth Press.

Kleinplatz, P. J. (2011). Arousal and desire problems: Conceptual, research and clinical considerations or the more things change the more they stay the same. *Sexual and Relationship Therapy, 26,* 3–15.

Kleinplatz, P. J. (2012). Is that all there is? A new critique of the goals of sex therapy. In P. J. Kleinplatz (Ed.), *New directions in sex therapy: Innovations and alternatives.* London, UK: Routledge.

Lemberger, M. E., & Lemberger-Truelove, T. L. (2016). Bases for a more socially just humanistic praxis. *Journal of Humanistic Psychology, 56*(6), 571–580. doi:10.1177/0022167816652750.

Masters, W. H., & Johnson, V. E. (1966). *Human sexual response.* Boston, MA: Little, Brown & Co.

Masters, W. H., & Johnson, V. E. (1970). *Human sexual inadequacy.* Boston, MA: Little, Brown & Co.

Miller, S. A., & Byers, E. S. (2010). Psychologists' sexual education and training in graduate school. *Canadian Journal of Behavioural Science, 42,* 93–100.

Rogers, C. R. (1957). The necessary and sufficient conditions of therapeutic personality change. *Journal of Consulting Psychology, 21*(2), 95.

Russell, E. B. (2012). Sexual health attitudes, knowledge and clinical behaviors: Implications for counseling. *The Family Journal, 20,* 94–101.

Sansone, R. A., & Wiederman, M. W. (2000). Sexuality training for psychiatry residents: A national survey of program directors. *Journal of Sex and Marital Therapy, 26,* 249–256.

Slife, B. D., & Fisher, A. M. (2000). Modern and postmodern approaches to the free will/determinism dilemma in psychotherapy. *Journal of Humanistic Psychology, 40*(1), 80–107.

Sokal, A. D., & Bricmont, J. (1998). *Fashionable nonsense: Postmodern intellectuals' abuse of science.* New York, NY: Picador.

Southern, S., & Cade, R. (2011). Sexuality counseling: A professional specialization comes of age. *The Family Journal, 19,* 246–262.

Tiefer, L. (2010). Beyond the medical model of women's sexual problems: A campaign to resist the promotion of "female sexual dysfunction." *Sexual and Relationship Therapy, 25,* 197–205.

Vermeulen, T., & Van Den Akker, R. (2010). Notes on metamodernism. *Journal of Aesthetics & Culture, 2,* 1–15.

Wampold, B. E. (2012). Humanism as a common factor in psychotherapy. *Psychotherapy, 49*(4), 445–449.

Weerakoon, P., Jones, M. K., Pynor, R., & Kilburn-Watt, E. (2004). Allied health professional students' perceived level of comfort in clinical situations that have sexual connotations. *Journal of Allied Health, 33*(3), 189–193.

CHAPTER 8

Counselor–Advocate–Scholar Model

A Postmodern Approach to Social Justice Counseling

MANIVONG J. RATTS

Society is unjust. Those who are marginalized in society experience daily harassment, discrimination, and hate crimes, and they are often denied access to services such as employment, health care, and a quality education. Living in an unjust world creates a culture of advantages for those who are privileged at the expense of those who are marginalized. Such injustices lead to a culture of intolerance, and it takes a psychological toll on the mental health and well-being of individuals from marginalized communities (Ratts & Pedersen, 2014). Moreover, oppression can lead those who are marginalized in society to be susceptible to developing depression, low self-esteem, substance abuse problems, and, in extreme cases, suicidality. These symptoms are but just some of the surface-level indicators of the toxic impact oppression has on clients from marginalized communities.

Counselors who use traditional talk therapy may not realize these aforementioned symptoms could be manifestations of oppression. Moreover, counselors who rely on using traditional, modernist approaches to helping, which are often intrapsychically based, often fail to understand how client problems may be connected to larger systemic factors. Such counselors are more likely to conceptualize client problems as being internally driven rather than externally based. When client problems are considered to be inside the client, it becomes easy for the focus of change to be on the client and not the environment. Although individual counseling can help clients gain insight, it does not alter the systemic barriers that clients may present with in counseling. Therefore, any change that clients seek will be short-lived because traditional counseling does not address the external basis of the problem.

A complicating matter is that clients rarely express openly how oppressive conditions contribute to their well-being. Instead, clients are more likely to discuss struggles around mental health issues such as depression and low self-esteem. This phenomenon exists for a few reasons. First, we are socialized to not see oppression. Oppression is integrated into the fabric of our culture, institutions, and everyday lives and thus renders itself invisible. It is difficult to see how oppression influences individuals on a daily basis unless it is overtly blatant. Second, we live in a country that is founded on the ideals of freedom and equality. All citizens are supposed to have the same opportunities to achieve their goals and reach their potential if they work hard enough. To discount this belief would crumble the very essence of what the United States was founded upon. Third, people are socialized to take personal responsibility and not blame others for their predicament. To do so would mean not taking responsibility for one's life. Fourth, people are socialized to not talk about oppression in public. Issues of racism, sexism, heterosexism, classism, ableism, and religious oppression are to be discussed in private.

The responsibility for exploring the extent to which client problems are influenced by oppression is with the counselor (Ratts & Pedersen, 2014). Counselors have an ethical responsibility to address injustices affecting clients. Unfortunately, counselors are not adept at addressing issues of equity impacting clients. Counseling continues to be a process wherein counselors help clients gain insight, change behaviors, and help clients experience sensations from within the comforts of an office setting. Exploring client thoughts, behaviors, and feelings goes only so far. Being able to address the social environment requires a social justice approach to counseling. This realization led to the social justice counseling movement.

Social justice counseling, also referred to as the "fifth force" among counseling paradigms, follows the psychoanalytic, cognitive-behavioral, existential-humanistic, and multicultural forces in the field (Lewis & Arnold, 1998). The ACA *Code of Ethics* (2014) defines social justice as "the promotion of equity for all people and groups for the purpose of ending oppression and injustice affecting clients, students, counselors, families, communities, schools, workplaces, governments, and other social and institutional systems" (p. 21). Similarly, Counselors for Social Justice, a division of the ACA, defines social justice as:

A multifaceted approach to counseling in which practitioners strive to simultaneously promote human development and the common good through addressing challenges related to both individual and distributive justice. Social justice counseling includes empowerment of the individual as well as active confrontation of injustice and inequality in society as they impact clientele as well as those in their systemic contexts. In doing so, social justice counselors direct attention to the promotion of four critical principles that guide their work; equity, access, participation, and harmony. This work is done with a focus on the cultural, contextual, and individual needs of those served. (Counselors for Social Justice, 2016)

Understood in these definitions is the belief that clients come to counseling with psychological issues that sometimes are attributed to their social environment. For this reason, counselors, consistent with a postmodern perspective, must take a contextual approach (Neimeyer, 2009). They can no longer separate the person from his or her environment. The belief is that oppression has a debilitating effect on human growth and development. This belief is supported by empirical research. Mani, Mullainathan, Shafir, and Zhao's (2013) research concluded that poverty negatively impacts cognitive functioning. A study by the Gay, Lesbian, and Straight Education Network (GLSEN) found that the use of harsh and exclusionary discipline policies (e.g., punitive responses to harassment and assault) contributed to higher dropout rates and a reliance on alternative education for lesbian, gay, bisexual, and transgender (LGBT) youth (GLSEN, 2016).

Social justice has long been a part of the counseling profession (Toporek, Gerstein, Fouad, Roysircar, & Israel, 2006). This history is reflected in Kiselica and Robinson's (2001) historical outline detailing the major figures and events that helped shape the social justice perspective in counseling. Lewis, Lewis, and Dworkin (1971) were among the first to speak about revolutionizing the counseling profession and connecting it with social change efforts. These activist scholars saw the connection between psychological disorders and social injustices. This realization led Lewis and Lewis (1971) to call on counselor educators to prepare students for a new reality that addressed social justice issues in counseling. However, mass calls for social justice in counseling did not gain traction until the early 2000s in part because they lacked a collective effort in the field. It was not until the creation of Counselors for Social Justice (CSJ), a division of the ACA in 2001, that the social justice movement became more than a grassroots effort by activist counselors, scholars, and counselor educators.

Evidence of the growing need to integrate social justice in counseling is reflected in the preamble of the ACA *Code of Ethics* (American Counseling Association, 2014), which considers "promoting social justice" (p. 3) to be fundamental to the work of professional counselors. Similarly, the 2016 Council for Accreditation of Counseling and Related Educational Programs (CACREP) training standards encourage counselor educators to teach students about social justice and advocacy. That social justice is embedded within the ethical codes and CACREP training standards speaks to its importance in the field.

What makes social justice counseling unique from other postmodern helping approaches is that it calls on counselors to work in the office using individual counseling and in the community using advocacy counseling. Moreover, individual counseling, which takes place within a traditional office setting, can help address psychological issues experienced by clients from marginalized communities such as internalized oppression. In contrast, advocacy counseling, which involves working in the community realm, is used to alter the social environment that is the root of psychological stress and disorders. Some situations will call for one-on-one traditional talk therapy. Other situations will require that counselors work in the neighborhoods and communities in which clients reside. Counselors who operate from a social justice framework are more equipped to handle the individual and systemic issues clients bring. Given this perspective, it is possible that an initial session would occur in the office environment and then follow-up sessions would occur outside the office setting. The challenge with this multilevel approach to counseling is that counselors are often not trained to do community-based work. Most are trained to work individually with clients, couples, and even families from within an office structure.

SOCIAL JUSTICE COUNSELING AS POSTMODERN

What makes social justice counseling postmodern? Social justice counseling shares many similarities with postmodern counseling approaches. First, the belief that counseling is an egalitarian process is an assumption that undergirds the social justice perspective in counseling. Client and counselor are equals. The challenge for counselors is how to establish an egalitarian counseling relationship given the imbalance of power between client and counselor. Although counselors may believe that counseling is a collaborative and egalitarian process, clients may not always believe this to be the case. Second, clients are experts regarding their own experiences. Clients know their experiences better than anyone. There is no way for counselors to fully understand client experiences no matter how empathic a counselor may be. They only know what clients share. Third, reality is in the eyes of the beholder. Clients come to counseling with their own set of values, beliefs, biases, and experiences. Social justice counseling and postmodernism are grounded in a social constructivist philosophy (Foucault, 1977). Both entail recognition that knowledge is constructed by the knower. Meaning is related to power; those who are more powerful impose their realities, including oppressive narratives, onto those who are less powerful (Brown, 2012). Counselors must acknowledge and validate clients' realities even when they differ from their own. This requires setting aside any preconceived notions and biases they may have of clients. When counselors are able to do this, they may realize that client issues can sometimes be rooted in their surroundings. Counselors should recognize when dominant narratives are oppressive and assist clients in co-constructing alternative, empowering narratives (Brown, 2012). This requires that counselors come to the counseling process without a set of pre-established theories from which to operate. This is easier said than done.

Yet another characteristic that makes social justice counseling postmodern is that it embraces the fact that identity is plural (Hansen, 2005). Modernism, by contrast, asserts that one's identity is a single, unified construct. However, postmodernism entails the notion that each of us necessarily possesses multiple selves. For example, both counselors and clients bring multiple backgrounds to the counseling relationship. Each comes to counseling with intersecting identities as well as privileged and marginalized statuses that shape their life experiences, including the counseling relationship. Counselors perform multiple roles (i.e., counselor, advocate, scholar) depending upon the needs of the client and the context.

Despite these salient commonalities, many in the counseling profession do not make the connection between social justice and postmodernism. This lack of awareness may be in part because of the popular belief that social justice is a political ideology rather than a helping paradigm.

SOCIAL JUSTICE COUNSELING APPROACH: THEORIES AND MODELS

Until recently, the literature on social justice has primarily focused on defining it and determining its relevance in counseling. Being able to define and describe what social justice entails in counseling has been important to creating a shared understanding of what social justice means to counseling professionals. Likewise, determining how social justice fits within the scope of the counseling profession has helped to ascertain the possibilities of what counselors can do to address issues of oppression afflicting clients. As the social justice counseling movement continues to evolve, more theoretical paradigms will be needed along with research to determine their efficacy in the field.

Unlike other postmodern theories, there is no signature theory or technique within social justice counseling. The lack of a true theoretical model to conceptualize client problems, to determine counseling techniques, and to conceptualize the overall process of counseling from a social justice perspective makes it challenging to implement social justice in clinical practice. However, there are theoretical frameworks that have been developed which can aid counselors in integrating social justice in counseling practice. This section of the chapter will highlight three theoretical models and frameworks that are instrumental to shaping social justice counseling practice: (1) Advocacy Competencies, (2) the counselor–advocate–scholar model, and (3) the newly created Multicultural and Social Justice Counseling Competencies. Each theoretical model illustrates the different approaches to applying social justice in clinical practice with clients.

Advocacy Competencies

Dr. Jane Goodman, then president of the ACA (2000–2001), commissioned a taskforce (Drs. Judy Lewis, Reese House, and Rebecca Toporek) to develop competencies around social justice advocacy (Ratts, Toporek, & Lewis, 2010). Members of the taskforce represented K-12, college, and mental health fields to ensure that the new competencies were applicable across various counseling settings. Competencies around social justice advocacy were needed because of the lack of established guidelines to help professional counselors in their advocacy work. Asking counselors to engage in social justice advocacy without clear guidelines on how to do so borders on being unethical. This concern led to the creation of the Advocacy Competencies.

The work of the taskforce led to the development of the Advocacy Competencies (J. Lewis, Arnold, House, & Toporek, 2002). The Advocacy Competencies provide a framework for working with, and on behalf, of clients at the microlevel (client/student), mesolevel (community collaboration), and macrolevel (public arena) (see Figure 8.1). Each level includes two domains. Microlevel interventions take place at the client/student empowerment and the client/student advocacy domains. Work at this level involves empowering clients and advocating on behalf of clients when situations arise. Mesolevel interventions occur within the community collaboration and systems advocacy domains. This work requires collaboration with community agencies and schools. Macrolevel interventions occur within the public information and social/political advocacy domains. These domains involve working with legislators and addressing social injustices through political advocacy. Such work requires counselors to develop political astuteness.

What makes the Advocacy Competencies postmodern is they value the client's personal view of reality, including a conceptualization of problems

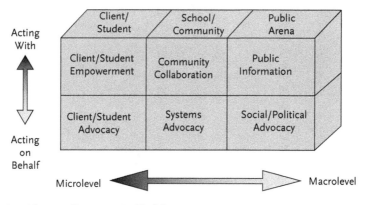

Figure 8.1: Advocacy Competencies Model

Source: Lewis, J., Arnold, M. S., House, R., & Toporek, R. (2002). ACA Advocacy Competencies, pp. 1–2. Retrieved from http://www.counseling.org/knowledge-center/competencies

as situated in the environment. Along the same lines as narrative therapy, the Advocacy Competencies entail externalizing the client's problem or conceptualizing the problem as something outside of the client (Combs & Freedman, 2012; Murdock, 2017). This approach contrasts with the dominant narrative, which commonly describes the problem as residing inside of the client. When counselors allow themselves to hear how client issues may be connected to their surroundings, they desire to do more than just listen (J. Lewis & Arnold, 1998). It leads counselors to want to intervene in two primary ways. First, perceiving the problem as external facilitates co-constructing an empowering alternative narrative. Second, this perception leads counselors to make necessary changes in the environment. Externalizing the problem enables counselors and clients to stand against social injustices (Murdock, 2017; Zimmerman & Dickerson, 2001). The Advocacy Competencies provide a framework to be able to listen to clients from their vantage point. When counselors use the Advocacy Competencies as a framework, they are able to situate client issues along the three levels of intervention: micro, meso, and macro.

Counselor–Advocate–Scholar Model

Ratts and Pedersen (2014) developed the counselor–advocate–scholar (CAS) model (see Figure 8.2). The CAS model is an offshoot of Mallinckrodt, Miles, and Levy's (2014) scientist-practitioner-advocate training model. The SPA model is used in psychology training programs to prepare psychologists for social justice work. The CAS model was developed

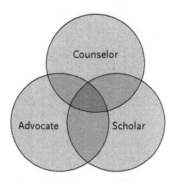

Figure 8.2: The Counselor–Advocate–Scholar (CAS) Model

Source: Ratts, M. J., & Pederson, P. B. (2014). Counselor-Advocate-Scholar model: Merging multiculturalism and social justice. In *Counseling for multiculturalism and social justice: Theory, integration, and application* (4th ed., pp. 51–58). Alexandria, VA: ACA.

to help practicing counselors integrate the roles of counselor, advocate, and scholar into their work with clients. The belief is that counseling, advocacy, and scholarship are critical roles for professional counselors who seek to do social justice work. Although professional counselors are familiar with enacting the role of counselor, they rarely engage in being an advocate, and even less so in being a scholar. Each role is articulated here in more detail.

Counseling involves working one-on-one with clients. Counseling typically occurs in an office setting. In this role, counselors explore the extent to which client problems are rooted in the environment. When counselors explore client issues more contextually, it provides them with insight into how advocacy and scholarship may be necessary because of the insight they gain from clients.

Advocacy entails working outside of the office to address an environmental barrier impeding on clients. Advocates understand that systemic barriers can impede psychological growth and development. The work advocates do in the community can provide rich insight into the ways social toxins such as oppression contribute to psychological stress and disorders for clients. This insight can inform an advocate's counseling work. Advocacy can also provide helping professionals with rich insight for developing meaningful scholarship. Moreover, being in the community and seeing firsthand the issues communities face can lead advocates to develop research that pertains to a specific community.

Scholars are critical thinkers. They use research in their quest to identify meaningful interventions that work with clients. Moreover, scholars understand that research can inform practice and that practice can inform research. To this end, they understand the value that qualitative and quantitative research has on their counseling and advocacy work. Practitioners in the field are ideal scholars. As counselors, they hear firsthand the struggles of clients; and as advocates, they see firsthand what occurs in the community. These direct experiences provide rich insight into ways to develop meaningful and culturally relevant research.

Consistent with postmodern ideology, the CAS model recognizes the need to conduct research that is not just quantitatively based. Postmodernism pushes against the belief that all things can be measured and that the best way to do this is through the scientific method. The CAS model assumes that research can be both qualitative and quantitative in nature. One method of research is not necessarily better than the other. Both types of research entail socially constructed knowledge. For example, in quantitative research the guiding hypotheses and the interpretation of the results represent constructed knowledge. In qualitative research, the data analysis commonly involves two or more researchers co-constructing agreed-upon themes. Whether one uses qualitative or quantitative methods for exploration should be based on the client and the situation. In other words, it is the client and the situation that should dictate what is appropriate and not a counselor's comfort with a research method. The challenge is that this perspective requires that counselors be skilled at both qualitative and quantitative research. Most people are skilled at either conducting qualitative- or quantitative-based research. To fulfill the scholar role, counselors will need to be adept at conducting mixed-methods research, which is a combination of qualitative and quantitative design.

Multicultural and Social Justice Counseling Competencies

The Multicultural and Social Justice Counseling Competencies (MSJCC) (see Figure 8.3) updates the Multicultural Counseling Competencies (MCC) (Ratts, Singh, Nassar-McMillan, Butler, & McCullough, 2016). In 2015 Dr. Carlos Hipolito-Delgado, president of the Association of Multicultural Counseling and Development (AMCD), commissioned a committee (Drs. Manivong J. Ratts, Anneliese Singh, Sylvia Nassar-McMillan, S. Kent Butler, and Julian McCullough) to update the MCC. The MSJCC is available on the ACA website: https://www.counseling.org/docs/default-source/competencies/multicultural-and-social-justice-counseling-competencies.pdf?sfvrsn=20. The MCC were updated to merge the multicultural and social justice counseling perspectives into one unified approach. Moreover, the MSJCC were developed to help counselors attend to intersectionalities in counseling and to provide a framework for a more contextual approach that balances individual counseling with social justice advocacy. The MSJCC are endorsed by the ACA, which suggests their relevance to the counseling profession.

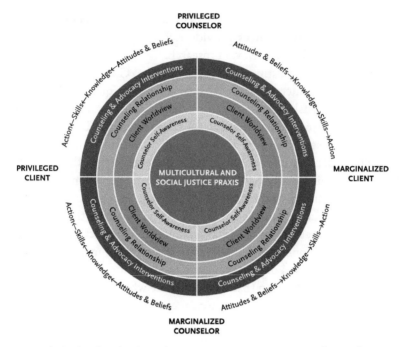

Figure 8.3: The Multicultural and Social Justice Counseling Competencies (MSJCC) Model

Source: Ratts, M. J., Singh, A. A., Nassar-McMillan, S., Butler, S. K., & McCullough, J. R. (2016). Multicultural and social justice counseling competencies: Guidelines for the counseling profession. *Journal of Multicultural Counseling and Development*, 44(1), 28–48.

Recall postmodernism's view of identity as plural rather than singular. In terms of intersectionalities, both clients and counselors bring to counseling a range of identities that shape the counseling relationship. Race, ethnicity, sexual orientation, social class status, age, ability status, and religion, to name a few, intersect in the lives of counselors and clients on a daily basis. Being cognizant of the counselor's and the client's intersecting identities is important to understanding their influence on the counseling relationship. The belief is that both client and counselor identities can influence the counseling relationship in positive and negative ways. For example, if a White counselor is uncomfortable and is not cognizant of one's White privilege, it may make it difficult to explore issues of racism with a client of color due to potential discomfort that may arise from such discussions. Likewise, a female survivor of domestic violence may have a preference for a counselor based on gender. Being able to explore this would be important to helping develop a meaningful counseling relationship for the client.

The MSJCC encourages counselors to take a contextual approach when exploring client problems and determining appropriate interventions and strategies. Once again, the postmodern perspective is plainly evident as counselors view competing narratives as socially constructed within diverse cultural contexts (Brown, 2012). The socioecological model (McLeroy, Bibeau, Steckler, & Glanz, 1988) is used as a framework for taking a contextual approach at the intrapersonal, interpersonal, institutional, community, and international/global levels. This multilevel approach allows counselors to attend to both individual- and systemic-based concerns. Understood within the socioecological model is that individuals influence, and are influenced by, their environment. Thus, counselors who separate clients from their environment are not gaining an accurate picture of a client's presenting concern because they only capture a limited aspect of a client's experience.

MSJCC focuses on intersecting identities between counselor and client. Postmodernism and MSJCC both recognize that each individual is unique and possesses multiple identities. Both client and counselor have unique identities that shape how they will perceive and experience each other in the counseling and advocacy relationship. Being cognizant of these identities as well as privileged and marginalized statuses will help counselors understand the ways that power, privilege, and oppression influence their interactions and communication.

There are a few similarities between the Advocacy Competencies, the CAS model, and the MSJCC worth mentioning. First, each framework was developed to address social inequities. The assumption is that current models of helping are not adequately addressing social injustices, which are often contextual in nature. For this reason, counselors need to understand the lethal impact oppression has on psychological stress and well-being. This understanding can help provide counselors insight into the ways to intervene. Second, each framework requires counselors to balance individual counseling with community-level interventions. The Advocacy Competencies offer three levels of intervention that begin with the client, extend to the community, and then reach the political arena. The CAS model discusses the need for advocacy in general and how advocacy can inform one's counseling and scholarship. The MSJCC incorporate the socioecological model as a framework for multilevel interventions that focus on various spheres of influence in the client's life. Third, implicitly understood within each framework is that counselors should not profess to be value neutral in their work. Consistent with the postmodern perspective framing knowledge and meaning as necessarily value-laden and constructed by the knower, counselors must recognize that a neutral stance is impossible. Simply listening and providing insight does not address issues of oppression. Counselors need to be socially and politically active in their communities so they can better understand issues that clients bring to counseling.

The distinctions between the Advocacy Competencies, the CAS model, and the MSJCC are also important to note. The Advocacy Competencies focus solely on advocacy strategies. There is also a component within the Advocacy Competencies that addresses how to bring social justice issues to public awareness. For example, the competencies around talking with media members can help counselors with knowing how to approach the media. These competencies can also aid in developing coalitions with allies in the community. The CAS model underscores the importance of using the counselor, advocate, and scholar roles in combination with each other. Counseling, advocacy, and scholarship are interconnected tasks that should not be used in isolation from the other if social justice is the goal. The challenge is determining when situations call for being a counselor, an advocate, and a scholar. The MSJCC addresses the need to attend to intersectionalities. In addition, the MSJCC addresses the need to intervene at the international/global level. This perspective is based on the growing understanding that international/global affairs directly, and indirectly, influence clients.

Being familiar with the similarities and distinctions between the Advocacy Competencies, the CAS model, and the MSJCC can be important in determining which framework is relevant for a given situation. For example, the Advocacy Competencies could be useful to bring social justice issues to public awareness. The competencies within the public arena level of the Advocacy Competencies provide information on ways to inform the public about social inequities. The CAS model is distinct because it encourages counselors to conduct research. This task requires counselors to embrace research. It also will require counselors working in agencies, schools, and colleges to restructure how they spend their time. The MSJCC can be useful for counselors who wish to explore how client and counselor identities shape the therapeutic relationship and the extent to which interventions need to occur at the individual and systemic levels.

CASE ILLUSTRATION

For purposes of this chapter, this case illustration highlights how the Advocacy Competencies, the CAS model, and the MSJCC come to life. Specifically, each framework will be used to illustrate how a contextual approach that uses a social justice lens benefits clients. Also discussed are challenges encountered when using each theoretical framework.

Description of Client

Van is a Vietnamese American male who sought counseling to address his inability to obtain a promotion at work. Van immigrated to the United

States as a refugee at 15 years old with his family in the late 1970s as a result of the Vietnam War. He holds a bachelor's degree in finance and a master's degree in business management. For the past 10 years he has worked in the finance department of a Fortune 500 company in an urban setting. Van has always received strong annual performance reviews at work. One year he was recognized as Employee of the Year. He has applied for, and been denied, management positions for the past 5 years with the company. He wonders if his accent has kept him from being promoted for management positions. Van indicated that he has been taking conversational English classes at a local community college to work on his accent. Van shared that the interview for management positions required that candidates be able to demonstrate they are "articulate" so they can effectively lead others. As a result, Van indicated that he has been taking conversational English classes at a local community college to work on his accent. Additionally, approximately 25% of the company consists of racial minorities and the number is growing. Yet over 95% of those in management positions are White.

Process Description

This section will illustrate use of the Advocacy Competencies, CAS model, and MSJCC with the case illustration. Moreover, it will highlight the strengths and limitations of using each framework.

Advocacy Competencies

When using the Advocacy Competencies in this case illustration, counselors should explore with clients the need to intervene at the micro, meso, and macro levels. The pros and cons to each level should be explored before taking any action. Taking the time to explore each level of intervention with Van helps to ensure that all possibilities are considered. In effect, the counselor deconstructs the context of the client's problem. Determining what action to take and at which levels should be done in consultation with Van.

Being able to identify Van's strengths would be an important starting point of counseling at the microlevel. For example, one could help identify and build on Van's strengths so that he could have confidence in building self-advocacy skills that would empower him. Similar to other solution-focused approaches, the counselor might ask Van to describe the optimal performance and outcomes resulting from self-advocacy efforts. The counselor then employs prompts to facilitate his detailed description of the strengths, behaviors, thoughts, and feelings that make up his optimal performance. Role plays could provide Van with an opportunity to enact his "solution" or constructed approach to self-advocacy. More specifically, role plays could also provide Van with practice opportunities to discuss with management his concerns about not getting a promotion. Such discussions could also lead to ideas about potential mentoring opportunities for leadership positions in the company. Alternately processing and repeating such role plays represents a process of constructing, deconstructing, and reconstructing his optimal performance to *thicken* his awareness and understanding of his optimal performance.

At the mesolevel, it may be important to explore the extent to which collaboration may be necessary with Van's employer. This form of advocacy involves working with Van to identify whether the possibility of assessing for institutionalized racism in his company could help. This discussion may lead to working with Van's employer to create a climate survey on issues of diversity in the organization. Such a survey could explore whether the company values the use of "proper" English, which tends to benefit those whose first language is English. Seeking permission from Van to collaborate with his company's Human Resource department to develop mentorship programs for racial minority employees is a possibility. If written permission is granted, a counselor could conceivably reach out to Van's company and explore with his Human Resource department possible ways to increase racial minorities in management positions. Such discussions could lead to the co-construction of viable solutions to address the institutional racism. For example, one solution might entail the creation of a diversity committee whose charge is to address issues of diversity and social justice in the company.

Macrolevel interventions could involve working with legislators to explore interventions that may influence companies to increase the racial diversity of their management. A counselor could email his or her local legislator to discuss the benefits of a having a company that is racially diverse at the management level. This narrative account of the benefits of increasing racial diversity at the management level would potentially serve as an alternative narrative inviting the local legislator to reconsider dominant narratives that are disempowering for diverse employees. Another intervention may involve helping to create legislation that provides incentives for companies to racially diversify their management. If reaching out to legislators is unsuccessful, developing a Twitter page to address the lack of racial minorities in management positions may be necessary. Sometimes public pressure via social media can lead organizations and community leaders to make changes.

When using the CAS model as a framework, helping professionals pay particular attention to the benefits and challenges to serving in the role of counselor, advocate, and scholar. Although each role may not be necessary, it is important to still explore each role with clients so they may understand their options. This exploration is particularly important since clients may not realize that counselors can also serve as advocates and scholars.

In terms of Van, the counselor role could be used to explore the extent to which he has negatively internalized his experiences. Possible indicators of internalized oppression include, but are not limited to, self-blame, depression, and/or negative self-talk. For example, Van indicated a desire to be able to speak English without an accent. This desire may be because he has bought into the belief that there is only one way to speak English. Rather than an absolute truth, this "belief" is a social construction that is a part of the dominant narrative. Deconstructing the dominant narrative (e.g., diversity characteristics are a liability when one assumes a leadership role) may help him to realize that he is not the problem, but in fact it is his work culture that is the problem. This realization, in turn, makes it possible for Van and his counselor to co-construct an alternative, more inclusive narrative or belief (e.g., Van's Vietnamese background is a strength). The work done in the counselor role could also be helpful to informing scholarship possibilities.

In the advocate role, what was suggested with the Advocacy Competencies could be used in this role. The difference is that there are no levels of intervention suggested. Additionally, the insight gained from collaborating with those in the company and in the community could help to inform one's scholarship. Being able to see firsthand the experiences of other racial minorities can provide insight into the types of advocacy needed, whether to advocate alongside or on behalf, and the type of scholarship that is necessary.

As a scholar, one would explore whether quantitative and/or qualitative research may be necessary. For example, it might be important to initiate conversation around the idea of developing and disseminating a climate survey. A climate survey could provide rich insight into the strengths and areas of growth of the company around issues of diversity. For example, results of a climate survey could help determine whether or not diversity training is needed at the company. A climate survey could also provide rich information on whether structural changes need to take place to help racial minorities seek promotions for management positions at work. Along the same lines as a solution-focused approach, it would be worthwhile to employ open-ended items to elicit recommended potential solutions from survey respondents.

If a climate survey is not possible, another option is to conduct a Photovoice study with Van and other racial minorities in the company. Photovoice is a participatory action research study where members of marginalized communities take photographs of their experiences and then share them with key stakeholders (Wang & Burris, 1997). The photographs are meant to reflect the voices of those in marginalized communities, and they might be viewed as constructed alternative narratives. The idea behind sharing photographs with key stakeholders is that it could help stakeholders better understand the experiences of marginalized communities. In turn, this awareness could lead to necessary social change. In Van's situation, emerging themes could be drawn from the photographs by meeting individually with participants using grounded theory methods. Grounded theory is a qualitative research method whereby two or more data analysts consensually identify important themes (Strauss & Corbin, 2007). In essence, the themes are the product of a social constructivist process. These themes could then be shared with key people within the company in the hopes that this will lead to changes in the organization.

Multicultural and Social Justice Counseling Competencies

When using the MSJCC in this case illustration, it would be important to explore how counselor and client identities influence the counseling relationship and the extent to which counseling and advocacy interventions should occur along the various spheres of influence in the socioecological model: intrapersonal, interpersonal, institutional, community, public policy, and international/global.

In terms of identities, incorporating into an intake form the various identities that client and counselor possess could be one strategy. This intake form could be used to initiate conversation about identities. Such conversations can be helpful in determining how privileged and marginalized aspects of identity influence the counseling relationship. For example, it might be helpful to explore whether Van prefers to see a counselor of color or a European American/White counselor. The assumption here is that the racial identity of a counselor could influence the degree to which Van is willing to share his experiences at work. Even if Van does not have a preference for a counselor based on racial identity, it would still be important to know how privileged and marginalized aspects of identity shape the counseling relationship. Such information could help determine how issues of power, privilege, and marginalization influence the counseling process.

Using the socioecological model as a framework, a counselor could determine the extent that interventions need to occur along the various spheres of influence. At the intrapersonal level, the interventions would be similar to what was suggested for the counselor role in the CAS model. What might be different is exploring how the environment at work influences Van's cognition, behaviors, and affect. Interpersonally, it would be important to explore individuals who are supportive and unsupportive of Van at work. Identifying such individuals could help to garner support for Van so that he doesn't feel alone in his desire to pursue management positions. Institutionally, a counselor could intervene with, and on behalf of, Van by talking with his employer to co-construct solutions that could help Van and other racial minorities. For example, reaching out to Van's employer while making sure to not mention Van by name could lead to potential professional development trainings on issues of diversity at the company. In terms of public policy, it would be important to explore whether policies exist within the company, whether intentional or unintentional, that hinder Van's ability to be promoted. These policies might need to be detected and deconstructed to promote increased understanding. For example, the need to be "articulate" as a management professional should be questioned. Does "articulate" mean being able to speak "proper" English, or does it mean being able to convey information to employees? Deconstructing the policy or narrative empowers the social justice counselor to more effectively determine its validity. Because narratives are related to relative amount of power held by different groups, there are always multiple narratives. A counselor can use his or her position to introduce and support alternative, empowering narratives for Van or other diverse individuals. For example, one such alternative narrative might state that internationally/globally, Van's ability to speak Vietnamese could be an advantage to a company that is growing in racial diversity. Helping the company see Van's bilingual skills to their benefit could help Van's pursuit of a promotion.

Counseling Outcomes and Discussion

Whether one uses the Advocacy Competencies, the CAS model, or the MSJCC, the focus is the same: determining whether to intervene at the individual and/or the systemic level. This focus must first begin with being able to see client problems using a contextual lens. Intrapsychic theories of helping do not allow for a contextual framework, which leads counselors to focus only on individual-level interventions. When counselors see (through counseling) and experience (through advocacy) client issues more contextually, they are able to gain a deeper understanding of individuals in the context of their environment. Moreover, they are able to hear and see firsthand how individuals influence, and are influenced by, their surroundings.

Such awareness can help determine if interventions need to occur with the individual and/or in the environment.

The need for a contextual approach is to make sure any barriers that impede client development are identified and removed so clients can reach their full potential. No rocks should go unturned because the consequences are too dire. Too often, counselors are quick to give clients a diagnosis when one is not warranted (Smith, Chambers, & Bratini, 2009). Misdiagnosing clients or giving a client a diagnosis when a problem is contextually based can impact a client for a lifetime. By addressing the root of client problems, counselors are able to help clients with making long-lasting changes.

LIMITATIONS OF SOCIAL JUSTICE COUNSELING

The social justice counseling approach is not without limitations. Arguably, one of the most significant limitations with implementing social justice in counseling practice is structural. The counseling profession is structured in a way that emphasizes individual interventions over systemic interventions. Part of this stems from the belief that counseling is an individual endeavor. The expectation is that clients come to counseling and share their concerns in an office setting. Counselors who seek to implement social justice counseling in their work will likely run into structural obstacles. For example, many mental health agencies are set up where a counselor is expected to see clients back to back throughout the day. This structure does not allow for counselors to do community-based work. Likewise, in schools the expectation is that school counselors work on school grounds. Not all schools are open to the idea of a school counselor working in a client's home or parent's workplace during school hours. These structural barriers make it difficult to be able to balance individual- and systems-level work.

Another limitation is related to the lack of training around social justice among counseling professionals. The lack of training in social justice presents challenges for counselors and counselor educators who wish to implement social justice into their work. For example, counselor preparation programs typically do not have a stand-alone course dedicated to social justice. The lack of a dedicated course on social justice counseling makes it difficult to implement this theoretical paradigm in the counseling field. In addition, counselor educators may feel inadequate in helping to prepare future counselors for social justice because they lack the proper training themselves. In turn, students in counseling programs feel underprepared to work from a social justice perspective because they were not adequately prepared for the realities of the field.

Another challenge to implementing social justice counseling has to do with the political nature of social justice itself. It is easier to acknowledge an individual's cultural differences than it is to validate an individual's experience with oppression. Similarly, it is easier to go along with the dominant narrative than it is to co-construct alternative, less oppressive narratives. Zinn (2002) asserts that individuals can not sit back and be passive observers when engaged in social justice work because oppression is not neutral. Yet there is a popular belief that counselors should be impartial and that counseling itself is a value-neutral process (Canfield, 2008). This belief is embedded in the counseling culture, which makes it challenging to incorporate social justice counseling into practice. This perspective is further supported by the ACA *Code of Ethics* (2014), which adds, "counselors are aware of—and avoid imposing—their values, attitudes, beliefs, and behaviors" (p. 5). There are many counselors who do not want to impose their values and beliefs onto clients. However, from a postmodern perspective, true neutrality is impossible. Further, oppression cannot be resolved simply by listening. Counselors who have a belief in a just world may find it challenging to refute the prevailing structures and narratives because of the belief by others that they are imposing their social justice values onto clients and communities.

IMPLICATIONS AND RECOMMENDATIONS FOR USE WITH CLIENTS

Social justice counseling is not a trend in the counseling profession. It is a helping paradigm that needs serious consideration if counselors are to address the social ills that clients, especially those from marginalized communities, bring to counseling. To further the social justice counseling perspective, several things need to occur. First, counseling professionals need training. The training counselors receive from their preparation programs is inadequate. For this reason, I suggest seeking out professional development opportunities embedded within the communities in which clients reside. Such training opportunities can provide insight into alternative approaches that better align with clients' cultural background and worldviews. Second, there is a need to conduct research on social justice counseling. For example, research on the Advocacy Competencies, the CAS model, and the MSJCC can help advance our understanding of social justice in counseling practice. Although these documents have promise in the field, they lack research to support their efficacy in the profession. Research can increase our understanding of the strengths and weaknesses within each framework. Third, to fully achieve the vision of social justice in counseling, recruiting different types of individual into the profession may be necessary. For example, individuals who already engage in political activism in their respective communities may be more open to engaging in social justice counseling than the traditional psychology student. Activist counselor educators are also needed. Such individuals possess the knowledge and skills needed to train aspiring social change agents.

Society is constantly evolving and so too must the counseling profession. A change is needed in the counseling profession to meet the shifting demands of society. The development of the counseling profession must incorporate social justice counseling, a postmodern approach, in the field. The profession can no longer rely on utilizing theoretical approaches that were developed for White, middle- to upper-class individuals. Such theories tend to be intrapsychic in nature, individualistic in design, and employ techniques that are office based. Clients, especially those from marginalized communities, need the field to shift to one that is more postmodern.

REFERENCES

American Counseling Association. (2014). *2014 ACA code of ethics*. Alexandria, VA: Author.

Brown, C. G. (2012). Anti-oppression through a postmodern lens: Dismantling the master's conceptual tools in discursive social work practice. *Critical Social Work, 13*(1), 34–65.

Canfield, B. S. (2008). Together, we make a difference. *Counseling Today, 50*(10), 5.

Combs, G., & Freedman, J. (2012). Narrative, poststructuralism, and social justice: Current practice in narrative therapy. *The Counseling Psychologist, 40*, 1033–1060.

Council for Accreditation of Counseling and Related Educational Programs (CACREP). (2016). 2016 CACREP standards. Retrieved from http://www.cacrep.org

Counselors for Social Justice. (2016). Definition. Retrieved from https://counseling-csj.org

GLSEN. (2016). *Educational exclusion: Drop out, push out, and school-to-prison pipeline among LGBTQ youth*. New York, NY: Author.

Hansen, J. T. (2005). Postmodernism and humanism: A proposed integration of perspectives that value human meaning systems. *The Journal of Humanistic Counseling, 44*(1), 3–15.

Kiselica, M. S., & Robinson, M. (2001). Bringing advocacy counseling to life: The history, issues, and human dramas of social justice work in counseling. *Journal of Counseling and Development, 79*(4), 387–397. doi:10.1002/j.1556-6676.2001.tb01985.x

Lewis, J., & Arnold, M. S. (1998). From multiculturalism to social action. In C. C. Lee & G. R. Walz (Eds.), *Social action: A mandate for counselors* (pp. 51–65). Alexandria, VA: American Counseling Association.

Lewis, J., Arnold, M. S., House, R., & Toporek, R. (2002). ACA Advocacy Competencies. Retrieved from http://www.counseling.org/knowledge-center/competencies

Lewis, M., & Lewis, J. (1971). Counselor education: Training for a new alternative. *The Personnel and Guidance Journal, 49*(9), 754–758.

Lewis, M. D., Lewis, J. A., & Dworkin, E. P. (1971). Counseling and the social revolution [Special issue]. *Personnel and Guidance Journal, 49*(9).

Mallinckrodt, B., Miles, J. R., & Levy, J. J. (2014). The scientist-practitioner-advocate model: Addressing contemporary training needs for social justice advocacy. *Training* and Education in Professional Psychology, 8(4), 303–311. doi:http://dx.doi.org/10.1037/tep0000045

Mani, A., Mullainathan, S., Shafir, E., & Zhao, J. (2013). Poverty impedes cognitive function. Science, 341, 976–980. doi:10.1126/science.1238041

McLeroy, K. R., Bibeau, D., Steckler, A., & Glanz, K. (1988). An ecological perspective on health promotions. Health Education and Behavior, 15, 351–377. doi:10.1177/109019818801500401

Murdock, N. L. (2017). Theories of counseling and psychotherapy: A case approach (4th ed.). New York, NY: Pearson.

Neimeyer, R. A. (2009). Postmodern psychotherapy: Distinguishing features. New York, NY: Guilford.

Ratts, M. J., & Pedersen, P. B. (2014). Counseling for multiculturalism and social justice: Theory, integration, and application (4th ed.). Alexandria, VA: American Counseling Association.

Ratts, M. J., Singh, A. A., Nassar-McMillan, S., Butler, S. K., & McCullough, J. R. (2016). Multicultural and social justice counseling competencies: Guidelines for the counseling profession. Journal of Multicultural Counseling and Development, 44(1), 28–48.

Ratts, M. J., Toporek, R. L., & Lewis, J. A. (Eds.). (2010). ACA Advocacy Competencies: A social justice framework for counselors. Alexandria, VA: American Counseling Association.

Smith, L., Chambers, D.-A., & Bratini, L. (2009). When oppression is the pathogen: The participatory development of socially just mental health practice. American Journal of Orthopsychiatry, 79(2), 159–168. doi:10.1037/a0015353

Strauss, A., & Corbin, J. (2007). Basics of qualitative research. Grounded theory: Techniques and procedures for developing grounded theory. Thousand Oaks, CA: Sage.

Toporek, R. L., Gerstein, L. H., Fouad, N. A., Roysircar, G., & Israel, T. (Eds.). (2006). Handbook for social justice in counseling psychology: Leadership, vision, and action. Thousand Oaks, CA: Sage.

Wang, C., & Burris, M. A. (1997). Photovoice: Concept, methodology, and use for participatory needs assessment. Health Education and Behavior, 24. doi:10.1177/109019819702400309

Zimmerman, J. L., & Dickerson, V. C. (2001). Narrative therapy. In R. J. Corsini (Ed.), Handbook of innovative therapy (pp. 415–426). New York, NY: Wiley

Zinn, H. (2002). You can't be neutral on a moving train: A personal history of our times. Boston, MA: Beacon Press.

Integrative Postmodern Therapeutic Models

INTRODUCTION

Consider what training was like for psychotherapists and counselors decades ago, particularly before the 1980s. In previous generations, talk therapists were usually trained in a single treatment approach and spent their careers implementing it (Fancher, 1995). In contrast to eras when fidelity to an exclusive orientation was the professional norm, contemporary therapists usually integrate multiple approaches and tailor these theoretical and technical hybrids to provide optimal help for their clients. This historical transition, from dogmatic theoretical allegiance to flexible, integrative models, is a notable and intriguing professional transformation. An important prerequisite for appreciating the various integrationist approaches that comprise this section of the book is an understanding of this transformation.

It may strike contemporary practitioners as odd that talk therapists from prior generations usually did not rely on integrated approaches. After all, in the current culture of practice, it is commonsensical to acknowledge that clients have various needs and that not all people are responsive to the same approach. Dogmatically insisting that one treatment orientation should work for everyone, then, is usually a strange and counterintuitive way of thinking about psychotherapy and counseling for modern practitioners.

An important reason for the intellectual divide between contemporary and past talk therapists on the issue of treatment integration is that the factors responsible for successful therapeutic outcomes only began to be identified in the late 1970s (Wampold & Imel, 2015). The complexities of talk therapy, including the vast number of interactions that constitute any treatment, contributed to the historical delay in identifying the factors that are associated with therapeutic outcomes (Hansen, 2014). That is, when a client reports improvement after talking to a therapist over a period of weeks or months, it is very difficult to determine the precise variables that were responsible for the change. However, thanks to over three decades of productive psychotherapy outcome research, we now have a far better understanding of the factors that contribute to client betterment than we did for most of the history of the helping professions. One of the important insights from this research is that treatment orientation generally has little to do with outcomes (Wampold & Imel, 2015). However, prior to the solidification of this and other outcome-based research findings, practitioners naturally assumed that their favored approach to psychotherapy and counseling was the answer to their clients' problems. To empathize with this dogmatic mindset, it is important to understand the intellectual climate that animated professional life during past eras.

Without firm scientific knowledge about the factors that contributed to psychotherapy outcomes, previous generations of practitioners usually relied on theoretical orientations for etiological explanations and treatment strategies (Fancher, 1995). For instance, the traditional behaviorist assumption that all behavior is the result of learning (Skinner, 1974) serves as the foundation for a compelling, reasonable, and internally consistent explanatory system, which offers causes of and solutions for client distress. Likewise, psychoanalysis, which posits that unconscious conflict is the root of human problems (Gabbard, 2010), is also a persuasive system of thought. Note, however, that the core assumptions of psychoanalysis and behaviorism are incompatible; if you endorse one as the truth about human nature, it is impossible to fully endorse the other. To summarize, past generations of practitioners operated in the following intellectual milieu: (a) little was definitively known about the factors that contributed to outcomes; (b) a variety of theoretical orientations posited answers to the outcome question; these theories were grounded in compelling, internally consistent core assumptions about human motivation and change; (c) the theories were generally incompatible; if one was endorsed, it was usually logically inconsistent to also endorse another. This professional milieu naturally served as a breeding ground for theoretical dogmatism (Fancher, 1995). Graduate schools were often dedicated to promulgating a particular orientation, and students became indoctrinated to view talk therapy through the lens of that orientation. Professionals read journals, joined associations, and engaged in other activities that were dedicated to their favored approach. When clients improved, practitioners attributed the improvement to the psychological insights and methods of their treatment orientation. This theoretical insularity and resulting tribalism strongly discouraged counselors and psychotherapists from considering alternative points of view.

The beginning answers to questions about therapeutic outcomes did not arrive until the late 1970s. Since that time, a consistent, highly replicated finding of outcome research has been that theoretical orientation and specific techniques, generally speaking, contribute negligibly to outcome variance (Wampold & Imel, 2015). As it turns out, then, theoretical orientation, a factor that was highly valued by past generations of practitioners, is of relatively trivial importance in the scheme of variables that constitute the practice of psychotherapy and counseling. These findings helped to launch a new era of integrative treatments. After all, if one approach generally does not have a significant advantage over any other, perhaps, theoreticians and researchers reasoned, various approaches might be integrated to optimally capitalize on the benefits of different orientations.

There are a number of ways that treatment orientations can be integrated (Harris, 2016). Although it is beyond the scope of this introductory section to provide an overview of every integrative strategy, suffice it to say that the theoretical postulates of approaches can be combined (i.e., theoretical integration); techniques of various orientations can be implemented according to client need, without regard for theoretical consistency (i.e., technical eclecticism); integration can occur along the lines of the common relational factors of all approaches (i.e., common factors); or practitioners can draw from secondary approaches to supplement their primary one (i.e., assimilative integration). Each of these integrative strategies has strengths, weaknesses, and implications for helping clients (Harris, 2016). The important point for this discussion, however, is that a new era of eclecticism and integrative approaches was initiated by the highly replicated outcome finding that factors other than theoretical orientation were the important contributors to client outcomes.

Furthermore, postmodern ideology added ideological steam to the integrative movement (Hansen, 2002). Recall that, unlike modernism, postmodernism rejects the assumption that theories are capable of reflecting the intrinsic nature of reality (Hansen, 2014). Modernism essentially posits that language, including the language of theories, can potentially be correspondent with truths about the world (Hansen, 2004). Prior to the introduction of postmodern ideas, therapists in past generations often used their modernist epistemological frame to bestow the attribution of truth on their favored theories, which, of course, caused them to appraise the inconsistent postulates of theoretical alternatives as misguided or outright false. The introduction of postmodern ideas in the talk therapy professions, generally beginning in the 1980s and 1990s, caused certain theorists to challenge the assumption that theories are capable of corresponding with truth (e.g., Gergen, 1991; Schafer, 1992; Spence, 1982; White & Epston, 1990). If, in postmodernist fashion, language is incapable of representing the supposed intrinsic nature of reality, then theories are simply narratives about the human condition, not systems of thought anchored in foundational truth. An important barrier to integration (i.e., concerns about combining theories that are grounded in inconsistent truths) is thereby substantially lessened by postmodernist ideology, which regards theories as narrative structures, not literal representations of reality (Hansen, 2002). In short, it is far less challenging to integrate various stories about human nature (i.e., postmodernism) than it is to integrate contradictory psychological truths (i.e., modernism).

As a result of this history, practitioners now operate in an era when the shackles of dogmatism have generally been shed and an emphasis on client betterment, through creative, integrative models, has been widely embraced. Contemporarily, most practitioners do not take pride in their unyielding allegiance to a particular system of thought. Rather, they focus on helping clients, generally without regard for ideological purity. Various integrative models have provided practitioners with novel ways to conceptualize treatment and new techniques to employ with their clients. These developments would have been highly unlikely in past eras when theoretical dogmatism ruled the talk therapy professions.

This section contains integrative models that have a postmodern element. Scholl and his colleagues creatively integrate postmodern and traditional career approaches for helping the ex-offender population. A seemingly unlikely, but extremely interesting and useful, integration of neuropsychology and narrative therapy for couples is offered by Monk and Zamani. Last, Clevenger and Teofilo Mattson provides practical, integrative insights for counseling men. Practitioners should find these chapters very useful, as they represent powerful postmodern, integrative means to therapeutic ends.

REFERENCES

Fancher, R. (1995). *Cultures of healing: Correcting the image of American mental health care.* New York, NY: Freeman.

Gabbard, G. (2010). *Long-term psychodynamic psychotherapy: A basic text* (2nd ed.). Washington, DC: American Psychiatric Publishing.

Gergen, K. (1991). *The saturated self: Dilemmas of identity in contemporary life.* New York, NY: Basic Books.

Hansen, J. T. (2002). Postmodern implications for theoretical integration of counseling orientations. *Journal of Counseling & Development, 80,* 315–321. doi:10.1002/j.1556-6678.2002.tb00196.x

Hansen, J. T. (2004). Thoughts on knowing: Epistemic implications of counseling practice. *Journal of Counseling & Development, 82,* 131–138. doi:10.1002/j.1556-6678.2004.tb00294.x

Hansen, J. T. (2014). *Philosophical issues in counseling and psychotherapy: Encounters with four questions about knowing, effectiveness, and truth.* Lanham, MD: Rowman & Littlefield.

Harris, J. E. (2016). Integrative theories of psychotherapy. In H. Tinsley, S. Lease, & N. Giffin Wiersma (Eds.), *Contemporary theory and practice in counseling and psychotherapy,* (pp. 434–464). Los Angeles, CA: Sage.

Schafer, R. (1992). *Retelling a life: Narration and dialogue in psychoanalysis.* New York, NY: Basic Books.

Skinner, B. (1974). *About behaviorism.* New York, NY: Knopf.

Spence, D. (1982). *Narrative truth and historical truth: Meaning and interpretation in psychoanalysis.* New York, NY: Norton.

Wampold, B. E., & Imel, Z. E. (2015). *The great psychotherapy debate: The evidence for what makes psychotherapy work.* New York, NY: Routledge.

White, M., & Epston, D. (1990). *Narrative means to therapeutic ends.* New York, NY: Norton.

CHAPTER 9

Career Support Workshop Series

A Postmodern Counseling Intervention Designed for the Ex-Offender Population

MARK B. SCHOLL, JASON PERRY, BRIAN CALHOUN, AND HEIDI ROBINSON

Community ex-offenders (sometimes referred to as *re-entrants*) often present with a considerable number of special limitations. Among these are relatively less developed job entry skills (e.g., interviewing skills), a history of poor outcomes in school and work settings, and lack of faith in their own ability to find a job (Varghese, Fitzgerald, Chronister, Cummings, & Forrest, 2013). Solution-focused therapy, grounded in postmodern ideology, has demonstrated effectiveness for promoting the career development of both the general population (Burwell & Chen, 2006) and for ex-offenders (Veysey, Christian, & Martinez, 2013). In this chapter, we describe a four-workshop series (e.g., interviewing skills, job search strategies) that we provide for community ex-offenders. The workshop series has been offered in Forsyth County, North Carolina, for approximately 3 years (Fall of 2014 through the fall of 2017) and evolved from an earlier career support group offered through the North Carolina Department of Public Safety in Washington, North Carolina (Scholl, Perry, Calhoun, & Robinson, 2016).

PRACTICAL AND PHILOSOPHICAL FOUNDATIONS

Rationale

Individuals who are on probation, parole, or postrelease supervision are often required to actively seek employment. Relative to the general population, ex-offenders are less prepared (e.g., possess fewer well-developed skills) for the job search and workplace entry process (Varghese et al., 2013). Another rationale for the provision of our services is the fact that career development appears to be one of the primary factors positively associated with successful community re-entry (Brown, Lent, & Noll, 2013; McWhirter, 2013; Varghese, et al., 2013). For a significant number of ex-offenders, desisting from a return to previous criminal activities poses a serious challenge. Relatedly, the acquisition of gainful employment has been identified as a reliable predictor of both criminal *desistance* (Devers, 2011; Laub & Sampson, 2001) and successful reintegration into society (Varghese & Cummings, 2012). Finally, whereas probation and parole services commonly include an emphasis on skills such as managing money and locating housing accommodations, these services do not typically include the provision of career information or support (Scholl et al., 2016).

Resilience Theory and Community Re-entry

We believe that resilience theory (Werner, 1996; Werner & Smith, 2001) bears particular relevance to the promotion of ex-offenders' successful community re-entry. Lewis (2012) defined *resilience* as "the human capacity to spring back from risk posed by adversity and ability to take actions to navigate satisfying life trajectories" (p. 191). As asserted previously (Scholl et al., 2016), we believe that our workshop series intervention has the potential to enhance the resilience of our participants.

Resilience theory posits that the relative influence of two primary forces, protective factors and risk factors, is critical with regard to an individual's life outcomes (Lewis, 2012). In the case of ex-offenders, risk factors such as living in an impoverished environment do not necessarily lead to negative outcomes such as participation in criminal activity for at least two important reasons. First of all, all humans have a *self-righting capacity*, which enhances their ability to correct a negative life trajectory (Lewis, 2012; Werner & Smith, 2001). Second, *protective factors* enhance ex-offenders' capacity for withstanding risk factors and experiencing a positive life trajectory. Examples of protective factors include hopefulness, being goal oriented, problem-solving abilities, and social competence (Benard, 1996). These protective factors are also, from a social cognitive career theory framework (Lent,

Brown, & Hackett, 1994), the same factors that promote positive career development and are plausibly promoted by our career development workshop series. A final protective factor, the opportunity to participate in a meaningful role in one's community (Lewis, 2012) is especially relevant to the current population. If ex-offenders are able to secure gainful employment, then they will also potentially bounce back from adversity (Scholl et al., 2016).

Lewis (2012) stated that, consistent with postmodernism, "both resilience theorists and humanists assert that people actively and intentionally construct meaning in their lives" (p. 193). Thus, one of our primary aims is to assist ex-offenders participating in our workshops to co-construct a positive, empowering worker identity and to co-construct a meaningful career path for themselves. In these ways, we believe that we can provide opportunities for ex-offenders to embrace their personal strengths and use these to construct a positive life trajectory (Masten, 1994; Scholl et al., 2016) that also entails meaningful participation in their surrounding communities.

An Integrative Postmodern Counseling Model

The present model of counseling is an *assimilative* integrative model; that is, a model in which the counselor maintains a primary commitment to one specific theoretical model but intentionally integrates techniques from other counseling perspectives (Messer, 1992). More specifically, this integrative model is primarily grounded in solution-focused therapy's (de Shazer, 1994) belief in the power of language to create reality. With regard to the actual practice of therapy, we have adopted some of the important assumptions of solution-focused therapy (O'Hanlon & Weiner-Davis, 2003), including the assumption that there are a variety of different views of a situation that are valid, and it is important to adopt a view (i.e., a solution-oriented view) that is more helpful or more likely to contribute to positive change. Views that are problem oriented are less helpful because they are less likely to bring about positive change. Thus solution-focused therapy serves as the primary theoretical orientation in our model, and additional theoretical orientations are integrated with this primary theoretical perspective.

One of these is narrative therapy. This perspective is highly compatible with solution-focused therapy, as it is also based on a postmodern perspective. From this perspective, power determines the versions of reality (i.e., dominant narratives) that are endorsed by society (Murdock, 2013; White & Epston, 1990). Power has a strong influence over the types of stories that individuals create to describe their lived experiences. Consequently, practitioners of narrative therapy encourage individuals to question and challenge dominant narratives that are stigmatizing or pathologizing. In the words of Doan (1998): "Narrative therapy concerns itself with the deliverance of clients from the weights of oppressive and totalizing stories via liberating the client's voice and preferences" (p. 219). For this reason, the techniques and practices in our workshop series emphasize the development of positive, strength-based *alternative* narratives (e.g., the individual learned from his or her mistakes), which run counter to the *dominant* narratives (e.g., the ex-offender is a "bad apple"), emphasizing the past and limitations of ex-offenders.

In addition, our integrative model incorporates social cognitive career theory (SCCT; Lent, Brown, & Hackett, 1994). This theory arguably includes modernist elements emphasizing social conventions associated with appropriate behaviors and practices more likely to lead to gainful employment. For example, there are social norms for specific behaviors such as characteristics of a good handshake, appropriate attire, and information that is appropriate and inappropriate to disclose when answering the question "Tell me about yourself" in an employment interview. Reflective of this theoretical perspective, our intervention includes exercises in which facilitators model appropriate interview behaviors, as well as provide constructive feedback pertaining to mock interview performance, and how to write a good resume. This approach, like narrative therapy, emphasizes the importance of emphasizing one's strengths throughout the job search process and, as a result, complements narrative therapy's emphasis on constructing useful alternative narratives.

In addition to SCCT, our career support intervention incorporates elements of Peavy's (1998) sociodynamic counseling model, which views the self as a project that is perpetually being constructed by the individual. Emphasizing intentional career identity construction is appropriate for the ex-offender population because it allows individuals who are at risk of viewing themselves as defined by a criminal act to construct alternative, more positive narratives. This perspective emphasizing identity construction also potentially fosters development of a *thicker* description of one's career identity. A more complete and fuller understanding of one's career identity can facilitate smoother movement across career transitions, including postrelease reintegration into society.

A Postmodern Perspective

Resilience theory is compatible with the postmodern perspective and related counseling approaches (e.g., solution-focused, narrative) because resilience theory is similarly based on a strengths-based perspective (Lewis, 2012). Werner and Smith (1992) viewed resilience as a quality that can be intentionally enhanced or amplified if the right conditions are provided. In their study of adolescents who succeeded in spite of obstacles (e.g., mental health problems, learning disorders), they described these individuals as learning "to perceive themselves as movers of their destiny rather than pawns in a power game played by outsiders" (Werner & Smith, p. 21). Along the same lines, our career support workshops include approaches that empower participating clients to become authors of their career identities.

As an assimilative intervention model with solution-focused therapy as the primary theoretical perspective, our workshop series includes four primary postmodern elements. First, this intervention model is based on a postmodern perspective on social justice in which the workshop facilitators join alongside the clients, forming an egalitarian alliance. The clients are viewed as competent and capable, and the counselor's role is to provide information, facilitate client skill development, and to partner with clients to assist them in networking and finding gainful employment. The counselors communicate this philosophy to the clients at the beginning of the first workshop. This perspective stands in direct contrast with a modernist perspective in which the counselors view themselves as assisting clients who are less powerful and need help in order to cope or succeed in the community (personal communication, Colette Dollarhide).

Second, a number of exercises throughout the four workshop series are intended to foster the clients' ability to construct personal meaning. Clients vary in their levels of readiness for the meaning construction process and in the degree to which they need orienting before they are ready to engage in the solution-focused therapy process (Neimeyer & Bridges, 2003). One informal approach for orienting or preparing a client for this process was recommended by Gelatt (1991). In this activity, occurring in the first workshop (i.e., Career Assessment), each participant reads a list of four metaphors (e.g., roller coaster, colossal dice game, great ocean, mighty river) and decides which one best matches the participant's view of his or her influence over the future (Kaufman, 1976). In addition, participants are encouraged to develop their own original metaphors.

Third, a number of the activities in the workshop are solution focused. For example, in one activity in the first workshop, clients identify three preferred possible future selves that are highly relevant to their occupational hopes. In the second part of this exercise, clients are asked to rank order the three future selves in order from most preferred to third most preferred. The counselor assists each client in exploring the cognitive, behavioral, and affective dimensions of his or her preferred future selves (Markus & Nurius, 1986; Robinson, Davis, & Meara, 2003), including interests, skills, and transferable skills. In this manner, clients are assisted in constructing a vision of the future that includes concrete details and, as a result, is potentially more compelling (Robinson et al., 2003).

Also in the Career Assessment workshop, clients deconstruct each preferred future self (e.g., restaurant manager) by identifying the transferrable skills that are typically required to enact the corresponding occupational role. Clients are encouraged to consider both their level of proficiency and how much they enjoy performing each skill. Deconstructing a possible future self in this way encourages clients to systematically consider how much they would like to actually enact the future self.

Fourth, some of the activities emphasize meaning making in the form of constructing stories in a manner consistent with narrative therapy (White, 2004, 2007; White & Epston, 1990). For many ex-offenders, the dominant narratives they are familiar with are ones in which they made bad choices which resulted in negative consequences (Morgan, 2000). These problem-saturated narratives emphasize their mistakes and often contain themes of hopelessness, helplessness, and internal flaws. One way to empower ex-offenders is to provide them with scaffolding to assist them in constructing alternative, empowering narratives. For example, in the Interviewing Skills workshop, we use the acronym STAR to assist clients in constructing alternative strength-based narratives. Clients are instructed to develop at least three stories illustrating their strengths and to strategically share these stories each time an interviewer asks a question about his or her assets or strengths. In the STAR acronym, S stands for situation, T is task, A is action, and R is a positive result. Clients are given an example of a success story using the STAR heuristic for story development. Then clients write three distinct stories illustrating three salient strengths they would like to share with a prospective interviewer. They share these stories in role plays, and afterward they are given feedback from peers and facilitators to help them make their stories more effective (e.g., includes a clearly communicated positive result of the client's actions).

Existing empirical evidence of the effectiveness of postmodern approaches for promoting the career development of community ex-offenders is limited. Postmodern approaches (e.g., constructivist, solution-focused) have demonstrated effectiveness for addressing the career needs of the general population (Burwell & Chen, 2006). In addition, another group has reported the effectiveness of narrative therapy for promoting hopefulness and optimism in ex-offenders (Veysey, Christian, & Martinez, 2013).

DESCRIPTION OF THE CAREER SUPPORT WORKSHOP SERIES

Purposes

The goals of the career support workshop series were guided by sociodynamic counseling theory (Peavy, 1998), solution-focused therapy (de Shazer, 1994; O'Hanlon & Weiner-Davis, 2003), and narrative therapy (White & Epston, 1990). These goals are to increase or enhance ex-offenders' (a) awareness and understanding of their preferred self-identity; (b) sense of self-efficacy regarding their ability to actively contribute to the construction of their preferred self-identity; (c) understanding of the interdependent role of their self in the context of a larger social support system; (d) adoption of a forward-looking solution-focused stance; (e) ability to construct narratives supporting a positive presentation of their skills and strengths; (f) sense of their capacity for meaning making, including identifying meaningful career options; (g) sense of self-efficacy regarding desired career outcomes (e.g., employment); (h) job search and career entry skills (e.g., networking, problem solving, interviewing); and (i) hopefulness and positive outcome expectations. From the perspective of resilience theory, these goals also represent protective factors or resilience traits (Benard, 1996; Benard & Marshall, 1997).

The original career support group, formed in the fall of 2012, was organic in the sense that the group would naturally move from one topic (e.g., from assessment to resume writing) at a rate that accommodated the developmental levels of the group members. Similarly, curriculum flexibility is built into the current workshop series to accommodate the developmental needs of participants in accordance with recommendations by researchers (Chronister & Davidson, 2010; Fitzgerald, Chronister, Forrest, & Brown, 2012). Each workshop series completer participated in a minimum of four 2-hour workshops. In some instances, participants met with the workshop facilitators after the workshop, communicated by telephone, or corresponded via email if they sought additional help mastering career concepts and skills.

Description of the Program and Topics

The participants in the workshops were all ex-offenders. The workshops ranged from three to seven members per workshop. Participation in the workshop series, or the earlier career support group, has always been entirely voluntary. Ex-offenders who qualified for participation were required to be clean and sober, take prescribed psychotropic medications, speak and write fluent English, and be either unemployed or underemployed.

Workshop 1: Career Assessment

The first group workshop presents a postmodern approach to help participants construct their own metaphor for the future and to construct several versions of future career opportunities of interest. The combination of activities included in this first workshop were selected to foster the client's self-efficacy with regard to the meaning-making process.

The first task was to introduce the postmodern perspective of social justice to the group members, including the notion that the facilitators and participants are allies who form an egalitarian alliance. Rather than *doing for* the participants, the facilitators' role is to foster the participants' ability to function optimally and independently. The facilitators shared their strength-based philosophy for the workshop series. They also discussed the importance of maintaining confidentiality regarding the self-disclosures of fellow participants.

In the initial workshop activity (Metaphors of the Future; Gelatt, 1991; Kaufman, 1976), participants articulate a metaphor representing their view of their relationship with the future. That is, they share a metaphor they believe reflects their current relationship with the future. They are given the option of either selecting from a list of four metaphors (i.e., roller coaster, river, dice game, or ocean) or alternately creating a personally meaningful metaphor (e.g., the future is a baseball game and I am stranded on third base). This activity emphasizes and supports each client's ability to construct personal meaning for herself or himself. The personal metaphor adopted by each participant is a flexible construct that they are encouraged to modify in accord with their changing views of themselves and their relationships to the future.

The second activity in the workshop, adopted from Markus and Nurius (1986), required participants to imagine three *preferred future selves* and then, on a worksheet, to rank order them from most preferred to third most preferred. Consistent with the solution-focused approach, participants were prompted to provide details, including the thoughts, behaviors, and feelings that would accompany each of the three future selves, a process known as *nuancing* (Neimeyer & Bridges, 2003). By providing these details, the clients were constructing an occupational identity representing a meaningful goal to attain. Clients' capacity for focusing on a solution-focused vision of the future is enhanced by the addition of concrete details (Robinson, Davis, & Meara, 2003).

Last, participants complete a transferable skills inventory. Participants identify the four skills they would most want to communicate to a potential employer, and they provide examples of work activities where they demonstrated they possess each of the four skills. In addition, participants were asked to identify the transferable skills inherent to their most preferred future self. By deconstructing their choice in this way they became more aware of the component activities and skills that make up their constructed selves, allowing them to more accurately assess their degree of preference for their constructed possible selves.

Workshop 2: Resume Writing

In the second session of the ex-offender workshop, the facilitators revisited the preferred future selves activity from the previous workshop. The workshop participants once again described their "preferred future self," followed by the identification of characteristics that are consistent with the future self. Importantly, these actions on the part of participants entail both constructing their preferred selves and identifying the component parts that make up their constructions.

The first handout listed examples of good and poor objective statements. Participants were asked to select examples of each type of objective statement and provide a rationale for judging an objective statement as well written or poorly written. Next, the participants composed objective statements reflecting their preferred future occupational identity and the transferable skills they would enjoy using in that occupation. Then the members read their objective statements aloud and participants provided feedback, including suggestions for improving their objective statements.

Participants were given two model resumes. Each model resume included a second page with a brief description of the individual's long-term career objective and a brief action plan detailing how the individual planned to achieve her or his long-term objective. The participants were then asked to share at least two action steps they were committed to completing to make their preferred occupational identity a reality. The identification of action steps addressed a common criticism that solution-focused counseling approaches frequently lack action elements (Reid, 2006). The action steps identified by the clients were included to form a bridge between the clients' current and future identities (Scholl & Cascone, 2010).

The last step in the workshop involved creating a resume using laptops provided for the resume workshop. The work on the resume began with participants typing their career objective that included a brief statement of the position they were seeking and their relevant skills and strengths. For positions they listed in their work history, participants were encouraged to be selective with regard to duties performed and to include action verbs representing functions they found meaningful and enjoyed performing.

Workshop 3: Interviewing Skills

The facilitators provided the participants with scaffolding, in the form of the STAR (Situation/Task/Action/Results) acronym to assist them in constructing narratives that vividly illustrate three or four of their greatest strengths. The facilitators emphasized that good stories impress employers and make them particularly memorable.

Workshop attendees shared their strengths, one area for improvement, and their preferred occupational position in 2–5 years. Facilitators advised participants to be concise in disclosing their criminal conviction record using a five-part approach articulated by Krannich and Krannich (2005). Participants and facilitators co-constructed the participants' self-disclosure statements. First, participants were given 15 minutes to construct a written self-disclosure statement. Next, participants took turns reading their statements aloud and received feedback on how to revise their statements so that they might be more positively received by prospective employers.

One particularly effective strategy shared by several participants involved detailing how they made positive use of time in prison through activities, including taking online courses, learning a work-related skill, and/ or volunteering for work opportunities. These examples demonstrated that even though a criminal conviction is potentially stigmatizing, it is possible for individuals to construct alternative narratives emphasizing their resilience. The participants were encouraged to construct alternative narratives of this nature in disclosing their criminal record because this narrative practice separates the individual from her or his problems in two important ways. First, the alternative solution-oriented narrative is adopted by the individual rather than the dominant, problem-saturated narrative frequently endorsed by society. Second, the alternative narrative emphasizes the individual's capacity for positive growth and change. As such, the individual does not allow the problem (i.e., conviction and incarceration) to define her or him and maintains a forward-looking, solution-oriented stance.

Workshop 4: Job Search Strategies

At the beginning of the workshop, the facilitators provided participants with a list of principles for conducting an effective job search (Krannich & Krannich, 2005). To empower clients to conduct a job search effectively, the facilitators shared a variety of strategies, including networking and conducting informational interviews. Participants were encouraged to use informational interviews as a "low-stakes" opportunity to practice effectively self-disclosing their criminal record. They were also encouraged to ask informants for suggestions regarding how to effectively and positively communicate their criminal records. This is consistent with the concept of social construction of more positive, alternative narratives (Scholl et al., 2016).

Clients completing all four of the workshops completed a survey that was approved by the Wake Forest University Institutional Review Board. The survey consisted of the following six open-ended items:

1. What did you learn or how did you benefit from participation in the workshop series?
2. How did what you learn, or ways you benefited, from the workshops change you or affect you as a person?
3. How did what you learned, or changes resulting from the workshops, influence your relationships with people in or outside of the workshops?
4. How will you apply what you learned from the workshops to your life in the future?
5. Think about your career skills, interests, and values, and your career identity. Based upon your identity and what you would like your life to look like in the future, describe the next chapter in your life. Where do you see yourself in 3 to 5 years? What type of work will you be doing and what type of skills will you be using? How will you feel and think about your role as a worker?
6. What recommendations do you have for changes or additions to the workshops that you believe would enhance or improve their quality?

A primary purpose of survey item 5 is to encourage participants to write narratives detailing how they were affected by their participation in the workshop series. Participants are encouraged to use I-statements in their responses. The prompts ask participants to include how the workshop series affected them on an intrapersonal level, including their career/self-identity. Consistent with narrative therapy (White, 2004, 2007; White & Epston, 1990), graduates were asked to describe "the next chapter" in their lives. Additional purposes of the final survey are to assist participants in gaining a sense of closure, as well as incorporating what they have gained from the workshops into their lives.

CASE ILLUSTRATION

Client Description

Sandy was a 44-year-old European American woman who presented as a first-time participant in our workshop series. Prior to her incarceration, she had worked as a certified registered nurse (CRN) and through hard work was promoted to supervisor after several years in her position. However, mounting pressures at home and work contributed to her development of serious addictions to heroin and prescription opiate drugs. Sandy was experiencing problems in her marriage, as well as feelings of stress, depression, and hopelessness. As a CRN, medications were accessible and she began to self-medicate using narcotic drugs to mask the hurt she was feeling in her life. Her problems with addictions grew, and she turned to illegal street drugs, such as cocaine. She eventually turned to criminal activity to support her drug use.

Sandy was eventually arrested, sentenced, and served time in prison. When released, she initially returned to illegal drug use, but then she decided that she wanted help with her problem. She expressed a desire to change her life when she spoke with her probation officer; however, she wasn't sure how to break the cycle. While on probation, Sandy tested positive once again for cocaine and was referred to a substance abuse counseling center for assessment and treatment. She completed a 6-month inpatient treatment program and was ready to start a new life. Sandy still had a desire to work with people but also realized that her criminal past would create a serious obstacle impeding her attempts to secure gainful employment. Sandy's probation officer informed her about the career development workshop series, and she decided to enroll. She was informed that participation was voluntary, and that the series consisted of four 2-hour workshops focusing on issues related to helping individuals with criminal backgrounds gain employment.

Process

Sandy attended the workshop series, completing the four sessions in a span of approximately 6 weeks.

Workshop 1: Career Assessment

From the outset, Sandy exemplified the postmodern spirit of the participants as constituting an allyhood. Her leadership ability was evidenced as she made announcements regarding a local business with an open call for employment applications, and also provided information regarding support groups for individuals suffering from a substance use disorder. During an exercise in which a participant in her mid-twenties had difficulty discussing her personal strengths, Sandy provided affirmations of strengths that she had observed in the young woman during the brief time she had interacted with her in the workshop. In these ways, she exemplified the postmodern ideal of workshop participants serving as resourceful allies for one another.

Early in the first workshop, clients constructed meaningful metaphors representing their views of the future (Kaufman, 1976). Sandy demonstrated that she was capable of constructing a personally meaningful metaphor. She offered that in her metaphor she was a baseball player and she was stranded on third base. One of the workshop facilitators explored the meaning inherent in her metaphor, and she disclosed that her metaphor entailed both a sense of personal accomplishment at having reached third base and a sense of feeling "stuck" as a result of being unemployed. In a later workshop session, a facilitator worked with Sandy to assist her in modifying the metaphor to incorporate her growing awareness of herself as having resources and increasing personal agency.

Later in the first workshop, Sandy participated in the solution-focused exercise in which she constructed a description of her preferred future self (Markus & Nurius, 1986). She shared that in the future she would like to work in an occupation that would allow her to help others who are also struggling with addictions. A part of her motivation for pursuing this particular occupational identity was a strong desire to reduce the pain and suffering of others. She stated that if she were able to achieve this preferred identity, she would feel a strong sense of confidence and a great deal of pride. She was also asked to identify some of her transferable skills that she would be able to utilize in this preferred future role. Some of these included *social perceptiveness, communicating information,* and *active listening.*

Among the intermediate steps she was willing to undertake to bridge the gap between her current and future preferred selves were completing Internet research to learn more about prospective occupations that fit her description of her preferred future self, and finding out what education and training the occupations would require.

Workshop 2: Resume Writing

During the second workshop, Sandy reported that she had read about several occupations that appeared to be well suited to her transferable skills and desire to help others suffering from addictions. Her most preferred occupation was mental health and substance abuse social worker. This position would require a 4-year degree. However, she could first work as a peer support specialist by completing a state certificate program. She explained to the group that a peer support specialist is a person recovering from a mental illness or substance abuse who provides emotional and social support to others living with the same condition. As a first step in composing her resume, she constructed an objective statement reflecting her interest in working as a peer support specialist. Under the Work History section, she listed her previous CRN positions, highlighting action verbs such as *cared for, motivated, informed,* and *coached,* which also reflected skills she would be expected to utilize as a peer support specialist.

Workshop 3: Interviewing Skills

During the Interviewing Skills workshop, Sandy used the STAR acronym (Strength/Task/Action/Result) to construct stories illustrating her strengths (e.g., empathic, good communication skills, and motivating others) consistent with the role of peer support specialist. For example, she shared a story in which she motivated a patient with high blood pressure to adopt healthier lifestyle habits. Importantly, her empowering stories were positive ones that she constructed, or co-constructed with assistance from facilitators or other participants, and ran counter to narratives portraying her as being flawed as a result of her criminal record.

With regard to an approach to disclosing her criminal record, she constructed an alternative story. Her story briefly presented her criminal past, and then emphasized how she constructively used her time in prison, and the steps she had taken to turn her life around since her release, including changing her peer group.

The workshop facilitator revisited Sandy's metaphor of the future in which she viewed herself as a baseball player stranded on third base. He pointed out that unlike herself, a baseball player on third base has little or no resources. She, on the other hand, could engage in numerous beneficial activities such as participating in mock interviews or conducting informational interviews with prospective employers. This process of pointing out potential discrepancies is known as *contrasting* (Neimeyer & Bridges, 2003). He also pointed out that unlike the baseball player, Sandy had access to supportive friends, counselors, and family. The workshop facilitator helped her to extend her metaphor to one in which her attempt to reach home (i.e., secure employment) is thwarted by a "rain delay" during which she is able to consult with coaches and trainers, and prepare mentally for going back into the game when the weather improves. Sandy accepted the co-constructed metaphor, which was more strength-based and entailed a greater sense of personal agency. This interpersonal process of extending the metaphor is known as *dilating* (Neimeyer & Bridges, 2003).

Outcomes

Following completion of the workshop series, Sandy provided written responses to the open-ended survey questions. In response to question 1, asking how she benefited from the workshop series, she wrote: "The workshop series increased my self-esteem and my confidence in myself and what I could accomplish." In this response one can recognize an increase in her sense of self-efficacy and in her career optimism for the future. As previously mentioned, survey question number 5 prompted workshop series completers to "describe the next chapter in your life." In response to this question, Sandy wrote: "I have decided to pursue a position as a Certified Peer Support Specialist, and attend the Human Services degree program at the local community college. Following completion of my Associate's Degree in Human Services, I will transfer to a university to complete a four-year degree in Social Work. After completing this degree, I plan on becoming a Substance Abuse Social Worker." This response clearly reflects an increase in Sandy's sense of purpose, as well as increased clarity regarding her career goals. She attributes her increased sense of purpose to her participation in the workshop series, and she explained that it gave her "the confidence to stand tall" and to move forward with her goals of helping others deal with addictions, homelessness, unemployment, and mental illness.

RESULTS

At the time of completion of the current chapter, the authors were in the process of collecting data for a qualitative study examining the outcomes for workshop series completers ($n = 12$) (Scholl et al., 2016). As previously mentioned, the authors received Wake Forest University Institutional Review Board approval to undertake this research.

The primary goal of this study in progress is to explore how the clients' career development skills (e.g., interviewing, networking) and attitudes (e.g., optimism, hopefulness) may have been influenced by their participation in the four workshops. In addition, we are interested in understanding how completing the workshop series may have influenced their functioning in areas beyond the scope of career or work (e.g., relationships outside of the group).

The study was conducted with a phenomenological approach (Moustakis, 1994) utilizing a conventional approach to qualitative content analysis of clients' responses to the six open-ended survey items. The immediate purpose of the qualitative content analysis is to provide a "subjective interpretation of the content of text data through the systematic classification process of coding and identifying themes" (Hsieh & Shannon, 2005, p. 1278). Because there are limited data available on the outcomes of this type of intervention with community ex-offenders, this type of design is appropriate because it is inductive and descriptive. Themes were independently identified by four raters and then consensually agreed upon, which is a conventional approach (Glaser & Strauss, 1967; Moustakis, 1994) to qualitative content analysis.

The preliminary results indicated that workshop series completers believed participation had contributed to development of their career skills (e.g., networking, interviewing skills) as well as career development attitudes (e.g., increased sense of hope and optimism for their future careers). In addition, the findings indicated that the participants believed the workshop series had contributed to their development in areas transcending their occupational identities. Examples of these transcendent themes inferred by the protocol raters included an increased sense of self-worth, increased feelings of empowerment, and increased sense of access to opportunity. Also, these findings tentatively indicate that the workshop series contributes to participants' growth in ways that may enhance their resilience and positive feelings associated with successful reintegration into the community.

DISCUSSION

From the preceding case illustration, it seems reasonable that participation in the career workshop series facilitated Sandy's self-righting capacity. According to resilience theory, a key factor promoting resilience is social competence (Benard, 1996). The workshops provided her with a supportive context where she could exhibit her social competence by encouraging, supporting, expressing empathy, and providing motivation for her peers. One can infer that she found providing these forms of support to her peers to be meaningful, and consistent with her selecting *peer support specialist* as her preferred occupation. She credited the group with giving her the confidence to follow through on her occupational goals. Thus, participation in the career support group appears to have promoted another important factor contributing to resilience—her sense of self-efficacy. She also credits the group with teaching her the "different avenues for getting and keeping a job." Sandy arguably has learned to recognize and tap into her internal qualities, including compassion, leadership, and personal knowledge gained from bouncing back from difficult life experiences. She is not allowing her criminal conviction to define her. Rather, an alternative narrative she appears to embrace is that her experiences of addiction and incarceration have increased her capacity for compassionate understanding and given her specialized knowledge she can use to empower others. Her aspirations of becoming a social worker and helping others to deal with a host of mental health problems indicate that she is both hopeful and goal oriented.

RECOMMENDATIONS

We advise counselors who endeavor to replicate this program in their own community to develop a close relationship with a community partner. One example of a viable community partner is the Department of Public Safety and, more specifically, a probation officer within that department. A second example is someone in the community who oversees the provision of services to the homeless population in an urban area. In our case, that individual, holding the title "peer support specialist," is an employee of the city's public library system. Forming partnerships with these individuals and their organizations provides us with a meeting place that is already familiar to a number of community ex-offenders. In addition, both the probation officer and the peer support specialist are excellent resources for planning the optimal meeting time for workshops.

Individuals who were recently released from prison sometimes present symptoms such as emotional numbing, difficulty trusting others, hyperarousal, and a startle response (Liem & Kunst, 2013). We usually present our workshops as a team of two or three counselors, which allows us to respond flexibly to the individual needs of one or more clients. If a client has difficulty participating in the group, one facilitator can take the client aside and work with her or him one on one. In some cases, we may decide that an individual is not able to function in the group, but we make every attempt to provide her or him with individual career development assistance (e.g., resume writing, mock interviews). Emphasize that the group is a resource for support, information, networking, and assistance. We have found that group members respond positively to this message and readily provide one another with support and encouragement. We recommend establishing a good collaborative relationship with a community mental health agency and consulting with clinical counselors as needed.

In addition, we commonly observe hopelessness or pessimism in clients. Receiving two stigmatizing labels (i.e., ex-offender, mentally ill) can cause an individual's optimism to plummet. For this reason, our workshop combines a climate of empathy and social support with a postmodern perspective. Because the ex-offender client commonly comes from a background of multiple setbacks, our approach is positive and forward looking. We help clients formulate solutions rather than dwelling on past problems or mistakes. We believe that constructing alternative narratives that emphasize a client's strengths, transferable skills, potential, and aspirations promotes hopefulness.

CONCLUSION

Two and a half years after completing the career workshop series, Sandy returned to speak at a Job Search Strategies workshop facilitated by the first two authors. She proudly informed the participants that she had been drug-free for over 3 years. She credited her participation in the career support sessions with enhancing her ability to cope successfully with her addictions.

For Sandy, and other community ex-offenders, the career development workshops appear to transcend the domain of career development by also enhancing the hopefulness, optimism, and sense of self-worth of participants. The postmodern techniques and practices utilized in the workshops emphasize adoption of a forward-looking, solution-focused attitude. This attitude serves as a springboard for the creation of compelling personal goals and passionate participation in meaningful work.

REFERENCES

Benard, B. (1996). From research to practice: The foundations of the resiliency paradigm. *Resiliency in Action, 1*(1), 7–11.

Benard, B., & Marshall, K. (1997). *A framework for practice: Tapping innate resiliency.* Minneapolis: University of Minnesota, Center for Applied Research and Educational Improvement, College of Education and Human Development.

Brown, S. D., Lent, R. W., & Noll, M. (2013). Applying social cognitive career theory to criminal justice populations: A commentary. *The Counseling Psychologist, 41,* 1052–1060. doi:10.1177/0011000013482380.

Burwell, R., & Chen, C. P. (2006). Applying the principles and techniques of solution-focused therapy to career counseling. *Counseling Psychology Quarterly, 19*(2), 189–203.

Chronister, K. M., & Davidson, M. M. (2010). Promoting distributive justice for domestic violence survivors with group intervention. In A. Singh & C. Salazar (Eds.), *Social justice in group work: Practical interventions for change* (pp. 115–123). New York, NY: Routledge.

de Shazer, S. (1994). *Words were originally magic.* New York, NY: Norton.

Devers, L. (2011). *Desistance and developmental life course theories* (Under Contract No. GS-10F0114L, Order No. 2008-F_08151). Washington, DC: Bureau of Justice Assistance, US Department of Justice.

Doan, R. E. (1998). Interviewing fear and love: Implications for narrative therapy. In M. F. Hoyt (Ed.), *The handbook of constructive therapies: Innovative approaches from leading practitioners* (pp. 219–240). San Francisco, CA: Jossey-Bass.

Fitzgerald, E. L., Chronister, K. M., Forrest, L., & Brown, L. (2012). OPTIONS for preparing inmates for community reentry: An employment preparation intervention. *The Counseling Psychologist, 41*(7), 990–1010.

Gelatt, H. B. (1991). *Creative decision making using positive uncertainty.* Los Altos, CA: Crisp.

Glaser, B. G., & Strauss, A. L. (1967). The discovery of grounded theory: Strategies for qualitative research. Chicago, IL: Aldine.

Hsieh, H. F., & Shannon, S. E. (2005). Three approaches to qualitative content analysis. *Qualitative Health Research, 15,* 1277–1288. doi:10.1177/1049732305276687

Kaufman, D. (1976). *Teaching the future.* Palm Springs, CA: ETC Publications.

Krannich, R., & Krannich, C. (2005). *The ex-offender's job hunting guide.* Manassas Park, VA: Impact Publications.

Laub, J. H., & Sampson, R. J. (2001). *Understanding desistance from crime.* Chicago, IL: The University of Chicago Press.

Lent, R. W., Brown, S. D., & Hackett, G. (1994). Toward a unifying social cognitive theory of career and academic interest, choice, and performance [Monograph]. *Journal of Vocational Behavior, 45,* 79–122.

Lewis, R. E. (2012). Ecohumanism: Integrating humanism and resilience theory. In M. B. Scholl, A. S. McGowan, & J. T. Hansen (Eds.), *Humanistic perspectives on contemporary counseling issues* (pp. 191–214). New York, NY: Routledge.

Liem, M., & Kunst, M. (2013). Is there a recognizable post-incarceration syndrome? *International Journal of Law and Psychiatry, 36,* 333–337.

Markus, H., & Nurius, P. (1986). Possible selves. *American Psychologist, 41*(9), 954.

Masten, A. S. (1994). Resilience in individual development: Successful adaptation despite risk and adversity. In M. C. Wang & E. W. Gordon (Eds.), *Educational resilience in inner-city America: Challenges and prospects* (pp. 3–25). Hillsdale, NJ: Erlbaum.

McWhirter, E. M. (2013). Vocational psychology, offenders and ex-offenders, and social justice: A critical psychology perspective. *The Counseling Psychologist, 41,* 1040–1051. doi:10.1177/0011000013482379

Messer, S. B. (1992). A critical examination of belief structures in integrative and eclectic psychotherapy. In J. C. Norcross & M. R. Goldfried (Eds.), *Handbook of psychotherapy Integration* (pp. 130–168). New York, NY: Basic Books.

Morgan, A. (2000). *What is narrative therapy? An easy to read introduction.* Adelaide, South Australia: Dulwich Centre Publications.

Moustakis, C. (1994). Phenomenological research methods. Thousand Oaks, CA: Sage.

Murdock, N. L. (2013). *Theories of counseling and psychotherapy: A case approach.* New York, NY: Pearson.

Neimeyer, R. A., & Bridges, S. K. (2003). Postmodern approaches to psychotherapy. In A. S. Gurman & S. B. Messer (Eds.), *Essential psychotherapies: Theory and practice* (2nd ed., 272–316). New York, NY: Guilford.

O'Hanlon, B., & Weiner-Davis, M. (2003). *In search of solutions* (rev. ed.). New York, NY: Norton.

Peavy, R. V. (1998). *Sociodynamic counseling: A constructivist perspective for the practice of counseling in the twenty-first century.* Victoria, British Columbia, Canada: Trafford.

Reid, H. L. (2006). Usefulness and truthfulness: Outlining the limitations and upholding the benefits of constructivist approaches for career counseling. In M. McMahon & W. Patton (Eds.), *Career counselling: Constructivist approaches* (pp. 30–41). New York, NY: Routledge.

Robinson, B. S., Davis, K. L., & Meara, N. M. (2003). Motivational attributes of occupational possible selves for low-income rural women. *Journal of Counseling Psychology, 50*(2), 156.

Scholl, M. B., & Cascone, J. (2010). The constructivist resume: Promoting the career adaptability of graduate students in counseling programs. *The Career Development Quarterly, 59,* 180–191.

Scholl, M.B., Perry, J., Calhoun, B., & Robinson, H. (2016). Career support workshop series: Promoting the resilience of community ex-offenders. *Career Planning and Adult Development Journal, 32*(1), 169–178.

Varghese, F. P. & Cummings, D. L. (2012). Introduction: Why apply vocational psychology to criminal justice populations? *The Counseling Psychologist, 41,* 961–989.

Varghese, F. P., Fitzgerald, E. L., Chronister, K. M., Cummings, D. L., & Forrest, L. (2013). Vocational psychology with criminal justice populations: Why not? *The Counseling Psychologist, 41*(7), 1072–1082.

Veysey, B. M., Christian, J., & Martinez, D. J. (2013). *How offenders transform their lives.* New York, NY: Routledge.

Werner, E. E. (1996). How children become resilient: Observations and cautions. *Resiliency in Action, 1*(1), 18–28.

Werner, E. E., & Smith, R. S. (1992). *Overcoming the odds: High risk children from birth to adulthood.* Ithaca, NY: Cornell University Press.

Werner, E. E., & Smith, R. S. (2001). *Journeys from adulthood to midlife: Risk, resilience, and recovery.* Ithaca, NY: Cornell University Press.

White, M. (2007). *Maps of narrative practice.* New York, NY: Norton.

White, M. (2004). Folk psychology and narrative practices. In L. E. Angus & J. McLeod (Eds.), *The handbook of narrative and psychotherapy: Practice, theory, and research* (pp. 15–51). Thousand Oaks, CA: Sage.

White, M., & Epston, D. (1990). *Narrative means to therapeutic ends.* New York, NY: Norton.

CHAPTER 10

Integrating Emerging Understandings of Neuropsychology and Affect for Narrative Therapy With Couples

GERALD MONK AND NAVID J. ZAMANI

Narrative therapy emerged in the latter part of the 20th century, drawing heavily on literary and Foucauldian theory. In their first major text, White and Epston (1990) located narrative therapy within specific strands of continental philosophy that emphasized the value of culture, discourse, and text. Narrative therapy embodied a linguistic turn away from liberal-humanistic philosophies that dominated psychotherapy and counseling. In many ways, it became an exemplar of the workings of poststructuralist and postmodernist concepts within the therapeutic realm. The primacy of narrative therapy has operated within the arena of discourse, culture, and the Foucauldian analyses of power (White & Epston, 1990). In fact, it has been one of the leading linguistic and poststructural therapies for more than 30 years. Certainly, the applications of narrative therapy with couples have primarily emphasized the discursive and linguistic elements of practice.

Because narrative therapy focuses on language as central to the construction of identity and relational life, researchers and practitioners working within a poststructural lens have largely ignored the research and scholarship focusing on the body, brain, emotion, and affect as part of a therapeutic process. However, this is now changing. In the last few years more narrative therapy scholars and practitioners are writing about the importance of including the fields of neurobiology and neurophysiology within the practice of collaborative therapies (Beaudoin, 2015a; Beaudoin & Duvall, 2017; Beaudoin & Zimmerman, 2011; Ewing, Estes, & Like, 2017). Ewing et al. (2017) scholarship is illustrative of this new trend where they describe a new therapeutic modality named narrative neurotherapy that emphasizes the relationship between narratives and physiology.

Within some subsets of neuroscience, psychology, and anthropology, there is now much more emphasis on human materiality. In many social science disciplines, this new interest in the primacy of the body and affect has led to what is now being referred to as the affective turn, a move beyond the linguistic explanations of human behavior (Price-Robertson & Duff, 2015). Wetherell (2012), a poststructural discursive scholar, has laid out a cogent argument for promoting the research on and scholarship of emotion and affect and linking this to a constructionist and discursive approach in mental health. Wetherell argues that some social science communities in the field of psychology have become bored with the 20–30 years of the discursive turn and have all but abandoned a discursive frame. However, she argues that although the study of human affect is beyond talk, texts, and cognition, the study of affect is inextricably linked with meaning making.

Our task in this chapter is to bring forward some of the new scholarship on affect and neuropsychology and its importance in understanding human behavior. More specifically, we begin to link this to narrative approaches to working with couples in therapy. In doing so, we pay attention to some of the patterns of relating in which a couple's physiology is aroused. We address the following:

1. Contemporary practices using narrative therapy with couples embedded within the discursive turn
2. How meaning making and affect are intricately interwoven in the human experience and how both need to be addressed to assist couples seeking therapy
3. How new understandings in the advancement in neuropsychological research help us better understand what is going on with couples in a psychological crisis
4. How research on neurophysiology, discourse, and affect can be incorporated into postmodern practice in couple therapy
5. How neurophysiology and the Foucauldian definitions of power engage with affect and the pursuer–withdrawer, pursuer–pursuer, and withdrawer–withdrawer dynamics in patterns of relating

In addition, we review the implications of these elements combined and integrated into the practice of narrative therapy.

Before introducing these new elements, we provide a brief case example, which will be used to illustrate specific concepts presented throughout the chapter.

A heterosexual couple, Helen and Gilbert, 2 years married, in their mid-twenties, sought counseling because their relationship was in serious trouble. Helen presented as deeply depressed and had low energy; she felt quite bleak about her life circumstances. Gilbert presented as confused and betrayed. He reported that their relationship had been perfect for 3 months and then Helen slowly started to withdraw and go into a shell. Then he described feeling like he was struggling to connect with Helen. He would try and reach out and Helen seemed disinterested in talking through the problems that were piling up. Gilbert spoke a lot in the first session, and Helen at times looked paralyzed to describe what was happening to their relationship and what she was feeling.

Both Helen and Gilbert were in graduate school and were both under stress attending to the various demands of their studies. While both were meeting demanding workloads outside their home, at home Helen was feeling like a failure and was struggling to meet her ideal of being a great homemaker. Gilbert was frustrated that Helen was not turning out to be the wife he was expecting her to be.

Next we present some of the contemporary practices of narrative therapy used with couples; we can then show where we can integrate new literature and new concepts developed from the affect literature and neuropsychology. Our purpose here is to better equip postmodern practitioners to serve the needs of couples in crisis.

KEY CONTEMPORARY NARRATIVE THERAPY PRACTICES WITH COUPLES

Freedman and Combs (2012), arguably the most prolific writers on using narrative therapy with couples, remind us that the narrative metaphor is not used as a problem-solving, communication skills training approach to addressing couple distress. Rather, it focuses on helping clients who are struggling to bring forth aspects of their life narratives that have been diminished by problem-saturated stories. The task of the narrative therapist engaging couples is to develop thick descriptions of alternative, more preferred narratives that allow people to live new versions of themselves, build new relational futures, and strengthen relational identities (Freedman & Combs, 2012). Readers familiar with narrative therapy know the primary focus is on helping couples by eliciting unstoried elements of their lives and relationships to build a preferred relational future. The client stories that narrative therapists work with are usually informed by dominant cultural ideas about the way their relationships should function. These dominant cultural ideas, or discourses as Foucault (1975, 1980) named them, influence couples to think, feel, and behave based on what they come to understand as true, fair, and right about how to be in relationship with their partners. As Combs and Freedman (2012) so deftly described, a narrative therapist's role is to create a context where couples "can lay claim to possibilities in their lives that are outside the box of dominant (presumably problem) narratives" (p. 272). Narrative therapists use the skills of heightened curiosity and persistence, allowing the practitioner to lay bare these new possibilities by asking pertinent questions and paying attention to helpful unstoried knowledge and life experience that were previously dormant, unexpressed, and unavailable to the couple in distress. Essentially, the steps and stages of narrative therapy practice have the following sequence, and this and is largely characteristic of doing narrative therapy with couples (Freedman & Combs, 2012; Monk, Winslade, Crocket, & Epston, 1997; White, 2007):

- The therapist evaluates with clients their current problem situation.
- Together, they externalize the problem and the discourses associated with the problem.
- Clients, with the help of the therapist, map the effects of problem situations on persons.
- Clients evaluate their relationship with the problem to invite accountability, action, and agency.
- Clients take a stand against the problem and explore lived experiences of the person's life that are part of a preferred narrative or counterstory.
- The therapist and client coauthor alternative stories constructed within the landscapes of action and identity.
- The therapist creates opportunities for telling and witnessing.

We concur with Hansen and Scholl (2018) that postmodern therapists can apply clear action steps and plans in setting the stage for a focused therapeutic contract. The therapist demonstrating expertise in developing a plan and laying out the process of therapy is important for a postmodern practitioner while at the same time being attuned to the clients and their expertise on their lives and their hopes for the future.

Narrative therapists typically start therapy with learning from the couple about the dominant stories that are shaping their relationship. Although many narrative therapists are reluctant to engage in goal setting and planning with their clients, many do explore the couple's ideas about future directions and specific life projects with which they are engaged. In this manner, narrative therapists do follow a relatively direct methodology when engaging with their clients. Partners are asked questions that encourage reflection on the effects of the problem story on each of their lives as well as the toll this is taking on their relationship. What follows is creating a therapeutic context in which the narrative therapist invites the couple to take responsibility or to experience themselves as agentic actors prepared to address the effects of the problem.

Narrative therapists focus on whose voices are privileged in the relationship and the discourses at play that contribute to parties closing communication down. Fundamental to narrative practice is the tracking of dominant discourses and their effects on clients. Michael White's (1991) transformative article titled "Deconstruction and Therapy" thrust the analysis of wider sociocultural and sociopolitical forces that affect people's mental health to the forefront in the minds of narrative therapists. White defined deconstruction as a procedure that subverts "taken-for-granted realities and practices" that subjugate and diminish people's lives. In fact, White and Epston's (1990) text *Narrative Means to Therapeutic Ends* coupled Foucauldian theory on discourse with the techniques of externalizing, an approach that White had invented many years before. Effectively, White's narrative mantra "the person is not the problem; the problem is the problem," the concept that supported the technique of externalizing, tied neatly into locating problems within discourses using externalizing practice. This discursive emphasis in therapy gave therapists new tools to explore the power relations that influence couple interaction. Couples could consider how discourses pertaining to gender, ethnicity, class, patriarchy, age, and other sociocultural and sociohistorical factors affect their relationship (Freedman & Combs, 2010). The work of Knudson-Martin (2013) and her colleagues has added important elements for therapists to explore with couples when doing deconstruction work with dominant gender discourses that can undermine gender equality and connectedness. This discursive work will be studied in more detail later in the chapter.

Identifying unique outcomes that are the building blocks of the preferred relational story is a significant part of work for narrative therapists working with couples. Narrative therapists track interactional events occurring between the couple that lie outside of the problem narratives shared early in the counseling sessions. Michael White's use of the concept "absent but implicit" is particularly helpful to track what is implied but left out when clients share about what is important to them (Carey et al., 2009; White, 2000). Adopting the technique of "double listening" to help the therapist listen for what is operating in the background that is shaping and influencing the client's actions is beneficial in revealing the client's preferences. For example, when a person experiences anger about an injustice that occurred in their relationship, the therapist can double listen for the kind of justice that the client embraces. This preferred justice can be elicited and lead to a construction around preferences and hopes for the future. Using the narrative metaphor, therapists help clients organize preferred events as plot lines, which are the makings of the preferred story. During therapy, these stories are told and the therapist and the parties present are witnesses to the telling, leading to building a new foundation on which these stories can be brought into being.

New stories are performed in what Bruner (1986) described as landscapes of action and landscapes of consciousness (or what he later termed landscape of identity). Unique outcomes are behaviors, thoughts, and feelings that occur within the landscape of action. Narrative therapists use this landscape to inquire about the volition and new agentic action displayed by the parties. This new action is then linked to the landscape of identity. For example, Freedman and Combs (1993) use what they describe as meaning questions that invite people to reflect on the landscape of action by considering the beliefs, values, and wishes that are being expressed within the person's actions. By exploring meaning in the action landscape, the door is opened to invite the couple to consider how their identities are being re-created in the landscape of action. At the heart of narrative therapy with couples is the creation of space for clients to develop within the relationship to become what Freedman and Combs (2012) call a place in the relationship "to become the person I want to be" (p. 284). There is a range of narrative techniques employed to facilitate a witnessing process that supports the performance of a preferred counternarrative of the couple's story. These techniques can include outsider witnessing, the internalized other questioning, and listening from relational perspectives.

This brief overview of the most recognizable elements of narrative therapy with couples gives us the opportunity later in the chapter to weave into mainstream narrative therapy practices new theoretical and therapeutic threads drawn from affect studies, neuropsychology, and specific practices utilized within the emotionally focused therapy (EFT) literature. In this next part of the chapter, we briefly summarize some of the recent scholarship on the affective turn.

THE AFFECTIVE TURN

Over the years, we have experienced students who are new to narrative therapy sometimes comment that this approach to therapy is too cerebral, too cognitively focused, and demonstrates an exaggerated interest in words and thoughts and neglects what people are experiencing in their bodies and their emotions. Some critics of narrative therapy say that this practice largely ignores affect and pays insufficient attention to bodily experience and feelings. Experienced practitioners of narrative therapy know this criticism to be inaccurate. On the contrary, the practice of narrative therapy can be thoroughly captivating of a person's entire human experience. Yet narrative therapists have not traditionally emphasized the value of engagement with affect and bodily experience. As we have noted earlier, there is now a commitment to using the contemporary knowledge found within the discipline of neurobiology and integrating this knowledge into the collaborative therapies and narrative therapy (Beaudoin, 2015a; Ewing, Estes, & Like, 2017). In this chapter, we too argue for a more deliberate, more intentional effort to engage with the field of neurophysiology and neuropsychology. We also emphasize in the chapter how the affective turn has us focus keenly on the body and emotion when working with couples from a predominantly poststructural orientation. We review the new literature on the study of affect and human materiality and the contributions this work can make to narrative and poststructural work.

We begin with a review of Margaret Wetherell's (2012) analysis of the affective turn. Wetherell's account of the affective turn is particularly interesting to poststructuralists because she has had a long history of articulating poststructural discursive applications in the field of psychology. Wetherell gives an account of how scholars on the study of affect (Ahmed, 2014; Brennan, 2004; Massumi, 2002; Sedgwick, 2003; Stewart, 2007; White, 1993) are analyzing feeling practices, to better understand the allegiances people have when they are meaning making and building an account of psychological actions. She suggests that affective practice helps us understand bodily possibilities. Affective practice engages with a nonconscious aspect of human functioning where habits form within deep-rooted relational patterns. There is a quality of human functioning where we sometimes are not aware of our bodily responses until after the fact. The study of affect is beyond text, words, and cognition and beyond a conscious account. Sharp bursts of affect invoke an action-oriented body. Affect constitutes a strong push to fight, flee, or freeze—to do something. In our case study of Helen and Gilbert's relationship, Helen describes a feeling of being paralyzed and struggling to engage Gilbert as he criticizes her failure to be present and active in the relationship. In the face of a psychological attack, she freezes or withdraws. It is more than psychological retreat. Her body feels the threat—her body is burdened, and there is a sense of heaviness, persistent tiredness, or wanting to sleep. Gilbert is active, in a pursuing mode, displaying a vigorous intensity, his tone of voice is harsh, his eyes are narrow, and his brow furrows—his body moves close wanting engagement, demanding engagement, setting up a new round of Helen's withdrawing, turning away, hunching over, her face pale and blank looking.

We understand affect when it is defined as the "experience of feeling"; it includes every aspect of emotion, physical reverberation, snarls, blushes, tears, sobs, levels of arousal, and dynamic changes in patterns of neural activity. Attention to affect requires us to come to terms with the body. Affect scholars (Beaudoin, 2015b; Siegel, 2012) emphasize the spontaneous automaticity of physiological reactions and the involuntary nature of bodily reaction. The central nervous system produces chemical transmitters that connect neural pathways. Neural circuits begin to fire rapidly, conveying information to the body. When there is an affective response, the body pumps out somatic gestures. Initiated in the reptilian brain and powered by the autonomic nervous system, changes in blood flow occur, heart and breathing rate change, and muscles move involuntarily, creating facial frowns, twisting, smiling, and wrinkling.

As we focus more on affect and the body, new adherents of the affective turn find poststructural discourse explanations somewhat limited in explaining and describing human behavior when considering the dynamic influences of affect in everyday life. Yet, despite this new attention to affect, Wetherell (2012) argues that the organization and interpretation of body possibilities is always culturally embedded and thus the subscription to the universal basic emotions thesis fundamentally misrepresents the complex investigation of the affective turn.

CONTRIBUTIONS OF NEW ADVANCES IN NEUROPSYCHOLOGY TO UNDERSTANDING COUPLE DYNAMICS

In the last 20 years, neuropsychology has seen a leap in technologies that allow researchers to examine the brain and neurological processes in a way that was not imaginable before. This includes an increased ability to connect this information with data from the body. Electrocardiograms, heart rate monitors, skin galvanization, and respiration instruments allow for instantaneous biofeedback on the physiological states of our bodies. These advancements have offered both researchers and practitioners much more nuanced understandings of the relationships between our brain, body, and environment in which we reside. Gergen (1991) proposes that the conceptual separation between the brain, body, and environment is a construct that we have created to help us understand these perceived components. This oversimplified classification can influence us to overlook the complexities between these systems. We suggest that narrative therapists are wise to consider affect and physiology as their own strands of narratives to be considered and reflected upon with their clients.

As scientific understandings of the body and brain expanded, ideas have developed of the "mental mind" and the "medical body" (Foucault, 1975; White, 2009). In this dichotomy, understandings of the self and the resulting treatments and interventions are split in their objectives of curing symptoms of the mind or symptoms of the body. These "symptoms" are understood to have their origins in *either* the brain or the body, but not both. Our understanding of ulcers is a wonderful example of this. Ulcers were originally assumed to originate due to stress or spicy foods. However, in the 20th century, scientists could identify the presence of a bacterium as the main perpetrator of this ailment. This information was initially rejected so widely that the scientist who developed this theory drank a petri dish full of the ulcer-responsible bacterium. He earned a Nobel Prize when he developed ulcers, and then was able to eliminate the ulcers by taking antibiotics. So, at this point, we had moved from a "mental" understanding of ulcers to a "bodily" understanding of ulcers. Now, research is indicating that certain affectual states can promote the growth of this bacterium, indicating the complex role of, believe it or not, both the body and mind as integral in the process (Overmier & Murison, 2012).

It can be argued that the inclusion of physiology and affect with the support of neuroscience understandings is beginning to capture the "wholeness" of one's experience. People are more than the summation of intellectual and discursive experiences in their lives, and they are also more than just a set of conditioned behavioral responses that are situated in purely biological processes. In fact, it is difficult to look at any facet of an individual's life without considering its relationship and interaction with other aspects and experiences in their lives, which can feel like a daunting challenge as a therapist! Lived experience both shapes and is shaped by the brain. Incorporating new advances in neuroscience in narrative therapy can create a richness in our therapeutic conversation with couples. Exchanges in these conversations incorporating affect and the bodily sensations generated between the therapist and the couple produce new experience, and through this *experience*, change occurs (Beaudoin, 2015b; Ewing, Estes & Like, 2017; Siegel, 2012). Using an affective lens, we encourage the naming of the bodily responses Gilbert and Helen bring into the room. Their bodies convey messages as important as the spoken problem-saturated narratives expressed by the couple. "Helen, I notice when Gilbert starts to talk and express frustrations, your shoulders drop, the color in your face is paler, your head looks down and away." "Gilbert, as you engage more with the sense of disconnection you are describing, your voice tone is a little sharper, your chest is rising and falling more quickly. You are leaning forward. There is brighter color rising in your neck." Naming what we are seeing and feeding it back to this couple in distress enriches the communication that's taking place. We discuss the therapeutic value of tracking affect and explore this later in the chapter.

Connecting the underpinnings of neuroscience concepts to the ways that a relational experience is processed in the body becomes a critical component when looking at the dynamics of a couple. It is commonly accepted that our brains are wired for relationships (Siegel, 2012). The structures and functions of our brain, our sensory organs, and even physiological expressions in our body, are hugely influenced by our relational contexts. So much so that the painful experience of losing a relationship is processed through the same neural systems and networks as physical pain (Eisenberger et al., 2006). This can explain why it literally hurts when we lose somebody we love. To further expand on the connectedness of the body and brain, neurons (cells that can learn and adapt, and exhibit traits of "neuroplasticity") have been discovered in both the heart and the gut, which has led to fields such as nuerogastroenterology and neurocardiology (Beaudoin & Zimmerman, 2015). Discoveries like this could begin to account for sensations of and physiological states associated with "heart-ache," the relationship between ulcers and affect, or even classic descriptions of physiological responses to emotional stimuli, such as "butterflies in my stomach." In fact, there have been cases where heart recipients can recall events in which they did not participate and are recollecting the memories "encoded" in the heart of the donor (Beaudoin, 2015).

Our experiences, our perception of ourselves through these experiences, are felt and stored throughout our bodies. There are numerous authors that suggest that the processes of perception, action, and expectation share the same neural pathways in the brain, also called the perception/action theory (Ewing, Estes, & Like, 2017; Proffitt, 2006; Witt, 2011). In this context, it is not necessary for an experience to be immediately occurring for it be "real" in the body. Ewing, Estes, and Like (2017) argue that the experiencing and naming of our identities in combination with their associated physiologies contributes to what they call an "identity state." When thinking about couples in distress, it can be helpful to consider the identity states that are constructed within the relational arena in which both partners engage. There are many strategies through which this consideration of identity state can occur: through asking questions that encourage the individual to be mindful of and connected with expressions of an experience in their bodies; enactments of the problem where the experience is "replicated" physically, mentally, and emotionally; and creative mediums such as art or music, which have been shown to enhance emotions and autobiographical memories (Jancke, 2008).

Central to this approach is that therapy is a learning process, rather than a healing process (Ewing, Estes, & Like, 2017). When individuals are in a relationship, we begin to learn about certain habits of relating, whether it is intentional or not. We begin to learn that certain statements and behaviors lead to certain reactions, certain tendencies start to create different emotional reactions in our partner, and so forth. This idea that we are not only learning about how to manage ourselves and our emotions in relationships but also the other has been named in neuroscience literature as the "social regulation of emotion" (Reeck et al., 2016). Research has even shown that a child's ability to socially regulate and attend to others' emotions enhances their ability to self-regulate in the future (Reeck et al., 2016). The converse is also present in research, that a child exposed to relational stress, particularly through "relational deprivation," can be more attuned to and responsive to stress (Patterson & Vakili, 2014). All these experiences begin to "teach" our brain about how things "typically" happen, which creates and reinforces very specific neural patterns and pathways, and therefore creates an "implicit bias." This implicit bias tends to hone in on and wire in negative affect (Beaudoin, 2015a). This was a helpful response when humans were just beginning to evolve, as it allowed us to connect with negative experiences, such as an encounter with a predator, and work hard to avoid them in the future. In today's world, this process shows up with experiences that are not immediately life threatening but are perceived to be stressful and dangerous. Therefore, therapy becomes a process where clients can begin to learn about themselves and their relationships, and begin to "rewire" some of the automatic functions and reactions of our brain to better fit their preferred identities and lives.

It should not be surprising to hear that intense emotion can override the brain's cognitive processes (Damasio, 2000; Nader & LeDoux, 2000). This process has been tracked in the brain. At the structural level, strong and well-developed connections exist between the amygdala (the section of our brain that seeks out threats in our environment) and the limbic system (where basic emotions and drives are housed) in the brain, and less neural pathways to the prefrontal cortex (where conscious thinking occurs). Functional magnetic resonance imaging scans of this process occurring in the brain show that the limbic system firing results in increased blood flow to the amygdala and decreases the blood flow to the prefrontal cortex, possibly indicating that experiences of anxiety and fear are heightened when the limbic system is overly activated, and the ability to engage in cognitive processes is more difficult. This heightened activity in the limbic system has been observed in individuals who identify with anxiety disorders and/or depression, and it provides a context for the strong relationship between these two diagnoses (Beaudoin, 2015a). This also speaks to the process of "flight, fight, or freeze," which we will cover in more detail later.

A result of approaching the therapeutic process as a learning one is that our proposition of conversations being experience driven becomes quite integral. Consider a school teacher that you felt had a significant impact on your learning. What was it about this teacher and his or her style that created such a rich learning context? Often, and in my (Navid) own experience, these teachers created tasks and assignments that emulated my lived experience, and it was through this experience that I learned. Compare that to a purely didactic context where a teacher tells you facts and encourages little engagement during the lecture. Therapeutic contexts can strive for a similar learning experience when they scaffold a conversation with questions, encouraging connection with a fuller experience that captures multiple aspects of our body's experience. White (2007) refers to "scaffolding" as a central feature of narrative therapy, which is drawn from Vygotsky's (1962) theoretical understandings of how children come to learn and understand new concepts. Neuroscience literature reflects that learning, and through our lived experience, we create structural and functional shifts throughout the brain (Kozorovitskiy et al., 2005). These shifts ultimately lead to the creation and development of biased neural pathways (Beaudoin & Zimmerman, 2015).

Invoking an experiential dialogue, where clients are able to connect with the "wholeness" of an experience, does not necessarily mean that you need to have the couple actually be in a fight or perform a dramatization of a preferred romantic gesture (such as acknowledging a preferred action through a compliment) for the process to be therapeutic. Simply put, bringing in notions of affect and emotion through questions and conversation that provoke a client to consider those connections can be hugely influential. It opens larger possibilities for accessing relevant memories. An individual is more likely to recall memories that were encoded in a similar emotional state, also referred to as "state-dependent recall" (Vazquez & Campbell, 1992). For instance, if a client is connecting to an identity state that elicits negative affect, he or she is more likely to recall negative memories, offering up more "plot points" for a problem-saturated story. When a client is situated in a preferred identity state, such as a partner talking about what it was like and how it felt to have a romantic gesture (like flowers) offered to them by their partner, they are much more likely to recall other positive memories, which begins to create a set of memories and experiences through which a reauthored and preferred narrative can be constructed (Beaudoin, 2016). It is critical that the associated physiology and affect are considered when in this preferred identity state. This is especially important as research supports that simply putting our bodies in a specific physical position that might be associated with a preferred identity state can allow us to better recall certain emotional experiences. For instance, a smile (even if fake or forced) can allow us to better recall emotional experiences associated with smiling (Critchley & Nagai, 2012; Davis, Senghas & Ochsner, 2009; Hennenlotter et al., 2009). This shift from a problem-saturated understanding to a "viscerally felt" preferred identity changes the brain's synaptic connections and firing (Siegel, 2012). As couples begin to understand the impact their partner has on their physiology and the impact they have on their partner's physiology, more opportunities open for addressing the relational issues emerging in the multiple landscapes of action and identity. Ewing, Estes, and Like (2017) have broadened the narrative therapy literature here to include exploring what is occurring within the individual's neurophysiology or what they term the "landscape of physiology." This exploration opens new options for practitioners to be mindful of the physiological condition of clients. When physiological arousal is soothed and quieted, structures in the brain are communicating without interference from an intense affective experience, so couples can attend to their relational dynamics with a higher level of ethical behavior and care.

DISCURSIVE AND AFFECTIVE DYNAMICS OCCURRING WITH COUPLES IN CRISIS

When speaking to the challenges of couples in crisis, habits of relating, and the neuroscience literature that surrounds these ideas, it can be a challenge to do so without seeming to adopt positivist and essentialist language that labels persons and categorizes lived experiences. This is not our goal. Rather, we are offering some contemporary knowledge in the field of neuropsychology and affect studies and how this work might fit into a postmodern practitioner's work.

An intimate relationship is a rich breeding ground for unchecked discourses and negative relational dynamics to occur. In this space, persons can be pathologized, identities corrupted, and the emotional well-being of the couple deeply disturbed. Often it is not just the couple who falls victim to these discourses but also the therapist who can become seduced and "sucked in" by the problems that are presented by the couple in distress. For this reason, a critical examination of the discourses surrounding not only intimate relationships but also the treatment modalities offered by the profession can offer an important escape from the ritualistic conversations about fixing the "communication." Instead, therapists can venture deeper into arenas of meaning-making and value systems that can be profoundly influential within a relationship.

When couples come in for counseling, they often arrive with the presenting concern of "communication problems" or "inability to talk to each other" (Gray, 2005; White, 2007). Although we are not suggesting that this is an invalid concern or an inaccurate description of what they are experiencing, we feel that this construction of the problem tends to obscure the more nuanced dynamics that are occurring and contributing to the pursuer–withdrawer "dance" that we will describe in more detail. Often these relational habits are occurring within the confines of gendered and discursive power, which are often not agreed upon nor explicitly stated positions within a relationship.

Therapy approaches to heterosexual couples in distress tend to assume that both partners are committed to a relationship of equality rather than a traditional patriarchal relationship where many men wield undue influence over their partners (Leslie & Southard, 2009; Lyness & Lyness, 2007). It is not uncommon for relationships that are in distress to be organized around the needs of the person with more influence, and typically this process is hidden as "normal" or "how it is." Furthermore, while most therapists recognize the importance of gender in the context of relationships, few tend to address it in a way that brings it forth as a prominent and influential voice in relationships (Leslie & Southard, 2009). Many heterosexual couples tend to organize their relational lives around a "gender legacy" where discourses of male privilege are prominent and influential (Knudson-Martin & Mahoney, 2005). The underlying effects of these unequal gendered understandings and behaviors are often neglected by therapists who, instead, have conversations almost exclusively about improving communication and attending to the "needs" of the other, which can unintentionally replicate issues of patriarchal discourse that are typically inherently present in heterosexual relationships (Knudson-Martin, 2013). The effects of patriarchal discourses that tend to privilege the needs and wants of men have significant effects of the couple's physiology. When men have expectations of their female partners about how their partners should look and behave, and ideas about what domestic and child care roles they should perform, these expectations easily turn into taken-for-granted entitlements. Unmet entitlements often lead to a "gender-familiar" display of emotion where many men move quickly to anger without having cognitive awareness that their body has moved to psychologically fight/attack stance or in some instances they are about to engage in physical violence. After the display of anger, the affective state often moves to a more culturally familiar stance of withdrawal. The display or anger in many men is culturally sanctioned in the ways it is not for many women. A complementary response in many women is to withdraw, to move to sadness and distress, or in some cases to attack or counterattack. It is not at all uncommon in therapy to see evidence of many women following such a display moving into a "pursuer" pattern to seek reengagement following a display of unsatisfied entitlement. Displaying vulnerability for many men is often held in check by then shutting down, stonewalling, or even placating. We immediately recognize that while naming this cultural pattern of emotional display, there are strong examples of gender action that do not fit this pattern at all. There is harm done in assuming this pattern of relating exists as some kind of essence within men and women and that it must be found by the therapist and confirmed to be so. In our example of Gilbert and Helen's relationship, there are prominent signs of a patriarchal rhythm taking hold. Gilbert has a taken-for-granted set of assumptions about what Helen should be doing in relation to domestic duties and emotional caregiving. These expectations easily turn into gender entitlements that invite Gilbert to expect more from Helen, even though Helen is working equally hard as Gilbert outside of their home. These gender entitlements work on Helen, too, leaving her feeling guilty and ashamed that she is not being a "better wife"—being more proficient on the domestic front and being an emotionally nurturing woman who caters to Gilbert's emotional needs. Gender entitlements are often woven into an affective landscape, leaving the couple reacting emotionally to one another driven by a narrow set of cultural imperatives of what a marriage should be.

In response to the "taken-for-granted" hierarchy that is often present yet unacknowledged in heterosexual relationships, a therapist is well situated to take an active role in the uncovering of these gender legacies (Almeida et al., 2008; Jordan, 2009). This is particularly critical, as those affected by male entitlement tend to be "less aware" and "less tuned into the needs and interests" of those who do not share equal power (Parker, 2009). Gray (2005) describes the difficulty men can have in accessing emotional language when they are steeped in patriarchal discourses. In the West, this can contribute to value systems structured around suppressing emotion, and only very specific expressions of emotion being acceptable (such as anger). In our case example, Helen and Gilbert are not conforming to stereotypical gender expressions of affect. Gilbert is making strong bids for connection, but these bids strike a discordant tone. He is longing to connect. He is wanting affection, yet the style of his engagement is aversive to Helen. In contrast, Helen has emotional habits closer to a stereotypical male gendered response, which is often to stonewall, to shut down, or to withdraw emotionally.

Gottman (2011) speaks to the destructive consequences with men who have more power, particularly when they are situated in negative affect. This fits in well with the neuroscience literature that we have discussed earlier, which largely suggests that negative affect significantly reduces blood flow to the frontal lobe, lessens the ability to connect with others, narrows attention, increases the production of cortisol, and engages the fight, flight, or freeze system (Cohen, 2005; Siegel, 2012). The opposite is equally true. By taking an active role and addressing patriarchal discourse in relationships, therapists are better situated to support their clients in achieving their desired outcomes. Research shows that both women and men do better in equal relationships (Steil, 1997), and that couples who were not organized around gender differences and shared decision making and a relationship built on equality reported feeling "understood," "respected," and "heard" (Knudson-Martin, 2013). For same-sex relationships, power discrepancies were identified, but they were more likely to be aware of them and engage in expressions of indebtedness and gratitude (Knudson-Martin, 2013). Gilbert and Helen's relationship does not model gender equality. Gilbert's expectations are driven by a patriarchal discourse, not an equity discourse.

While we are speaking about the background influences of patriarchal discourse here, it is important to note that it does not show up so plainly in conversations. Additionally, power is not a fixed commodity that is held by a specific person (or gender) at all times; rather, it is a fluid relational dynamic that is hugely influenced by many variables. As we discussed earlier, notions and actions of power are typically conveyed through the vehicle of discourse. Therefore, it is not that *men* walk into relationships with power and begin to wield it blindly, but rather that romantic partners show up in relationships under the influence of strong patriarchal discourses. This is true for both men and women. The influence of discourse can be so powerful that it can encourage "horizontal oppression," where it is women who conform to patriarchal discourses and maintain the status quo (Monk, Winslade, & Sinclair, 2008). I (Navid) have certainly been privy to conversations where a woman has asked her female friend why "she doesn't stay at home to take care of the children," or that her friend can "make [her] man happy by meeting his needs when he gets home from work." Both these statements are soaked in gendered and relational discourses that begin to create very specific expectations for relationships.

Knudson-Martin (2013) describes four qualities of a "postgender" relationship (couples who are not organized around gender differences and share power and relational responsibility, and have mutual vulnerability, mutual attunement, and mutual influence). Shared relational responsibility refers to a practice where both partners are "sensitive and accountable" for their actions within the relationship and take an active role in maintaining the relationship. Mutual vulnerability refers to the willingness and sense of safety each partner has in being able to admit weakness, uncertainty, or mistakes in their partner's presence, and bringing a "spirit of openness, curiosity, and self-honesty" to the relationship. Mutual attunement is an ongoing awareness and interest in the needs of the other, typically without the expectation of reciprocity. And mutual influence is being able to allow your partner to have an impression on and influence your thoughts, feelings, and actions. Not only do these qualities promote an egalitarian relationship, but they also fit into the idea that we are constantly socially regulating others' emotions, and that this process is more than just a neuropsychological habit but also a political action. Gottman refers to this process within relationships as an "interlocking influence process," which he identified as being present in successful couples (Gottman, 2011).

NEUROPHYSIOLOGY AND THE PURSUER–WITHDRAWER, PURSUER–PURSUER, AND WITHDRAWER–WITHDRAWER DYNAMICS IN PATTERNS OF RELATING

Our brain activates our physiological and psychological resources to deal with perceived threats that result in fearful and anxiety-focused reactions. As mentioned earlier, the brain is designed to protect and create safety. Our brains are designed to streamline mental processes. The amygdala and thalamus work in tandem to make sure the body has the physiological resources it needs to react to threat. The brain fires instantaneously with limited cognitive information. The body acts. Our responses to perceived threats normally produce at least three habitual reactions (Cannon, 1929; Jansen, Nguyen, Karpitskiy, Mettenleiter & Loewy, 1995). The most familiar habitual human response is flight—an action to get away from threat. A fleeing from psychological threat is characterized by psychological withdraw. A psychological withdrawal tends to produce human reactions that lead to placation, shutting down, or giving in to the threat. We can see strong evidence of Helen being subjected to the flight dynamic and retreating to find psychological safety. The second habitual response is to physically fight the perceived threat or to psychologically respond with an angry or aggressive attack in order to subdue the threat. The attacking psychological response turns into a heightened and intense form of reaction that can involve anger, aggression, pursuing, intense criticism, and anxiety to get a response. Gilbert is participating in this pursuing and fighting dynamic. The third habitual response is to freeze, like a deer in headlights. It often psychologically translates to immobilization, passivity, and inaction. These reactions we describe here are by no means new to the mental health field and have been described in the literature for decades (Cannon, 1929). We want to explore some of the therapeutic techniques we can use in couple therapy based upon these ideas but use them within a poststructural frame.

Building upon the family systems literature of the 1970s and 1980s, Susan Johnson (2004) who founded emotionally focused therapy (EFT) has eloquently described the pursuing and distancing dance. Her efforts to resurrect an analysis of these dynamics from the earlier systems theory work is an important contribution we have paid attention to in our couple work. In this chapter, advocates of EFT will be disappointed to discover that we ignore many of the fundamental verities of emotionally focused work as articulated by Johnson and her colleagues (Furrow, Johnson, & Bradley, 2011; Kallos-Lilly & Fitzgerald, 2015). This occurs because we have misgivings in how EFT largely ignores the dominating influences of patriarchy, gender dynamics, heterosexism, ethnic diversity, socioeconomic effects, and all dominant discursive influences occurring in any social location that human beings engage. This occurs largely because EFT has a universalistic and liberal-humanist analysis that often unintentionally ignores the discursive frame. We find we can incorporate the pursuer and distancing patterns of relating in our therapeutic practice without having to adopt a purely universal set of descriptions of human behavior.

Johnson makes a link with the flight and fight response with the pursuer–withdrawer dynamic. In this next section, we review Johnson's (2004) research and scholarship that describes what occurs with couples displaying these flight–fight, pursuer–withdrawer dynamics. We then make a case for why there is value in examining and integrating these cyclical habits of relating in couple therapy for practitioners using a literary, text-based discursive frame. We want to be clear that we do not subscribe to categorizing persons as pursuers or withdrawers, which would be a rudimentary, simplistic, and essentializing analysis that shows complete disregard for context and social location. Instead, we will argue that these cyclical patterns of relating can play out with particular couples in particular circumstances. If the individuals in a relationship habitually participated in one kind of relational dynamic with one another, we argue that participation in the pattern can change at a different stage of their lives or change because of different life circumstances. In addition, if individuals in one intimate relationship demonstrated a particular habitual style of relating and then these individuals became involved in a different intimate partnership, their habitual style of engagement could completely change with this new person.

The most recent scholarship on these patterns of relating for couples (Kallos-Lilly & Fitzgerald, 2015) falls into three different categories: the pursue–withdraw, the pursue–pursue, and the withdraw–withdraw. We describe the pursuing and withdrawing behaviors and motivations. Not surprisingly, in many instances there is a strong gender component to the habitual patterns of relating. Interestingly, in the case example we cite with Gilbert and Helen, the stereotypical pattern is reversed. Gilbert features some classical pursuer patterns of relating, whereas Helen exhibits a withdrawing or distancing dynamic.

The pursuing habit is often driven by the threat of being alone, feeling isolated, feeling like one does not matter, and fear of abandonment. Pursuing is often an attempt to close an inaccessibility gap. Behaviors can be intense, clinging, and filled with angry criticism. Blame, complaining, demanding, and trying to control are often at play with a pursuing dynamic. The body's physiology is fighting for engagement. The pursuing dynamic is not to be confused with tactics that accompany patterns of behavior that use physical and psychological violence to stalk, try to control a partner's activities, and suffocate a person's choices of relating to others. These are classical patriarchal patterns of behavior that emanate from the dominant discursive themes that many men are affected by that are discussed in the previous section on power and privilege.

The withdrawing dynamic is primarily driven by the flight to psychological safety. A person withdrawing feels anxious and incompetent in the face of an attacking pursuing dynamic. An avoidant withdrawing is an effort to quiet the physiology, regulate fears of rejection, and limit the threats accompanying a sense of failure, feelings of being unworthy of care, and being overwhelmed. The behaviors can often present as defended, stonewalling and dismissing, numbed out, or shut down and avoiding. Not surprisingly, many men who have been raised in traditional gendered relational patterns can often be located in a withdrawing dynamic, which can often be accompanied by a lack of language to express emotion (Gray, 2005). Many men are not raised to develop relational patterns that enable them to be emotionally available and vulnerable; therefore, retreat becomes an emotional withdrawing habit. The flight dynamic diminishes the prospect of being emotionally vulnerable. Without the couple understanding what is physiologically occurring, trying to merely suppress the pattern is an ineffective strategy because it often heightens the body's arousal and bodily reaction leaks out in facial expressions and voice tone that can reinforce the habitual pattern. Helen and Gilbert report that they react to particular facial expressions or voice tones displayed by the other, and this invigorates the pursuer–withdrawer dynamic. The bodily responses occur so rapidly that they can rarely be controlled consciously. Johnson (2004) claims that the suppression of affect in one partner can increase affective responses in the other. Couple therapy must focus on reducing the threats the couple experience in the flight–fight dynamic. Additionally, once the brain has begun a negative affective turn, it initiates a set of responses that creates an unhelpful context to begin to reflect on and speak about what the client is experiencing, as mentioned previously. The therapist's task is to provide a context to build psychological safety and develop a therapeutic process for helping the couple diminish their fears that usually trigger the habitual responses. The pursuing–withdrawing dynamic, which attempts to keep psychological threats at bay, paradoxically keeps fear alive in the relationship. Fear keeps Helen and Gilbert from reaching for care, contact, and comfort from the other in an emotionally straightforward and vulnerable way. Paying attention to the affective turn and the robust neuropsychological discoveries we are making about the human body help us understand how emotions can organize social interactions and orient and prime our behavioral responses.

Withdraw–Withdraw Dynamic and Pursue–Pursue Dynamic

The *withdraw–withdraw dynamic* and the *pursue–pursue dynamic* patterns have all the characteristics of the elements described earlier except rather than having the complementary dynamic pursuer–withdrawer, this habitual dance has a symmetrical theme. Withdraw–withdraw tends to have an appease, avoid rhythm where individuals resolve a perceived threat to their well-being by retreating. A pursue–pursue dynamic often occurs where an individual who more typically withdraws in the face of a fight or attacking response turns to counterattack. In the remainder of the chapter we lay out some of the specific techniques in our couple work that incorporate these cyclical patterns of relating.

INCORPORATING NEUROPHYSIOLOGY, AFFECT, AND HABITS OF RELATING AROUND FLIGHT, FIGHT, AND FREEZE INTO NARRATIVE/POSTMODERN PRACTICE WITH COUPLES

Narrative and the postmodern therapies stand securely on their own epistemological ground resting within the linguistic and discursive turn. As we laid out in the beginning of this chapter, poststructural theory underpinning this orientation as well as the practices that emanate from it have had enormous favorable impact on the marriage and family therapy field as well as systems and constructionist practices for decades. Narrative adherents will keenly defend narrative therapists' contributions, especially on the commitment to the broader macrolevel analysis of problems being located within the sociohistorical and sociocultural landscape. This chapter is not an effort to weaken this analysis in any way. Narrative therapy has a highly evolved political analysis and invites therapists to engage as political activists in addressing social justice (Monk & Gehart, 2003) in the wider community and within the intimate environment of the therapy room. We are fierce advocates of these social justice agendas. Defenders of narrative therapy may worry that some of the material presented in this chapter could contribute to an effort to "water down" the theoretical purity of narrative therapy and perhaps even contaminate some of the therapeutic practices that arise from narrative work. To be clear, this chapter is not an effort to open the gates to a freewheeling assault on narrative therapy. Neither are we presenting a thin edge of the edge to alien ideas that are often viewed as fitting into a liberal-humanist home.

We do acknowledge that we are advocating for specific affective ideas that come from both affective scholarship and neuropsychological studies, and even remnants of older systemic knowledge such as the systemic literature on vicious/virtuous cycles (White, 1984) and elements of Johnson's work on EFT (Johnson, 2002). What we are not trying to do in this chapter is build a hybrid version of couple work combining narrative therapy with EFT. Instead, we find that there are some specific ideas and techniques that we use that were developed within EFT, and we incorporate them in specific ways into the narrative work that we discuss next. We discuss specific therapy techniques that we believe complement and can be connected to a narrative couple therapy approach based upon neurophysiology, affect, and habits of relating around flight, fight, and freeze.

EXAMPLES OF APPLICATIONS OF NEUROPSYCHOLOGY AND AFFECT IN NARRATIVE PRACTICE WITH COUPLES IN THE EARLY PHASES OF THERAPY

Due to the limited space to describe incorporating the applications of neuropsychology, affect, and negative relational cycles within a narrative therapy frame, we review some of the elements we pay attention to early in the therapeutic process.

Developing a tentative overview of the therapeutic process and explicitly laying out what the therapist will be focusing upon invites a level of intentionality and transparency that helps build a stronger therapeutic alliance and trust between clients and therapist. Asking about conversations that were held about coming to therapy achieves a range of insight to both the couple and the therapist. From a narrative perspective, such conversations and invitations to share about private reflections about why the couple decided to come to therapy right now reveals emerging preferences for a new outcome. Gilbert was very clear he had been longing to be closer to Helen and had reflected on how he wanted the emotional closeness he had treasured with his mother growing up to be replicated with Helen. Helen, on the other hand, expressed concern about not being pathologized and blamed in the relationship for emotional distance and expressed an interest in wanting to be supported without judgment. Declaring hopes and reflections about therapy is not only a rich contribution to a conversation but also allows the partner to be witness to some of the preferences and dreams of his or her partner. Furthermore, we might get access to turning points in their motivation or become more informed about the extent of the distress the couple are experiencing in preparation for mapping the effects of the current trajectory of the problem-saturated narrative.

A practice common to many narrative therapists (Freedman & Combs; White, 2007) is getting to know clients as separate from the problem. For example, asking questions such as "Tell me about when the [problem]'s influence didn't have as much power in your life" or "What did it take for you both to come to therapy?" Getting to know the couple in these brief exchanges early on in therapy sets in motion entry points to track unique outcomes, the building blocks for preferred story development. When therapy begins with talking about hopes for the future and discovering strengths outside of the problem that brought them to therapy, it begins therapy on an optimistic and lighter note, and the beginning conversation between therapist and client can be less burdensome. There is great value in talking with the couple about what attracted each of them to one another at the onset of their romantic relationship. Helen spoke of how she was besotted with Gilbert on immediately meeting him for the first time at a university event. She was drawn to his charisma and his warmth and attentiveness. These qualities described by Helen are recorded by the therapist and can be resurrected in the therapy going forward as part of the lived experiences and plot events central to the preferred story of their relationship. Gilbert was immediately drawn to Helen's beauty and her lighthearted playfulness. He was captured by her quiet confidence and willingness to speak her mind about things she cared about but doing so in the most nonthreatening way. These remembrances can bring a lightness to the mood at the beginning of therapy and invite the couple to engage with one another and reflect on the forces of attraction that would have been otherwise marginalized by the feelings of despair that have come with them to therapy. This is an intentional practice of shifting the affectual state that the couple resides in, from "despair" (presumably negative in this context) to "lighthearted playfulness" (presumably positive affect).

The early interactions of this kind provide opportunities to not just explore the landscapes of preferred action but also open prospects for exploring the landscapes of identity which invite conversations on one's preferred identities of the self and relationship. These conversations invite some openness to new possibilities and that at least some hopes that have brought the couple to therapy can be realized. We can ask, "What does this say about you when you are thinking about your relationship in these ways that you prefer? What is it that you draw upon when you decide to face the problems that have brought you to therapy?" We can ask how the couple have worked through difficult dynamics in the past and the therapist's role is to identify her new actions that created opportunities for change. Even in these early phases of therapy we can see the application of narrative-oriented practices using externalizing conversations, mapping effects skills, preference questions, tracking unique outcomes, and exploring the landscapes of action and identity. Narrative therapists can be seduced into working with problem-saturated stories first and feeling that the problem story must be explored before preferred trajectories are touched upon. The approach mentioned earlier moves away from a problem-bound conversation as the only conversation that occurs in the first few sessions.

There is a risk in exclusively inhabiting preferred experiences, desirable events, and unique outcomes when the couple are often wanting to unload their distressing concerns. Therefore, it is wise to consider leaving room for some early unburdening of pent-up distressful feelings and experiences. However, we do not want to let negative reactive emotions dominate the therapeutic landscape. As we have mentioned, the initiation of a conversation and experience that elicits negative affect can severely limit the scope and possibilities of a conversation. The therapist oversees a process that should not encourage a free-for-all of angry and intense negative reactions by an upset couple. Trust and safety are invoked by the therapist when the therapist asserts clear boundaries about what kinds of interactions will be supported in the therapy room.

Including the Affective Turn

A postmodern therapist drawing upon the affective turn material will take care of strengthening the therapeutic alliance, building trust and confidence in the couple that their concerns will be taken seriously. Helen and Gilbert are asked by the therapist, "How will I know when you begin to trust me and this therapy process?" Being explicit about the importance of the therapeutic relationship and the focus on the display of trust provides the therapist with a lot more information on how to build a safe environment for Gilbert and Helen to be vulnerable with one another and take psychological risks to disclose primary heartfelt emotions.

The beginning of our sessions with couples has been modified from the traditional narrative approach. Although we include the classic narrative ideas such as getting to know the individuals and the couple outside of the problem story, exploring the couple's ideas about future directions and specific life projects, we are explicitly interested in the couple's emotional landscape. Helen and Gilbert each respond to the question, "What did you learn in your family about being emotional and vulnerable and about comfort and connection?" Gilbert spoke of the emotional warmth he felt with his mother in his childhood and how close he felt to her while feeling the emotional distance of his father. He commented on the pursuing pattern of his mother with his father and how his father would remove himself physically from his mother when there was any tension between them. Gilbert described making a decision very early in his life that he would not be emotionally distant because of the loss of relationship he felt with his father. Connections are made between these familial discourses and habits of relating, and what is going on in their current relationship. Helen, in contrast, had an emotionally distant relationship with her mother as she was preoccupied with the despair her mother experienced following the divorce from her father. Helen had very little emotional warmth from both parents as a child but had a nurturing and warm relationship with her maternal aunt, which helped her get through so many difficulties in her childhood. We explore this emotional history to survey the contours of their relationship with affect and beginning to explore habitual styles of relating around the pursing, distancing, or withdrawing dynamic. This is developed further with questions like: "What do you remember happening when you were little and you were hurt? Who did you turn to? What was their response? How have you tried to find comfort in past relationships?" Other examples include: "Do you remember feeling safe with someone in your family? If yes, who was it and how did you know you were safe? How did you let this person know that you need connection and comfort?" Not only do these questions incorporate practical examples of drawing out elements of the affective life of the parties, but we also are cognizant of the neuropsychological landscape as this pertains to primal patterns of relating around flight and fight.

Identifying pursuer–withdrawer dynamics early in the therapy while exploring the impact of the problem-saturated narratives is an added resource to the narrative practitioner. Not only can problem discourses be externalized in this phase of therapy but a negative interactional cycle of a pursuer–withdrawer can be integrated into an externalizing conversation. The inclusion of the negative relational cycles responding to the primal human responses of flight, fight, and freeze in narrative couple therapy invites practitioners to pay greater attention to the affective turn in a postmodern therapeutic context. The 22 therapy sessions conducted with Helen and Gilbert placed a great emphasis on the distancing dynamic that Helen was captured by and the pursuing pattern demonstrated by Gilbert. The therapist linked the narrative constructions built around these cyclical dynamics to problem-saturated stories. The effects of these problem-saturated patterns of relating were mapped on to the couple's interactional styles when conflicts occurred between them. As Gilbert and Helen became more clear about the effects of the cycles and the suffering this caused both of them, they became quite motivated to begin seeking more preferred relational interactions. The vulnerable and heartfelt expressions of hurt and desires for connection were woven into emerged preferred narratives of emotional closeness and a shared vision of their relationship. This therapeutic work was accompanied by deconstructing the patriarchal gendered dynamics that impacted Gilbert's unequal expectations on how Helen should be performing in their relationship. Gilbert's entitled interactions were brought to light, and these were helpful for him to engage in more equitable interactions with Helen. Helen felt strengthened in her interactions to not conform to stereotypical gendered expectations, and she increasingly found her voice to reposition herself in response to making choices to participate in domestic tasks without being governed by a sense of duty, responsibility, or feeling guilt and shame for not conforming to patriarchal roles. This chapter provides a small window into some new possibilities and additions to the power of combining affect work within a discursive lens. A fuller, more detailed articulation of our efforts to integrate these new elements into couple work is provided in our text *Integrating the Affective Turn, Relational Cycles, Neuropsychology and Discursive Therapy With Couples.*

CONCLUSION

This chapter argues for the inclusion of affect, neuropsychology, and expressions of emotion linked to physiology, while acknowledging the culturally embedded discursive frame in narrative couple therapy. This is an early iteration on exploring the intersections of neuroscience, therapy, and postmodernism. This therapeutic project serves to encourage a much larger conversation on the study of affect, the body, and discourse in couple work. This is the beginning of an affective embrace, an honoring of human materiality, a recognition of all that occurs within and between text and talk. There is much room for these approaches and understandings to be expanded significantly by the potential that these ideas offer.

There is still much to be discovered about the complex interactions that occur within the body during an experience, particularly surrounding relational contexts. The understandings that have emerged over the last several decades offer significant implications for practices, and technological advances will continue to expand on current understandings and offer new ones that may have a very influential impact on the ways the field conceptualizes change.

We are encouraging the narrative spirit of curiosity and the exploration of different landscapes as they may be connected to our work and our lives. Our hope is that you might be able to consider some of these ideas as you sit with couples in distress and to keep present the influence of affect and the neuroscience that is beginning to support many of the theoretical approaches that narrative work offers.

REFERENCES

Ahmed, S. (2014). *The cultural politics of emotion* (2nd ed.). Edinburgh, Scotland: Edinburgh University Press.

Almeida, R. V., Dolan-Del Vecchio, K., & Parker, L. (2008). *Transformative family therapy: Just families in a just society*. Boston, MA: Pearson Education.

Beaudoin, M. (2015a). Broadening the scope of collaborative therapies: Embodied practices arising from neurobiology, neurocardiology, and neurogastroenterology. *Journal of Systemic Therapies, 34*(4), 1–12. doi:10.1521/jsyt.2015.34.4.1

Beaudoin, M. (2015b). Flourishing with positive emotions: Increasing clients' repertoire of problem counter-states. *Journal of Systemic Therapies, 34*(3), 1–13. doi:10.1521/jsyt.2015.34.3.1

Beaudoin, M., & Zimmerman, J. (2011). Narrative therapy and interpersonal neurobiology: Revisiting classic practices, developing new emphases. *Journal of Systemic Therapies, 30*(1), 1–13. doi:10.1521/jsyt.2011.30.1.1

Brennan, T. *The transmission of affect*. Ithaca, NY: Cornell University Press, 2004.

Bruner, E. M. (1986). Anthropology and human studies. *Cultural Anthropology, 1*(1), 121–124.

Cannon, W. B. (1929). *Bodily changes in pain, hunger, fear, and rage*. New York, NY: Appleton-Century-Crofts.

Carey, M., Walther, S., & Russell, S. (2009). The absent but implicit: A map to support therapeutic enquiry. *Family Process, 48*(3), 319–331. doi:10.1111/j.1545-5300.2009.01285.

Cohen, J. D. (2005). The vulcanization of the human brain: A neural perspective on interactions between cognition and emotion. *Journal of Economic Perspectives, 19*(4), 3–24.

Combs, G., & Freedman, J. (2012). Narrative, poststructuralism, and social justice: Current practices in narrative therapy. *The Counseling Psychologist, 40*(7), 1033–1060. doi:10.1177/0011000012460662

Critchley, H. D., & Nagai, Y. (2012). How emotions are shaped by bodily states. *Emotion Review, 4*(2), 163–168.

Damasio, A. (2000). *The feeling of what happens: Body and emotions in the making of consciousness*. New York, NY: Mariner.

Davis, J. I., Senghas, A., & Ochsner, K. N. (2009). How does facial feedback modulate emotional experience? *Journal of Research in Personality, 43*(5), 822–829.

Eisenberger, N. I., Jarcho, J. M., Lieberman, M. D., & Naliboff, B. D. (2006). An experimental study of shared sensitivity to physical pain and social rejection. *Pain, 126*(1), 132–138. doi:10.1016/j.pain.2006.06.024

Ewing, J., Estes, R., & Like, B. (2017). Narrative neurotherapy (NNT): Scaffolding identity states. In M. N. Beaudoin & J. Duvall (Eds.), *Collaborative Therapies and Neurobiology: Evolving Practices in Action* (pp. 87–99). New York, NY: Routledge.

Foucault, M. (1980). The history of sexuality: Interview. *Oxford Literary Review, 4*(2), 3–14. doi:10.3366/olr.1980.002

Foucault, M. (1975). *Discipline and punish: The birth of the prison.* New York, NY: Random House.

Freedman, J., & Combs, G. (1993). Invitations to new stories. Using questions to explore alternative possibilities. In S. Gilligan & R. Price (Eds.), *Therapeutic conversations* (pp. 291–303). New York, NY: Norton.

Furrow, J. L., Johnson, S. M. & Bradley, B. A. (2011). *The emotionally focused casebook: New directions in treating couples.* New York, NY: Taylor & Francis Group.

Gergen, K. J. (1991). *The saturated self: Dilemmas of identity in contemporary life.* New York, NY: Basic Books.

Gottman, J. M. (2011). *The science of trust: Emotional attunement for couples.* New York, NY: Norton.

Gray, M. C. (2005). Narrative couple's therapy with feeling resistant men. *Revue Des Sciences De L'Education De McGill, 40*(1).

Hansen, J. T., & Scholl, M. B. (2018). Chapter 1: Introduction to postmodern perspectives on contemporary counseling issues. In M. B. Scholl & J. T. Hansen (Eds.), *Postmodern perspective on contemporary counseling issues: Approaches across diverse settings.* New York, NY: Oxford University Press.

Hennenlotter, A., Dresel, C., Castrop, F., Ceballos-Baumann, A. O., Wohlschläger, A. M.,& Haslinger, B. (2009). The link between facial feedback and neural activity within central circuitries of emotion—New insights from botulinum toxin induced denervation of frown muscles. *Cerebral Cortex, 19*(3), 537–542.

Jansen, A., Nguyen, X., Karpitskiy, V., & Mettenleiter, T.C., & Loewy, A. D. (1995). Central command neurons of the sympathetic nervous system: Basis of the fight-or-flight response. *Science, 270,* 644–646.

Johnson, S. M. (2002). *Emotionally focused couple therapy with trauma survivors: Strengthening attachment bonds.* New York, NY: Guilford Press.

Johnson, S. M. (2004). *The practice of emotionally focused couple therapy* (2nd ed.). New York, NY: Brunner-Routledge.

Jordan, J. (2009). *Relational-cultural therapy.* Washington, DC: American Psychological Association.

Kallos-Lilly, V. & Fitzgerald, J. (2015). *An emotionally focused workbook for couples: The two of us.* New York, NY: Routledge.

Knudsen, B. T., & Stage, C. (2015). Introduction: Affective methodologies. In Knudsent, B.T. & Stage, C. (Eds.), *Affective Methodologies: Developing Cultural Research Strategies for the Study of Affect* (pp. 1–22). Basingstoke: Palgrave Macmillan.

Knudson-Martin, C. (2013). Why power matters: Creating a foundation of mutual support in couple relationships. *Family Process, 52*(1), 5–18. doi:10.1111/famp.12011

Knudson-Martin, C., & Mahoney, A. (2005). Moving beyond gender: Processes that create relationship equality. *Journal of Marital and Family Therapy, 31,* 235–246.

Kozorovitskiy, Y., Gross, C. G., Kopil, C., Battaglia, L., Mcbreen, M., Stranahan, A. M., & Gould, E. (2005). Experience induces structural and biochemical changes in the adult primate brain. *Proceedings of the National Academy of Sciences, 102*(48), 17478–17482. doi:10.1073/pnas.0508817102

Leslie, L. A., & Southard, A. L. (2009). Thirty years of feminist family therapy: Moving into the mainstream. In S. A. Lloyd, A. L. Few, & K. R. Allen (Eds.), *Handbook of feminist family studies* (pp. 328–339). Los Angeles, CA: Sage.

Lyness, A. M., & Lyness, K. P. (2007). Feminist issues in couple therapy. *Journal of Couple and Relationship Therapy, 6,* 181–195.

Massumi, B. (2002). *Parables for the virtual: Movement, affect, sensation.* Durham, NC: Duke University Press.

Monk, G., & Gehart, D. (2003). Sociopolitical activist or conversational partner? Distinguishing the position of the therapist in narrative and collaborative therapies. *Family Process, 42*(1), 19–30.

Monk, G., Winslade, J., Crocket, K., & Epston, D. (1997). *Narrative therapy in practice: The archaeology of hope*. San Francisco, CA: Jossey-Bass.

Monk, G., Winslade, J., & Sinclair, S. (2008). *New horizons in multicultural counseling*. Thousand Oaks, CA: Sage.

Nader, K., & Ledoux, J. (2000). How the brain learns about danger. *Brain, Perception, Memory: Advances in Cognitive Neuroscience*, 253–266. doi:10.1093/acprof:oso/9780198524823.003.0017

Parker, L. (2009). Disrupting power and privilege in couples therapy. *Clinical Social Work Journal, 37*, 248–255.

Patterson, J. E., & Vakili, S. (2014). Relationships, environment, and the brain: How emerging research is changing what we know about the impact of families on human development. *Family Process, 53*(1), 22–32. doi:10.1111/famp.12057

Price-Robertson, R., & Duff, C. (2015). Realism, materialism, and the assemblage: Thinking psychologically with Manuel DeLanda. *Theory & Psychology, 26*(1), 58–76. doi:10.1177/0959354315622570

Proffitt, D. R. (2006). Embodied perception and the economy of action. *Perspectives on Psychological Science, 1*(2), 110–122. doi:10.1111/j.1745-6916.2006.00008.x

Reeck, C., Ames, D. R., & Ochsner, K. N. (2016). The social regulation of emotion: An integrative, cross-disciplinary model. *Trends in Cognitive Sciences, 20*(1), 47–63. doi:10.1016/j.tics.2015.09.003

Sedgwick, E. K. (2003). *Touching feeling: Affect, pedagogy, performativity*. Durham, NC: Duke University Press.

Siegel, D. (2012). *The developing mind: How relationships and the brain interact to shape who we are* (2nd ed.). New York, NY: Guilford.

Steil, J. (1997). *Marital equality: Its relationship to the well-being of husbands and wives*. Newbury Park, CA: Sage.

Stewart, K. (2007). *Ordinary affects*. Durham, NC: Duke University Press.

Wetherell, M. (2012). *Affect and emotion: A new social science understanding*. Thousand Oaks, CA: Sage.

White, M. (1984). Pseudo-encopresis: From avalanche to victory, from vicious to virtuous cycles. *Family Systems Medicine, 2*(2), 150–160.

White, M. (1991). Deconstruction and therapy. *Dulwich Centre Newsletter*, No. 2.

White, G. (1993). Emotions inside out: The anthropology of affect. In M. Lewis and J. M. Haviland (Eds.), *Handbook of emotions* (pp. 29–40). New York, NY: Guilford.

White, M. (2000). Re-engaging with history: The absent but implicit. In M. White (Ed.), *Reflections on narrative practice* (pp. 35–58). Adelaide, South Australia: Dulwich Centre.

White, M. (2007). *Maps of narrative practice*. New York, NY: Norton.

White, M. (2009). Narrative practice and conflict dissolution in couples therapy. *Clinical Social Work Journal, 37*(3), 200–213. doi:10.1007/s10615-009-0192-6

White, M., & Epston, D. (1990). *Narrative means to therapeutic ends*. New York, NY: Norton.

Witt, J. K. (2011). Action's effect on perception. *Current Directions in Psychological Science, 20*(3), 201–206. doi:10.1177/0963721411408770

Vygotsky, L. (1978). Interaction between learning and development. In L. Vygotsky (Ed.), *Mind and society: The Development of Higher Psychological Processes* (pp. 79–91). Cambridge, MA: Harvard University Press.

CHAPTER 11

Obscuring Masculine Truths

A Postmodern, Clinical Framework for Counseling Men

ADAM M. CLEVENGER AND CORINA MARIA TEOFILO
MATTSON

Jim is a White man in his mid-thirties, who currently lives with his girlfriend of 3 years. The couple is childless and unmarried, though he reports future plans for marriage and children without a distinct timeline for either. Jim works a low-paying service job and believes he will receive a promotion once he pays his dues by working the lower rung of the corporate ladder. Jim is able-bodied and denies significant physical health concerns. However, he describes increasing mood-related symptoms that are beginning to impact his professional and personal life. Jim comes to counseling seeking to improve his mood, though he is quick to refute the likelihood of depression. He is currently requesting a "quick-fix" from you, his therapist, to help him learn how to start resolving his depressive symptoms on his own.

Jim is from a traditional, working family; he grew up in a poor, rural community where many families were struck by substance abuse and addiction, including many of his childhood friends. Jim has escaped the addiction that plagues his hometown, though he struggles with guilt related to his own success and his distance from family and friends. Jim differentiates himself from his family, even though he describes a strong sense of responsibility to them. Unlike his family, Jim has fairly liberal social and political beliefs, and seeks to surround himself with people different from the community he knew growing up. Jim describes a strong desire to support his girlfriend's career aspirations and speculates he will soon be relocating to support the growth of her career. Jim laughs while acknowledging he has become the target of family jokes based on his willingness to support his girlfriend's career above his own. Though he is proud of the flexibility and encouragement he can provide, Jim describes internal conflict experienced from his desire to prove himself a man and model the type of financial success and breadwinner status he was taught in childhood. Jim worries that his support may come across as laziness. Jim fears becoming the "black sheep" like his older brother— the guy who continually "goofs up" and is hardly taken seriously. Jim describes efforts to distance himself from perceived failures by his brother. He worries that he will be unable to simultaneously meet the expectations of his girlfriend and family.

Jim describes feeling "stressed" and "overwhelmed" by felt-responsibility, and describes a sense that he is "slowing down," noticing a lack of motivation and energy to accomplish even the most routine tasks at home. Jim describes low frustration tolerance and the ease at which he is beginning to find himself in conflict with others. He reports increasing irritability and further describes cognitive and emotional lethargy—changes to which he cannot identify a specific trigger. His affect is somewhat muted though he remains engaged in the therapy session. He continues to blame himself for perceived failures while working hard to mask those failures from others. As Jim describes to you his growing sense of failure, his eyes begin to fill with tears until he laughs, and says, "Dude! Get it together!" pushing the welling emotion away. "What do I do?" he says. "Do you think I'm fixable?"

INTRODUCTION

The mental health professions are grounded in theories that posit a true reality (Hansen, 2004). From the perspective of these traditional theories, uncovering hidden personal truths is the primary means to bring about change. Traditional therapeutic practice was founded on the belief that the identification of certain "truths" can ultimately provide mental, emotional, and spiritual liberation from the confines of mental illness and social dysfunction (Hansen, 2007).

Postmodern therapeutic perspectives deny an objective, discoverable truth and instead view truth and reality as a human construction (Hansen, 2004; Hayes & Oppenheim, 1997; Leary 1994; Rosen, 1996; Ryan, 1999). This chapter explores how to apply a postmodern approach to clinical work with men, like Jim, who experience conflicting messages and desires related to masculine expression and modern role fulfillment. The chapter will (1) explore general ideological principles of postmodernism in comparison to modernism; (2) explore how postmodernism applies to the culture of men and masculinity, specifically; and (3) explore how to apply postmodern, ideological principles to clinical practice with men. Throughout the chapter the case study of Jim will be used to illustrate these ideas.

MODERNISM VERSUS POSTMODERNISM

A modernist perspective assumes a knowable reality (Hansen, 2004; Hayes & Oppenheim, 1997; Leary, 1994; Rosen, 1996; Ryan, 1999). In relation to men, a modernist perspective might suggest there is an objective, natural truth concerning men and masculinity—supporting a "right" way of being a man through traditional, masculine measures at work, in relationships, and other life arenas. As it relates to Jim's experience in counseling, a modernist clinician may focus on helping Jim construct and achieve clinical goals through understanding, achieving, and aligning himself with traditional, cultural expectations of masculine behavior and decision making.

Postmodern approaches allow for an innately playful understanding of meaning and truth that can be used to deconstruct and reconstruct sociocultural forces inhibiting growth and wellness. A postmodern framework challenges gender "truths" by illuminating and questioning the psychological adoption of arbitrary cultural standards of masculinity.

Because they do not endorse the idea of universal truth, postmodernists are likely to deny an inherent "right" way of being a man, and they may further deny any particular legitimacy in the ways gender and masculinity are constructed, or performed, at any point in time; instead, postmodernists would more likely view the subjective experience of men and masculinity as a cultural phenomenon where male objects become gendered subjects (i.e., men) through a series of social, cultural, and interpersonal processes that begin from the moment of birth. In Jim's case, a postmodern therapist would explore the meaning and impact of masculinity and gender expectations on Jim's life, while helping Jim deconstruct rigid gender beliefs and expectations.

Both the modernist and postmodernist approach would likely address very similar clinical questions, and they would further apply considerations for diversity and other environmental and contextual factors within the case conceptualization. However, the clinical assumptions and therapeutic goals would likely vary.

Consider, again, the case of Jim: How might your clinical approach shift if Jim were a Black man, working third shift and requesting your clinical support while "coming out" as bisexual to his boss and colleagues? Or, how would your clinical approach change if Jim had a physical disability that limited mobility? How does the approach change if we manipulated other variables like socioeconomic status, religion, substance use, trauma history, marital status, mental health status, first language, and cultural influence? Similarly, how does your identity and gender expression as the therapist impact the therapeutic exchange, as well as the construction and meaning of gender and gender expression in the therapeutic relationship?

All of these questions highlight obvious therapeutic considerations. For example, a therapist may conceptualize a disability status from a framework of privilege, helping the client to navigate loss of privilege while improving the client's quality of life by addressing challenges. Another therapist may help build coping skills and cognitive reframes to help empower the client and build resilience within the context of the disability. Each of these approaches would be helpful; however, they assume innate meaning and truth in the client's disability. A postmodern therapist, alternatively, may identify the ways certain abilities are interpreted as a disability or a challenge to overcome, through cultural interaction and assumed belief. The postmodern therapist will instead engage the client in a collaborative, meaning-making process filled with alternative perspectives that may help develop new, positive conceptualizations of differing ability statuses that generate new possibilities and enrich experiences without needing to accept assumed loss or a state of difference.

A POSTMODERN PROPOSAL FOR GENDER-AWARE THERAPY WITH MEN

Clinical research on men and masculinities in counseling is limited, though attention to men's issues and gendered experiences appears to be increasing (Brooks, 2010; Englar-Carlson, Evans, & Duffey, 2014; Evans, 2013; Evans, Duffey, & Englar-Carlson, 2013; O'Neil, 2014). Men have been traditionally overrepresented in empirical research. However, men are often selected for research as standardized subjects rather than gendered subjects, so underlying issues associated with men's gender socialization and masculinity have not been widely explored in the literature (O'Neil & Renzulli, 2013). Gender, itself, has been often construed to mean "woman," or pertaining to women's issues and political causes, so similar questions of men's diversity and the variability of lived experience among men are not often considered from a gender perspective. Future research is needed to validate the diagnostic criteria for diverse men (Rochlen, 2005); to identify cultural competency standards for men and masculinities (Liu, 2005); and to develop an empirically supported method or paradigm to provide effective, gender-aware counseling with men (O'Neil, 2014).

Existing literature is consistent in concluding that men are hesitant, and generally less likely than women, to seek professional help (i.e., Evans et al., 2013; Rochlen, 2005)—a reality that is in direct contrast to men's need for clinical support. Men experience high rates of depression (approximately 6 million men are diagnosed annually; Addis, 2008) and the highest rates of completed suicide (Courtenay, 2003). Men's depression often manifests in other externalizing behaviors or disorders characterized by addiction, anger, violence, and problematic sexual behavior (see Addis, 2008; Courtenay, 2003). Not surprisingly, men experience the highest rates of trauma-related accidents and injury (Brooks, 2001; Centers for Disease Control and Prevention, 2011). Men experience the highest rates of alcohol and substance use and abuse (Center for Behavioral Health Statistics and Quality, 2015).

Men's negative health consequences are consistently linked to restrictive gender practices and beliefs maintained through a culture of masculine discourses and relational hierarchies (see Brooks, 2001; Courtenay, 2003; Englar-Carlson, 2014; Good et al., 2005; O'Neil, 2008). Widespread (and largely unrecognized) trauma and abuse among men contribute to men's mental and physical health consequences (Englar-Carlson, 2014). Men are more likely to be the victims and the perpetrators of physical and emotional abuse (Brooks, 2001); thus, it is not surprising that men account for 93.3% of the US prison population (Federal Bureau of Prisons, 2016). Although fewer men are thought to experience sexual assault compared to women, men and boy's sexual victimization is believed to be vastly underreported and a significant community health concern (see McLean, 2013). Men's traumatic experiences are frequently unacknowledged or misunderstood unless the victim is significantly and physically wounded, or otherwise responsible for provoking the violence. The myth of men's low risk and experience of victimization ignores recurring patterns of masculine socialization that are likely traumatic themselves: hazing rituals, bullying, competition, physical aggression, and other humiliations that have become part of the common narrative for men's right of passage into adulthood.

The number of men seeking therapy has grown exponentially in the last decade (Evans, Duffey, & Englar-Carlson, 2013). Like Jim, many of these men are experiencing shame, guilt, and frustration related to perceived or realistic failures to achieve the socially prescribed expectations for men across multiple contexts and life arenas. Men today are expected to adhere to rigid, traditional masculinity standards while successfully managing modern role shifts and emerging responsibilities as partners, fathers, colleagues, and leaders—roles that require interpersonal skills and emotional awareness traditionally associated with femininity (Good, Thomson, & Brathwaite, 2005). Culturally valued men are now expected to be both feared and personable; strong and vulnerable; independent and emotionally expressive; career oriented and family focused; both hard and soft, dominant and gentle. The paradox of modern masculinity, and the awareness of common gender-related conflicts and value contradictions experienced by men, are important for the assessment, diagnosis, and treatment of men's clinical issues.

In general, men are thought to benefit from an explicit focus on gender beliefs and practices during mental health treatment with the help of culturally competent therapists (Brooks, 2001; Duffey & Haberstroh, 2014; Evans et al., 2013; Kahn, 2011; Liu, 2005; Mahalik et al., 2005; Reed, 2014; Shen-Miller, Isacco, Davies, St. Jean, & Phan, 2013). A postmodern paradigm may help some men to develop the personal flexibility and skill set to improve emotional, social, and spiritual functioning that are incongruent with traditional, masculine socialization experiences. Limited research has been conducted on the use of postmodern therapies with men as gendered subjects. However, postmodern narrative approaches may have some benefit for men when attempting to facilitate new and unique constructions of masculinity for improved wellness; the development of realistic self-concepts; and shame-reduction (Evans, Carney, & Wilkinson, 2013; Falicov, 2010; Schermer, 2013). Motivational interviewing is another approach consistent with a postmodern paradigm that may be useful for working with men (Scholz & Hall, 2014). Motivational interviewing relies on nonhierarchical, therapeutic partnership; the therapist's total acceptance of the client's worth and inherent strengths; and a compassionate view of men that may help deconstruct modernist views of men and masculinity.

The application of a postmodern paradigm for gender-aware therapy with men requires one to be familiar with the culture of men and masculinity and the social construction of gender and sex. Postmodern perspectives on men and the culture of masculinity will be conceptually introduced using seminal, epistemological theories of gender and the impact on gendered truths and societal knowing from other social science fields (i.e., Butler, 1990; Connell, 2005; Schippers, 2007; West & Zimmerman, 1987). Every society throughout history has had a "sex/gender system" that produces gender norms and expectations in relation to gender performances, gender beliefs, and sexuality (Rubin, 1975). A postmodernist view of gender challenges the assumed truth of innate gender differences and recognizes the societal influence on the current, American sex/gender system.

Cultural Constructions of Gender and Sex

The distinction between "gender" and "sex" is not always acknowledged but is the most formative component to postmodern views of men and masculinities. The terms are sometimes used interchangeably to describe assumed biological gender differences relating to personality strengths, innate ability, and aesthetic difference (Connell, 2005). Gender and sex were indistinguishable in the social sciences until the 1950s (Muehlenhard & Peterson, 2011). Though inconsistencies remain, most modern social scientists agree that gender is closely associated with sociocultural effects, whereas sex is closely tied to biology (Muehlenhard & Peterson, 2011). For the purposes of this chapter, sex will be a reference to biology, whereas gender will connote the social, cultural, and political symbolism of biological difference.

In Western society, sex is often considered to determine gender, though gender is probably best understood as a cultural interpretation of sex (Butler, 1990). Rubin (1975) writes, gender is less an expression of innate difference and more a "suppression of natural similarities" (p. 40), challenging the frequently assumed truth behind observed sex/gender differences. It is increasingly commonplace within the social sciences to conceptualize gender as a social construction, rather than an innate predeterminant, which emphasizes gender difference rather than similarity. West and Zimmerman (1987) famously theorized that gender differences, and the societal construction of gender, are maintained through a type of learned performance, or the act of "doing gender." Doing gender creates a process of accountability where every individual is policed, by one's self and by others, about the performance of our respective genders to ensure appropriate conformity to gender norms from the moment we are born. Learning to perform our gender as a man or woman is often considered a cultural achievement so long as sex, gender, sexual behavior, and sexual desire meet heteronormative assumptions (Butler, 1990; Connell, 2005).

Hegemonic masculinity is the most culturally valued way of doing gender for men (i.e., assertive, emotionally restricted, independent, powerful, etc.). The complete achievement of hegemonic masculinity is unrealistic, though it is culturally enticing for many men; the top of the hierarchy would hypothetically help one avoid shame, embarrassment, and gendered consequences that men often experience when their masculinity is called into question (White & Peretz, 2010). Men who are unable or unwilling to uphold the hegemonic standards of masculinity will be symbolically feminized, socially sanctioned and stigmatized, and will often experience physical threat and verbal admonishment (Schippers, 2007); however, despite the cultural ideal, men have unique expressions and experiences of gender. The differential access to power and privilege among men, as well as the diversity of lived experiences among men, is an important aspect of postmodern clinical approaches with men and masculinities. Recognizing and affirming the heterogeneity among men will help illuminate social and cultural effects on men's lived experiences, and this will further help the therapist identify appropriate and unique interventions for each individual man.

One important component to the construction of the sex/gender system found throughout Western societies is the interdependence between masculinity and femininity. Western constructions of cultural masculinity are generally in direct contrast to anything considered feminine (Butler, 1990; Connell, 2005; Schippers, 2007), which means that masculinity cannot even exist without femininity. This relational arrangement has fluctuated throughout cultural and historical changes but consistently maintains a hierarchical power structure of masculine dominance and feminine subordination. The distribution of power is a productive force that ingrains and characterizes who men and women are, and what the relationship between men and women should be (Schippers, 2007). Hence, masculinity (or femininity) cannot be considered fixed characteristics but rather dynamic, relational, institutionalized structures that reify themselves through conscious and unconscious interactions (Connell, 2005).

The Culture of Men and Masculinities

The culture of American masculinity is often understood in contrast to anything considered feminine, and it can be further characterized by frequent displays of power and control through competitive interaction between men (Kimmel, 2012). One man's individual value and access to gender privilege is often dependent on his ability to prove himself a man by obtaining power in relation to other men, and by differentiating himself and his interests from women. Other identities like race, ethnicity, class, age, and sexuality can change the perception of some men's value and authenticity among other men and in relation to women, further impacting some men's access to gendered power and privilege (Kimmel, 2012). Intersectionality (Crenshaw, 1989) refers to the experience of multiple, overlapping identities (i.e., age, race, class, sexuality) within a broader system of domination, discrimination, and oppression. The experiences of African American men, for example, who experience gender privilege relative to Black women will likely experience lesser gender privilege relative to White men. The intersection of multiple identities diversifies the experiences of American men so that it becomes nearly impossible to describe one homogenous narrative. Thus, literature pertaining to men's gender in a clinical setting will often reference "masculinities" (i.e., Connell, 2005) as a theoretical understanding of the different displays of masculinity, and the varying levels of access men experience to the cultural power and privilege traditionally bestowed on men. Three, interrelated themes associated with traditional gender beliefs and practices among men in the United States are significant to understanding men's common mental health consequences and related gendered conflicts: competition, and the cultural achievement of hegemonic masculinity; shame-related effects on men's lived experiences; and the relationship to women and femininity.

IMPORTANT CLINICAL THEMES

Competition and the Achievement of Hegemonic Masculinity

Hegemonic, American masculinity has been historically defined by power, domination, and control over others (Kimmel, 2012). Although men's power and control over women is often the focus of gender relations, the hegemonic, gender system in the United States also creates a competitive, hierarchical relationship between men (i.e., Connell, 2005; Kahn, 2011). Competition through sport; capital gain; and violence are markers of cultural masculinity that often reinforce traditional masculinity and suppress other forms of self-expression (Connell, 2005; Kahn, 2011; O'Neil, 2008). The competitive nature of men's relationships creates the perception of "realness" (i.e., "the real man")—characterizing one man's status over another.

Competition between men defines who is the "better," "bigger" man—allowing one to boast to another and say, "Who's THE man?" Kimmel (2012) writes, "manhood is less about the drive for domination and more about the fear of others dominating us, having power or control over us" (p. 4). The fear activates a cycle of power and control over others—particularly women, and other men who are unable to uphold hegemonic standards of masculinity. American men are afraid of "not measuring up to some vaguely defined notions of what it means to be a man" and afraid to be seen as "weak, timid, [and] frightened" (Kimmel, 2012, p. 4). The dynamic alludes to the gendered emphasis on success and failure among men as workers, partners, and gendered persons, while perpetuating expectations for independence and self-reliance to be the top competitor without the help of others with whom he is competing (theoretically, this would include everyone!).

Problematic competition, and the achievement of masculinity, may manifest clinically through one's perceived performance failures as a man, a worker, a father, or partner, and in various other roles. Perceived performance failures, matched with guilt and shame, may motivate further competition and a desire for status among other men or in relation to women. A client may be unwilling or unable to engage in narrative development or feedback processes in treatment if the therapist is perceived as a competitor; the client may be motivated to "man-up" and distance himself from the therapeutic exchange to avoid loss of power and authority. For this reason, power dynamics within the therapeutic relationship should be addressed early in treatment. The therapist is encouraged to help explore the client's experiences of giving and receiving feedback throughout masculine socialization processes, while increasing awareness of the ways gender policing has negatively impacted the client's life.

The social construction of men and masculinities is deeply rooted in shame (Connor, 2001; Osherson & Krugman, 1990; Wright, 1994). Shame itself is complex—experienced as a psychological response that includes "cognitive (self-attacking thoughts), affective (emotional pain), and behavioral components (submissive facial and postural expressions, as well as social withdrawal actions)" (Shepard & Rabinowitz, 2013, p. 451). Shame is correlated to depression—characterized by anger and rage toward the self and others; a desire to disappear; low self-worth; and believing one is inherently "bad" or "deficient" (p. 451). Experienced or perceived vulnerability will often trigger shame responses in men. Efthim, Kenny, and Mahalik (2001) found that "intellectual inferiority, expressing tender emotions, physical inadequacy, and performing in work and sexual activity" (p. 435) are likely to evoke a shame response in men.

Masculinity socialization creates a particular vulnerability to experiencing shame (Connor, 2001; Osherson & Krugman, 1990; Shepard & Rabinowitz, 2013; Wright, 1994). From an early age, boys are taught to act like "real" men through "repeated humiliations and reprimands" that become a controlling force in men's lives (Shepard & Rabinowitz, 2013, p. 452). The threat or actual loss of masculine power and privilege within the hierarchical status structure among men creates a shame response that "animates" (Kimmel, 2012, p. 5) the domination and control over others by emphasizing himself as bigger, better, and stronger than others to avoid future humiliation. Power and control are not motivating factors in and of themselves; power and control are tools men use to avoid feelings of shame by upholding gendered boundaries and proving themselves as men.

A postmodern approach to men's clinical issues must include exploration of shame experiences and the underlying causes of shame to support men's full, human potential and access to healthy, dynamic relationships. The therapeutic process itself can be shame inducing for some men if vulnerability is perceived as a loss of masculinity, so the therapist must be careful to avoid language and assumptions that continue the cycle of shame in men's lives. A postmodern therapist would likely use curiosity in response to the demonstrations of shame within the therapeutic relationship, inviting the client to be curious about the triggers for these feelings and the roots of those triggers. The postmodern therapist might invite the client to consider the context in which shame was learned and the ways that this shame may have served to reinforce cultural norms related to performing masculinity. A postmodern therapist might even wonder with the client about the ways that the shame has manifested in the client's relationships with other men, and the degree to which the client may have policed others for their performances of culturally informed gender expectations.

Distance From Women and Femininity

Competition and shame among men are fundamentally linked to a fear of femininity (Kierski & Blazina, 2009; Wright, 1994). Men avoid expressing themselves in ways associated with femininity because feminine traits are associated with feelings of shame. Women and symbolic femininity act as a "negative pole" from which men must distance themselves in order to prove and maintain their masculinity and gendered perception of self (Kimmel, 2012, p. 5). Symbolic femininity is a controlling, "disciplinary force" in men's lives that reinforces the hegemonic sex/gender structure through political, moral, cosmetic, and somatic expectations of men (Hennen, 2008, p. 56). Femininity, real or perceived, is associated with a loss of power or general powerlessness.

The therapeutic process relies on characteristically feminine processes like the expression and communication of emotion, so the therapeutic process itself might bring about shame in men. Femininity, and the fear of appearing feminine, must be addressed in the clinical setting to help the client combat possible stigma associated with his participation in the therapeutic process (Kierski & Blazina, 2009). In addition, expanding notions of masculinity to include the positive characteristics of femininity will further help clients develop emotional and relational strengths that are needed to navigate today's contradictory messages experienced by men. This requires attention to, and preparation for, potential negative reactions from those in a client's life who might be most invested in supporting, reinforcing, and avoiding deviation from the aforementioned versions of masculinity. Challenging the avoidance of cultural femininity will help the client renegotiate masculine stances and behaviors that may be limiting full engagement and life potential.

POSTMODERN THERAPEUTIC PRACTICE WITH MEN

These authors propose a broad, postmodern framework to clinically address men's gendered health consequences and intrapsychic conflict. The proposed, postmodern framework includes three therapeutic processes: (1) increase awareness of the culture of masculinity and the constructionist view of gender; (2) increase insightful understanding of the helpful and unhelpful meaning making, and restrictive gendered practices, that have produced negative health consequences; and (3) integrate therapeutic opportunities for men to construct new, alternative masculinities and gendered meaning to reduce intrapsychic conflict. This postmodern framework for therapeutic practice with men will evoke men's emotional depth, empathy, and vulnerability—reflective of a broader "paradigm shift" in the literature that emphasizes a nontraditional view of men's emotionality that is infrequently considered in treatment conceptualizations for men (O'Neil, 2014, ix).

The postmodern framework will challenge the societal impulse to blame men for existing problems rather than acknowledge the negative impact of restrictive gender beliefs and practices on men's negative health outcomes (O'Neil, 2014). The proposed framework will prioritize the use of fundamental counseling practices that work well with men to help decrease blame and shame related to men's negative health outcomes, including empathic listening, unique conceptualizations that value men's diversity, and a collaborative approach that includes discussion of goals and counseling processes (Duffey & Haberstroh, 2014).

Masculine behaviors and discourses (i.e., avoidance of open emotionality and resistance to help seeking) are not well suited for therapy, and yet very few treatment models exist for men, specifically, that address the discrepancy between men's social learning and therapy standards (O'Neil, 2014). Liu (2005) discusses the need for masculine sensitive therapies and cultural competency by the therapist for effective clinical work with men. The postmodern framework will incorporate "masculine-friendly adjustments" to improve engagement by men in the broader therapeutic process to address the need for cultural sensitivity (Englar-Carlson, 2014, p. 19). These adjustments may include replacing clinical jargon with masculine discourses that align with men's socialization and relational style through the use of humor, small talk, and metaphors affirming his masculine cultural orientation (i.e., sports analogies, work metaphors, and clinical examples involving specific, relational aspects of men's lives). Active participation by the therapist and goal-oriented processes resemble common relational themes in men's lives (i.e., coach/mentor/consultant) and can be emphasized to provide a sense of direction and accomplishment that supports engagement in the therapeutic process. The appropriate use of therapist self-disclosure is another important adjustment that may help eliminate power imbalances in the therapeutic relationship and feelings of shame by men in the therapeutic process (Englar-Carlson, 2014, p. 22). The suggested adjustments can be easily incorporated into the following postmodern, treatment tools and modalities meant to support increased understanding and recognition of societal expectations and dominant cultural messages that impact men's experiences.

TREATMENT TOOLS AND MODALITIES

Assessment

The use of assessment tools like the Conformity to Masculine Norms Inventory (CMNI; Mahalik et al., 2003) or the Gender Role Conflict Scale (GRCS; O'Neil, Helms, Gable, David, & Wrightsman, 1986) may be useful tools to initiate conversation about gender beliefs and practices from a postmodern lens (Mahalik, Talmadge, Locke, & Scott, 2005; O'Neil, 2013). These assessment tools may also be appropriate for identifying gendered health consequences experienced by men in treatment. Once the clinical concerns have been identified through self-report and assessment, the therapist can begin helping the client explore internal and external expectations that may be complicating the change process. In the case study at hand, Jim is obviously struggling with expectations for self and the expectations of others. Notions of responsibility, success, and failure are controlling his ability to identify behavior change or a new perspective that may help alleviate his increasing depression symptoms.

The CMNI consists of 94 items on a Likert scale that can be used to help men become aware of the invisible effect of masculinity in their lives that may otherwise be so closely adhered to, and culturally salient, that it is not easily identifiable without purposeful intervention. Using a tool like the CMNI can help increase self-awareness; identify coping resources and personal strengths; identify masculinity-related beliefs and cognitions that create impairment or dysfunction; and further help explore role conflict and issues of work–life balance.

The GRC consists of 37 items on a Likert scale that measures direct and indirect intrapsychic conflicts with traditional gender role expectations. Jim struggles with ideals and values he has used to create new identity in adulthood and controlling gendered expectations permeating his progressive lifestyle. Perceived failures he may experience as a man in relation to those expectations are the culmination of gender role conflict (O'Neil, 1981). Clinical approaches relying on gender role conflict theory redirect clinical attention to a broader focus on problematic patterns of masculine socialization rather than on specific, pathological behaviors presenting in treatment (Wester, 2008). The GRC scale can help identify problematic patterns of socialization that are possibly limiting Jim's self-expression and outcome potential.

Treatment Models

In addition to narrative and motivational interviewing approaches previously discussed, feminist and multicultural treatment models align well with the proposed, postmodern framework for masculine-sensitive therapy (Kahn, 2011; Liu, 2005). Feminist therapy has greatly influenced the psychological understanding of human behavior as it relates to gender socialization and the expectation for gender practice. This therapeutic modality promotes less restrictive gender beliefs and practices through direct problem solving, behavior change, and self-awareness (Kahn, 2011). Being that feminist theorists were influential in helping differentiate gender from sex, feminist therapy could serve as a very helpful treatment modality to address men's gender negotiations while providing a forum to discuss diverse masculinities and societal expectations of men. Feminist therapy challenges the innate hierarchy that exists in a counseling relationship, addresses power in context and related stigma, and normalizes the strain of gendered experiences—all of which are important for men in the therapeutic process (Englar-Carlson, 2014; O'Neil, 2014). Similarly, multicultural models of treatment encourage the ongoing construction of gender and further ensure recognition of the client's worldview and the context in which he or she lives and encounters gender-reinforcing messages (Liu, 2005). The multicultural approach creates responsibility for the therapist to challenge his or her own biases and remain aware of gender perspectives in order to avoid reinforcing controlling, restrictive gender messages. The multicultural approach also ensures recognition of the diversity among men and the multidimensionality impacting men's lived, gender experiences.

An adapted version of Mary Jo Barrett and Linda Stone Fish's (2014) collaborative change model for persons experiencing trauma offers a framework for postmodern clinical work with men. This model takes a collaborative approach to developing initial trust and safety in the therapeutic relationship. Stage one is an opportunity for the therapist and client to understand how the symptoms (i.e., aggression, shame) arose as an adaption to life experiences. In the case of trauma, symptoms are understood as an adaption to the traumatic experiences specifically. In the case of working with men, aggressive and competitive behavior can be understood as tools for avoiding shame and connection to femininity. The clinician works with the client to understand the sequences in which these symptoms are reinforced. In subsequent stages of the work, observed defensiveness, reactivity, and other therapist–client relational challenges in the work are indicators that a return to stage one is needed.

Stage two of Barrett and Fish's (2014) model may include deconstructing current conceptualizations of gender and masculinity by welcoming questions, curiosity, and challenge to the status quo. This stage would include exploring and experimenting with alternative constructions of what it is to be a man. Stage three looks ahead to plan for, and practice, managing stress while sustaining the new and helpful patterns of behavior and belief.

Duffey and Haberstroh (2014) explore the use of developmental relational counseling (DRC) with men in therapy, a model that emphasizes greater intra- and interpersonal awareness and further encourages flexibility, management of feedback, and appropriate use of power to better facilitate full, healthy relationships between men and the women in their lives. Rather than conceptualizing men as deficient and incapable of meeting their needs in socially desirable ways, DRC challenges popular discourses and identifies ways that men do connect in their relationships and make meaning in their lives. Similarly, a positive masculinity approach "emphasizes the adaptive character strengths, emotions, and virtues of men that promote well-being and resiliency in self and others" (Englar-Carlson & Kiselica, 2013). By relying on a positive masculinity approach and avoiding deficit-focused treatments, men are empowered to improve themselves and their communities. Clinicians can help men identify personal strengths that have been used to challenge and resist patriarchal forces in their lives. This insight may connect men to feelings of shame and guilt around experienced or perceived deviations from hegemonic norms and standards of masculinity. This process may also allow for greater self-exploration that includes an examination of different ways of being a man than the one way that society prescribes. The clinician should work to understand men from a specific context, or worldview, that allows for greater empathy and understanding when working with, or experiencing, traditional masculine behaviors in the therapy setting that may otherwise seem off-putting to the clinician.

Clinical Application

Return to the case study at the start of this chapter:

> As Jim's therapist, you curiously ask Jim why he said "Get it together?" earlier. While Jim initially responds with defensiveness, saying "What do you mean?," he eventually shares that he doesn't understand why he would become emotional while discussing these challenges. You ask him, "Why wouldn't you become emotional?"
>
> This leads Jim to share that he has experienced an increase in the frequency of moments of emotionality of late. Jim shared that until recently he had typically found that focusing on work had been an effective strategy for managing emotions as they occurred.
>
> As his therapist, you ask Jim how this new increase in emotionality has played out in his relationship. Jim notes that he has excused himself from social interactions and moments with his girlfriend when he begins to feel overwhelmed by feelings. In the past this would have led to an increase in productivity at work, whereas now Jim reports that finishing tasks feels almost impossible. Jim then looked at his feet and shared that his sex drive has been very low, which has led his girlfriend to worry that he is not sexually

interested in her. Jim's girlfriend reportedly tells Jim that he seems to have almost no emotion about anything. Jim finishes up describing his symptoms by saying, "I just can't seem to get out of my head."

Throughout the course of your work together Jim shares about a broad diversity of experiences in which he was told by peers, parents, teachers, and coaches that his brother had been a failure. Jim shared that he eventually intuited that he should avoid that path at all costs. Jim remembered distancing himself from his brother. Jim shares that even now he worries when he sees any indicators that they might be similar, and his struggles with motivation lean on this particular source of anxiety.

Jim recounted a number of stories in college, and in the professional world, in which he has felt incredibly angry with people who "don't do their part." As Jim becomes more comfortable in therapy, he shares a sense that he is unable to do as much as he should in work, which causes Jim great fear of losing his job and his girlfriend. At one point Jim shares, "I wish I could have more time with my girlfriend too, but you know how it is." As his therapist, you say, "Please, tell me what you mean." These kinds of curious explorations of Jim's engagement in the world are initially frustrating to Jim, but he learns to tolerate them over time. He eventually even says, "Yeah. I know what you are going to say. How did I learn that, right?"

From a postmodern approach, Jim's therapist could bring empathic curiosity to demonstrations of manliness as they occur in the therapy room. The therapist could invite Jim to recollect memories of his gendered, social learning, exploring the ways that he learned to perform manliness; identifying masculine role models in his life; and further identifying the explicit and implicit gendered messages received during his youth. As safety develops in the relationship, the therapist might even disclose to Jim how it feels to be on the receiving end of his demonstrations of masculinity as well as how it feels to be on the receiving end of Jim's initial exploration of a more flexible variation of his gender expressions. From a postmodern view, demonstrations of competition, shame, and distance from femininity should be understood as coping skills for managing historical and current social and familial pressures. The therapist could respond to Jim by empathizing with those inclinations while also inviting curiosity into both the strengths and limitations of exhibited behaviors and beliefs. This kind of relational knowing (i.e., learning through relational experiences, knowing by observing, knowing by feeling) is well suited to a postmodern framework. The therapist inherently becomes a part of the therapeutic work as therapist observations become an element of potential knowledge co-constructed with the client. Therapists may contribute intuitive knowledge, for example, asking:

- "What is it like for you to be in this room with me as a woman/man/ nonbinary therapist?"

- "How is this similar or different to your experiences with people that you have perceived as having a similar gender expression in the past?"
- "How are you different with me than in other contexts, and how is that influenced by our genders?"

As Jim nears the end of treatment, greater flexibility in gender beliefs and practices may be co-constructed to further counter traditional masculine socialization associated with negative health outcomes. The therapist would additionally help him integrate new forms of expression and identity into his broader social world. This may include inviting his partner and/or family into the therapeutic process. Or the therapist could co-construct a game plan to help Jim practice new forms of self-expression through interpersonal techniques in therapy to feel increasingly prepared to bring new skills to his relationships outside of therapy. It will be important for the therapist to attend to the real-life consequences that Jim might face in reconsidering, and potentially shifting, his understanding and performance of gender. Jim does not live in a vacuum, and changes that he makes may cause negative reactions from others. Depending on the degree of value put on gender expression and performance, Jim's parents, siblings, partner, employers. and others may negatively respond to Jim's decisions to modify his conceptions and performance of gender expression.

With these potential consequences in mind, therapists might find a systemic framework useful when exploring gender constructions and the consequences of the same. A systemic framework takes into account the context in which we have grown, developed, and currently live. A systemic framework recognizes that change in one member of a system impacts other members of the system. A systemic framework also invites intervening with multiple members of a system when possible. In Jim's case this could include inviting Jim's partner, or family members, into treatment as Jim explores and understands the negative health impacts of his current gender construction. This would allow for systemic change to occur in the context of those who have an investment in a given construction of gender and relationships.

CLINICAL CONSIDERATIONS AND LIMITATIONS

A postmodern framework used to counsel men ultimately requires clinicians to understand men and masculinity within a cultural framework. Therapists must have an understanding of the cultural values and expectations imposed on men, while approaching their clinical work with a willingness to expand their own assumptions associated with masculinity. It is also important that clinicians address their own biases and misconceptions about men's gender expression to ensure that they are not reinforcing stereotypes and societal conceptualizations of masculine performance that lead to negative gender health consequences. In addition, therapists must be flexible and engender cognitive flexibility in their clients, in regard to the construction of men and masculinity. Flexibility will allow for diverse expression and combat gendered consequences when one does not fit, or chooses to subvert, traditional masculinity. This may be a challenge for therapists who are grounded in more traditional, naturalist assumptions regarding gender and biological sex. It may be additionally challenging for those therapists who have not had the opportunity, or who have been unwilling, to explore their own gender narratives.

This particular approach to affirming men's gendered experiences may require intensive exploration of individual experiences that may not be well suited for some brief-therapy models found within the postmodern paradigm. When utilizing the approach outlined earlier, and addressing men's socialization processes, the clinician may experience resistance from the clients. When addressing men's cultural power, some men may perceive that their self-concept (i.e., hard-working, in control, nonemotional) is being challenged and may, in turn, react defensively. Others may experience anxieties related to the self-reflexive process and increased self-awareness. Through self-reflection around gender issues, some clients may begin to recognize personal experiences of injustice or former acts of perpetration that may lead to further identification of losses, insecurities, and emotions that were not previously identified. Given that the clients will be asked to explore socialization processes and the negative gender messages received, some men may experience a loss of meaning and safety that can further provoke anxieties and personal insecurities. Thus, emphasizing cultural strengths associated with masculinity in relation to character strengths can help ensure personal resources and coping strategies are not depleted.

It is inevitable that the therapeutic trajectory will look different depending on the therapist who is chosen by the client. The therapist's visible and nonvisible identities will undoubtedly influence the process of therapy. It is also true that the client's assumption of similarity to the therapist will influence the therapeutic process. While this effect could certainly be an added strength and a valuable part of the process, the presence of certain identities may inhibit important dialogue more than others. For example, Jim may be less likely to consider alternative perspectives with a woman therapist if his conceptualization of masculinity is based on situating himself in positions of power over others, or specifically women in this example. Similarly, Jim may be less likely to openly explore conceptualizations with a man therapist because of his fear of judgment, guilt, and shame associated with being perceived as less than a man. Similarity by the therapist, in addition to a lack of nuanced understanding and cultural observation by the therapist, may inhibit the incorporation or creative development of alternative perspectives and ways of "knowing" oneself as a gendered person.

SUMMARY

The postmodern paradigm offers promising clinical approaches for the facilitation of therapeutic work with men. Postmodern ideology underscores important considerations for the nature of gender and masculinity that can be useful when addressing gendered health consequences and intrapsychic conflict experienced by modern men. New meaning and healthy constructions of gender and masculinity stemming from a postmodern view may help support individual awareness and healthy behavior change that can increase men's individual potential.

Postmodern treatment approaches are not the only way of facilitating gender awareness in men. However, these authors believe postmodern approaches offer a nonhierarchical, collaborative experience between client and the therapist that may help men to engage more authentically in the therapeutic process. Perceived partnership between client and therapist will help develop a team-like approach that will additionally help eliminate power struggles and competition in the therapeutic relationship while encouraging active participation and motivational support to accomplish treatment goals.

Perhaps most impotant, postmodern approaches to clinical treatment with men will challenge the cultural compulsion to label (or gender) men as uniquely *men* without recognition of their full, human potential to be something other than a culturally prescribed stereotype (O'Neil, 2014). Recognizing men as gendered *humans* may help elicit compassionate, empathetic, and strength-centered views of men, while combatting harmful gender conceptualizations, beliefs, biases, and discourses in the therapy room that negatively affect men's lived experiences. By conceptualizing men more holistically from a postmodern treatment approach, men in therapy will be given permission to embrace their authentic selves and to challenge cultural standards and constraints to experience their greatest human potential.

REFERENCES

Addis, M. E. (2008). Gender and depression in men. *Clinical Psychology: Science and Practice, 15,* 153–168.
Barrett, M. J., & Stone Fish, L. (2014). *Treating complex trauma: A relational blueprint for collaboration and change.* New York, NY: Routledge.

Brooks, G. R. (2001). Masculinity and men's mental health. *Journal of American College Health, 49*(6), 285–297.

Brooks, G. R. (2010). *Beyond the crises of masculinity: A transtheoretical model for male-friendly therapy.* Washington, DC: American Psychological Association.

Butler, J. (1990). *Gender trouble: Feminism and the subversion of identity.* Philadelphia, PA: Taylor & Francis.

Center for Behavioral Health Statistics and Quality. (2015). Behavioral health trends in the United States: Results from the 2014 National Survey on Drug Use and Health (HHS Publication No. SMA 15-4927, NSDUH Series H-50). Retrieved from http://www.samhsa.gov/data/sites/default/files/NSDUH-FRR1-2014/NSDUH-FRR1-2014.pdf

Centers for Disease Control and Prevention (CDC). (2011). Fact Sheet—CDC health disparities and inequalities report—U.S., 2011. Retrieved from http://www.cdc.gov/minorityhealth/CHDIR/2011/FactSheet.pdf

Connell, R. W. (2005). *Masculinities* (2nd ed.). Berkeley, CA: University of California Press.

Connor, S. (2001). The shame of being a man. *Textual Practice, 15*(2), 211–230.

Courtenay, M. H. (2003). Key determinants of the health and the well-being of men and boys. *International Journal of Men's Health, 2*(1), 1–27.

Crenshaw, K. (1989). Demarginalizing the intersection of race and sex: A black feminist critique of antidiscrimination doctrine, feminist theory, and antiracist politics. *The University of Chicago Legal Forum, 1*(8), 139–140.

Duffey, T., & Haberstroh, S. (2014). Developmental relational counseling: Applications for counseling men. *Journal of Counseling & Development, 92,* 104–111.

Efthim, P. W., Kenny, M. E., & Mahalik, J. R. (2001). Gender role stress in relation to shame, guilt, and externalization. *Journal of Counseling & Development, 79,* 430–438.

Englar-Carlson, M. (2014). Introduction: A primer on counseling men. In M. Englar-Carlson, M. P. Evans, & T. Duffey (Eds.), *A counselor's guide to working with men* (pp. 1–31). Alexandria, VA: American Counseling Association.

Englar-Carlson, M., Evans, M. P., & Duffey, T. (2014). *A counselor's guide to working with men.* Alexandria, VA: American Counseling Association.

Englar-Carlson, M., & Kiselica, M. S. (2013). Affirming the strengths in men: A positive masculinity approach to assisting male clients. *Journal of Counseling & Development, 91,* 399–409.

Evans, A. M., Carney, J. S., & Wilkinson, M. (2013). Work-life balance for men: Counseling implications. *Journal of Counseling & Development, 91,* 436–441.

Evans, M. P. (2013). Men in counseling: A content analysis of the journal of counseling & development and counselor education and supervision, 1981–2011. *Journal of Counseling & Development, 91,* 467–474.

Evans, M. P., Duffey, T., & Englar-Carlson, M. (2013). Introduction to the special issue: Men in counseling. *Journal of Counseling & Development, 91,* 387–389.

Falicov, C. J. (2010). Changing constructions of machismo for Latino men in therapy: "The devil never sleeps." *Family Process, 49*(3), 309–329.

Federal Bureau of Prisons. (2016). Inmate gender. Retrieved from https://www.bop.gov/about/statistics/statistics_inmate_gender.jsp

Good, G. E., Thomson, D. A., & Brathwaite, A. D. (2005). Men and therapy: Critical concepts, theoretical frameworks, and research recommendations. *Journal of Clinical Psychology, 61*(6), 699–711.

Hansen, J. T. (2004). Thoughts on knowing: Epistemic implications of counseling practice. *Journal of Counseling & Development, 82,* 131–138.

Hansen, J. T. (2007). Counseling without truth: Toward a neopragmatic foundation for counseling practice. *Journal of Counseling & Development, 85,* 423–430.

Hayes, R., & Oppenheim, R. (1997). Constructivism: Reality is what you make it. In. T. Sexton & B. Griffin (Eds.), *Constructivist thinking in counseling practice, research, and training* (pp. 19–40). New York, NY: Teachers College Press.

Hennen, P. (2008). *Faeries, bears, and leathermen: Men in community queering the masculine.* Chicago, IL: The University of Chicago Press.

Kahn, J. S. (2011). Feminist therapy for men: Challenging assumptions and moving forward. *Women & Therapy, 34*, 59–76.

Kierski, W., & Blazina, C. (2009). The male fear of the feminine and its effects on counseling and psychotherapy. *The Journal of Men's Studies, 17*(2), 155–172.

Kimmel, M. (2012). *Manhood in America: A cultural history.* New York, NY: The Free Press.

Leary, K. (1994). Psychoanalytic "problems" and postmodern "solutions." *Psychoanalytic Quarterly, 63*, 433–465.

Liu, W. M. (2005). The study of men and masculinity as an important multicultural competency consideration. *Journal of Clinical Psychology, 61*(6), 685–697.

Mahalik, J. R., Locke, B. D., Ludlow, L. H., Diemer, M., Scott, R. P. J., Gottfried, M., & Freitas, 2003. Development of the conformity to masculine norms inventory. *Psychology of Men and Masculinity, 4*, 3–25.

Mahalik, J. R., Talmadge, W. T., Locke, B. D., & Scott, R. P. J. (2005). Using the conformity to masculine norms inventory to work with men in a clinical setting. *Journal of Clinical Psychology, 61*(6), 661–674.

McLean, I. A. (2013). The male victim of sexual assault. *Best Practice & Research Clinical Obstetrics and Gynaecology, 27*, 39–46.

Muehlenhard, C. L., & Peterson, Z. D. (2011). Distinguishing between sex and gender: History, current conceptualizations, and implications. *Sex Roles, 64*, 791–803.

O'Neil, J. M. (1981). Male sex-role conflict, sexism, and masculinity: Implications for men, women, and the counseling psychologist. *The Counseling Psychologist, 9*, 61–80.

O'Neil, J. M. (2008). Summarizing 25 years of research on men's gender role conflict using the gender role conflict scale: New research paradigms and clinical implications. *The Counseling Psychologist, 36*(3), 358–445.

O'Neil, J. M. (2013). Gender role conflict research 30 years later: An evidence-based diagnostic scheme to assess boys and men in counseling. *Journal of Counseling and Development, 91*(4), 490–498.

O'Neil, J. M. (2014). Foreword. In M. Englar-Carlson, M. P. Evans, & T. Duffey (Eds.), *A counselor's guide to working with men* (pp. ix–xix). Alexandria, VA: American Counseling Association.

O'Neil, J. M., Helms, B., Gable, R., David, L., & Wrightsman, L. (1986). Gender role conflict scale: College men's fear of femininity. *Sex Roles, 14*, 335–350.

O'Neil, J. M., & Renzulli, S. (2013). Introduction to the special section: Teaching the psychology of men—a call to action. *Psychology of Men & Masculinity, 14*(3), 221–229.

Osherson, S., & Krugman, S. (1990). Men, shame, and psychotherapy. *Psychotherapy, 27*(3), 327–339.

Reed, E. E. (2014). Man up: Young men's lived experiences and reflections on counseling. *Journal of Counseling & Development, 92*, 428–437.

Rochlen, A. B. (2005). Men in (and out of) therapy: Central concepts, emerging directions, and remaining challenges. *Journal of Clinical Psychology, 61*(6), 627–631.

Rosen, H. (1996). Meaning-making narratives: Foundations for constructivist and social constructionist psychotherapies. In H. Rosen & K. Kuehlwein (Eds.), *Constructing realities: Meaning making perspectives for psychotherapists* (pp. 3–51). San Francisco, CA: Jossey-Bass.

Rubin, G. (1975). The traffic in women: Notes on the "political economy" of sex. In R. Reiter (Ed.), *Toward an anthropology of women* (pp. 157–210). New York, NY: Monthly Review Press.

Ryan, B. (1999). Does postmodernism mean the end of Barrett science in the behavioral sciences, and does it matter anyway? *Theory and Psychology, 9*, 483–502.

Schermer, T. W. (2013). The story of manhood: Using a narrative approach to facilitate unique constructions of masculinity. *Journal of Creativity in Mental Health, 8*, 136–150.

Schippers, M. (2007). Recovering the feminine other: Masculinity, femininity, and gender hegemony. *Theory & Society, 36*, 85–102.

Scholz, R., & Hall, S. R. (2014). Motivational interviewing and masculine sensitive therapy. In M. Englar-Carlson, M. P. Evans, & T. Duffey (Eds.), *A counselor's guide to working with men* (pp. 325–346). Alexandria, VA: American Counseling Association.

Shen-Miller, D. S., Isacco, A., Davies, J. A., St. Jean, M., & Phan, J. L. (2013). The men's center approach: Ecological interventions for college men's health. *Journal of Counseling & Development, 91*, 499–507.

Shepard, D. S., & Rabinowitz, F. E. (2013). The power of shame in men who are depressed: Implications for counselors. *Journal of Counseling & Development, 91*, 451–457.

West, C., & Zimmerman, D. H. (1987). Doing gender. *Gender & Society, 1*(2), 125–151.

Wester, S. R. (2008). Male gender role conflict and multiculturalism: Implications for counseling psychology. *The Counseling Psychologist, 36*(2), 294–324.

White, A. M., & Peretz, T. (2010). Emotions and redefining black masculinity: Movement narratives of two profeminist organizers. *Men and Masculinities, 12*(4), 403–424.

Wright, F. (1994). Men, shame, and group psychotherapy. *Group, 18*(4), 212–224.

Counselor Education From a Postmodern Perspective

INTRODUCTION

In Chapter 12, "Counselor Education From a Postmodern Perspective: Empowering Students," Dr. Colette T. Dollarhide and her coauthors call attention to a pervasive tension between modernist and postmodern elements in current counselor education practices. They establish the significance of the problem through the application of postmodern adult education principles. In their critique of contemporary counselor education practices, they invoke the voices of renowned postmodern educators, including Paulo Freire, Marcia Baxter Magolda, Jack Mezirow, and Parker J. Palmer. These theorists are united by a firm belief that constructionist learning is transformative or capable of promoting an expansion of consciousness for the learner (e.g., Freire, 1970; Mezirow, 1991).

Paulo Freire (1970), the earliest of these pedagogues, railed against what he called a *culture of silence* in which dominant teachers prevent oppressed learners from engaging in critical and egalitarian dialogue. Freire (1970) proposed a form of education in which teachers and learners interact as equals as the solution to oppression and the culture of silence. Such a relationship would provide oppressed learners with the opportunity to express themselves openly and authentically. Freire's philosophy is postmodern in two important ways. First, learning occurs through co-constructed dialogue among equals. In his pedagogy of liberation (Freire, 1970), there is no student–teacher dichotomy because such a dichotomy necessarily entails oppression of the student's voice by the teacher. In addition, Freire's philosophy of education emphasizes a view of the learner as actively and intentionally constructing her or his identity. Another way of viewing this is to say that learners are *self-authoring* (Baxter Magolda, 2008; Freire, 1970).

In the field of counselor education, authors have previously examined methods for integrating postmodern social justice pedagogy into graduate courses (Brubaker, Puig, Reese, & Young, 2010; Odegard & Vereen, 2010), and they have even explored methods for using supervision to prepare counselors-in-training for client advocacy roles (Glosoff & Durham, 2010). Yet, by and large, the methods for implementation of postmodern social justice andragogy in counselor training appear to have been largely neglected by scholars in the field (Barrio Minton, Wachter Morris, & Yaites, 2014). Why is this topic important? It is important for at least two primary reasons. The first reason relates to the need for an approach to instruction that is more holistic and, as a result, optimally engaging for counselors-in-training. A postmodern approach is more likely to engage students through the provision of a good teacher–student relationship and to engage students on both intellectual (e.g., learning objectives) and emotional (e.g., values, preferences) levels. The degree of engagement in learning is important because it can have a significant influence on students' persistence, skill acquisition, and knowledge retention (Appleton, Christenson, & Furlong, 2008; Scholl, Hayden, & Clarke, 2017; Scholl, Gibson, Despres, & Boyarinova, 2014; Yates, Brindley-Richards, & Thistoll, 2014).

A second reason that it is important to implement a postmodern form of andragogy in counselor training pertains to preparing counselors-in-training to provide their clients with the same sort of egalitarian, dialogic, and empowering relationships. It is the responsibility of counselor educators to model and prepare their students for the day they will form egalitarian alliances with clients from all walks of life. A postmodern approach to counselor education in which the learner is active, equal to the educator, and self-authoring is an exemplar of the postmodern, empowering approach to counseling that has the potential to promote self-authoring in clients. For this reason, counselor educators should encourage and challenge their counselors-in-training to continue to maintain an egalitarian, antioppression stance with their clients after completing their professional training (Poole, 2010).

The recommendations made by Dollarhide and her associates echo the values that are both integral to the role of counselor and relevant to an antioppression philosophy of education. Critical values they call attention to include cultivating and amplifying the learner's inner voice and contextualizing skills in a manner that benefits and builds one's local community. Their recommendations are compelling as they entail processes in which learners are active co-constructors of knowledge integral to their ongoing professional identity development. Moreover, the authors have written a chapter that artfully blends abstract principles with concrete descriptions of methods for implementing innovative techniques in the classroom. The authors recommend five postmodern techniques for counselor educators, and they go into considerable depth and detail in explaining how to implement each technique. For example, one technique, the creation of *brave spaces*, entails learners demonstrating the courage to challenge inequities and also to express themselves honestly and openly. A guiding principle for creating and maintaining brave spaces is embracing *controversy with civility* (Arao & Clemens, 2013, p. 144). They propose this rule as suitable for replacing a common rule in safe spaces known as *agree to disagree*. Controversy with civility is more likely to engender productive socially co-constructed dialogue, and for this reason it is more consistent with a postmodern social justice perspective.

Chapter 12 provides a good example of how authors can transform the printed page into a *brave space* (Arao & Clemens, 2013) characterized by *challenge*, exploration of *dissonance*, and authentic expression of each individual's inner *voice*. One of the most important implications of this chapter is that counselor educators and counselors-in-training are collaborators engaged in a critical enterprise. If graduates of professional programs (e.g., counselors, social workers, psychologists) are to serve as effective agents of social justice and advocate for the oppressed in their communities, then the onus is on educators to employ postmodern pedagogical methods that foster egalitarian attitudes and practices in graduate students (Fook, 2002; Poole, 2010; Tolliver & Burghardt, 2016). Counselors who are exclusively modernist learners and practitioners will prove far less capable of empowering their clients. Both counselor educators and counselors-in-training have a shared stake in the development and maintenance of an egalitarian, community-building workforce in our society (Tolliver & Burghardt, 2016). In their chapter, Dollarhide and associates provide timely recommendations for providing counselors-in-training with educational experiences designed to promote their ability to contribute to such a workforce.

REFERENCES

Appleton, J. J., Christenson, S. L., & Furlong, M. J. (2008). Student engagement with school: Critical conceptual and methodological issues of the construct. *Psychology in the Schools, 45,* 369–386. doi:10.1002/pits.20303

Arao, B., & Clemens, K. (2013). From safe spaces to brave spaces: A new way to frame dialogue around diversity and social justice. In L. M. Landreman (Ed.), *The art of effective facilitation: Reflections from social justice educators* (pp. 135–150). Herndon, VA: Stylus.

Barrio Minton, C. A., Wachter Morris, C. A., & Yaites, L. D. (2014). Pedagogy in counselor education: A 10-year content analysis of journals. *Counselor Education & Supervision, 53*(3), 162–177.

Baxter Magolda, M. B. (2008). Three elements of self-authorship. *Journal of College Student Development, 49*, 269–284.

Brubaker, M. D., Puig, A., Reese, R. F., & Young, J. (2010). Integrating social justice into counseling theories pedagogy: A case example. *Counselor Education & Supervision, 50*(2), 88–102.

Fook, J. (2002). *Social work: Critical theory and practice.* London, UK: Sage.

Freire, P. (1970). *Pedagogy of the oppressed.* New York, NY: Continuum.

Glosoff, H. L., & Durham, J. C. (2010). Using supervision to prepare social justice advocates. *Counselor Education & Supervision, 50*(2), 116–129.

Mezirow, J. (1991). *Transformative dimensions of adult learning.* San Francisco, CA: Jossey-Bass.

Odegard, M. A., & Vereen, L. G. (2010). A grounded theory of counselor educators integrating social justice into their pedagogy. *Counselor Education & Supervision, 50*(2), 130–149.

Poole, J. (2010). Progressive until graduation? Helping BSW students hold on to anti-oppressive and critical social work practice. *Critical Social Work, 11*(1), 2–11.

Scholl, M. B., Gibson, D. M., Despres, J., & Boyarinova, N. (2014). Using the film *October Sky* to teach career counseling theories to counselors-in-training. *Journal of Humanistic Counseling, 53*(1), 2–21.

Scholl, M. B., Hayden, S. C. W., & Clarke, P. B. (2017). Promoting optimal student engagement in online counseling courses. *Journal of Humanistic Counseling, 56*(3), 197–210.

Tolliver, W., & Burghardt, S. (2016). Education and training of a race-conscious workforce. In A. J. Carten, A. B. Siskind, & M. Pender Greene (Eds.), *Strategies for deconstructing racism in the health and human services* (pp. 33–50). New York, NY: Oxford University Press.

Yates, A., Brindley-Richards, W., & Thistoll, T. (2014). Student engagement in distance-based vocational education. *Journal of Open, Flexible and Distance Learning, 18*, 29–44.

CHAPTER 12

Counselor Education From a Postmodern Perspective

Empowering Students

COLETTE T. DOLLARHIDE, ALLISHA M. BERENDTS,
TODD A. GIBBS, SEAN R. GORBY, AND J. P. OEHRTMAN

D ebates about educational effectiveness are ongoing, with the pendulum of opinion swinging from modern to postmodern perspectives. Research within the last decade has demonstrated some advantages of conventional instruction methodology when compared to various postmodern pedagogical practices for K-12 students; this has reinforced some use of modernistic pedagogy. For example, when face-to-face instruction was compared to online instruction, individuals receiving face-to-face instruction received significantly higher scores on two out of three tests and assignments (Ferguson & Tryjankowski, 2009). Higher scores were also recorded through standardized testing by middle-school math and science students when teachers invested more time implementing lecture-style instruction than when more time was spent utilizing problem-solving activities (Schwerdt & Wuppermann, 2011). However, other significant research has also pushed the pendulum of opinion in support of a more postmodern perspective. Problem-based learning, a postmodernistic pedagogy, was found to be more effective than traditional teaching methods where teacher instruction, textbooks, discussion, and questioning were implemented (Tasoglu & Bakac, 2010). Further complicating the debate are studies that yield no significant difference between traditional instruction and postmodern pedagogical practices. When students' perceived understanding and ability to apply learned material were examined, no difference was found between traditional lecture and a postmodern pedagogy involving cooperative learning (Ali, 2011). Research has affirmed that in the complex gestalt of instructor, learner, setting, and subject matter in K-12 education, both modern and postmodern pedagogies have documented advantages (Eggen & Kauchak, 2013).

However, in an increasingly complex and diverse world, learners need thinking strategies that encourage creative problem-solving and inspire innovation (Shields, 2013). Some postmodern approaches, especially the emphasis on collaboration between teacher and student to co-create learning, foster this inventive learning perspective. In counselor education and supervision, a new learning perspective is required, one in which epistemological complexity is paramount in both cognitive and affective domains (Anderson et al., 2001; Krathwohl, Bloom, & Masia, 1964). In an ideal classroom, this complexity is developed in a learning *community*, which would enable counseling students to experience trust in self, instructor, and learning process; where learning is a shared responsibility between learner and instructor; and where the voices of students are as valuable as the voice of the facilitators (Palmer, 1998). But to attain true community, the dynamics of power (of the instructor, supervisor, and profession) and viable professional/educational goals must be contextualized, and current pedagogical practices must be understood as a point of departure.

PEDAGOGY IN COUNSELOR EDUCATION AND SUPERVISION

Current practices in counselor education logically reflect the full continuum of learning structures: from structured, instructor-centered pedagogy to evidence-based, student-based pedagogy (Malott, Hall, Sheely-Moore, Krell & Cardachiotto, 2014). Pedagogic strategies in counselor education range from modernistic to constructivistic (Guiffrida, 2005), without clear consensus about preferred instructional or evaluative methods for these strategies (Malott et al., 2014). Many counselor educators and supervisors are approaching the age of retirement (Bureau of Labor Statistics, n.d.) and may be using pedagogical approaches grounded in modernistic assumptions that were in effect during their training in counselor education and supervision (Guiffrida, 2005). It is no wonder that Mallot et al. (2014) express concern about current practices of training in teaching in counselor education and supervision.

Teaching about teaching should be a high priority in counselor education. Barrio Minton, Wachter Morris, and Yaites (2014) conducted a content analysis of peer-reviewed counseling journals to determine how pedagogy is addressed. The purpose of this study was to see if the literature contained evidenced-based pedagogy that was consistent with accreditation standards, and to highlight present trends and implications for future focus. According to Barrio Minton et al., of the 230 articles examined from January 2001 through December 2010 in 16 different counseling journals, approximately 9% was focused on pedagogy and 6% on teaching and learning. The majority of the articles focused on techniques, foundations, and other content areas (Barrio Minton et al., 2014). As the counseling profession grows in awareness of social justice, so should the profession grow in the way we teach and train new counselors (Brubaker, Puig, Reese, & Young, 2010; Chang, Crethar, & Ratts, 2010; Odegard & Vereen, 2010; West, Bubenzer, Cox, & McGlothlin, 2013). Yet this does not appear to be happening.

The emphasis of postmodern pedagogy is knowledge as a social construct, so our objective should be to design learning goals that focus on the construction of knowledge and meaning through reflection, dialogue, and collaborative learning (West et al., 2013). The teacher should be a part of the collaborative learning, not the expert imparting knowledge to the students (Bemak & Chung, 2011; Fong, 1998). This is a shift in education: from the teacher as expert *passing along* knowledge, to the teacher and student learning and creating knowledge and meaning *together as equals*, sharing power in the classroom (Freire, 2009; Nelson & Neufeldt, 1998). Both the teacher/supervisor and student are to be involved as "an active participant[s] in socially co-considering, questioning, evaluating, and inventing information" (Nelson & Neufeldt, 1998, p. 79). By using the teacher/supervisor–student relationship to refer to power relations, the student can observe and redefine the power differential in a counselor–client relationship (Lonn, Tello, Duffey, & Haberstroh, 2014; Nelson & Neufeldt, 1998).

Power in relationships in counselor education and supervision are found in both the instructor–learner relationship in the classroom and the supervisory relationship in field experience, both pre- and post-graduation. In fact, these power dynamics are as visible in the field between supervisor and supervisee as they are in the classroom between instructor and student (Bernard & Goodyear, 2014). For this reason, pedagogical implications related to supervision will be offered throughout this chapter, as one of the primary goals of supervision is to refine and polish prior learning (Bernard & Goodyear, 2014).

Measures of Learning in Counselor Education and Supervision

Learning in counselor education is variously measured by program accreditation status and student academic performance. Both of these strategies for assessing program quality and student success suggest a modernist foundation, and pressure to perform on each of these measures is an example of the power of the profession to mold programs in "desirable" modernistic shapes (Hansen, 2012).

First, the accreditation process (regardless of accreditation body or level) emphasizes program self-assessment as one primary way to determine worthiness for accreditation and defines the quantitative measures that must be collected on applicants, students, and graduates. For the counseling profession, the Council for Accreditation of Counseling and Related Programs [CACREP] requires large amounts of quantitative data. (See the *CACREP 2009 Standards*, Section I, Evaluation, p. 8; and *Draft 2 of the 2016 CACREP Standards*, CACREP, 2014, Section IV, p. 15). In these self-assessment processes, programs demonstrate accountability through collecting data for presentation to the accreditation agency, requiring the quantification of student learning to facilitate the measurement and comparison of the program over time. While the metrics themselves may be variously defined, what is mandated is a *process* of quantification, data collection, and data tracking.

A second example of modernistic forces in counselor education can be seen in ways that student performance is measured, usually on tests, grades, and other individual metrics. Learning in counselor education is more than taking tests, yet testing is an important measure by which students and programs are compared. Scores on licensure exams, for example, are used to compare program to program. This forces a modernist approach of didactic teaching that prepares students for exams as the primary focus of the educational endeavor. Further, it invites comparison of student to student, as competition for jobs or positions in doctoral study facilitates the use of an easily comparable number (GPA or licensure exam score) to award employment or admission.

Deconstructing Modernistic Measures of Learning

From a modernist perspective, it makes sense to use numbers or other quantifiable, explicit criteria to measure "quality." We would all prefer to drive a car that has demonstrated a significant safety record in accidents, as measured by the percentage of fatally damaged crash-test dummies. But the expediency of such measurements does not justify the practice in a human endeavor such as education, and especially not in programs of counselor education and supervision—a notably humanistic endeavor (Hansen, 2003). We might feel pressure to collect such data to preserve accreditation status, but we do not need to allow it to define our pedagogical realities. Just as counseling cannot be mechanistic, neither can be the measures we use to assess its successful demonstration (Hansen, 2010). Quality in counselor education must be measured by more than the databits we collect, whether it is for accreditation or for program accountability.

Postmodern pedagogy helps future counselor to learn about self and client in ways that will inform future practice; students are encouraged to learn and adopt counseling perspectives in self-reflective ways. Students should learn about social justice and emancipation as experience, not just as concepts on an upcoming test (Bemak & Chung, 2011; Brubaker et al., 2010). As one example of a postmodern approach, constructivist teaching promotes students' creation of knowledge by discovering and understanding through a narrative process and by critically evaluating frameworks that work for them (Guiffrida, 2005). In another example, counselors-in-training take part in social justice activities as a "classroom without walls" experience to extend counseling into communities that are currently or historically oppressed (Bemak & Chung, 2011).

To understand if a counselor-in-training is moving toward responsible clinical practice, Hansen (2010) proposes self-definitions of professional identity that would be co-constructed with the social group in which the new professional is currently participating, resulting in definitions of professional identity that are locally responsive and guided by prag-matic considerations. As such, professional identity and counselor educa-tion would be in constant flux, as discussions of professional identity and standards would be constructed and reconstructed in the training process (Hansen, 2010). In this reflexive dialogue, new professionals would experi-ence responsibility for learning, self-advocacy, and appreciation for diverse voices in the counseling milieu (Hansen, 2010).

Appreciation for diverse and alternative discourses is important for the understanding and contextualization of power dynamics in counseling (Brubaker et al., 2010). Prilleltensky (1997) coined the term "emancipa-tory communitarianism" to explore how postmodern views could be ex-panded in the effort to empower oppressed groups in the effort to build just communities. In this view, Prilleltensky emphasizes the value of *distributive justice* (equal access to resources), *collaboration*, and *compassion*, stating that communitarianism underscores the balance between rights and responsibilities, highlights the common good, and acknowledges commitment to social obligations to share power. In an extension of eman-cipatory communitarianism, one could argue that the building of commu-nity in a counseling classroom and in supervision accomplishes important goals: Students learn to co-create their professional identities, they learn to take responsibility for collaboration and compassion, and they learn the value and power of community (Brubaker et al., 2010). This means that emancipation becomes a viable educational goal, one that coexists with professional identity as a critical outcome of counselor education.

EMANCIPATORY COMMUNITARIANISM AS A GUIDING
PHILOSOPHY IN COUNSELOR EDUCATION AND SUPERVISION

Drawn from communitarian philosophies that emphasize the building of communities using caring, compassion, mutual responsibility, and collaboration, and from liberation theories that address the value of distributive justice and rights of access, emancipatory communitarianism brings together the dynamic interplay of core humanistic, postmodern values: individual agency *and* the need for community (Prilleltensky, 1997). As an educational philosophy, facilitation of emancipatory communitarianism for students will allow for educational practices that are guided by the values of communion (efforts for the common good), emancipation and distributive justice, mutual responsibility and power sharing, and the balance of individual agency with community. In practice, education based on emancipatory communitarianism would involve shared responsibility between teacher/supervisor and student to design educational/supervisory strategies, educational/supervisory goals, and pedagogical/supervisory tools that would bring about community; distribution of knowledge and resources fairly and equitably; and the balance of individual interpretation of meaning with community interpretation of meaning. What makes this "emancipatory" is the emphasis on student/teacher/supervisor co-responsibility for learning; the student and teacher/supervisor share power with each other as equals in the educational process. What makes this education "communitarian" is the overall goal to become a community, which is described by Palmer (1998).

In this community, learners/teachers gather around a subject worthy of study using "complex patterns of communication—sharing observations and interpretations, correcting and complementing each other, torn by conflict in this moment and joined by consensus in the next. The community . . . is circular, interactive, and dynamic" (Palmer, 1998, p. 103). In this way, all participants of the community are concurrently learners, teachers, questioners, challengers, provocateurs, and clarifiers (Palmer, 1998). All members of this community are responsible to each other to function as facilitators of individual and collective knowledge, which is the shared resource, the coin of distributive justice, available to all equally and equitably.

Palmer (1998) goes on to describe the paradoxes of the learning context:

1. Topics are bounded and focused, yet concurrently open to new interpretations.
2. The learning context is hospitable and inviting, yet concurrently offers compelling reasons to risk being vulnerable during learning.

3. The context is respectful of the voice of the individual, yet concurrently responsible to and for the collective understanding and growth of the group in an iterative process.
4. The learning conversation honors the individual stories of learners yet concurrently honors the larger stories of the discipline being studied.
5. The learning context supports thoughtful reflection yet concurrently offers the resources of the learning community for mutual growth.
6. The learning community invites both silence and speech to allow learners to communicate in timing and ways that are reflective of deeper learning.

In these paradoxical conditions of community and learning, counselors-in-training become emancipated from being passive consumers of information to becoming active partners in the co-creation of their professional being. They take responsibility for their learning, their colleagues' learning, and by extension, for their future clients.

Postmodern Models of Learning in Counselor Education and Supervision

Within the aforementioned *philosophy of education*, we are contextualizing educational effort using *three postmodern models of learning* that provide structure for the educational process. Integrating these models provides an overview of how learning happens for the learner and will provide structure for the suggested learning activities that will be presented.

Self-Authorship

Self-authorship is defined as a capacity for holistic meaning making that is characterized by an internalization of beliefs, values, and loyalties, such that the individual can take responsibility for his or her thoughts, feelings, and actions (Boes, Baxter Magolda, & Buckley, 2010). As a constructive-developmental theory, self-authorship fits with the broader constructivist paradigm that realities are multiple, bound by context, and socially negotiated (Lincoln & Guba, 2000). Within the context of adult learning, movement toward self-authorship may be sparked when the external formulas that have proved capable of guiding the learner's life up to that point are no longer sufficient to make meaning of their current experience. Students thus find themselves at a crossroads, where they must learn to listen to and cultivate their own voice in the midst of competing narratives and directives (Baxter Magolda, 2009).

Counselor educators and supervisors may make use of this theory by looking and listening for the presence of these crossroads experiences. For counselors-in-training, each of these moments has the potential to provide greater ownership of preferred identities, both personal and professional. Movement toward greater self-authorship is often an introspective process, so assignments that prompt reflective activity may propel counseling students' development of this capacity. Self-authorship may also be facilitated by providing spaces for meaningful dialogue and exploration of alternative views of self, others, and the world we share. In the context of counselor education, this can occur in a variety of ways, including group discussions and individual consultations between students and supervisors or faculty members. Each opportunity for meaningful exploration is termed a "holding space," within which students learn to trust their own voice in a manner that supports internal foundations for creating the personal and professional life they desire for self and others (Baxter Magolda, 2009). Numerous research agendas related to self-authorship continue to expand this developmental theory. Counselor educators and supervisors may therefore benefit from attending to and potentially contributing to future directions in understanding self-authorship, including the integration of cultural identities and the role of intersectionality in the process of individual meaning making (Baxter Magolda, 2010).

Transformational Learning

Transformational learning is a theory of learning and development that parallels self-authorship by situating adult learning as an experience that moves students from absolute and simple ways of knowing to more complex and contextualized forms of understanding (Taylor, 2008). Transformational learning is potentiated when students' prior meaning perspectives have been challenged, thus prompting the expansion or alteration of one's worldview (Mezirow & Taylor, 2009). These *initial disruptions* (Mezirow, 2012) may occur in any context, although they may be particularly prevalent in social justice and multicultural coursework, or during immersion in practica and internship field placements, as students intentionally encounter diverse perspectives and are required to provide empathy, align with others, and respond with cultural competence.

Mezirow (1991, 2000) highlighted both cognitive and affective domains as important dimensions of transformational learning for adults. Within the cognitive domain, reflective analysis is identified as a key component of transformational learning (Mezirow, 2012). Mezirow (1991) identified differing levels of reflection as *content*, *process*, and *premise* reflections.

Each level represents a necessary increase in the depth of processing for counselors-in-training. *Content* reflection involves contemplation of the nature of a problem, such as giving consideration to a client's presenting concerns (Rosin, 2015). *Process* reflection integrates an added level of reflection by considering the interaction between counselor and client. *Premise* reflection, or critical reflection, involves consideration of underlying beliefs and assumptions on the part of the counselor-in-training. Students engaged in premise reflection question and challenge previously held presuppositions, and this is therefore the level of reflection that is most likely to prompt any transformation of worldview (Rosin, 2015).

Presuppositional beliefs and values are also linked to the affective domain of experience, which suggests that awareness of emotional responses is a necessary component of the reflective process. The presence of strong emotions may provide a powerful deterrent to premise reflection. For instance, when counselors-in-training feel threatened by interpersonal challenges, they may become more entrenched in previously held perspectives. Identification of emotions and opportunities for affective processing in reflection or intentional conversation with educators and supervisors can promote greater acceptance of these affective reactions, and they can reframe perceived threats into potential growth opportunities. Moreover, experiences of critical dialogue and exploration of diverse worldviews offer students an opportunity to reformulate their sense of self within this new perspective (Mezirow, 2012).

Professional Identity Development

Professional identity is a lifelong process, but it is one that begins during training (Auxier, Hughes, & Kline, 2003; Brott & Myers, 1999; Moss, Gibson, & Dollarhide, 2014). According to Gibson, Dollarhide, and Moss (2010), the three learning activities through which professional identity is developed involve (a) external validation; (b) coursework, experience, and commitment; and (c) internal validation. The outcomes of these three activities yield three "transformational tasks" (Gibson et al., 2010): self-labeling as a professional, integration of professional skills and attitudes, and the perception of context in a professional community. The parallels with self-authorship and transformational learning are striking, and they are presented in Table 12.1. In professional identity development, the perception of context in the professional counseling community is a critical part of the development of a counselor-in-training's professional identity (Gibson et al., 2010), and, for doctoral students in counselor education, the acceptance of responsibility for being a counselor educator is a transformational

Table 12.1. PARALLEL PROCESSES OF LEARNING

SELF-AUTHORSHIP Baxter Magolda, 2009	TRANSFORMATIONAL LEARNING Mezirow, 2012	PROFESSIONAL IDENTITY DEVELOPMENT Gibson, Dollarhide, & Moss, 2010	
		Process	Concurrent Goals
Following external formulas	Initial disruption (of previous ways of viewing the world)	External validation	1. Self-labeling as a professional
Crossroads (listening to one's internal voice, cultivating one's voice)	Reflective analysis (critical thinking and dialogue, exploration of alternative worldviews and sense of self in that world)	Coursework, experience, and commitment	2. Integration of professional skills and attitudes, 3. The perception of context in a professional community
Self-authorship (trusting the internal voice, building an internal foundation, securing internal commitments)	Verification and integration (making decisions, taking action, developing confidence)	Self-validation	

task identified for the development of a counselor educator professional identity (Dollarhide, Gibson, & Moss, 2013).

A synthesis of all three models yields a tripartite developmental structure:

1. An externally derived sense of self is challenged (termed *challenging*).
2. The learner struggles with the dissonance through exploring, thinking, and reflecting (termed *dissonance*).
3. The learner derives an internally sourced response to the dissonance, learning to trust in self during the process (termed *voice*).

Each of these developmental structures resonates with the constructivist nature of postmodern counselor education and supervision. The movement toward internalization and formation of new attitudes and knowledge are accessed through reflective and dialogical processes, and they promote distinctive, individualized responses to dissonance in a manner that can enhance efficacy and agency according to the preferred identities of each individual student. Both counselor educators and supervisors may play key roles as facilitators of these developmental processes in order to support counselors-in-training through the challenging journey toward a co-created professional identity.

Using the models of learning outlined earlier, we can now apply the philosophy of emancipatory communitarianism to examine learning strategies, seen in a new light. The strategies presented next are offered as a springboard for further exploration by counselor educators and supervisors interested in practicing emancipatory communitarianism. The foundation for these strategies is the tripartite model and all lend themselves to *challenging* (challenge externally defined perceptions), *dissonance* (explore and reflect on the resulting dissonance), and *voice* (articulate internally derived solutions to the dissonance). Further, each strategy allows students and educators/supervisors to co-create learning, break down power differentials, and foster an authentic learning community. The strategies are presented in a chronological structure mirroring the learning/supervision process (designing the learning situation, learner interactions, and assessment of learning), and they include learning contracts, creating brave spaces, peer learning strategies, problem-based learning, and portfolios.

Learning Contracts

Implementing learning contracts is an effective way for counselor educators and supervisors to utilize the emancipatory communitarian framework and foster shared responsibility in the learning process and an atmosphere conducive for communal learning. Contract learning is a form of self-directed learning that developed out of the movement toward independent learning that began in the 1920s and gained form in the 1960s and 1970s with the manifestation of andragogy in literature as a concept of learning (Knowles, 1986). A learning contract, also referred to as a learning plan or a learning agreement, is a written agreement between two individuals that outlines five aspects of the individual's learning.

The first component of a learning contract addresses the learning objectives (Knowles, 1986). In this section, the contract begins by specifying what the learner will gain or acquire through the process of executing the contract. The learning objectives are often written as the obtainment of skills, knowledge, values, or attitudes. The second component of a learning contract outlines the learning strategies, which are the methods that will be utilized by the learner to complete the learning objectives. The third component of the learning contract is the target completion date for the learning objectives, and the fourth and fifth components indicate the evidence that will be produced to demonstrate the completion of the learning objectives as well as how that evidence will be validated.

When utilizing learning contracts, the responsibility that under modernistic pedagogy fell entirely on the educator diffuses to the classroom community, the learner, and the instructor equally. Unlike a syllabus outlined by the educator to be upheld by the learner, the learner generates the learning contract with the assistance of the educator to be adhered to and carried out by both learner and educator (Knowles, 1986). The learner is responsible for constructing the learning contract between the educator and the learner but should not do so without support and input from both classmates and the educator. The learner would draft the five aspects of the learning contract over a period of time, determined by the educator to best fit the structure of the specific course, while meeting one on one with the instructor to discuss the contract. This process provides the learner the autonomy to create the self-directed content of the learning contract while providing direction through scaffolding via the instructor. In this model, the instructor is a facilitator of knowledge and resources and ought to be utilized by the learner to construct and execute the contract (Knowles, 1986). The pedagogical tool demands the instructor to be active, available, and accessible to the learner throughout the process. It is in this negotiation of learning that *challenge, dissonance,* and *voice* are fostered.

One danger of utilizing the learning contract in the classroom is the misconception that the responsibility to complete the learning objectives is solely on the learner. This is where the emancipatory communitarian framework of the learning contract is different from the postmodern pedagogy of independent study, where the learner is fully responsible for the learning that takes place. Although on the surface it may appear that learning contracts require less time, energy, and effort from the instructor, this is not the case. With learning contracts the instructor may spend more time, energy, and effort with individual students, especially in the beginning as the students are constructing their contracts (Knowles, 1986).

Fellow classmates are a key resource to the construction and execution of the learning contract in the classroom. The beauty of diversity within a class lies in the perspective and influence that diverse views can offer the class community as a whole. Since learning contracts are self-directed and are constructed to push the development of the specific individual, there are usually experiences of fellow classmates that, if shared, prove beneficial to the construction and completion of a specific student's learning objectives. This is much more prominent in a doctoral classroom where the individuals are likely to be at different points in their counseling career, whether it be fresh out of their master's program, young in their clinical career, or a seasoned veteran. Nonetheless, in both master and doctoral courses, providing numerous opportunities for interaction and consultation between students throughout the process (during the construction, the execution, and the completion of the contract) to discuss their learning contracts enriches the learners' experiences and provides the communitarian aspect to the learning process. Learning contracts can be utilized judiciously for specific projects within the counselor education classroom or supervision, or they may be more effectively implemented to demonstrate the learner's completion of learning objectives for the entire program or supervisory period. Whatever the format, providing time at the end of the learning experience to discuss both the process and the product of the contracted learning experience can be valuable learning for the classroom community, and it emancipates students from passive learning orientations.

Learning contracts are also a great way to implement an emancipatory communitarian framework into supervision. Contracts are already utilized in the supervision process and therefore can have a great impact on the learning process of the supervisee with low preparation on the part of the supervisor (Bernard & Goodyear, 2014). Much like the classroom, learning contracts in supervision shift responsibility from the supervisor to shared responsibility with the supervisee. Learning contracts force growth and learning through the intrapersonal processing required for the supervisee to construct the same five aspects of the contract as those used in the classroom. The supervisor and the supervisee, along with any other active parties in a clinical supervisory setting, ought to spend a small portion of time prior to creating the contract discussing aspects of the contract. This may take place over the span of several days, or even several weeks. Through the discourse of supervisee strengths, weaknesses, growth edges, future goals, and other topics relevant to the construction of a learning contract, both the supervisor–supervisee relationship and the potential learning contract are strengthened. Just as in the classroom, the supervisor and the other individuals responsible for overseeing the work of the supervisee are facilitators of knowledge and resources that the supervisee may call upon throughout the process, along with student- or practitioner-colleagues who constitute the training site community.

Creating Brave Spaces

A common educational strategy for adult learning environments is the creation of a *safe space*, within which all students can participate fully in dialogical learning without fear of ridicule. The concept of safe space is particularly salient when challenging issues, especially those related to social justice, comprise the course content (Holley & Steiner, 2005). Safe spaces are usually defined and maintained through the establishment of ground rules that frame guidelines for class discussions (Hardiman, Jackson, &

Griffin, 2007). It is presumed that within these socially constructed class-room environments, all students can share experiences and create transfor-mational learning experiences together.

However, Arao and Clemens (2013) question the notion of safe spaces, suggesting that this concept is incompatible with the inherent risk that is necessary for authentic learning. Within the context of classroom environments, this can become especially salient when students represen-tative of target and agent groups interact within discussions of challenging topics. For target group members, there is a keen awareness that naming experiences of oppression is an inherently unsafe activity (Leonardo & Porter, 2010). By contrast, the insistence upon safety by agent groups as a condition for participation in discussions regarding social justice has been described as an expression of profound privilege (Wise, 2004).

Arao and Clemens (2013) propose a new concept of *brave spaces* as a reformulation of the more traditional approach of safe spaces. Instructors who explicitly articulate the need to maintain brave spaces for learning emphasize the need for courage rather than the maintenance of perceived safety. Bravery is required of all students, as learning involves not only risk but also the challenge of relinquishing prior worldviews in order to find new perspectives, beliefs, and values (Boostrom, 1998). It is clear that this strategy would foster the *challenge, dissonance,* and *voice* that learning requires, and it may have applicability beyond the classroom environment for counseling students. While the formation of brave spaces has the poten-tial to benefit classroom dialogue, it may also reinforce students' resilience as they move out into field placements and initial professional positions. Rather than feeling a need for safety as counselors-in-training, the expe-rience of brave spaces in the educational process may facilitate students' capacity for courage in the new endeavors required for effective growth and presence in client sessions, supervision sessions, and professional interviews.

The creation of brave spaces for learning begins when educators use this terminology explicitly with students, and provide opportunities for students to reflect upon the meaning behind the linguistic shift. Ground rules remain an elemental component for the generation of brave spaces. Some suggested guidelines include what Arao and Clemens (2013) term *controversy with civility, own your intentions and your impact, challenge by choice, respect,* and *no attacks. Controversy with civility* refers to the ability to expect and honor differing views while continuing to work toward common solutions. *Owning intentions and impact* indicates that one's in-tended outcomes do not always align with the impact of one's actions, but each individual must assume responsibility for both, even in the presence of a discrepancy between the two. *Challenging by choice* allows all students to determine the degree to which they will participate in any given exercise, and to reflect upon the factors that influence their level of participation. Mutual *respect* is generally a well-accepted ground rule for discussion, but it may benefit from some dialogical exploration of what respect looks like and how others may receive certain actions or statements. Finally, *attacks* are perceived as statements or feedback directed toward individuals rather than toward behaviors, or statements that are articulated with extreme disrespect (Arao & Clemens, 2013). The ability to honor these ground rules may facilitate students' willingness to embody greater courage within classroom interaction in a manner that may also inform their overarching trajectory as emerging professional counselors.

Peer Teaching and Jigsaw Groups

Peer teaching is a collaborative learning model that integrates cognitive strategies, motivational theory, and social strategies in classroom, group, or supervision settings. When students are also the teachers, they are able to more readily internalize and personalize course information. Through this model, students take more responsibility for their learning, and learning becomes more meaningful through interaction and cooperation with peers (Rubin & Hebert, 1998).

This learning strategy fosters *challenge* as learners navigate the material to be learned, *dissonance* as they reflect on ways to integrate the learning, and *voice* as they share their discoveries with fellow learners. The benefits of peer teaching accrue to both the student who is teaching and the student who is learning (Mackinnon, Haque, & Start, 2009), as increased knowledge, greater skills, deeper learning, and greater understanding have been found in participants (Mackinnon, Haque, & Stark, 2009). Other benefits include increased awareness of intellectual and interpersonal skills, increased confidence in the classroom, and active participation in learning (Klein, 2003). Community is created and fostered through various and complex interactions with peers in which teaching and learning coexist in the same mutually beneficial relationships, and students experience emancipation through ownership over and co-creation of knowledge in diverse conversations.

Elliot Aronson and his colleagues developed a type of peer learning called "jigsaw learning" in 1978. In Aronson's (1978) version of jigsaw learning, the class is divided into groups of six, and each member is assigned a portion of the academic material. Then members of different groups team up with students from other groups who were assigned the same portion, forming "expert groups" (Young & Hadgraft, 1997, p. 12).

This creates motivation and interest in listening to others to learn about all content (Young & Hadgraft, 1997). In a modification done at Johns Hopkins University, students are broken up into small groups of four or five and assigned a specific topic. Once the group has gathered the needed information on their specific topic, they split up and create new groups that consist of one person from each topic group. In this way, they form a new small group where each person teaches others about the topic they were originally assigned (Klein, 2003; Young & Hadgraft, 1997).

In counselor education, peer teaching can be used in a variety of ways and in many different courses. Divide the students into small groups, giving each a topic to research and the students in each small group design a lesson plan to teach their fellow students in a large group setting. For example, jigsaw learning could easily be used in a Theories course. Assign students in groups of four or five, and ask each group to research one theory (person-centered, reality, existential, etc.). The students would then work in their small group to learn about this theory and come up with the information they want to share with their peers. Then the groups would break up and one person from each of the original groups would form a new group and teach each other about their theory. So within each group, the students would learn about four or five different theories from their peers. This could always be done in several cycles if there are more students and/or theories.

Peer teaching would look slightly different in a supervision setting. Existing supervision groups (Bernard & Goodyear, 2014) can be designed to allow supervisees to teach each other. Such groups can also be designed as a jigsaw, similar to the classroom setting, in which new topics for supervisees to learn or case presentations can take place. In these situations, supervisees present a case to their peers to brainstorm clinical strategies or information to be gathered. Such peer teaching in supervision would allow supervisees to refine their clinical "voice" and increase professional confidence, concurrently increasing their co-constructed professional identity. The community built by the learner now expands to include not only fellow students and counselor educators but also professional colleagues and supervisors.

Problem-Based Learning

Problem-based learning (PBL) is another postmodern teaching technique where the students construct their own learning through experience. "PBL is a . . . teaching method that structures knowledge in clinical contexts, strengthens motivation to learn, develops clinical reasoning skills, and enhances self-directed and lifelong learning" (Baker, Pesut, McDaniel, &

Fisher, 2007, p. 215). In PBL, the students do not gain mastery over content knowledge before the problem is presented. By experiencing the problem in stages, students desire additional knowledge to fully understand the problem. This is typically done within a small group setting so students can access knowledge from each other as well as from the teacher, assistant, or facilitator. The facilitator asks questions and monitors interactions and group processes to further the learning (Baker et al., 2007).

PBL is typically focused on a particular curriculum area. Through group work, students are able to identify gaps in their knowledge (*challenge*), which creates cognitive *dissonance*, leading them to pursue independent research (*voice*) to fill the gaps. By sharing their new knowledge with their peer group and facilitator, they are able to self-direct their learning and teach others as well, reinforcing community and emancipation of self-defined learning needs. The theory behind PBL is constructivism, self-directed learning, collaboration, and contextual learning theory, which highlight the benefits to the student (Thurley & Dennick, 2008).

This learning tool can be used in several different courses and a variety of formats. An example would be using problem-based learning in a counseling techniques course. Begin the course giving general information about a client/situation. Each week, as students learn new techniques, they would practice in a dyad or triad and add new techniques each class. Additional information regarding the client and/or the counseling issue would be added each class to go along with the techniques the students are learning.

Applying this tool to supervision can be accomplished in an individual or group setting in an activity similar to case consultation (Bernard & Goodyear, 2014). Supervisees could bring in a real experience from a session where they felt they had a gap in their knowledge. With the supervisor as the facilitator, the supervisees could discuss the knowledge that they have regarding the situation and brainstorm ideas about how to fill that knowledge gap. They could then research the information on their own and bring it back to the group at another time and teach the others.

Portfolios

Counselor educators should be aware of different ways to evaluate the skills and knowledge of counselors-in-training. Utilizing a variety of assessment strategies can help counselor educators improve the training of future counselors. One strategy that can be employed is portfolio development throughout the training and supervision processes. The portfolio strategy can help counselors-in-training take personal responsibility for their own knowledge and skills and provide them with a strategy for continued reflection throughout their careers. This type of strategy will encourage self-authorship, transformational learning, and professional identity development as students confront what they don't yet know (*challenge*), work with the *dissonance,* and make plans and commitment to address those learning gaps, cementing their internal professional *voice* in the process.

One of the many benefits from using portfolios as a strategy for assessment of learning is that it allows students the opportunity to reflect on what they have learned throughout their graduate program. Portfolios enhance students' and supervisees' autonomy as learners and future professionals (Yildrim, 2013). As students begin to compile artifacts for the portfolio, there are five important processes they will experience (Jones, 2013). The first process is collecting all samples of work, which in the second process, undergoes reflection and selection as examples of learning. If the student is not pleased with a specific example, then he or she may undertake a new practice in order to generate better evidence. The third process is annotation, where the student demonstrates how each piece of evidence is demonstrative of learning and growth. The final two processes are reflection and projection, where the student identifies growth that has taken place and sets goals in order for continuous improvement (Jones, 2013). Students can earn long-term benefits that occur as a result of goal setting (Ripley, 2012), which allows students to be self-reflective about which professional areas they would most like improvement and how they plan to achieve their goals. As a part of portfolio development, this practice will help students become more autonomous, emancipated learners. When this process is undertaken in the context of a community of developmental similarity (all students at graduation, for example), it creates support and resources for learners.

In terms of counselor education, portfolio development throughout the course of a program can allow students to identify ways in which knowledge and theory can be applied in practice. Johnson, Renzulli, Bunch, and Paino (2013) found that a portfolio project increased sociological thinking and identity in sociology students. This type of transformation learning could also benefit counselors-in-training. Periodic checks of a student's portfolio development would allow faculty members to identify gaps in student understanding and then plan to address those gaps through coursework (Parker, Ndoye, & Ritzhaupt, 2012; Ripley, 2012).

In terms of emancipatory communitarianism, a portfolio project throughout a student's program will help the student to become a more autonomous learner (Baltimore, Hickson, George, & Crutchfield, 1996; Carney, Cobia, & Shannon, 1996). The student will begin to trust his or her inner voice when choosing what examples of learning he or she selects to include in a portfolio. The reflective analysis of her or his work will help the student to develop confidence in her or his skills as a counselor. The student can include demonstrations of performance from the beginning, middle, and final stages of the program to document the growth he or she achieved (Baltimore et al., 1996). The application of theory to practice in portfolio development (Jones, 2013) can help the student begin to build a professional identity as a counselor. Through both external validation from periodic checks from the advisor, and self-validation through the selection of artifacts, the student will begin to identify himself or herself as a counselor.

The portfolio can also be a valuable tool during supervision, as a supervisee can share with the supervisor examples of current learning. The supervisee will have autonomy on the examples that are selected to share with the supervisor. As the counselor-in-training progresses through the training process, the supervisor can use the portfolio to guide the beginning counselor to identify areas of needed development (Ripley, 2012). The supervisor can help the supervisee plan activities that will lead to additional development of skills and knowledge (Baltimore et al., 1996). The supervisor can also use previous examples from the supervisee to help demonstrate the progress shown by the supervisee. This shared connection between the supervisee and supervisor helps to build community between the two, and it can help emphasize the mutual responsibility for continual professional development.

Limitations and Conclusions

As with any model, following the letter without the spirit of the endeavor will be met with failure, just as assigning students learning contracts just to get out of working with them is unprofessional and unethical. Emancipatory communitarianism in the classroom will require that counselor educators and supervisors recognize and modify modernistic structures of learning, an effort that requires courage and commitment. It will require challenging modernistic forces in counselor education and supervision, such as quantification of learning evidenced in testing, scores, and assessment reports— no easy task. Further, as new models develop and emerge as research continues on learning and self-authorship, so too will our educational tools.

Postmodern philosophy, and its extension into emancipatory communitarianism, is designed to address the absolutism of modernism, and to bring the soul of human endeavor back into educational dialogue. However, it is not possible to successfully apply these strategies without careful consideration of the basic premises of self-authorship within a professional community, distributive justice, and shared voice and responsibility found in communitarianism. If we want to elevate counselor education and supervision out of the modernistic realm of objective knowing, dead-White-men-know-all, knowledge as pain and sacrifice earned only by the worthy, then we need to examine ways that we empower students into their professional identities. We need to acknowledge our power as educators and supervisors, and give that power back to the learner. We need to show students that emancipation and community are possible and show them what that feels like so that they can re-create those conditions for their clients.

REFERENCES

Ali, H. (2011). A comparison of cooperative learning and traditional lecture methods in the project management department of a tertiary level institution in Trinidad and Tobago. *Caribbean Teaching Scholar, 1*(1), 49–64.

Anderson, L. W., Krathwohl, D. R., Airasian, P. W., Cruikshank, K. A., Mayer, R. E., Pintrick, P. R., Raths, J., & Wittrock, M. C. (Eds.). (2001). *A taxonomy for learning, teaching, and assessing: A revision of Bloom's Taxonomy of Educational Objectives* (abridged ed.). New York, NY: Longman.

Arao, B., & Clemens, K. (2013). From safe spaces to brave spaces: A new way to frame dialogue around diversity and social justice. In L. M. Landreman, (ed.). *The art of effective facilitation: Reflections from social justice educators* (pp. 135–150). Herndon, VA: Stylus.

Aronson, E. (1978). *The jigsaw classroom.* Beverly Hills, CA: Sage.

Auxier, C. R., Hughes, F. R., & Kline, W. B. (2003). Identity development in counselors-in-training. *Counselor Education & Supervision, 43*(1), 25–38.

Baker, C. M., Pesut, D. J., McDaniel, A. M., & Fisher, M. L. (2007). Evaluating the impact of problem-based learning on learning styles of master's students in nursing administration. *Journal of Professional Nursing, 23*, 214–219.

Baltimore, M. L., Hickson, J., George, J. D., Crutchfield, L. B. (1996). Portfolio assessment: A model for counselor education. *Counselor Education and Supervision, 36*(2), 113–121.

Barrio Minton, C. A., Wachter Morris, C. A., & Yaites, L. D. (2014). Pedagogy in counselor education: A 10-year content analysis of journals. *Counselor Education & Supervision, 53*(3), 162–177.

Baxter Magolda, M. B. (2009). The activity of meaning making: A holistic perspective on college student development. *Journal of College Student Development, 50*(6), 621–639.

Baxter Magolda, M. B. (2010). Future directions: Pursuing theoretical and methodological issues in the evolution of self-authorship. In M. B. Baxter Magolda, E. G. Creamer, & P. S. Meszaros (Eds.), *Development and assessment of self-authorship: Exploring the concept across cultures* (pp. 267–284). Sterling, VA: Stylus.

Bemak, F., & Chung, R. C. (2011). Applications of social justice counselor training: Classroom without wall. *Journal of Humanistic Counseling, 50*, 204–219.

Bernard, J. M., & Goodyear, R. K. (2014). *Fundamentals of clinical supervision* (5th ed.). Columbus, OH: Pearson.

Boes, L. M., Baxter Magolda, M. B., & Buckley, J. A. (2010). Foundational assumptions and constructive-developmental theory: Self-authorship narratives. In M. B. Baxter Magolda, E. G. Creamer, & P. S. Meszaros (Eds.), *Development and assessment of self-authorship: Exploring the concept across cultures* (pp. 3–23). Sterling, VA: Stylus.

Boostrom, R. (1998). "Safe spaces": Reflections on an educational metaphor. *Journal of Curriculum Studies, 30*(4), 397–408.

Brott, P. E., & Myers, J. E. (1999). Development of professional school counselor identity: A grounded theory. *Professional School Counseling, 2*(5), 339–348.

Brubaker, M. D., Puig, A., Reese, R. F. & Young, J. (2010). Integrating social justice into counseling theories pedagogy: A case example. *Counselor Education & Supervision, 50*(2), 88–102.

Bureau of Labor Statistics. (n.d.). *Employment projections.* Retrieved from http://data.bls.gov/projections/occupationProj

Carney, J. S., Cobia, D. C., & Shannon, D. M. (1996). The use of portfolios in the clinical and comprehensive evaluation of counselors-in-training. *Counselor Education and Supervision, 36*(2), 122–132.

Chang, C. Y., Crethar, H. C., & Ratts, M. J. (2010). Social justice: A national imperative for counselor education and supervision. *Counselor Education & Supervision, 50*(2), 82–87.

Council for Accreditation of Counseling and Related Educational Programs [CACREP]. (2009). *CACREP standards 2009.* Retrieved from http://www.cacrep.org/

Council for Accreditation of Counseling and Related Educational Programs [CACREP]. (2014). *Draft II of the 2016 CACREP standards.* Retrieved from http://www.cacrep.org/about-cacrep/2016-cacrep-standards-revision-process/

Dollarhide, C. T., Gibson, D. M., & Moss, J. M. (2013). Professional identity development of counselor education doctoral students. *Counselor Education & Supervision, 52*(2), 137–150. doi:10.1002/j.1556-6978.2013.00034.x

Eggen, P. D., & Kauchak, D. P. (2013). *Educational psychology: Windows on classrooms* (9th ed.). Columbus, OH: Pearson.

Ferguson, J., & Tryjankowski, A. M. (2009). Online versus face-to-face learning: Looking at modes of instruction in master's-level courses. *Journal of Further and Higher Education, 33*(3), 219–228.

Fong, M. L. (1998). Considerations of a counseling pedagogy. *Counselor Education & Supervision, 38*(2), 106.

Freire, P. (2009). *Pedagogy of the oppressed.* New York, NY: Continuum.

Gibson, D. M., Dollarhide, C. T., & Moss, J. M. (2010). Professional identity development: A grounded theory of transformational tasks of new counselors. *Counselor Education & Supervision, 50*(1), 21–38.

Guiffrida, D. A. (2005). The Emergence Model: An alternative pedagogy for facilitating self-reflection and theoretical fit in counseling students. *Counselor Education & Supervision, 44*(3), 201–213.

Hansen, J. T. (2003). Including diagnostic training in counseling curricula: Implications for professional identity development. *Counselor Education & Supervision, 43*(2), 96–106.

Hansen, J. T. (2010). Consequences of the postmodernist vision: Diversity as the guiding value for the counseling profession. *Journal of Counseling & Development, 88*, 101–107.

Hansen, J. T. (2012). Extending the humanistic vision: Toward a humanities foundation for the counseling profession. *Journal of Humanistic Counseling, 51*(2), 133–144.

Hardiman, R., Jackson, B., & Griffin, P. (2007). Conceptual foundations for social justice education. In M. Adams, L. Bell, & P. Griffin (Eds.), *Teaching for diversity and social justice* (2nd ed., pp. 35–66). New York, NY: Routledge.

Holley, L. C., & Steiner, S. (2005). Safe space: Student perspectives on classroom environment. *Journal of Social Work Education, 41*(1), 49–66.

Johnson, D. R., Renzulli, L., Bunch, J., & Paino, M. (2013). Everyday observations: Developing a sociological perspective through a portfolio term project. *Teaching Sociology, 41*(3), 314–321. doi:10.1177/0092055X13480642

Jones, E. (2013). Practice-based evidence of evidence-based practice: Professional practice portfolios for the assessment of work-based learning. *Quality in Higher Education, 19*(1), 56–71. doi:10.1080/13538322.2013.772467

Klein, S. R. (2003). Peer teaching. *Journal of Teaching in Marriage & Family, 3*, 215–226.

Knowles, M. S. (1986). *Using learning contracts.* San Francisco: CA: Jossey-Bass.

Krathwohl, D. R., Bloom, B. S., & Masia, B. B. (1964). *Taxonomy of educational objectives.* New York, NY: Longman.

Leonardo, Z., & Porter, R. K. (2010). Pedagogy of fear: Toward a Fanonian theory of "safety" in race dialogue. *Race, Ethnicity and Education, 13*(2), 139–157.

Lincoln, Y. S., & Guba, E. G. (2000). Paradigmatic controversies, contradictions, and emerging confluences. In N. K. Denzin & Y. S. Lincoln (Eds.), *Handbook of qualitative research* (2nd ed., pp. 163–188). Thousand Oaks, CA: Sage.

Lonn, M. R., Tello, A. M., Duffey, T., & Haberstroh, S. (2014). Relational-cultural theory as pedagogy: Preparing doctoral student leaders for the counselor education workforce. *Journal of Counselor Leadership and Advocacy, 1,* 140–151. doi:10.1080/2326716X.2014.954164

Mackinnon, R., Haque, A., & Stark, P. (2009). Peer teaching: By students for students. A student-led initiative. *Clinical Teacher, 6*(4), 245–248.

Malot, K. M., Hall, K. H., Sheely-Moore, A., Krell, M. M., & Cardaciotto, L. (2014). Evidence-based teaching in higher education: Application to counselor education. *Counselor Education and Supervision, 53,* 294–305. doi:10.1002/j.1556-6978.2014.00064.x

Mezirow, J. (1991). *Transformative dimensions of adult learning.* San Francisco, CA: Jossey-Bass.

Mezirow, J. (2000). Learning to think like an adult: Core concepts of transformation theory. In J. Mezirow (Ed.), *Learning as transformation* (pp. 3–34). San Francisco, CA: Jossey-Bass.

Mezirow, J. (2012). Learning to think like an adult: Core concepts of transformation theory. In E. W. Taylor, P. Cranton, and associates (Eds.). *The handbook of transformative learning: Theory, research, and practice* (pp. 73–96). San Francisco, CA: Jossey-Bass.

Mezirow, J., & Taylor, E. W. (2009). *Transformative learning in practice: Insights from community, workplace, and higher education.* San Francisco, CA: Jossey-Bass.

Moss, J. M., Gibson, D. M., & Dollarhide, C. T. (2014). Professional identity development: A grounded theory of transformational tasks of counselors. *Journal of Counseling & Development, 92*(1), 3–12. doi:10.1002/j.1556-6676.2014.x

Nelson, M. L., & Neufeldt, S. A. (1998). The pedagogy of counseling: A critical examination. *Counselor Education & Supervision, 38*(2), 70–89.

Odegard, M. A., & Vereen, L. G. (2010). A grounded theory of counselor educators integrating social justice into their pedagogy. *Counselor Education & Supervision, 50*(2), 130–149.

Palmer, P. J. (1998). *The courage to teach: Exploring the inner landscape of a teacher's life.* San Francisco, CA: Jossey Bass.

Parker, M., Ndoye, A., & Ritzhaupt, A. D. (2012). Qualitative analysis of student perceptions of e-portfolios in a teacher education program. *Journal of Digital Learning in Teacher Education, 28*(3), 99–107.

Prilleltensky, I. (1997). Values, assumptions, and practices: Assessing the moral implications of psychological discourse and action. *American Psychologist, 52,* 517–535. doi:10.1037/0003-066X.52.5.517

Ripley, D. (2012). Implementing portfolio-based language assessment in LINC programs: Benefits and challenges. *TESL Canada Journal, 30*(1), 69–86.

Rosin, J. (2015). The necessity of counselor individuation for fostering reflective practice. *Journal of Counseling & Development, 93*(1), 88–95.

Rubin, L., & Hebert, C. (1998). Model for active learning. *College Teaching, 46*(1), 26.

Schwerdt, G., & Wuppermann, A. C. (2011). Is traditional teaching really all that bad? A within-student between-subject approach. *Economics of Education Review, 30,* 365–379.

Shields, C. M. (2013). *Transformative leadership in education: Equitable change in an uncertain and complex world.* New York, NY: Routledge.

Tasoglu, A. K., & Bakac, M. (2010). The effects of problem based learning and traditional teaching methods on students' academic achievements, conceptual developments and scientific process skills according to their graduated high school types. *Procedia Social and Behavioral Sciences, 2,* 2409–2413.

Taylor, E. W. (2008). Transformative learning theory. *New Directions for Adult and Continuing Education, 119*(Fall), 5–15.

Thurley, P., & Dennick, R. (2008). Problem-based learning and radiology. *Clinical Radiology, 63,* 623–628.

West, J. D., Bubenzer, D. L., Cox, J. A., & McGlothlin, J. M. (Eds.). (2013). *Teaching in counselor education: Engaging students in learning.* Alexandria, VA: Association for Counselor Education and Supervision.

Wise, T. (2004). *No such place as safe: The trouble with white anti-racism.* Retrieved from http://www.timwise.org/2004/07/no-such-place-as-safe-the-trouble-with-white-anti-racism/

Yildrim, R. (2013). The portfolio effect: Enhancing Turkish ELT student-teachers' autonomy. *Australian Journal of Teacher Education, 38*(8), 92–110.

Young, W., & Hadgraft, R. (1997). An application of jigsaw learning to teaching. *European Journal of Engineering Education, 22,* 1.

CHAPTER 13
Conclusion

MARK B. SCHOLL AND JAMES T. HANSEN

This book has reviewed a wide range of approaches that were inspired by postmodern ideology. Many of these approaches would not have been possible without a postmodern reconceptualization of the way that counseling processes operate. For instance, the technique of externalizing the problem (White & Epston, 1990) arguably could not have been conceived within a modernist epistemological frame. This is because counseling theories based on modernist ideology generally presume that the true causes of client complaints reside within the client (e.g., unconscious conflict, erroneous cognitions; Gergen, 1999). Proceeding from the modernist assumptions of truth and internality, it naturally follows that expert helping requires the identification of objectively true, internal causes of distress. The epistemological soil of modernism, then, does not provide the ideological nutrients to support the creation and growth of postmodern approaches to counseling, such as externalizing the problem (i.e., placing the problem outside of self; White & Epston, 1990) or the miracle question (i.e., creating new possibilities rather than discovering truths; de Shazer et al., 2007). These novel ways of helping require a rejection of modernist foundations, particularly the core assumptions that there are foundationally true causes of mental misery, which are located within client selves. In short, if the modernist goal of discovering truths about selves is abandoned and is instead replaced by the critical, postmodern ideas that truths are created and a hypothetical self-structure should no longer be the central unit of treatment concern, the horizons of therapeutic possibility expand considerably (Hansen, 2010).

It should be no surprise that the generation of treatment methods is constrained by the ideologies that produce them. As an illustrative analogy, cognitive theorists have noted that the way we think about the world determines how we navigate our lives (e.g., Ellis & Grieger, 1977). For instance, if I firmly believe that becoming involved in new relationships will inevitably lead to the pain of abandonment, this belief system will place constraints on my relational life. By challenging this cognitive template, and adopting alternative assumptions, I can widen the scope of my psychological options in relationships. Similarly, challenging the traditional, modernist assumptions of objective truth and self, and adopting alternative foundations, can generate novel theories and methods to help clients.

The idea that talk therapy, for most of its existence, has been locked into a modernist ideological straitjacket, which has placed severe limits on the potential to create new theories and approaches to helping clients, suggests several questions: (a) Why did the talk therapy professions endorse modernist assumptions in the first place? (b) Why did it take so long to consider alternative ideological foundations? (c) What is the logical basis for critiquing modernist assumptions? Each of these questions is examined next.

Regarding the endorsement of modernist assumptions, talk therapy was invented by Freud at the end of the 19th century (Shorter, 1997). During this era, the modernist, scientific paradigm was responsible for many exciting developments in diverse fields, such as biology, physics, and medicine. Freud, a trained neurological researcher, conceptually designed psychoanalysis to have the same modernist, scientific foundation that had been so successful in the natural sciences (Gay, 1988). Psychoanalysis was launched, therefore, with the idea that psychotherapists should use psychoanalytic methods to objectively observe the unconscious conflicts of patients, just as a biologist might use a microscope to observe a specimen. With this scientific foundation, early psychoanalysts presumed that the psychoanalytic method would lead to the gradual discovery of general laws of mental functioning, which could be used to continually advance the treatment of mental health problems (Spence, 1982). This optimism about modernist principles was shared, albeit in a different form, by behaviorists, who believed that objective observation and manipulation of environmental contingencies would lead to the discovery of general laws of learning, which, ultimately, could be used to solve social and behavioral problems (Skinner, 1974; Watson, 1919).

Given the era in which the talk therapies and the social sciences were launched, it is understandable that pioneering theorists were highly optimistic that the application of modernist, scientific principles to the study and treatment of people would result in rapid theoretical, technical, and practical advances, just as they had in the natural sciences. Of course, it did not work out that way (Hillman & Ventura, 1992). Whereas medicine, for instance, has made tremendous advances over the past century, progress in the behavioral sciences has been disappointingly slow. During the past 100 years, medical science has eliminated polio, transformed diabetes into a manageable condition, and extended the average lifespan by decades. In contrast, we are still stuck with depression, schizophrenia, crime, poverty, and other mental health and social problems, which social science pioneers had hoped would be resolved by the application of a modernist, natural science approach to the study of human beings.

Why have there been such differential rates of progress between the natural and social sciences? This is a complex question and the answer undoubtedly involves innumerable variables. However, a part of the answer might be that the modernist, epistemological foundation, which has worked so well for the natural sciences, is a poor fit for disciplines whose primary subject matter is human behavior (Polkinghorne, 1988, 1992). Perhaps the modernist goal of gradually discovering the laws of nature via objective, scientific observation is an inappropriate aim for the study of human beings, who, instead of being subject to universal laws, continually make up and follow their own personal and cultural belief systems (Hansen, 2016). Even if one is prone to defend the notion that modernism is an appropriate ideological foundation for the study of people, the differential rate of progress evidence suggests that it would at least be reasonable for social and psychological investigators to experiment with alternative epistemological foundations.

This discussion leads to the second question: Why did it take so long for theorists and researchers who study human beings to consider alternatives to modernism? Indeed, postmodernism, as an ideological system, has only been adopted very gradually by talk therapy professionals over the past three decades or so. Even with this gradual adoption, there has arguably been widespread professional resistance within the talk therapy professions to giving up the scientific, modernist approach to the study of people. Research funding sources, universities, and third-party reimbursement organizations generally continue to support the modernist view, even though postmodern ideology has proved extraordinarily generative (e.g., qualitative research methods, narrative therapies, etc.) and progress made by endorsing modernist foundations has arguably been disappointing.

One relatively obvious reason that postmodern ideology did not influence the talk therapy professions at an earlier point in their history is that postmodernism only recently coalesced into a compelling system of thought. Although various philosophical forerunners to postmodernism have arguably been in place since the 19th century, these ideological strands were not woven together into a semicoherent system of thought until the mid-20th century (Anderson, 1990; Hicks, 2004). Naturally, given this timeline, the talk therapy professions only began considering postmodern ideas during the 1980s and 1990s. Furthermore, because the intellectual infrastructure of the social and psychological sciences has historically been built around modernist ideals, the adoption of an alternative epistemology has understandably been a slow process.

Apart from the obvious reasons noted above, perhaps there is another, more insidious, reason that the talk therapy professions have been slow to adopt postmodern perspectives: the cultural prestige and status of modernism. Modernist ideals, such as the use of the scientific method, technological innovations, objective observation, and the discovery of truth are rewarded in our culture with money and status (Hansen, 2016). For example, medicine, which embodies these modernist ideals, generally has far more cultural status than professions that are not primarily investigative, technical, or truth-finding in nature, such as education. Perhaps, as Flax (1990) has argued, professional status is a gendered phenomenon, with high cultural value placed on prototypically male traits, such as active problem solving, hunting for truths, and emotionally removed technical expertise. In contrast, feminine motifs, such as relational engagement and caretaking, are generally devalued in the professional arena. Whatever the reasons, professions structured by modernist ideals tend to be awarded greater status than ones that are not. Perhaps, then, the talk therapy professions have clung to modernism, despite its drawbacks, for the cultural and financial payoffs.

For the third question in this section I have asked whether there are logical bases for critiquing modernism. Certainly, as noted earlier, there are reasons to look beyond modernism as an ideological foundation for the talk therapy professions. However, in addition to the fact that it has not inspired much success, are there other reasons, derived from philosophical logic, to challenge the assumptions of modernism? Is postmodernism a reasonable alternative foundation for the talk therapy professions?

The answers to these questions have been offered in previous sections of this book. However, some of the primary reasons for philosophically critiquing modernism are worth reviewing here. In this regard, modernism generally maintains that reality is structured by universal laws, which human beings are capable of discovering through objective observation (primarily with the scientific method; Hansen, 2004). This modernist ideal of discovering singular, universal truths, though, does not hold up very well to the evidence that various people and communities have different, but perfectly legitimate, perspectives (Hansen, 2014). A physicist might justifiably assert that a chair merely has the illusion of solidity but actually consists mostly of vast realms of empty space between subatomic particles. This perspective would not be shared by the designer of the chair, the person who merely wants to sit in it, or the antique dealer who appraises the value of it. All would have different, but completely justifiable, versions of truth about the chair. Therefore, the modernist ideal of singular truth is inconsistent with the regular observation that so-called truth is often plural.

Of course, even with the existence of a plurality of perspectives, only select conclusions about the world are officially endorsed as true within particular societies and during certain historical eras. As postmodern philosophers have noted, it is no coincidence that culturally sanctioned truths tend to benefit the people in power (Foucault, 1980). For instance, the majority culture has long benefitted from ignoring the truths of the oppressed. Another compelling reason to question the ideals of modernism, then, is that so-called truth is always entangled with power. Under these ideological circumstances, it seems reasonable to consider a philosophical system of thought that acknowledges the legitimacy of multiple truths rather than one that locks us into singularity.

Perhaps the most compelling critique of modernism as applied to the talk therapy professions, though, is that people, at least for the most part, are probably not determined by unchanging, universal laws (Hansen, 2016). It is perfectly reasonable to presume that chemicals, and other objects of study in the natural sciences, are, indeed, subject to natural laws. For instance, if mixing a certain quantity of chemical A with chemical B under particular conditions produces a predictable reaction, then this resultant reaction is a good candidate for a universal law of chemistry. The objects of the natural sciences are passively beholden to the rules of nature, which scientists, using modernist ideological foundations, progressively aim to discover.

In contrast to inanimate objects, however, people are influenced by the belief systems that they create (Hansen, 2016). Cells, chemicals, and rocks are passively determined by the rules of nature. Humans, however, actively create their own rules. With human behavior, even a simple, seemingly obvious law, such as people will avoid pain, cannot be deemed universally true. For the most part, people avoid pain. However, certain individuals and cultures (e.g., religious devotees who engage in self-flagellation, self-cutters, extreme exercise aficionados) have developed meaning systems that result in deliberate exposure to pain. The natural science strategy of discerning natural laws in order to predict and control phenomena quite obviously falls short when the subjects of study are sentient beings who create and follow their own laws.

What should be done when the subject of study does not follow the singular truth rulebook of modernism? Perhaps we should consider adopting a new rulebook. This book has been about this new, postmodern rulebook and the innovative treatment methods it has generated.

At the same time, we recognize that readers might be concerned about the potential downside of adopting such a rulebook. Because more cultural prestige is associated with modernist ideology and related approaches, readers might question the wisdom of endorsing or adopting a postmodern ideological perspective. In response to this skepticism, we would like to remind readers of several examples of prestigious or popular therapy trends that were later rejected as inferior, ineffective, or worse. Perhaps most noteworthy among these is the lobotomy, involving the surgical destruction of a portion of a patient's frontal lobes to treat psychosis (Shorter, 1997; Whitaker, 2002). In spite of the fact that patients undergoing this procedure also routinely incurred severe damage to their higher executive functioning, the lobotomy was the toast of the international psychological community in the 1940s and 1950s (Hansen, 2014), and its inventor, Antonio Moniz, was awarded the Nobel Prize (Whitaker, 2002). Another example of a popular trend that has recently fallen into disfavor is the belief, prevalent during most of the 20th century, that White males represent the mental health ideal by which all other demographic groups should be measured. More recently, it has become widely recognized that all diverse groups have unique strengths, and that no group represents the mental health ideal. Yet another example is the once widespread belief, during the 1920s through the 1950s, that substance addiction was a sign of a flawed character (Hansen, 2014) that should be treated through the use of "fairly aggressive confrontational strategies" (White & Miller, 2007, p. 13). However, research failed to support the effectiveness of confrontation in the treatment of addiction (Boardman, Catley, Grobe, Little, & Ahluwalia, 2006) and today evidence-based, nonconfrontational, motivational interviewing (Miller & Rollnick, 2013) has become ascendant. The primary point of the preceding discussion is that prestige or political support for a treatment should not be used as a selection criterion because prestige is no guarantee that a treatment will stand the test of time.

An outdated belief, once regarded as objective truth by many counseling theorists and practitioners, disputed by the originators of solution-focused therapy (de Shazer, et al., 2007), is the belief that therapeutic change must occur slowly over an extended period of time. For example, proponents of psychoanalysis in the middle of the 20th century asserted that effective treatment required years of therapy. Solution-focused therapists and other practitioners operating from a postmodern perspective (e.g., narrative therapy, collaborative therapy) assert that therapeutic change can be rapidly achieved (O'Hanlon & Weiner-Davis, 2003). Empirical support, though modest, has been accruing in support of this claim (e.g., Knekt et al., 2008).

The modernist perspective places a premium value on *objective* truths. A logical inconsistency at the heart of this perspective is that a number of highly revered truths in the helping professions are actually social constructions. A noteworthy example is the *Diagnostic and Statistical Manual of Mental Disorders* (American Psychiatric Association, 1952), currently in its fifth edition (*DSM-5*; American Psychiatric Association, 2013), which was originally derived from a process of social construction by a group of individuals. Although the diagnostic labels in the *DSM* were defined on the basis of observable criteria, the criteria were also selected and described through a process of social construction. As previously mentioned, truth is entangled with power. The individuals who developed the *DSM*, and the more recent *DSM-5*, possessed the power necessary to co-construct knowledge that is widely respected. However, it would be a misnomer to refer to the diagnostic labels in the *DSM-5* as *objective* truths.

The literature reviews and applications contained in the chapters of this book provide evidence that postmodern ideology is gaining in credibility and popularity among professional counselors. In Chapter 2, Drs. Michelle S. Hinkle and Caroline Perjessy detail the effective application of solution-focused therapy to the treatment of an adolescent survivor of sexual abuse. These authors point out that with the use of conventional treatment approaches grounded in modernist ideology, problems may endure because "words and conversation . . . entrap people within a particular narrative." As the authors note, the postmodern perspective opens up new possibilities for the client (Ashley), including a conceptualization of the problem as external, less oppressive, or not a problem at all, to name a few alternatives. Conversations between the counselor and client are egalitarian. Through such conversations, Ashley experiences a shift from a view of herself as a victim, to a more agentic view of herself as a capable and competent survivor who also serves as a resource for her peers. This shift, predicated on an openness to the existence of multiple realities, is made possible by the solution-focused counselor's implementation of a postmodern perspective. Drs. Hinkle and Perjessy provide an excellent overview of existing empirical evidence supporting the effectiveness of solution-focused therapy. This substantial support includes the results of five meta-analytic studies (Corcoran & Pillai, 2009; Franklin, Zhang, Froerer, & Johnson, 2016; Gingerich & Peterson, 2012; Kim, 2008; Stams, Dekovic, Buist, & de Vries, 2006) representing more than 120 individual studies. All five of these meta-analytic studies yielded statistical results that supported the effectiveness of solution-focused therapy.

In Chapter 3, Dr. Todd F. Lewis presents an overview and case illustration of the use of solution-focused therapy in the treatment of substance addiction. Although empirical support for the effectiveness of solution-focused therapy with substance use issues is modest (e.g., Smock et al., 2008), there are increasing numbers of outcome studies being conducted on solution-focused therapy's effectiveness with counseling concerns, including depression, burnout, domestic violence, and couple counseling (Nelson & Thomas, 2014). Dr. Lewis provides a detailed description of the counseling process. This description focuses on collaboratively building solutions with the client, including the implementation of engaging techniques such as *scaling* and the *miracle day.*

As previously mentioned, so-called objective truths are entangled with power. It is no coincidence that postmodern therapies commonly effect positive outcomes by disentangling or disassociating truth and power. An excellent example of how this separation can be promoted by a counselor is described by Dr. Juleen K. Buser in Chapter 6, titled "Acceptance, Empowerment, and Meaning." More specifically, the collaborative therapist disentangles truth and power through the provision of an egalitarian relationship. The counselor, Sylvie, takes a great deal of care to honor the client's perspective. In counseling Chloe, a client who might be described as displaying "subclinical eating disorder symptoms," Sylvie is careful not to use diagnostic labels or clinical jargon which could serve to communicate a hierarchical relationship and inhibit Chloe's meaning-making process. She shows great respect and interest in Chloe's story, regarding it as one of a kind. As they collaboratively work to co-construct a more flexible and adaptive identity for Chloe, Sylvie is careful to show support for Chloe's ability to be self-authoring. Researchers have reported that collaborative therapy is effective with a range of problems, including homelessness (Feinsilver, Murphy, & Anderson, 2007) and the treatment of psychosis (Haarakangas, Seikkula, Alakare, & Aaltonen, 2007; Seikkula, Alakare, & Aaltonen, 2001; Seikkula, 2002; Seikkula et al., 2003).

An exemplar of the postmodern principle that people are influenced by the belief systems they create can be found in Chapter 5, titled "Restorying the Survivor Narrative With Sexually Abused Adolescents." Drs. Webber and Mascari powerfully illustrate this narrative principle through the case of Angel, a 16-year-old adolescent who restories her experience by creating a narrative titled "My Survivor Story: Artist, Actress, Daughter, Friend." Their case illustration is highly informative and inspiring. In a similar manner, Drs. Wheat and Whiting (Chapter 4, "Sacred Privilege: Using Narrative Reconstruction as a Postmodern Approach With Grieving Children and Adolescents") share the case of Alexis, a 16-year-old who is struggling to cope with the recent death of her 8-year-old brother, Mateo. The authors vividly illustrate the narrative approach of the counselor who encourages Alexis to expand her story, make herself the central character, and perhaps most intriguing, find a way to make Mateo a part of her ongoing life narrative. Rather than attempting to help the client resolve her grieving process, client and counselor effectively reconstruct a resilient narrative that is intended to support the client's ongoing meaning-making process—a process that is therapeutic, healing, and hopeful. Researchers have found that treatments involving the co-construction of positive and hopeful narratives are associated with better client adaptation to grief (Holland, Currier, & Neimeyer, 2006).

Yet another chapter in support of the postmodern assumption that many so-called truths are in reality cultural constructions is Chapter 11 by Drs. Clevenger and Teofilo Mattson. In their chapter, "Obscuring Masculine Truths: A Postmodern Clinical Framework for Counseling Men," they effectively illustrate the application of a *positive masculinity approach* to the case of a man who is unduly limited by his perceptions of mainstream society's definition of masculinity. The counselor facilitates the client's exploration of his beliefs about the meaning of *masculinity*, including the strengths and limitations inherent to conventional definitions of this construct. Together, they co-construct a healthier and more adaptive *masculinity* that is expanded to allow for greater awareness and expression of the client's emotions. Their original approach integrates constructivist theory and practice features from the counseling literature on approaches to counseling men.

An important point that we should make at this point is that we are not advocating the adoption of a postmodern ideology entailing the rejection of modernism entirely. Recall from Chapter 1 that we endorsed a neopragmatic *postmodernism*. For example, in Chapter 7, Drs. Speciale and Lemberger, in applying dialectical humanism, caution counselors that the modernist perspective *grounds* the more visionary postmodern one. Also, Dr. Scholl and colleagues apply an integrative model with ex-offenders in Chapter 9. This model includes not only solution-focused and narrative elements but also incorporates pragmatic world of work knowledge (e.g., appropriate dress, tips for answering common interview questions). Finally, in Chapter 10, titled "Integrating Emerging Understandings of Neuropsychology and Affect for Narrative Therapy With Couples," Drs. Gerald Monk and Navid J. Zamani achieve a superb synthesis of modernist and postmodern paradigms.

Another interesting aspect of Chapter 10 is that its integration encompasses multiple system levels. Dr. Robert Neimeyer (2009) emphasized that a distinctive feature of postmodern therapies is that these therapies address the ways meaning varies as a function of system levels. Smaller systems are contextualized within larger systems of increasing size (e.g., "bio-genetic systems" reside within larger "personal-agentic systems"; Neimeyer, 2009, p. 24). Because truth is entangled with power, a pragmatic postmodernism must acknowledge that the meaning-making client is nonetheless also vulnerable to fundamental "truths" that have been defined by individuals and groups with power. To promote successful client adaptation, counselors must promote both individual meaning making and the ability to navigate existing realities (e.g., rules, laws, conventions) in institutions, communities, and greater society (e.g., the "cultural-linguistic system"; Neimeyer, 2009, p. 24).

Counselors not uncommonly find themselves in systems (e.g., the workplace, the community) where they are required to fulfill more than one professional role. This is consistent with the postmodern view of identity as plural. The current text presents two chapters calling attention to additional, but no less important professional roles that are commonly played by counselors. In Chapter 8, titled "Counselor–Advocate–Scholar Model: A Postmodern Approach to Social Justice Counseling," Dr. Manivong J. Ratts describes the ways in which the postmodern ideology informs and enriches the roles of *researcher* and *social justice advocate* that counselors may assume when working with oppressed clients. In Chapter 12, titled "Counselor Education From a Postmodern Perspective: Empowering Students," Dr. Colette T. Dollarhide and associates present their argument for the incorporation of postmodern social justice ideology into the methods of the *counselor educator*. She effectively argues that postmodern teaching methods should be used to educate and prepare counselors-in-training for their eventual role in the workplace. Importantly, postmodern approaches to education, relative to modernist approaches, are more likely to engage the learner on both intellectual and affective levels. Postmodern counselor education is founded on principles including a view of knowledge as being co-constructed by instructors and students, respect for the counselors-in-training as self-authoring, and the central position of co-constructed dialogue in the learning process. Ultimately, employing egalitarian postmodern methods in educating counselors-in-training better prepares them for assuming the role of a counselor, who similarly forms egalitarian relationships with clients. These egalitarian relationships, in turn, empower clients to be autonomous and self-authoring.

We hope that the exemplars of individuals benefiting from postmodern therapies and techniques in this text will serve to inspire and encourage counselors-in-training and practitioners to adopt elements of postmodern ideology and related practice features. As the case illustrations throughout the book vividly illustrate, postmodern interventions have the potential to serve as vehicles for therapeutic growth, healing, and empowerment. In this text, we have deliberately presented postmodern therapies that are both well established and nascent. There is substantial empirical support for the well-established therapies. The evidence for many of the more nascent therapies and techniques is either modest or slowly accruing. What cannot be denied is that the postmodern therapies and techniques presented in this book's pages are unequivocally people responsive.

REFERENCES

American Psychiatric Association. (1952). *Diagnostic and statistical manual of mental disorders* (1st ed.). Washington, DC: Author.

American Psychiatric Association. (2013). *Diagnostic and statistical manual of mental disorders* (5th ed.). Washington, DC: Author.

Anderson, W. (1990). *Reality isn't what it used to be: Theatrical politics, ready-to-wear religion, global myths, primitive chic, and other wonders of the postmodern world.* San Francisco, CA: Harper & Row.

Boardman, T., Catley, D., Grobe, J. E., Little, T. D., & Ahluwalia, J. S. (2006). Using motivational interviewing with smokers: Do therapist behaviors relate to engagement and therapeutic alliance? *Journal of Substance Abuse Treatment, 31,* 329–339.

Corcoran, J., & Pillai, V. (2009). A review of the research on solution-focused therapy. *British Journal of Social Work, 39,* 234–242. doi:10.1093/bjsw/bcm098

de Shazer, S., Dolan, Y., Korman, H., McCollum, E., Trepper, T., & Berg, I. K. (2007). *More than miracles: The state of the art of solution-focused brief therapy.* Binghamton, NY: Haworth.

Ellis, A., & Grieger, R. (1977). *Handbook of rational-emotive therapy.* New York, NY: Springer.

Feinsilver, D., Murphy, E., & Anderson, H. (2007). Women at a turning point: A transformational feast. In H. Anderson & D. Gehart (Eds.), *Collaborative therapy: Relationships and conversations that make a difference* (pp. 269–290). New York, NY: Routledge/Taylor & Francis Group.

Flax, J. (1990). *Thinking fragments: Psychoanalysis, feminism, and postmodernism in the contemporary West.* Berkeley, CA: University of California Press.

Foucault, M. (1980). C. Gordon (Ed.), *Power/knowledge; selected interviews and other writings 1972–1977* (C. Gordon, L. Marshall, J. Mepham, & K. Soper, Trans.). New York, NY: Pantheon.

Franklin, C., Zhang, A., Froerer, A., & Johnson, S. (2016). Solution focused brief therapy: A systematic review and meta-summary of process research. *Journal of Martial and Family Therapy.* doi:10.1111/jmft.12193

Gay, P. (1988). *Freud: A life for our time.* New York, NY: Norton.

Gergen, K. (1999). *An invitation to social construction.* Thousand Oaks, CA: Sage.

Gingerich, W. J., & Peterson, L. T. (2012). Effectiveness of solution-focused brief therapy: A systematic qualitative review of controlled outcome studies. *Research on Social Work Practice, 23,* 266–283.

Haarakangas, K., Seikkula, J., Alakare, B., & Aaltonen, J. (2007). Open dialogue: An approach to psychotherapeutic treatment of psychosis in northern Finland. In H. Anderson & D. Gehart (Eds.), *Collaborative therapy: Relationships and conversations that make a difference* (pp. 221–233). New York, NY: Routledge.

Hansen, J. T. (2004). Thoughts on knowing: Epistemic implications of counseling practice. *Journal of Counseling & Development, 82,* 131–138. doi:10.1002/j.1556-6678.2004.tb00294.x

Hansen, J. T. (2010). Consequences of the postmodernist vision: Diversity as the guiding value for the counseling profession. *Journal of Counseling & Development, 88,* 101–107. doi:10.1002/j.1556-6678.2010.tb00156.x

Hansen, J. T. (2014). *Philosophical issues in counseling and psychotherapy: Encounters with four questions about knowing, effectiveness, and truth.* Lanham, MD: Rowman & Littlefield.

Hansen, J. T. (2016). *Meaning systems and mental health culture: Critical perspectives on contemporary counseling and psychotherapy.* Lanham, MD: Lexington Books.

Hicks, S. (2004). *Explaining postmodernism: Skepticism and socialism from Rousseau to Foucault.* Milwaukee, WI: Scholarly Publishing.

Hillman, J., & Ventura, M. (1992). *We've had a hundred years of psychotherapy and the world's getting worse.* New York, NY: HarperCollins.

Holland, J. M., Currier, J. M., & Neimeyer, R. A. (2006). Meaning reconstruction in the first two years of bereavement: The role of sense-making and benefit-finding. *Omega, 53,* 175–191. doi:10.2190/FKM2-YJTY-F9VV-9XWY

Kim, J. (2008). Examining the effectiveness of solution-focused brief therapy: A meta-analysis. *Research on Social Work Practice, 32,* 49–64.

Knekt, P., Lindfors, O., Harkanen, T., Valikoski, M., Virtala, E., Laaksonen, M. A. et al. (2008). Randomized trial on the effectiveness of long-and short-term psychodynamic psychotherapy and solution-focused therapy on psychiatric symptoms during a 3-year follow-up. *Psychological Medicine, 38*(5), 689–703.

Miller, W. R., & Rollnick, S. (2013). *Motivational interviewing: Helping people change* (3rd ed.). New York, NY: Guilford.

Neimeyer, R. A. (2009). *Postmodern psychotherapy: Distinguishing features.* New York, NY: Guilford.

Nelson, T. S., & Thomas, F. N. (Eds.). (2014). *Handbook of solution-focused brief therapy: Clinical applications.* New York, NY: Haworth.

O'Hanlon, B., & Weiner-Davis, M. (2003). *In search of solutions* (Rev. ed.). New York, NY: Norton.

Polkinghorne, D. (1988). *Narrative knowing and the human sciences.* Albany, NY: State University of New York Press.

Polkinghorne, D. (1992). Postmodern epistemology of practice. In S. Kvale (Ed.), *Psychology and postmodernism* (pp. 146–165). Thousand Oaks, CA: Sage.

Seikkula, J. (2002). Open dialogues with good and poor outcomes for psychotic crises: Examples from families with violence. *Journal of Marital and Family Therapy, 28*(3), 263–274. doi:10.1111/j.1752-0606.2002.tb01183.x

Seikkula, J., Alakare, B., & Aaltonen, J. (2001). Open dialogue in psychosis II: A comparison of good and poor outcome. *Journal of Constructivist Psychology, 14*(4), 267. doi:10.1080/107205301750433405

Seikkula, J., Alakare, B., Aalotonen, J., Holma, J., Rasinkangas, A., & Lehtinen, V. (2003). Open dialogue approach: Treatment principles and preliminary results of a two-year follow-up on first episode schizophrenia. *Ethical Human Sciences & Services, 5*(3), 163–182.

Shorter, E. (1997). *A history of psychiatry; from the era of the asylum to the age of Prozac.* New York, NY: Wiley & Sons.

Skinner, B. (1974). *About behaviorism.* New York, NY: Knopf.

Smock, S. A., Trepper, T. S., Wetcher, J. C., McCollum, E. E., Ray, R., & Pierce, K. (2008). Solution-focused group therapy for level 1 substance abusers. *Journal of Marital and Family Therapy, 34*(1), 107–120.

Spence, D. (1982). *Narrative truth and historical truth: Meaning and interpretation in psychoanalysis.* New York, NY: Norton.

Stams, G. J. J., Dekovic, M., Buist K., & de Vries, L. (2006). Effectiviteit van oplossingsgerichte korte therapie: een meta-analyse [Efficacy of solution focused brief therapy: a meta-analysis]. *Gedragstherapie, 39,* 81–95.

Watson, J. (1919). *Psychology from the standpoint of a behaviorist.* Philadelphia, PA: Lippincott. doi:10.1037/10016-000

Whitaker, R. (2002). *Mad in America: Bad science, bad medicine, and the enduring mistreatment of the mentally ill.* Cambridge: MA: Perseus.

White, M., & Epston, D. (1990). *Narrative means to therapeutic ends.* New York, NY: Norton.

White, W., & Miller, W. (2007). The use of confrontation in addiction treatment: History, science, and time for change. *Counselor, 8*(4), 12–30.

AUTHOR INDEX

Hayes, R., 262
Hays, K. W., 169
Hebert, C., 301
Hedtke, L., 112
Heinonen, E., 54
Helwig, A. A., 122
Hennen, P., 271
Hennenlotter, A., 245
Henning, K., 31
Herbison, G. P., 38
Herman, J., 121, 123, 124, 127, 133, 134
Herraiz, A., 29
Hester, R., 65
Hicks, S., 6, 313
Hickson, J., 304, 305
Hiersteiner, C., 123, 133
Hillman, J., 312
Hinkle, M., 316
Hocking, C., 104
Hoek, H. W, 151
Hoffman, R. M., 37, 56
Holland, J. M., 99, 102, 103, 104, 105, 318
Holley, L. C., 299
Holma, J., 161, 163, 317
Hooper, S. R., 34
Hopper, E. K., 99
House, R., 189
Hoyt, M. F., 41
Hsieh, H. F., 227
Hudson, J. I., 151
Hughes, F. R., 295
Hull, K., 33
Humphrey, N., 54
Humphry, T. A., 149, 150, 154
Hwang, W. C., 34

Imel, Z. E., 134, 207, 208, 209
Isacco, A., 266
Israel, T., 187

Jackson, B., 299–300
James, L., 95, 97
Janoff-Bulman, R., 101
Jansen, A., 249
Jarcho, J. M., 242
Järvikoski, A., 54
Jayawickreme, N., 29
Jensen, P., 16
Jimenez-Chafey, M. I., 34
Johnson, D. R., 304
Johnson, S., 55, 316

Johnson, S. M., 249–251, 250, 253
Johnson, V. E., 170
Jones, E., 304, 305
Jones, M. K., 169
Jordan, J., 247

Kahn, J. S., 266, 269, 274
Kallos-Lilly, V., 250
Kant, I., 10
Kaprio, J., 151
Karpitskiy, V., 249
Kashak, E., 170
Kater, K., 149, 150, 156
Kauchak, D. P., 288
Kaufman, D., 217, 220, 225
Kazdin, A. E., 31
Keane, T. M., 124
Keesee, N. J., 105
Kelly, G. A., 104
Kendall-Tackett, K. A., 30, 38
Kenny, M. E., 270
Keski-Rahkonen, A., 151
Kessler, R. C., 29, 30
Kierski, W., 271
Kilburn-Watt, E., 169
Kim, J. S., 54, 55, 316
Kimmel, M., 268, 269, 270
Kiselica, M. S., 187, 275
Kiser, D., 18
Kiser, L. J., 102
Kitzinger, R., 122
Klass, D., 95, 102, 104
Klein, S. R., 301, 302
Kleinplatz, P. J., 170
Kleinst, D. M., 133
Kline, W. B., 295
Knekt, P., 54, 55, 315
Knowles, M. S., 297, 298
Knudsen, K., 32
Knudson-Martin, C., 237, 246, 248
Koch, P., 160
Kohm, L., 34
Kolko, D. J., 31
Kopil, C., 244
Korman, H., 310, 315
Kowalski, K., 122
Kozorovitskiy, Y., 244
Krannich, C., 222
Krannich, R., 222
Krantz, A. M., 35
Krathwohl, D. R., 288

Plato, 5–6
Polanyi, M., 10–13, 12, 13, 16, 17
Polk, G. W., 77
Polkinghorne, D., 14, 89, 312
Ponzi, D., 37
Poole, J., 284
Pope, H. G., 151
Porter, R. K., 300
Price-Robertson, R., 234
Prilleltensky, I., 291, 292
Prochaska, J. O., 71–72, 155
Proffitt, D. R., 242
Propst, O., 129
Prosch, H., 10, 12, 13
Puig, A., 284, 289, 291
Pynor, R., 169

Rabinowitz, F. E., 270
Raevuori, A., 151
Rambo, A., 52
Rasinkangas, A., 161, 163, 317
Raths, J., 288
Ratican, K. L., 30, 38
Ratts, M. J., 146, 185, 186, 189, 191, 193, 319
Ray, D. C., 18
Ray, R., 317
Reeck, C, 243
Reed, E. E., 266
Reese, R. F., 284, 289, 291
Reichenberg, L. W., 70, 85
Reid, H. L., 221
Reinherz, H. Z., 29
Renzulli, L., 304
Renzulli, S., 264
Reuter, T., 8
Reynolds, V. V., 32
Rhodes, M. L., 17
Ribeiro, A. P., 105
Ricciardelli, L. A., 149, 150, 154
Richards, P. S., 150, 156
Riley, S., 56
Ripley, D., 304, 305
Rissanen, J., 54
Ritzhaupt, A. D., 304
Rober, P., 140
Robinson, B. S., 217, 220
Robinson, H., 213, 214, 215, 222, 227
Robinson, M., 187
Rochlen, A. B., 264
Rodenburg, R., 35
Rodríguez-Jazcilevich, I., 160–161

Rogers, C. R., 171, 176
Rohde, P., 150, 152
Rollnick, S., 11, 155, 315
Romans, S. E., 38
Ronan, K. R., 33
Root, T. L., 151
Rorty, R., 5, 6, 13, 14
Rosa-Alcázar, A. I., 35
Rose, A. J., 37
Rosen, H., 93, 262
Rosenau, P., 4
Rosin, J., 295
Ross, M., 38
Rossouw, W., 29
Rothschild, B., 123, 124, 126, 129, 130, 131
Roysircar, G., 187
Rubin, G., 266, 267
Rubin, L., 301
Rubin, S. S., 95, 102
Rudes, J., 15
Runte, J. K., 122
Russell, E. B., 169
Russell, S., 237
Ruzek, J. I., 32
Ryan, B., 262

Salgado, J., 105
Salloum, A., 99, 100
Sampson, R. J., 214
Sánchez-Meca, J., 35
Sandoz, E. K., 149, 150, 156
Sansone, R. A., 169
Saul, J., 99, 102
Saywitz, K. J., 30, 32
Scaletti, R., 104
Schafer, R., 210
Schermer, T. W., 266
Schippers, M., 266, 267, 268
Schmidt, L. L. P., 122
Scholl, M. B., 3, 17, 18, 163, 213, 214, 215, 221, 222, 227, 236, 284, 318
Scholz, R., 266
Schüler, J., 149, 150, 154
Schut, H., 98
Schwerdt, G., 287
Scott, N., 125
Scott, R. P. J., 266, 273
Sedgwick, E. K., 239
Seedat, S., 29
Seikkula, J., 161, 162, 163, 317
Seligman, L., 70, 85

SUBJECT INDEX

Note: Tables and figures are indicated by an italic *t* and *f* following the page number.

Couples. *See* narrative therapy (couples)
Culture of silence, 283

Darwinian evolution, 8–9
*Diagnostic and Statistical Manual of Mental
    Disorders,* 316
Dialectical humanism. *See also* sexuality
    counseling
  clinical applications, 182
  limitations, 182
  principles, 171–75
  techniques, 175–76

Eating disorders, 150–52, 162–63. *See also*
    collaborative therapy
Education. *See* counselor education
Emancipatory communitarianism,
    292–96, 296t
Enlightenment, 7
Ex-offenders. *See* career support workshops

Gender-aware therapy. *See* men and
    masculinity
Gender Role Conflict Scale (GRCS), 273
Grief, grieving
  adolescence, 97–98
  benefit finding, 103
  case study, 105–13
  coauthoring therapeutic relationship, 101,
      103, 106–9, 114
  continuing bonds, 104
  conventional interventions, 99–100
  dance movement therapy, 104
  developmental progression, 94–95
  disenfranchised grief, 94
  early, middle childhood, 95–97
  expressive arts interventions,
      103–4, 110–12
  imaginary audience, 98
  literature review, 103–5
  meaning making, 100–105
  narrative-dialogical processes, 105
  narrative reconstruction applications,
      102–3, 114–15
  narrative reconstruction
      limitations, 113–14
  narrative reconstruction rationale,
      100–102
  overview, 93–94
  personal constructs, 104–5
  personal fable, 98

psychological first aid, 99–100
resilience narrative, 100–103, 109–13
ritual creation, 104
trauma-focused CBT, 99, 116

Helping professions theories
  intellectual dualisms in, 6
  overview, 1–4
  reason as path to truth, 7, 9
  search-for-truth paradigm, 5–7
  unconscious motivations, 7

Identity development, in adolescent sexual
    abuse survivors, 30

Jigsaw groups, 301–2

Learning contracts, 297–99

Men and masculinity
  American culture, 268
  assessment tools, 273
  case study, 261–62, 275–77
  clinical applications, 275–77
  collaborative change model, 274
  competition, 267, 269
  developmental relational counseling, 275
  feminist therapy, 273–74
  gender as learned performance,
      267, 275–76
  gender-aware therapy, 264–66, 318
  gender privilege, 268
  gender/sex cultural constructions, 266–68
  hegemonic masculinity, 267, 269, 271
  hidden personal truths, 262
  intersectionality, 268
  masculinity-femininity
      interdependence, 267–68
  meaning making, 276–77
  modernism *vs.* postmodernism, 262–64
  motivational interviewing, 265
  multicultural approach, 274
  narrative therapy, 265
  negative health consequences, 264–65
  postmodern therapeutic framework,
      271–72, 279
  power relationships, 267–68, 270,
      271, 278
  sexual victimization of, 265
  shame, 270–71
  social expectations of, 265

psychoanalysis *vs.*, 312–13
  reauthoring and envisioning
      process, 15–16
  relatedness in, 64–65
  rulebook, adoption of, 314–15
  social constructivism, 15
  therapeutic change time frame, 315–16
  truth as social construction, 316
  varieties of, 13
Power relationships
  career support workshops, 218, 220
  counselor education, 289
  men and masculinity, 267–68, 270,
      271, 278
  narrative therapy (couples), 234, 237, 239,
      245–49, 256–57, 318–19
  postmodernist concepts of, 314, 317
  social justice counseling, 188–89
Problem-based learning, 302–3
Psychoanalysis
  limitations of, 209–10, 311
  outcomes, factors affecting,
      207–9, 311–12
  postmodernism *vs.*, 312–13
  theoretical assumptions in, 4–5, 9, 311
PTSD, in adolescent sexual abuse, 29, 124,
      130, 136

Re-entrants. *See* career support workshops
Resilience theory, 214–17

Safe spaces, 299–300
Scaling questions, 43–44, 48–49, 75, 317
Self-authoring, by learners, 283–84
Self-authorship, 293–94, 296t
Sexuality counseling
  alternative contact theory, 174
  case study, 177–82
  dialectical humanism applications, 182
  dialectical humanism limitations, 182
  dialectical humanism principles, 171–75
  dialectical humanism techniques, 175–76
  dialectical method, 174
  heteronormativity, 170, 175
  living on the frontier, 146
  meaning clarification, 179–80
  overview, 169–70
  possibilities, reimaging, 181
  postmodern approaches to, 170–71
  script deconstruction, 180–81

therapeutic relationship establishment, 179
  traditional models of, 170–71
Sexual trauma. *See* adolescent sexual abuse
Social cognitive career theory, 216
Social justice counseling. *See also* counselor-
      advocate–scholar (CAS) model
  advocacy, 198
  Advocacy Competencies model, 190–91,
      191f, 195–99
  case study, 196–202
  clinical applications, 203–4
  identity as plural, 189, 200
  limitations of, 202–3
  macrolevel interventions, 198
  model, 186–88
  oppression, effects of, 186, 199
  as postmodern, 188–89
  power relationships, 188–89
  redefining reality, 146
  self-advocacy, 197–98
  theories, models, 189–90
  traditional counseling *vs.*, 185–86
  workplace discrimination, 146
Sociodynamic counseling model, 216
Solution-focused therapy generally. *See also*
      postmodernism
  action steps development, 17–18
  benefits of, 316–20
  counselor's skills, 17
  cultural divide in, 18
  quantitative research, 18
  superficiality, 18
STAR acronym, 218, 221–22, 226
Substance addiction treatment
  abstinence contract, 72
  case study, 70–76, 78–83
  change, progress conceptualization, 70
  change as constant, 66–67, 81–82
  clients as experts, 69
  clinical applications, 84–86
  clinician responsibilities, 69–70
  co-construction in, 64–65
  cognitive-behavioral therapy, 63–64
  conventional therapies, 63–64
  exceptions, 67, 70, 74, 79–80
  externalization of problems, 67–69
  future-oriented questions, 74–75, 81–82
  goal setting, 71–73, 78–82
  key questions, 71
  language/behavior influences, 67, 72

Substance addiction treatment (*cont.*)
    miracle days, 76, 82–83, 317
    miracle questions, 74, 79–80
    outcome research, 76–78
    as postmodern, 64–65
    practical advantages of, 65–66
    relationship-oriented questions, 75
    scaling questions, 75
    solution-focused brief therapy, 77
    solution-focused group therapy, 77, 84–85
    solutions, exploring, 73–76, 80–81
    strengths, limitations of, 83–84
    taking a break, 75–76, 81
    theoretical approach, 66–69
    treatments, 62–63
Supervision. *See* counselor education
Synanon, 63

Talk therapy. *See* psychoanalysis
Transformational learning, 294–95, 296t
Trauma-informed care, 99

Workplace discrimination. *See* social justice
    counseling